STRESS AND COPING
IN LATER-LIFE FAMILIES

STRESS AND COPING IN LATER-LIFE FAMILIES

Edited by

Mary Ann Parris Stephens
Janis H. Crowther
Stevan E. Hobfoll
Daniel L. Tennenbaum

Kent State University, Ohio

⬤HEMISPHERE PUBLISHING CORPORATION

A member of the Taylor & Francis Group

New York   Washington   Philadelphia   London

STRESS AND COPING IN LATER-LIFE FAMILIES

1 2 3 4 5 6 7 8 9 0   E B E B   9 8 7 6 5 4 3 2 1 0

This book was set in Janson by Hemisphere Publishing Corporation. The editors were Lisa A. Warren and Deanna D'Errico; the production supervisor was Peggy M. Rote; and the typesetters were Cynthia B. Mynhier, Linda Andros, and Deborah S. Hamblen. Cover design by Debra Eubanks Riffe. Printing and binding by Edwards Brothers, Inc.

A CIP catalog record for this book is available from the British Library.

Library of Congress Cataloging-in-Publication Data

Stress and coping in later-life families/edited by Mary Ann Parris Stephens . . . [et al.]
    p. cm.—(Series in applied psychology)
        Based in large part on the 1989 Kent Psychology Forum which took place in April at the Inn at Honey Run in the Amish country of central Ohio.
        Includes bibliographical references.

    1. Aged—Mental health—Congresses. 2. Stress (Psychology)—Congresses. 3. Adjustment (Psychology) in old age—Congresses. 4. Aging—Psychological aspects—Congresses. I. Stephens, Marry Ann Parris. II. Kent Psychology Forum (1989: Inn at Honey Run) III. Series: Series in applied psychology (New York, N.Y.)
        [DNLM: 1. Aged—congresses. 2. Family—psychology—congresses. 3. Social Environment—congresses. 4. Social Support. 5. Stress, Psychological—congresses. WT 30 S915 1989]
RC451.4.A5S777   1990
155.67—dc20
DNLM/DLC
for Library of Congress   90-4263
                                                                                      CIP

ISBN 0-89116-928-8
ISSN 1048-8146

To four generations who, in different ways, have helped me know the value of family bonds—my parents, my husband, our four children, and our grandchild.—M.A.P.S.

To my grandmother and my parents, for their loving support and wisdom about families.—J.H.C.

To my dad, Ed Hobfoll, still young at 70.—S.E.H.

To my wife, Iris, who so lovingly cared for her mother, Margaret Kotovsky, during her mother's lengthy terminal illness.—D.L.T.

Contents

Contributors

CAROLYN M. ALDWIN, Normative Aging Study, Boston Veterans Administration Outpatient Clinic, Boston, Massachusetts 02108.

TONI C. ANTONUCCI, Institute for Social Research, University of Michigan, Ann Arbor, Michigan 48106.

ANGELA BRIDGES, Department of Psychology, Kent State University, Kent, Ohio 44242.

TIMOTHY H. BRUBAKER, Department of Home Economics, Miami University, Oxford, Ohio 45056.

BRUCE CARPENTER, Psychology Department, University of Tulsa, Tulsa, Oklahoma 74104.

JANIS H. CROWTHER, Applied Psychology Center, Department of Psychology, Kent State University, Kent, Ohio 44242.

ANITA DeLONGIS, Department of Psychology, University of British Columbia, Vancouver, British Columbia, Canada V6T 1Y7.

BARBARA J. FELTON, Psychology Department, New York University, New York, New York 10003.

MELISSA M. FRANKS, Department of Psychology, Kent State University, Kent, Ohio 44242.

ROSE C. GIBSON, Institute for Social Research, University of Michigan, Ann Arbor, Michigan 48106.

ROBERT O. HANSSON, Psychology Department, University of Tulsa, Tulsa, Oklahoma 74104.

STEVAN E. HOBFOLL, Applied Psychology Center, Department of Psychology, Kent State University, Kent, Ohio 44242.

JAMES S. JACKSON, Institute for Social Research, University of Michigan, Ann Arbor, Michigan 48106.

NEAL KRAUSE, Health Gerontology Program, School of Public Health, The University of Michigan, Ann Arbor, Michigan 48109-2029.

JACOB LOMRANZ, Department of Psychology, Tel Aviv University, Ramat Aviv, Tel Aviv 69 978 Israel.

BRENDA PAPINCAK LOREN, Department of Psychology, Kent State University, Kent, Ohio 44242.

VIRGINIA KLINE NORRIS, Department of Psychology, Kent State University, Kent, Ohio 44242.

TESS O'BRIEN, Department of Psychology, University of British Columbia, Vancouver, British Columbia, Canada V6T 1Y7.

PAULA K. OGROCKI, Department of Psychology, Kent State University, Kent, Ohio 44242.

KAREN S. ROOK, Program in Social Ecology, University of California at Irvine, Irvine, California 92717.

MARY ANN PARRIS STEPHENS, Applied Psychology Center, Department of Psychology, Kent State University, Kent, Ohio 44242.

DANIEL L. TENNENBAUM, Applied Psychology Center, Department of Psychology, Kent State University, Kent, Ohio 44242.

ALOEN L. TOWNSEND, Benjamin Rose Institute, Cleveland, Ohio 44115-1989.

STEVEN H. ZARIT, Department of Individual and Family Studies, Pennsylvania State University, University Park, Pennsylvania 16802.

Preface

Over the past several years, a plethora of publications has appeared concerning social issues related to the aging of the human population. Interest has focused in particular upon the problems that older adults and their families encounter. Given the abundance of scientific and popular writings currently available on these topics, we took on a significant challenge when we set out to assemble a publication that would make a unique contribution to this growing literature. We believe that *Stress and Coping in Later-Life Families* has met this challenge successfully. It is truly a unique volume with respect to the topic areas covered, the contributors it brings together, and the processes involved in its development.

In planning this volume, our goal was to invite outstanding scholars in three areas related to social gerontology—stress, social support, and caregiving. Although researchers in these areas typically have worked independently of one another, it was our contention that they share much in common and that a cross-seeding of their perspectives could provide important new insights into later-life family processes. This volume includes some of the best and most creative thinkers in each of the three content areas and focuses their collective attention on a problem of growing social concern—how older adults and their families cope with the vicissitudes of later life. The result is a rich blend of empirical findings and theorizing about this multifaceted and intriguing area.

We initiated a somewhat unusual plan for contributors to participate in the creation of the volume. In large part, the volume is a product of the 1989 Kent Psychology Forum, where the volume's contributors presented their ideas about various facets of later-life families, challenged the ideas of others, and had their own ideas challenged in return. Thus each chapter not only has been written by one of the leading scholars in the field, but also has undergone the scrutiny and has profited from the input of the other chapters' contributors. We believe that the lively exchanges among the contributors at the 1989 Kent Psychology Forum enhanced the volume's quality and cohesiveness.

The Kent Psychology Forum was sponsored by the Applied Psychology Center at Kent State University. The Applied Psychology Center has as its primary mission the facilitation and dissemination of applied psychological research, and the concept of the Forum evolved as one means of achieving these goals. Unlike most research meetings and conferences where large registration and broad topic coverage are sought, the Forum seeks to limit participation to a small number of invited researchers and active professionals whose shared expertise is focused on a specific topic. The intent is to foster intense and free-ranging discussions of research, theory, and practice in various arenas of applied psychology.

The 1989 Forum on later-life families was the first in a series of forums that focus in various ways on families and health. The chair of this first Forum was Mary Ann Parris Stephens, and co-chairs were Stevan Hobfoll, Janis Crowther, and Daniel Tennenbaum. The 11 scholars who were invited were Carolyn Aldwin (Veterans Administration Outpatient Clinic and Boston University School of Public Health), Toni Antonucci (The University of Michigan, Institute for Social Research), Timothy Brubaker (Miami University, Family and Child Studies Center), Anita DeLongis (University of British Columbia), Barbara Felton (New York University), Robert Hansson (University of Tulsa), Neal Krause (School of Public Health and the University of Michigan Institute of Gerontology), Jacob Lomranz (Tel Aviv University), Karen Rook (University of California, Irvine), Aloen Townsend (Margaret Blenkner Research Center, Benjamin Rose Institute), and Steven Zarit (The Pennsylvania State University). Graduate students from the Department of Psychology at Kent State University who participated were Angela Bridges, Melissa Franks, Brenda Loren, Virginia Norris, and Paula Ogrocki. Other invitees, who represented a wide range of professions serving older adults, were Matthew Baldwin (Ohio Department of Aging), Carl Brahce (Gerontology Center at Kent State University), Robert Eckardt (Cleveland Foundation), Paula Hartman-Stein (Akron General Medical Center), Jennifer Kinney (Bowling Green State University, Gerontology Program) and James Kvale (St. Elizabeth's Hospital and Medical Center at Youngstown, Ohio).

The 1989 Forum took place during four days in April at the Inn at Honey Run in the Amish country of central Ohio. Sequestered in the beauty of springtime in the countryside, and amply nourished with the delights of Amish cooks, Forum participants developed constructive and productive working relationships with one another that lasted throughout. From the Forum emerged friendships as well as ideas. We believe that *Stress and Coping in Later-Life Families* reflects the collaborative and creative spirit of the processes that spawned it.

This edited volume will be useful to researchers who are concerned with a variety of issues in social gerontology, especially those involving family relationships. It is appropriate as a supplemental text in graduate gerontology courses in disciplines such as psychology, sociology, and family studies. Because of the applied nature of the topics covered, it will also be useful to practitioners who plan and provide services to older adults and their families.

Mary Ann Parris Stephens
Janis H. Crowther
Stevan E. Hobfoll
Daniel L. Tennenbaum

Acknowledgments

We would like to acknowledge the contributions of several people whose efforts and resources made the volume possible. We are indeed grateful to the Ohio Board of Regents whose Academic Challenge Award funded the Applied Psychology Center and its mission of promoting applied psychological research. We want to thank Seymour Sarason and Camille Wortman, whose ideas and encouragement about the Forum were invaluable in its creation. We also want to thank our colleagues in the Department of Psychology at Kent State University who provided many forms of tangible and emotional support in the development of the Forum concept, and in the preparation of this volume. Special thanks are also extended to Patricia John for her secretarial assistance and personal involvement in these activities, and to Melissa Franks and Jaime Carr for their careful attention to the laborious tasks of proofreading.

SOCIAL RELATIONSHIPS AS COPING RESOURCES IN LATER-LIFE FAMILIES

Mary Ann Parris Stephens

Kent State University

One of the most important societal changes occurring in the 20th century has been the aging of the human population. The number of older adults is increasing not only in absolute numbers but also in proportion to the total population. In the United States in 1900, adults over the age of 65 years numbered about 3 million (representing approximately 4% of the total population), and in 1985 they numbered over 28 million (representing 12% of the total population). Demographic projections indicate that by 2030 these older adults could number more than 64 million and represent as great as 21% of the total population. The most rapidly growing segment of the older adult population comprises those individuals whose ages are 85 years and older (American Association of Retired Persons [AARP], 1986; Gilford, 1988). These figures indicate that the older adult population is not only growing larger, but it is also growing older. Evidence also suggests that these older persons frequently remain closely tied to their families. In fact 82% of older men and 55% of older women reside in a family setting (Gilford, 1988). These settings include residing with a spouse as well as with other family members, especially children.

These demographic estimations not only raise concerns about the quality of life that older adults themselves are likely to face, but they also raise concerns about the lives of their families as well. Most older adults are embedded in some form of complex family structure and in valued interpersonal relationships with their family members; therefore, whatever problems they experience are not theirs alone but are shared by their families. Thus, in a very real sense, the problems of aging are not simply problems that are experienced at the individual level by older people. They are also social problems that are felt at both the primary group level and by society. Chapters in this volume address various facets of this complex and pressing social issue, in particular, how older adults and their families cope with the stressors of later life.

This chapter provides an overview of existing theory and research that bears on stress and coping in these families. I review psychosocial theory and research concerning the following questions. What are the problems and stressors that older adults typically encounter? How can these problems be understood in the context of family systems? How do older adults cope with these problems, and how do their families function as sources of assistance in times of need? What is the impact on family members of providing sustained assistance to an older relative? In the final section of the chapter, I attempt to integrate knowledge related to these questions in order to provide a context for the chapters that follow.

STRESSORS IN LATER LIFE

It often has been observed that life is never free from stress, but rather is characterized by a continuing process of adaptation to struggles and challenges, or stressors, that tax coping resources to a greater or lesser degree. Thus, stressful encounters in later life are not new experiences for older adults, because they have weathered a lifetime of coping challenges. The very fact that old age has been reached implies a certain level of successful adaptation. The particular kinds of stressors that any individual is likely to face vary to some extent, however, as a function of the point he or she has reached in the life span. As such, older adults, by virtue of their age and its concomitant physiological, psychological, and social changes, are more likely to encounter certain stressful events that are younger people. In this section I describe some of these events and their implications for family relationships.

In contrast to stereotypic beliefs about older adults, most are fully independent in their activities of daily living and are cognitively intact (Rowe, 1985). Many of the problems experienced by older adults are health-related. Approximately 86% of older adults experience at least one chronic illness (Office of Technology Assessment, 1985). Nearly one-fifth require at least some assistance with activities such as bathing and grooming or in transportation or preparing meals (Gilford, 1988). These functional limitations also are reflected in self-reports of health. Nearly one-third of older adults rate their health status as fair or poor as compared to younger adults, of whom less than one-tenth rate their health as fair or poor (AARP, 1986).

Not only do older adults experience problems of somatic health and functional disability, but also they often experience significant mental health problems. Approximately 15% to 25% of those over age 65 demonstrate symptoms of mental illness. Older people represent about one-fifth of all first admissions to psychiatric hospitals and occupy almost one-fourth of all psychiatric beds. Although many of these psychiatric problems appear to be organic, it is widely believed that many nonorganic problems, such as depression, are undiagnosed. Even so, the documented rates of depression range from 10% to 30% among older adults (Brody & Kleban, 1983; Kay & Bergmann, 1980). Many of these figures exceed the relative proportion of older adults in the population and suggest that mental health is often a key problem for older people.

In spite of these often considerable health problems, only about 5% of all older adults reside in institutional settings at any given time (AARP, 1986). National surveys indicate that there are twice as many ill elderly people living at home as there are in institutions. It appears that a key factor in the prevention of institutional placement is the availability of viable family relationships to provide assistance (Shanas, 1979).

In addition to the dependency and disability resulting from physical and mental health problems, older adults often experience a variety of other stressful life changes such as retirement, bereavement, and the lessening of authority and feelings of control (Bohm & Rodin, 1985). Although retirement from work is usually a planned event to which the retiree has looked forward, this change often creates large and sometimes unexpected negative alterations in the life style of the retiree and his or her family. Death of peers is another frequent experience for older adults. These losses may include long-term intimate relationships such as those with spouses, friends, and family members of the same generation. Almost all of the major life changes of older adulthood, including declining health and loss of important roles and interpersonal relationships, have implications for the family networks of these individuals. Because older adults' needs for assistance from others often are increasing at a time when their involvement with and access to the social world are decreasing, a mismatch between needs and resources may result. In such times of need, it appears that older people turn first to their families for support and assistance. Family members often respond with many forms of assistance such as providing services and emotional support and making regular visits (Shanas, 1979; Weeks & Cuellar, 1981).

It is clear that the social and health-related stressors in later adulthood have far-reaching consequences that extend beyond the older person who experiences them directly. The family of this older person may be affected as well, sometimes in profound ways. Not only may family members be called upon to provide assistance and support to their older relative who experiences a stressful life situation, but also they often have to make adjustments to accommodate the stressful situation itself (McCubbin & Dahl, 1985). Thus families function as systems such that a change in any family member makes it necessary for other family members to adapt to this change. Several theoretical formulations have been proposed that describe family systems and their underlying dynamic relationships, and how these systems adapt to stressful life changes.

FAMILIES UNDER STRESS

The *Oxford English Dictionary* defines a family as a group of persons consisting of parents and their children, whether actually living together or not, or the unity formed by those who are connected by blood or affinity. A more psychosocial definition describes families as groups composed of individuals who have mutual obligations to provide a broad range of emotional and material support to one another (Dean, Lin, & Ensel, 1981).

Although a family unit in modern society is a highly complex entity that defies all but the most general definition, all families are considered to possess a number of important features, including structure, functions, assigned roles, modes of interacting, resources, a life cycle, and a set of individual members with unique histories (Turk & Kerns, 1985). Thus the family social system is an organization consisting of intricately related social positions that have complex sets of roles and norms. Families serve a wide variety of functions including reproduction, socialization, and emotionally intimate interaction. They also provide psychosocial protection for family members and accommodation to and transmission of a culture (Minuchin, 1974). In carrying out these functions, families appear to strive toward some sort of stability or predictability of preferred behavior among their members (Hess & Handel, 1985). Although different theories about family systems emphasize different aspects of family relationships, two dimensions related to family functioning, cohesion and adaptability, are prominent features of several theories. Because these dimensions may help shed light on the processes families use in coping with late life stressors, they are briefly discussed here.

Cohesion and Adaptability

Cohesion usually refers to the mutual attraction or attachment among members of a family unit. It has been defined as the degree of bonding or connection that family members have with one another (Olson, Sprenkle, & Russel, 1979). Cohesion from this perspective includes both the emotional bonding among members and the degree of individual autonomy each experiences. It has also been conceptualized within two constructs labeled *affective responsiveness* and *affective involvement* (Epstein, Bishop, & Levin, 1978). Affective responsiveness refers to the ability of the family to respond to a broad range of situations with appropriate feelings and emotional expression, whereas affective involvement refers to the degree to which family members value the activities and interests of one another. The focus is on how much and in what way family members can show an interest in and invest themselves in each other.

A second major dimension of family functioning, adaptability, refers to the family's capacity to adjust to and accommodate change with little psychological or organizational discomfort (Burr, 1982). It has been defined as the potential that a family system has for changing its power structure, role relationships, and relationship rules in response to situational and developmental stress (Olson et al., 1979). Adaptive flexibility is a related concept and refers to a family's ability to negotiate, function, and deal effectively with stressful situations (Beavers, 1977). Families that possess a high degree of adaptability are thought to have greater freedom to evolve and differentiate. Family problem-solving is closely related to adaptability and refers to a family's ability to resolve problems at a level that maintains effective family functioning.

Common to the major theories of family systems is the assumption that families often are confronted with stressful situations that require change or accommodation. Other theories have been developed to explain relations between a family's experience of crisis or disruption and its adaptation to this change.

Response to Crisis

Theories of family stress define family stressors as events that are perceived as disrupting or changing the family social system. These events represent something more than the normal changes that are expected as part of a family's regular routine. Rather, they are sufficiently unusual in that the family system itself changes (Hansen & Hill, 1964). Family crises evolve and are resolved over a period of time; therefore, families are seldom dealing with a single stressor. Instead, they often experience an accumulation of stressful events, especially following a major stressful life change (McCubbin & Patterson, 1983).

During times of stress, the family initially attempts to make adjustments in its pattern of interaction, with minimal change or disruption of the family's established patterns of behavior and structure. However, families in crisis often come to realize that in order to restore functional stability or family satisfaction, they need to restructure. Restructuring efforts may include modifications in established rules, goals, or patterns of interaction. To assist in this process, families call upon a variety of resources including psychological, social, interpersonal, and material contributions of individual family members. These resources may be old and established or they may be newly developed or strengthened in response to the demands emerging out of the stressful situation (McCubbin & Patterson, 1983).

Coping efforts such as restructuring and resource utilization are directed at restoring organization and unity within the family and promoting growth and development among its members. Adaptation, which encompasses the long-term effects of stressors on family functioning, represents the outcome of coping efforts. Such efforts highlight the paradox of family stress. Stressors present the family unit and its members with the opportunity for personal and family system changes and growth, while making the family increasingly vulnerable to emotional distress and family instability (McCubbin, Cauble, & Patterson, 1982).

From a family systems perspective, families that possess greater organizational adaptability or flexibility have the potential to respond to the demands for change with less psychosocial discomfort and disruption in normal functioning. Members of well-organized families have the ability to redefine or alter role functions with relative ease so as to accommodate changes imposed by stressors. In addition, the strong emotional bonds that exist among these individuals provide important interpersonal resources for coping efforts that include socially supportive interactions.

Although family systems theories posit that cohesion among family members is a key ingredient for optimal family functioning, its effects may not be wholly positive, either for the person who receives the support or for the family members who supply it. From the recipient's perspective, families may represent unique reservoirs of tangible and interpersonal support, and as such, they often provide critical assistance during periods of stress. However, in the course of receiving this assistance, there is always the potential that feelings of dependency, inadequacy, and resentment will be engendered in the recipient. From the perspective of the support provider, being able to help a member of one's family who is in need often provides inherent satisfaction and may fulfill a variety of social expectations about family members' responsibilities. At the same time, the sustained needs of an individual for this support can deplete a family's resources and substantially alter its functioning and stability. Thus it appears that, as is the case in all systems, any alteration in a family's established pattern of behavior sets into motion a variety of other changes, the effects of which sometimes are beneficial and sometimes are costly.

COSTS AND BENEFITS TO RECIPIENTS OF SUPPORT

Turning to others in times of need, as older adults frequently do with their families, reflects an active form of behavioral coping. Relationships with others can serve as sources of instrumental, emotional, and informational resources. Instrumental or material resources refer to tangible commodities such as money, goods, and services (Cohen & McKay, 1984). Emotional resources are the feelings of being loved and valued by others and the opportunity to reciprocate those feelings (Cobb, 1976). Informational resources are available when others make suggestions about the meaning of events, offer recommendations, or provide feedback concerning one's behavior (Cohen & McKay, 1984). During times of stress, the assistance of family and friends can be a significant aid to coping, especially if one is satisfied with the resources received (Cohen & Wills, 1985; Sarason & Sarason, 1984). Social support, or the exchange of instrumental, emotional, and informational resources that assist recipients in attaining their goals, is an important indicator of what transpires within a relationship and therefore can be seen as a measure of the quality of one's social life.

Recent research indicates that, for a number of populations and life situations, informal networks of interpersonal relations provide significant emotional assistance, information, and material support. Successful social relationships appear to foster good health and health-related behaviors, provide useful resources in stressful situations, and offer helpful feedback for maintaining appropriate behavioral practices (Cobb, 1979; Cohen & Wills, 1985; DiMatteo & Hays, 1981; Hammer, 1981; Wellman, 1981). Among older people who frequently experience decrements in physical stamina and social and financial resources, social relationships appear to play an important role in well-being. Some of the earliest research concerning this issue demonstrated that access to a confidant helps to safeguard the mental health of older persons experiencing certain types of life events (e.g., widowhood or retirement) that often reduce contact with less intimate network ties (Lowenthal & Haven, 1968).

One of the most consistent findings from research on social relationships and aging is that family members are major providers of assistance for older people (Hofer, 1981). Among a variety of ethnic groups, older people typically turn to their families in times of need (Hochschild, 1973; Johnson, 1971; Weeks & Cuellar, 1981). Families provide a wide range of support to their older relatives regardless of living arrangements or the older person's degree of impairment. However, these situational factors appear to affect the types of resources provided.

For relatively healthy older people residing in urban communities, their adult children have been shown to provide substantial assistance with activities such as personal care, shopping, household repairs, and transportation (Cantor, 1975). Even for residents of planned housing where many services are provided by the housing facility, family members continue to play a vital role in social systems (Stephens & Bernstein, 1984). These families often provide instrumental resources such as assistance with transportation and meals. Despite the exchange of these tangible resources, interpersonal resources such as sharing feelings and providing information seem to represent the core of residents' relationships with their families. However, when older adults experience health problems that severely limit their abilities to function independently, patterns of resource exchanges may be somewhat altered. For seriously disabled older people who have had a stroke, tangible help from their family members (e.g., aid with basic and instrumental activities of daily living) appears to represent the bulk of resources exchanged. In addition to this instrumental aid, emotional and informational resources also seem to be important resources received from family members, especially those that contained positive expressions about the older person's progress toward recovery (Stephens, Kinney, Norris, & Ritchie, 1987).

Both the mental and physical status of older people have been shown to influence the amount and kind of social support they receive (Arling 1976; Cohen & Sokolovsky, 1979, 1980), but relations between social support and psychological outcomes such as satisfaction, morale, and alienation are less clear. Some researchers have reported enhanced psychological functioning with increased support from others (Larson, 1974; Wood & Robertson, 1978), whereas other studies have shown little or no covariation (Cohen & Sokolovsky, 1980; Conner, Powers, & Bultena, 1979; Mancini, Quinn, Gavigan, & Franklin, 1980). These findings suggest that interactions with one's social network are not always beneficial and that both positive and negative outcomes can result from social relationships.

Recent evidence suggests that some interactions with others can, indeed, have deleterious effects on individuals undergoing life crises. Interactions regarded by such people as being undesirable have included discouraging the expression of feelings, urging quick resolution, and trivializing the crisis by relying on stereotypic support responses (Wortman & Lehman, 1985). In studies of such age-related psychosocial crises as widowhood (Rook, 1984), caregiving for a spouse with Alzheimer's disease (Fiore, Becker, & Coppel, 1983), and recovery from stroke (Stephens et al., 1987), both positive and negative interactions have been examined simultaneously. Across these investigations, a consistent pattern revealed that negative interactions generally were more strongly related to psychological distress than positive interactions were related to psychological adjustment.

It is intuitively obvious that any relationship within a social network may have both positive and negative features. When the social network is viewed as a system of mutual obligation, it is clear that the network not only provides support but also demands it in return. For the most part, the net effects of this exchange of support are beneficial. However, in some instances, the demands of the network may be excessive and burdensome, and this imbalance may account for some of the negative effects of social interactions (Antonucci & Depner, 1982).

Interpersonal relationships involving help to an older person who is experiencing some kind of life crisis are likely to be inequitable in that the older person receives more resources than he or she is able to reciprocate. Under these conditions, recipients' reactions to help may be in part determined by their perceptions of the amount of inequity between themselves and the person providing the help (Greenberg, 1980; Greenberg & Westcott, 1983; Hatfield & Sprecher, 1983). Such inequity, or indebtedness, is thought to be an aversive state that is experienced when there is an unfavorable correspondence between what one gives and what one receives in a relationship. When older people are recipients of help, they may be experiencing diminished health and income that often accompany old age. These conditions tend to increase their dependence on others and to reduce the capacity to reciprocate support provided by others

(Cicirelli, 1983). Thus demands for reciprocity from one's network may seem especially excessive to older people who are experiencing highly stressful situations and whose personal resources for coping are low. Under such conditions these demands may further erode the older person's well-being.

The way in which the recipient's self-concept is affected by the receipt of assistance may be one mechanism through which these inequitable relationships gain their psychological significance. Help from others frequently contains a mixture of both self-enhancing elements such as its instrumental value or evidence that one is cared for, and self-threatening elements such as evidence that one has failed, is inferior, or is dependent. The consequences that receiving help holds for the self-concept may strongly influence how one reacts to that help.

Whereas threats to self-esteem communicated through help appear to produce negative reactions in the recipient, it is also the case that the esteem enhancement involved in help forms the primary component of exchanges that are regarded as supportive (Heller, Swindle, & Dusenbury, 1986; Thoits, 1985). Thus, when self-esteem is threatened, social interactions that may be intended as supportive could evoke negative reactions from recipients. Therefore, it may not only be the inequity of helping relationships per se that determines their effects, but also how that help is perceived and interpreted by recipients in terms of their own self-worth.

COSTS AND BENEFITS TO FAMILIES PROVIDING SUPPORT

Although early research on the interplay between older adults and their families tended to focus on the assistance that was received by the older person, recent research has begun to document the effects that providing such support has on family members. This research has most often examined families who provide support to chronically ill and disabled older relatives. Several factors may help to explain this tendency to focus on illness. Illness and disability constitute common and often severe stressors in old age, and families provide the bulk of health care for these ill older adults. Additionally, the amount of family support required to offset the functional limitations that are due to illness and disability is often great and is needed for an extended period of time. For these reasons families often have to make major adjustments to accommodate the older person's needs. The case of illness provides an important arena for learning how the long-term provision of assistance can affect support providers.

At those times when families are challenged by illness, family roles and relationships often must be redefined or modified. The outcome of such restructuring efforts can range from the undesirable, such as distancing among family members or dissolution of the family unit, to the more desirable, such as an increase in family cohesiveness and in a sense of well-being in its members

(Boss, 1987; Johnson, 1988). According to family systems theory, roles (including both status and behavioral expectations) are clearly defined and coordinated in a well-organized family. Additionally, these family units are cohesive and effective in solving problems and reducing psychological distress that is due to life crises. Therefore it would be expected that the crisis of illness in a family member would have a more devastating impact on a poorly organized family. It can also be expected that a well-organized family will be negatively affected, especially if the experience of illness is novel. The first experience of chronic illness in an adult may pose unanticipated demands and require coping responses that are not part of existing role expectations or skills. The ambiguities inherent in such novelty may bring to the forefront questions about the legitimacy of obligations and the legitimacy of requests for assistance that are not typically considered in everyday family interactions (Levanthal, Levanthal, & Nguyen, 1985).

In times of illness, social expectations and pressures often are brought to bear on family members who are expected to provide assistance to its ill member. Although families in Western culture are characterized by relative flexibility in forming and maintaining relationships (Furstenberg, 1981; Hagestad, 1981), norms of obligation or duty to family also operate and may evolve from strong feelings of affection (Finley, Roberts, & Banahan, 1988). These norms influence both the ill person's expectations about the family member's obligations to provide support and the family member's willingness to comply.

Other pressures for the family to provide help during times of illness may be based on norms of reciprocity, which suggest that help is given in return for the ill person's aid and support in the past. These norms have been described as the principle of give and take that underlie the stability of all social systems (Gouldner, 1960). Although this principle holds that there is no overt calculation as to what one gives and receives in a relationship, the abrogation of this norm can lead to a breakdown of the relationship. In later-life families, spouses and adult children form the core reciprocal relationships of the ill older adult (Johnson, 1988). Strong feelings of obligation and reciprocity may explain why these family members frequently assume major caregiving roles for their ill older relatives.

One of the most striking features of research on the psychosocial impact of giving care to a dependent older family member is the high degree of variability among caregivers' responses to the chronic demands of their role. Although initially is was assumed that caregivers' mental and physical health status would steadily decline throughout the course of giving care, some research has indicated that many caregivers adapt well to their role. In many cases improvement rather than deterioration is the norm (Townsend, Noelker, Deimling, & Bass, 1989). Overall, caregiving families have been found to have impressive adaptive capabilities (Horowitz, 1985).

Some aspects of caregiving have been shown to be positive experiences that produce feelings of mastery and satisfaction in the caregiver (Danis, 1978; Moss, Lawton, Dean, Goodman, & Schneider, 1987; Seelbach, 1978). Personal satisfaction and increased self-respect are commonly cited by caregivers as some of the rewards of their role. They also cite other rewards such as an improved relationship with and greater understanding of the ill family member, placing other life stressors in better perspective, and relief from worry about the care the ill family member receives. Even among caregivers to individuals with dementia, when role demands are often very high, small satisfactions with caregiving are reported surprisingly often (Kinney & Stephens, 1989).

Despite the gratification that family caregivers may derive from their role, research indicates that caregiving can produce a substantial amount of stress especially if the ill person's condition is severe and prolonged (Johnson, 1983). The impact on the family member who is most responsible for giving care (the primary caregiver) includes changes in psychological and somatic health and personal life style, as well as depletion of financial resources. When compared to social and emotional stressors, financial demands seem to be easiest to deal with and are the least frequently reported as being stressful (Horowitz, 1985).

Clearly the greatest impact on caregivers is in the area of emotional well-being. Reports of distress among caregivers are widespread (Cantor, 1983), usually resulting in feelings of depression, anxiety, low morale, and loneliness (Brocklehurst, Morris, Andrews, Richards, & Laycock, 1981; Kinney & Stephens, 1989; Poulshock & Deimling, 1984). In the area of somatic health, caregivers frequently report changes in their own health, increases in medical treatment, and in use of tranquilizers and antidepressants (Brocklehurst et al., 1981). Changes in life style, especially restrictions on time and freedom, are some of the social consequences of caregiving (Horowitz, 1985). In addition, other social relationships may be eliminated, or caregivers' attitudes may change so that they withdraw from their friends and become more tense and anxious (Chenoweth & Spencer, 1986). Not only are primary caregivers often affected negatively by the chronic stressors of caregiving, but evidence suggests that such effects are also felt by other members of their families (Brody, 1981).

As has been previously noted, relationships between caregivers and care-recipients often are inequitable. In contrast to care-recipients who frequently are overbenefitted, caregivers are likely to be underbenefitted in that they most often give more in these relationships than they receive. Being underbenefitted is thought to be the more aversive state (Austin & Walster, 1974). Furthermore, such inequities are likely to persist over long periods of time. Thus, although caregivers may have accepted their roles in response to the norms of reciprocity based on past interactions with the ill older person, the inability of the ill person to reciprocate in the present may help to explain some of the negative consequences of caregiving.

Just as self-esteem may mediate the ill person's reactions to the help he or she receives, feelings of esteem may also mediate the caregiver's reactions to the help he or she provides. On the one hand, providing assistance to an ill family member could enhance the caregiver's sense of self-worth through knowing that the recipient's needs are being met, fulfilling family obligations and responsibilities, and mastering the skills required to care for another person. On the other hand, a caregiver's sense of self-worth could be threatened through other situations such as believing that one's assistance is not appreciated by the care-recipient, that one's other roles are compromised because of the time and effort spent in caregiving, and that caregiving efforts are not successful in restoring or maintaining the ill person's health or behavior. Thus, the negative reactions of the caregiver may not only be due to the lack of reciprocity from the care-recipient, but also by the ways in which the self-esteem of caregivers is implicated in the help they provide.

PURPOSE OF THIS VOLUME

This overview suggests that both helping and being helped are key components of family members' interactions with one another, and they represent part of what it means to be a member of a cohesive family unit. In later-life families, older adults often call on their families for help in times of need, and their families generally respond affirmatively to these requests. Although on the surface such supportive exchanges appear to be an indication of healthy family functioning, research on receiving and providing aid strongly indicates that the effects of these interactions are not wholly positive and that family functioning under these conditions is not always optimal. Theories of family stress point out that stressful circumstances not only present families with possibilities of dysfunction and dissolution but also they hold opportunities for growth and enhancement.

Although theory and research on receiving and providing support within families have strong implications for one another, little communication exists between these areas. For example, researchers interested in the experiences of family caregivers most often conceptualize these experiences in terms of the stressors that caregivers encounter in their role rather than examining this role in the context of dyadic relationships. The focus is usually on the caregiver and the role demands that she or he encounters rather than on the relationship between the caregiver and care-recipient. The psychosocial impact of the caregiver's role demands is undoubtedly influenced by characteristics of the dyadic interaction, such as the care-recipient's inability to adequately reciprocate the help that has been provided by the caregiver.

Researchers concerned with the negative effects experienced by the recipients of help tend to engage in a similar kind of one-sidedness. They often accept their findings that some interactions have deleterious consequences without asking why these negative interactions occur. Especially when the focus is on individuals whose needs for assistance are chronic, too little consideration has been given to the demands created by providing sustained support and how these demands may exhaust the caregiver's personal resources. Exhaustion of personal resources can lead to friction and disharmony in the dyad that can produce undesirable consequences for support providers, as well as for support recipients.

The primary purpose of this volume is to bring together theory and research in three major areas pertaining to stress and coping in later-life families. Because giving and receiving help frequently occur in the context of an acute crisis or a more enduring stressful event, the first section of this volume focuses on the kinds of stressors that are commonly experienced in later-life families and the mechanisms underlying these stressors. The second section addresses issues pertaining to older people's needs for socially supportive relationships during times of stress and how these relationships may impact their psychosocial well-being. The third section focuses on the effects of providing long-term support to an older family member.

Although chapters in this volume are concerned with somewhat different aspects of coping in later-life families, there are many commonalities in the problems and processes they address. Figure 1 is designed to depict these commonalities. Boxes in the figure contain descriptors of the general constructs that are dealt with in the volume. Arrows are used to indicate the links among constructs that are the foci of various chapters; they are not intended to imply direction of causation, or all possible linkages.

The top row of boxes displays the experiences, responses, and adaptation of the older adult who is undergoing some type of life stress, and the bottom row of boxes displays the experiences, responses, and adaptation of their family members under such stressful conditions. Stressors encountered by the older adult (Box A) may include any event or change that is perceived as taxing or exceeding personal resources and threatening well-being. These stressors may be acute or chronic (e.g., sudden death of an important person or a physically disabling disease), they may be large or small in magnitude (e.g., retirement from a career or constantly misplacing things around the house), and they may stem from a variety of sources (e.g., physical environment and interpersonal relationships). What is common among stressors is the appraisal by the person who experiences them that personal resources are inadequate to cope with the demands imposed by the stressful situations, and that well-being is jeopardized. The older person may respond to the stressor in a variety of ways (Box B), including attempting to manage the problem itself or its concomitant emotions, seeking help and support from others, and reacting to the responses that others make to the situation. In some cases, older people may respond to their own needs by becoming involved with and assisting others. All these responses ultimately play a role in determining how older people will adapt to the stressful experience, that is, how their psychological, social, and somatic health will be affected (Box C).

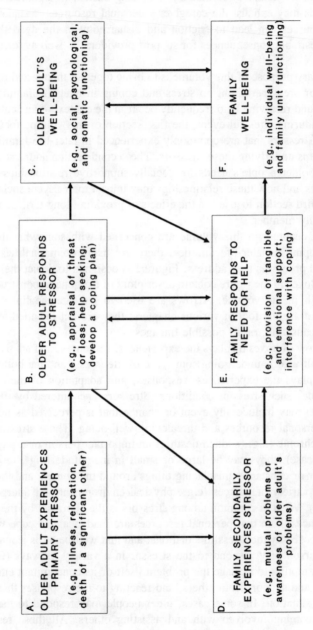

FIGURE 1 Relationships among constructs featured in *Stress and Coping in Later-Life Families.*

The boxes in the figure read:

A. OLDER ADULT EXPERIENCES PRIMARY STRESSOR
(e.g., illness, relocation, death of a significant other)

B. OLDER ADULT RESPONDS TO STRESSOR
(e.g., appraisal of threat or loss; help seeking; develop a coping plan)

C. OLDER ADULT'S WELL-BEING
(e.g., social, psychological, and somatic functioning)

D. FAMILY SECONDARILY EXPERIENCES STRESSOR
(e.g., mutual problems or awareness of older adult's problems)

E. FAMILY RESPONDS TO NEED FOR HELP
(e.g., provision of tangible and emotional support, interference with coping)

F. FAMILY WELL-BEING
(e.g., individual well-being and family unit functioning)

14

As is indicated in the bottom row of Figure 1, the older person's family members become aware of the stressful situation confronting their relative (Box D). Such awareness may come about through a number of channels. The family may gain this knowledge through shared experiences (e.g., death of a mutual friend) or by direct observation (e.g., observing the older person's symptoms of illness), or the information may come from the older person (e.g., through a request for help). Based on this awareness, family members respond to the older person's needs (Box E), very often resulting in some form of aid or support. However, sometimes family members' responses may interfere with the older person's coping efforts. Ultimately, the psychological, social, and somatic adaptation of family members will be affected (Box F).

Each chapter in this volume emphasizes constructs in at least two boxes that are connected by an arrow in Figure 1. Overviews preceding each section describe the constructs and relationships from Figure 1 that are emphasized in each chapter of that section. It is the intent of this volume to offer opportunities for researchers in several different areas to communicate with one another and to help develop a better understanding of how later-life families cope with the stressors that frequently beset one of their older members and that have implications for the family as a whole.

REFERENCES

American Association of Retired Persons. (1986). *A profile of older Americans.* (PF3049-1086-D996). Washington, DC: Author.

Antonucci, T. C., & Depner, C. E. (1982). Social support and informal helping relationships. In T. A. Wills (Ed.), *Basic processes in helping relationships* (pp. 233–254). New York: Academic Press.

Arling, G. (1976). Resistance to isolation among elderly widows. *International Journal of Aging and Human Development, 7,* 67–86.

Austin, W., & Walster, E. (1974). Reactions to confirmations and disconfirmations of expectancies of equity and inequity. *Journal of Personality and Social Psychology, 30,* 208–216.

Beavers, W. (1977). *Psychotherapy and growth: A family systems perspective.* New York: Brunner/Mazel.

Bohm, L. C., & Rodin, J. (1985). Aging and the family. In D. C. Turk & R. D. Kerns (Eds.), *Health, illness and families: A life-span perspective* (pp. 279–310). New York: Wiley.

Boss, P. (1987). Family stress. In M. B. Sussman & S. K. Steinmetz (Eds.), *Handbook of marriage and the family* (pp. 695–723). New York: Plenum Press.

Brocklehurst, J. C., Morris, P., Andrews, K., Richards, R., & Laycock, P. (1981). Social effects of stroke. *Social Science and Medicine, 15,* 35–39.

Brody, E. M. (1981). "Women in the middle" and family help to older people. *The Gerontologist, 21,* 471–480.

Brody, E. M., & Kleban, M. H. (1983). Day-to-day mental and physical health symptoms of older people: A report on health logs. *The Gerontologist, 23,* 75–85.

Burr, W. (1982). Families under stress. In H. I. McCubbin, A. E. Cauble, & J. M. Patterson (Eds.), *Family stress, coping and social support* (pp. 5–25). Springfield, IL: Charles C Thomas.

Cantor, M. H. (1975). Life space and the social support system of the inner city elderly of New York. *The Gerontologist, 15,* 23–27.

Cantor, M. (1983). Strain among caregivers: A study of experience in the United States. *The Gerontologist, 23*(6), 597–604.

Chenoweth, B., & Spencer, B. (1986). Dementia: The experience of family caregivers. *The Gerontologist, 26*(3), 267–272.

Cicirelli, V. G. (1983). Adult children's attachment and helping to elderly parents: A path model. *Journal of Marriage and the Family, 45,* 815–825.

Cobb, S. (1976). Social support as a moderator of life stress. *Psychosomatic Medicine, 38,* 300–314.

Cobb, S. (1979). Social support and health through the life course. In M. W. Riley (Ed.), *Aging from birth to death: Interdisciplinary perspectives* (pp. 93–106). Boulder, CO: Westview Press.

Cohen, C. I., & Sokolovsky, J. (1979). Health-seeking behavior and social networks of the aged living in the single-room occupancy hotels. *Journal of the American Geriatrics Society, 27,* 270–278.

Cohen, C. I., & Sokolovsky, J. (1980). Social engagement versus isolation: The case of the aged in SRO hotels. *The Gerontologist, 20,* 36–44.

Cohen, S., & McKay, G. (1984). Social support, stress, and the buffering hypothesis: An empirical and theoretical analysis. In A. Baum, J. E. Singer, & S. E. Taylor (Eds.), *Handbook of psychology and health* (Vol. 4, pp. 253–263). Hillsdale, NJ: Erlbaum.

Cohen, S., & Wills, T. A. (1985). Stress, social support and the buffering hypothesis. *Psychological Bulletin, 98,* 310–357.

Conner, K. A., Powers, E. A., & Bultena, G. L. (1979). Social interaction and life satisfaction: An empirical assessment of late-life patterns. *Journal of Gerontology, 34,* 116–121.

Danis, B. G. (1978, November). *Stress in individuals caring for ill relatives.* Paper presented at the meeting of the Gerontological Society of America, Dallas, TX.

Dean, A., Lin, N., & Ensel, W. M. (1981). The epidemiological significance of social support systems in depression. *Research in Community Mental Health, 2,* 77–109.

DiMatteo, M. R., & Hays, R. (1981). Social support and serious illness. In

B. H. Gottlieb (Ed.), *Social networks and social support* (pp. 117–148). Beverly Hills: Sage.

Epstein, N., Bishop, D. S., & Levin, S. (1978). The McMaster model of family functioning. *Journal of Marriage and Family Counseling, 4,* 19–31.

Finley, N. J., Roberts, M. D., & Banahan, B. F. (1988). Motivators and inhibitors of attitudes of filial obligation toward aging parents. *The Gerontologist, 28,* 72–78.

Fiore, J., Becker, J., & Coppel, D. B. (1983). Social network interactions: A buffer or a stress. *American Journal of Community Psychology, 11,* 423–439.

Furstenberg, F. (1981). Remarriage and intergenerational relations. In R. W. Fogel, E. Hatfield, F. Kieser, E. Shanas, & J. G. March, (Eds.), *Aging: Stability and change in the family* (pp. 115–142). New York: Academic Press.

Gouldner, A. W. (1960). The norm of reciprocity: A preliminary statement. *American Sociological Review, 25,* 161–178.

Gilford, D. M. (Ed.). (1988). The aging population in the twenty-first century. Washington, DC: National Academy Press.

Greenberg, M. S. (1980). A theory of indebtedness. In K. J. Gergen, M. S. Greenberg, & R. H. Willis (Eds.), *Social exchange: Advances in theory and research* (pp. 3–26). New York: Plenum.

Greenberg, M., & Westcott, D. (1983). Indebtedness, as a mediator of reactions to aid. In J. D. Fisher, A. Nadler, & B. M. DePaulo (Eds.), *New directions in helping: 1. Recipient reactions to aid* (pp. 85–112). New York: Academic Press.

Hagestad, G. (1981). Problems and promises in the social psychology of intergenerational relations. In R. W. Fogel, E. Hatfield, F. Kieser, E. Shanas, & J. G. March, (Eds.), *Aging: Stability and change in the family* (pp. 11–46). New York: Academic Press.

Hammer, M. (1981, January). *Impact of social networks on health and disease.* Paper presented at the meeting of the American Association for the Advancement of Science, Toronto.

Hansen, D., & Hill, R. (1964). Families under stress. In H. Christenson (Ed.), *Handbook of marriage and the family* (pp. 782–819). Chicago: Rand McNally.

Hatfield, E., & Sprecher, S. (1983). Equity theory and recipient reactions to aid. In J. D. Fisher, A. Nadler, & B. M. DePaulo (Eds.), *New directions in helping: 1. Recipient reactions to aid.* New York: Academic Press.

Heller, K., Swindle, R. W. Jr., & Dusenbury, L. (1986). Component social support processes: Comments and integration. *Journal of Consulting and Clinical Psychology, 5,* 466–470.

Hess, R. D., & Handel, G. (1985). The family as a psychosocial organization. In G. Handel (Ed.), *The psychosocial interior of the family* (pp. 33–46). New York: Aldine.

Hochschild, A. R. (1973). *The unexpected community.* Englewood Cliffs, NJ: Prentice-Hall.

Hofer, A. (1981, November). *The emerging role of the family support system for the elderly living at home.* Paper presented at the meeting of the Gerontological Society of America, Toronto.

Horowitz, A. (1985). Family caregiving to the frail elderly. In M. P. Lawton & G. L. Maddox (Eds.), *Annual review of gerontology and geriatrics* (Vol. 5, pp. 194–246). New York: Springer.

Johnson, C. L. (1983). Dyadic family relations and social support. *The Gerontologist, 23,* 377–383.

Johnson, C. L. (1988). Relationships among family members and friends in later life. In R. M. Milardo (Ed.), *Families and social networks* (pp. 168–189). Beverly Hills: Sage.

Johnson, S. K. (1971). *Idle haven: Community building among the working class retired.* Berkeley: University of California Press.

Kay, D. W. K., & Bergmann, K. (1980). Epidemiology of mental disorders among the aged in the community. In J. E. Birren & B. R. Slone (Eds.), *Handbook of mental health.* Englewood Cliffs, NJ: Prentice-Hall.

Kinney, J. M., & Stephens, M. A. P. (1989). Hassles and uplifts of giving care to a family member with dementia. *Psychology and Aging, 4,* 402–408.

Larson, C. J. (1974). Alienation and public housing for the elderly. *International Journal of Aging and Human Development, 5,* 217–230.

Levanthal, H., Levanthal, E. A., & Ngyuen, T. V. (1985). Reactions of families to illness: Theoretical models and perspectives. In D. C. Turk & R. D. Kerns (Eds.), *Health, illness, and families: A life-span perspective* (pp. 108–145). New York: Wiley.

Lowenthal, M. F., & Haven, C. (1968). Interaction and adaptation: Intimacy as a critical variable. *American Sociological Review, 33,* 20–30.

Mancini, J. A., Quinn, W., Gavigan, M. A., & Franklin, H. (1980). Social network interaction among older adults: Implications for life satisfaction. *Human Relations, 33,* 543–554.

McCubbin, H. I., Cauble, A. E., & Patterson, J. M. (1982). In H. I. McCubbin, A. E. Cauble, & J. M. Patterson (Eds.), *Family stress, coping and social support* (pp. xi–xvii). Springfield, IL: Charles C Thomas.

McCubbin, H., & Dahl, B. B. (1985). *Marriage and family: Individuals and life cycles.* New York: Wiley.

McCubbin, H. I., & Patterson, J. M. (1983). Family stress and adaptation to crises: A double ABCX model of family behavior. In D. H. Olson & B. C. Miller (Eds.), *Family studies yearbook* (Vol. 1, pp. 87–106). Beverly Hills: Sage.

Minuchin, S. (1974). *Families and family therapy.* Boston: Harvard University Press.

Moss, M., Lawton, M. P., Dean, J., Goodman, M., & Schneider, J. (1987,

November). *Satisfactions and burdens in caring for impaired elderly persons.* Paper presented at the meeting of the Gerontological Society of America, Washington, DC.

Office of Technology Assessment. (1985). *Technology and aging in America.* (OTA Publication No. BA-264). Washington, DC: U.S. Government Printing Office.

Olson, D., Sprenkle, D., & Russel, C. (1979). Circumplex model of marital and family systems: 1. Cohesion and adaptability dimensions, family types, and clinical applications. *Family Processes, 18,* 29-44.

Poulshock, S. W., & Deimling, G. T. (1984). Families caring for elders in residence: Issues in the measurement of burden. *Journal of Gerontology, 39,* 230-239.

Rook, K. S. (1984). The negative side of social interaction: Impact on psychological well-being. *Journal of Personality and Social Psychology, 46,* 1097-1108.

Rowe, J. W. (1985). Health care of the elderly. *New England Journal of Medicine, 312*(13), 827-835.

Sarason, I. G., & Sarason, B. R. (1984). Life changes, moderators of stress and health. In A. Baum, S. E. Taylor, & J. E. Singer (Eds.), *Handbook of psychology and health: 4. Social psychological aspects of health.* Hillsdale, NJ: Erlbaum.

Seelbach, W. C. (1978). Correlates of aged parents filial responsibility, expectations, and realizations. *Family Coordinator, 27,* 341-350.

Shanas, E. (1979). The family as a social support system in old age. *The Gerontologist, 19,* 169-174.

Stephens, M. A. P., & Bernstein, M. D. (1984). Social support and well-being among residents of planned housing. *The Gerontologist, 24,* 144-148.

Stephens, M. A. P., Kinney, J. M., Norris, V. K., & Ritchie, S. W. (1987). Social networks as assets and liabilities in recovery from stroke by geriatric patients. *Psychology and Aging, 2,* 125-129.

Thoits, P. A. (1985). Social support and psychological well-being: Theoretical possibilities. In I. G. Sarason & B. R. Sarason (Eds.), *Social support: Theory, research, and applications* (pp. 51-72). The Hague, The Netherlands: Martinus Nijhoff.

Townsend, A., Noelker, L., Deimling, G., & Bass, D. (in press). Longitudinal impact of interhousehold caregiving on adult children's mental health. *Psychology and Aging.*

Turk, D. C., & Kerns, R. D. (1985). The family in health and illness. In D. C. Turk & R. D. Kerns (Eds.), *Health, illness and families: A life-span perspective* (pp. 1-22). New York: Wiley.

Weeks, J. R., & Cuellar, J. P. (1981). The role of family members in the helping networks of older people. *The Gerontologist, 21,* 388-394.

Wellman, B. (1981). Applying network analysis to the study of support. In

B. H. Gottlieb (Ed.), *Social networks and social support*. Beverly Hills: Sage.

Wood, V., & Robertson, J. F. (1978). Friendship and kinship interaction: Differential effect on the morale of the elderly. *Journal of Marriage and the Family, 40,* 367–375.

Wortman, C. B., & Lehman, D. R. (1985). Reactions to victims of life crises: Support attempts that fail. In I. G. Sarason & B. R. Sarason (Eds.), *Social support: Theory, research, and applications* (pp. 463–489). The Hague, The Netherlands: Martinus Nijhoff.

I

STRESS IN LATER-LIFE FAMILIES

2

OVERVIEW

Brenda Papincak Loren
Melissa M. Franks

Kent State University

Many stress and coping theorists agree that the stressfulness of an event is a function of the characteristics of the organism experiencing the event. When the organism is a family, the event is experienced not only by individuals, but also by the entire family system. Stressful experiences are frequent in later-life families that are exposed to the sometimes unexpected and merciless changes that threaten the well-being of their older members. Family members may be exposed to the aging adult's emotional reactions to stressful situations and are often directly involved in the management of their relative's problems. The novelty, chronicity, and intensity of many later-life problems may tax the coping resources of the family unit as well as the resources of individual family members. Additionally, structural and dynamic changes that alter relationships within the aging family may complicate both the older adult's ability to ask for and accept assistance and the family's ability to provide it. As the size and age of the older adult population increases, so does the need for us to understand the stress encountered by these individuals, and the factors that influence how they and their families cope during later life.

The chapters in this section have the important task of laying the foundation for sections to follow by exploring the unique aspects of later-life stress as experienced by both older adults and their families. Brubaker begins this process by introducing us to the later-life family, which, as a distinct family system, is contracting in size as a result of the launching of children and the loss of loved ones due to death. The family caregiving situation is used to illustrate later-life family processes and the ways in which these processes influence

23

family stress. Brubaker proposes a contextual theory of family stress in later life in which caregiving stress, and responses to it, develop in the context of individual, interpersonal, familial, and societal networks over time. This multifaceted context is thought to allow for the great variety seen in the responses of older adults and their families to stressful events and the stress associated with caregiving. It also helps us understand the reciprocal relationship between the older adult's well-being and that of the family.

The focus on stress in later-life families sets Brubaker's ideas apart from those of other family stress theorists. Given that most other theories of family stress are limited to the family during child-rearing years, Brubaker's chapter represents a pioneering effort to extend family stress theory to the post–child-rearing period. His focus on the complex context of the caregiver–care-recipient relationship and interpersonal dynamics offers valuable insights into the inner workings of these families. Understanding how these dynamics affect the development of caregiving stress will become increasingly important as the number of caregiving families grows, and as society becomes more demanding of solutions to the concerns and problems of older adults.

Aldwin calls our attention to those stressors in later life that arise from the older adult's concern for others. Her unique contribution lies in her integration of developmental theory and a phenomenological approach to stress. Drawing from Erikson's developmental theory of generativity, she proposes that stress experienced by significant others (which she refers to as nonegocentric stress), becomes more salient in later life as a consequence of reaching the developmental stage of generativity where nurturing and guiding others is a central concern. Generativity is thought to alter appraisal processes in later life, thereby changing the older adult's perception and experience of stress. As older adults become more concerned with difficulties encountered by loved ones, they tend to appraise these other-related problems as stressful, while minimizing all but the most life-threatening personal or "egocentric" stressors. They become attuned to the well-being of others and frequently become actively involved in providing assistance and social support to those for whom they are concerned. Aldwin believes that the presence of nonegocentric stress reflects a healthy, adaptive mechanism by which older adults minimize their own often uncontrollable problems, remain involved with others, and maintain a sense of purpose and meaning in their lives.

Krause further expands our understanding of later-life stress by examining stress that occurs when older adults experience changes in the social roles they occupy. Loss or change in important social roles is a hallmark of later life, and it constitutes a major potential source of stress for older adults. The degree of stress and its impact is thought to vary as a function of the social role involved and its importance to the individual. Krause maintains that role-related stress operates by eroding feelings of self-esteem and personal control, ultimately resulting in psychological distress. Changes in highly salient roles are thought to have a greater impact on self-esteem, feelings of control, and psychological well-being, when compared to the impact of changes in less important social roles. Furthermore, social support is thought to offset the deleterious effects of stress by bolstering self-esteem and feelings of personal control in the face of these role-related changes.

Krause's major contribution is his formulation of a testable causal model that delineates the effects of the stress process and social support on self-esteem, personal control, and psychological well-being within salient social roles. He explicitly describes detailed methods for identifying and measuring salient social roles, role-specific stressful events, role-specific self-esteem and personal control, and supportive social relations. He provides statistical guidance for modeling causal relationships among these variables and identifies modeling limitations inherent in the estimation of nonlinear effects of social support. Although the statistical sections of this chapter may be difficult for the uninitiated, they represent a methodological advance in efforts to translate theory into testable hypotheses that can be used by researchers who investigate complex psychosocial phenomena.

Thus far, the chapters in this section have been limited to relatively normative aspects of later-life stress in individual, interpersonal, familial, and social contexts. Lomranz's chapter introduces us to the stages and developmental consequences of traumatic stress, and discusses its impact on the aging process in the later-life families of Holocaust survivors. This chapter constitutes an important bridge between the stress and trauma literature, as well as a needed contribution to the understanding of a specific trauma that affected millions of families. Like Aldwin and Krause, he discusses the impact of stress on the older adult's personal well-being. He also echoes Brubaker and Aldwin in their recognition of the relationship between the older adult's well-being and that of the family. Lomranz's special contribution, however, lies in his emphasis on historical events and their impact on individual and family dynamics. He describes the ways in which long-term adaptation to a traumatic event, namely, the Holocaust, has altered the developmental experience of aging for both elderly Holocaust survivors and their families.

Whereas Brubaker emphasizes family history in terms of family members' shared experiences, Lomranz emphasizes past events experienced by the older adult alone that later come to bear on that person's family. Particular attention is given to intergenerational and role-related problems that are often caused by the ways in which elderly Holocaust survivors have coped with their traumatic experience. Coping with trauma is also discussed as it relates to the ability of these individuals to deal with more normative stressors such as illness or the loss of a spouse. Although the focus of the chapter is on the potential negative impact of personal trauma on both the individual and family in later life, Lomranz points out that many Holocaust survivors have adapted successfully and that they represent a fruitful arena for stress and coping research.

In addition to focusing on later-life stress as it affects the older adult, the chapters in this section also address the impact of stress on the older adult's family. Families generally are concerned and involved when their elders experience difficulty, typically offering support meant to offset the effects of stress on the older adult's well-being. However, such involvement requires that the family adjust to the changes encountered by the older adult, often by altering their own roles or taking on new ones. Brubaker helps us understand how these changes, especially those involved in giving care to an aged parent, can be stressful both for the recipient of this care and for the family that provides it. Stress may develop as a result of the difficulty that a caregiver has accepting a parent's increasing dependency or as a result of role overload. For example, caregiving demands may be placed on an adult child who may also have a variety of other role-related demands such as those associated with being a spouse, parent, and breadwinner. Family resources, personal characteristics of the caregiver and care-recipient, and the history of their relationship set the context in which caregiving demands are encountered, appraised, and managed. Together, they determine the level of stress experienced by caregivers, as well as that experienced by older adults themselves. Lomranz's chapter adds societal history to this list of factors and provides an excellent example of how families can be affected by stress experienced long ago by their aging loved ones.

Taken together, these four chapters provide a solid foundation for understanding the nature of stress in later-life families. They also leave us with three broad points to consider. First, stress in later life is qualitatively different from that associated with other stages of the family life cycle. It tends to more deeply involve role changes and role loses, and it may involve increasing concern with stressful events being experienced by loved ones. Such stress is profoundly influenced by a multiplicity of individual, interpersonal, familial, and societal factors, the presence and influence of which vary widely from individual to individual and from family to family across time.

Second, stress in later life may differ quantitatively from stress associated with other stages of the family life cycle and, therefore, may have a greater impact on both the individual and the family. Later-life stress is often more taxing because of the novelty of the problems encountered or because of the intense, often life-and-death, nature of the demand involved. These demands also tend to be chronic, giving little opportunity for the day-to-day accumulation of the effects of stress to subside. Intensity, novelty, and chronicity are recognized as potent determinants of the stressfulness and degree of impact of a given stressor. As such, later life represents a time of increased exposure to stressors that have greater potential to negatively affect the well-being of both older adults and their families.

Finally, the systems perspective taken by the authors reminds us that stress in later life does not occur in a vacuum, but that stress affecting older adults and their families is reciprocal in nature. Families do not sit back as their elders struggle with problems. Occasionally, their attempts to help actually exacerbate the older adult's difficulties or cause new ones. Similarly, older adults are often aware of any burden their presence places on the family, and they may react emotionally or behaviorally in ways that further burden the family. An accelerating spiral of later-life stress fed by the actions and reactions of both the older adult and the family often results. A greater understanding of this shared experience of later-life stress will be necessary if we are to effectively assist later-life families in their attempts to manage the never before experienced events associated with the later stages of the family life cycle.

3

A CONTEXTUAL APPROACH TO THE DEVELOPMENT OF STRESS ASSOCIATED WITH CAREGIVING IN LATER-LIFE FAMILIES

Timothy H. Brubaker

Miami University

Within the past decade, later-life families have received increasing attention within gerontology and family studies. Long-term marriage; intergenerational relationships; relationships among work, retirement, and family; and health and family relationships have been addressed. Family caregiving to dependent older adults has also received a great deal of attention within the past few years. As individuals live longer, these issues, as well as others related to the later portions of the family life cycle, will continue to be attractive to gerontologists and family scholars.

This chapter focuses on later-life families and, in particular, the development of family stress that is due to caregiving. I discuss the unique aspects of later-life families and review research on family structure, caregiving, and stress. Finally, based on family stress literature, I present a contextual approach to the development of family stress in caregiving families.

Families that consist of older members have needs, stresses, resources, and experiences that are different from those of families consisting of newlyweds or couples with young children. Using the family development approach (Duvall, 1977) as a basis, I have defined later-life families as those whose members are in the middle and later years of their lives. Later-life families begin when a family unit starts to define itself as dealing with tasks related to the "contraction" of its structure and, in many cases, interaction patterns (Brubaker, 1985).

Later-life families have been defined as "families who are beyond the child-rearing years and have begun to launch their children" (Brubaker, 1983, p. 9).

The focus of these family units is on the changing structure of the nuclear unit. Specifically, "the emphasis is on the *remaining members* of the family of orientation *after* the children have initiated their own families of procreation" (Brubaker, 1985, p. 13).

This definition is not directly related to chronological age. Rather, the crucial factor for determining the ages at which parents enter the later stages of the family life cycle is the parents' ages at their children's birth. For example, if a mother is 18 years of age when her first child is born and her child leaves home at age 18, the mother has the potential of beginning to deal with contraction of the family at age 36 years. Other families may not experience issues associated with contraction of the family unit until one or both of the parents is aged 50 years or more. In either case, these families are addressing issues related to the structural contraction of family.

FAMILY HISTORY AS A UNIQUE CHARACTERISTIC OF LATER-LIFE FAMILIES

Later-life families have several unique characteristics that may either enable them to or inhibit them from dealing with the changes associated with later life (Brubaker, 1985). These families have a lengthy family history as they enter the later years. Husbands, wives, children, siblings, and other relatives have been part of the family network for many years. The frequency and content of interactions and the ethos that guides interactions may vary. For example, it has been noted in gerontological literature that older parents and their children are in frequent contact (Circirelli, 1981; Kivett, 1988; Powers & Brubaker, 1985; Shanas, 1979). This contact, however, may be with only one child out of two or more children in the family network. It is possible that the other children have little or no contact with the parents' generation. The contact may have been disrupted many years ago, and neither the parents nor the children turn to each other to deal with later-life changes.

Families with young children do not have the same option to regulate interaction. If a young mother fails to interact with her child, she can be adjudicated for neglect. Later-life families are unique because the parent and child generations have a lengthy history on which their relationship is built as well as the option to alter or change the family legacy. Thus, as the later-life family is contracting, older and younger generations have the opportunity to establish either frequent or infrequent patterns of interaction. The history of the interaction patterns between the generations is a crucial variable when studying later-life families.

Historically, the content of the family interaction is another unique factor associated with later-life families. The content of the interaction within later-life families may vary between the generations or individual family members. Content of the interactions may focus on instrumental or expressive aspects of the family relationships. The grandparent–grandchild interactions may provide an illustration. These relationships may be instrumental and focus on the moral development of the younger generation, or they may be expressive and address affectional issues (Matthews & Sprey, 1984; Robertson, 1977; Thompson & Walker, 1987; Wood & Robertson, 1976). Patterns of caregiving within later-life families demonstrate the divergent content of later-life family interactions. Sheehan and Nuttall (1988) and Matthews and Rosner (1988) reported both instrumental and expressive patterns of caregiving within family caregiver samples. The differing content of the interactions appears to be related to earlier patterns of interactions within the family (Matthews & Rosner, 1988).

The family ethos of affection and obligation may also be influenced by the lengthy family track record that is characteristic of later-life families. Over time, families develop a definition of who is responsible to help with 'the changes experienced in later life. Do family members seek to interact with and provide assistance to older family members because they are obligated or because they feel affection to do so? Families in which autonomy is emphasized and both generations discuss the need to encourage independence may develop an ethos of affection. Consequently, they may interact or provide assistance because of feelings of affection. Other families may discuss the responsibility to provide help in the later years and may do so because they feel obligated. They may wish to reciprocate parental sacrifices from earlier years.

There is some evidence that feelings of affection and obligation may be influenced by structural factors. Gender, conflict with other roles, and types of family relationships (parent or parent-in-law) have been shown to be crucial variables in the balance between affection and obligation (Finley, Roberts, & Banahan, 1988). The affection component seems to be more salient for women, and competing role demands (work vs. children) tend to lessen the feelings of obligation. Although a family ethos concerning caregiving obligations and affection may be crucial, structural factors (gender, children, and work) are likewise influential.

The family ethos (Blieszner, McAuley, Newhouse, & Mancini, 1987; Brubaker & Brubaker, 1989; Thomas, 1988) may influence the choice of who the family defines as being responsible for providing assistance if help is needed. Individual family members may be defined as being responsible, whereas other family members are not. For example, in some Amish families, an unmarried daughter is seen as being responsible for helping her elderly parents, whereas other married children are held less responsible (Brubaker & Michael, 1987). Family expectations about who is responsible can lead to family conflict if the expectations are not met (Fisher, Reid, & Melendez, 1989). In some cases, the family ethos may dictate that responsibility is assigned to individuals or groups outside the family (Brubaker & Brubaker, 1989). Recently, Borgatta and Montgomery (1987) questioned whether public policies should hold individuals responsible for the care of dependent family members.

To emphasize the role that family histories play, consider the salience of an antagonistic family history, or track record, highlighted by Matthews and Rosner (1988). They have shown that long-held animosities may influence the way in which children participate in the care of dependent older parents and that the feelings of caregiving spouses can also be influenced by the family history of interaction. Family history provides a glimpse of the way families differentiate family activities from past experience. As Gubrium (1988) noted, family history

> informs us that people have their own ways of assigning meaning to parts of everyday life. They partition and assemble their lives on their own terms, against their pasts, in ways that might be at odds with the categories we might, as social researchers, use to analyze their contemporary existence. (p. 204)

EFFECTS OF CAREGIVING ON FAMILY MEMBERS

As the eldest members of a family age and experience more health difficulties, issues related to family caregiving become more crucial. It is clear that families provide extraordinary care for older family members who need assistance (Brody, 1981; Cicirelli, 1981, 1983; Horowitz, 1985a; Seelbach, 1984; Stephens & Christianson, 1986; Stolar, Hill, & Tomblin, 1986). Not only are they providing care but they are also receiving little assistance from individuals or organizations outside the family. National long-term care surveys (Comptroller General, 1977; Doty, Liu, & Wiener, 1985) have indicated that these family caregivers utilize little extrafamilial assistance. Who are these caregivers, and which family members are most likely to be providing assistance?

Numerous studies (Brody, 1981; Cantor, 1983; Horowitz, 1985b; Sheehan & Nuttall, 1988; Stoller, 1983) have noted that gender is a differentiating structural variable. Female family members are likely to provide primary assistance within the family. Two recent reports (American Association of Retired Persons [AARP], 1988; Stone, Cafferata, & Sangl, 1987) of national caregiver surveys indicated that approximately 75% of the family caregivers are women. Although women are more likely to provide care than are men, a portion of the primary care is, however, derived from male caregivers (AARP, 1988; Horowitz, 1985a, 1985b; Miller, 1987; Patterson, 1987; Smallegan, 1985; Stoller, 1983; Stone et al., 1987). Examining caregivers as a unit of analysis, it was found that 23% were wives who provided care for their husbands and 29% were daughters who assisted parents, whereas only 13% of the caregivers were husbands who cared for wives and still fewer sons (9%) assisted their parents (Stone et al., 1987). The remainder of the caregivers were other relatives or nonrelatives.

Age of the caregiver often varies considerably. The AARP (1988) study reported that 28% of the primary caregivers were under 35 years of age, 29% were aged 35–49 years, 26% were aged 50–64, and the remaining 15% were 65 years or older. In the Stone et al. (1987) report, the average age of all caregivers was 57.3 years; nearly 22% were 14–44 years of age, 42% were ages 45–64 years, 25% were 65–74 years old, and 10% were 75 years or older. Age is likely to combine with other structural factors to influence the caregiving relationship. For example, the younger caregivers, who are most likely to be female, often are married and have children. These caregivers become the "women in the middle" (Brody, 1981) or the "sandwiched" members of a family (Miller, 1981). The older caregivers are likely to be husbands caring for their spouses (Stone et al., 1987).

A small majority of family caregivers are married. Stone et al. (1987) indicated that more than half of the caregiver daughters (56%) and sons (53%) were married. The dynamics of negotiating the demands of marriage and providing care to an older parent are complex. Although caregivers differ in the way in which they deal with the demands of marriage and caregiving, Matthews and Rosner (1988) noted that the competition between marriage and caregiving demands is an important concern because married caregivers have less flexibility in providing care. Often the situation between the caregiving daughter and the dependent parent is influenced by the caregiver's spouse and the spouse's relationship with the older dependent person.

Some caregivers have dependent children within the household and, consequently, need to juggle the demands of caregiving, marriage, and parenthood. Stone et al. (1987) reported that 25% of the caregiving daughters had children less than 18 years of age in the household. The AARP study (1988) indicated that one-third of all caregiving households had children. The presence of children in the caregiver's household further complicates the caregiver's life.

Employment outside the home adds another dimension to the caregiver's situation. National studies (AARP, 1988; Stone et al., 1987) have suggested that a large portion of caregivers are employed outside the home. For example, half of the caregivers in the AARP study were employed full-time (38%) or part-time (12%), whereas in the Stone et al. (1987) report, 44% of the caregiver daughters were employed. Employment and caregiving contribute to the complexity of the caregiving relationship, and the ways in which caregivers deal with this situation vary markedly. For example, some may decrease the hours they devote to employment or discontinue working, whereas others develop rigid schedules to meet the demands of the competing roles (Brody, Poulshock, & Masciocchi, 1978; Cantor, 1983; Lang & Brody, 1983). Several studies (Brody & Schoonover, 1986; Cantor, 1983; Lang & Brody, 1983; Stoller, 1983) have indicated that employed caregivers frequently provide assistance at the same levels as do comparable nonemployed caregivers, but the type of care may vary. Furthermore, Thomas (1988) suggested that compromises about work and caregiving can be made so that the elderly care recipients are satisfied with the caregiving relationship. Combining work and caregiving can create a difficult situation; however, caregivers often use a variety of coping strategies that older care recipients perceive as satisfying.

The income level of the caregiver and older person may influence the caregiving relationship. Stone et al. (1987) reported that nearly one-third had incomes at or near poverty level, and approximately 56% had low to middle incomes. The AARP (1988) study found a $25,700 median income for primary caregivers. The availability of financial resources may enable caregivers and older dependent persons to purchase assistance (Brody & Schoonover, 1986), thereby reducing the demands of family caregiving.

The older person's level and type of disability are two factors that can be important to the relationship between the caregiver and care recipient (Brubaker & Brubaker, in press; Thomas, 1988). For example, as an older person's level of dependency increases, family caregivers are more likely to use extrafamilial support services (Noelker & Bass, 1989). Family caregivers provide assistance to the elderly on a long-term basis (Brubaker, 1987; Stoller & Earl, 1983), although the caregiving tasks become more difficult as the level of dependency increases. Also, the type of dependency (e.g., financial, physical, or socioemotional) may influence the amount of assistance provided by a family caregiver.

Structural factors such as gender, age, marital status, presence of children, outside employment, and income contribute to a multifaceted role with many competing demands. Although some data (Finley et al., 1988; Noelker & Wallace, 1985) suggest that these competing demands lessen the caregiver's feelings of obligation, it appears that many caregivers are providing care by negotiating the complex expectations associated with the roles of caregiver, spouse, parent, and worker. Feelings of stress are a consequence of the multiple expectations that often compete with one another. The amounts of stress and the ways in which families deal with the stress vary. Thus, the consequences of stress on family relationships differ.

Family caregiving can potentially cause stress among family members in a variety of ways. First, caregiving may result from a change in the functional capacity of an elderly family member. Stress may ensue because neither the caregiver or the older person may understand the aging process and how to deal with the functional changes (Johnson, 1978; Springer & Brubaker, 1984). Second, the stress may be a consequence of difficulty in redefining a parent as being dependent and vulnerable (Lowy, 1985). It may be difficult for an adult child to assist an elderly parent because the adult child is reluctant to deal with the parent's dependencies. Third, especially for middle-aged caregivers, it may be difficult to negotiate the demands of caregiving and marriage, parenthood, and employment (Brody, 1981; Cantor, 1983; Lang & Brody, 1983; Miller, 1981). The expectations of the various roles may be excessive and result in a "role overload" and, eventually, a "role burnout." Eventually, these caregivers may use extrafamilial support, such as in-home services, if their physical or emotional resources become strained (Noelker & Bass, 1989).

Research has identified a number of symptoms of the stress experienced by caregivers. For example, physical fatigue and health difficulties (Rabins, Mace, & Lucas, 1982), social isolation (Crossman, London, & Barry, 1981; Fengler & Goodrich, 1979), conflicts within the family (Grad & Sainsbury, 1968; Rabins et al., 1982), and symptoms such as depression, sleeplessness, guilt, and irritability (Grad & Sainsbury, 1968; Lazarus, Stafford, Copper, Cohler, & Dyken, 1981; Poulshock & Deimling, 1984) have been identified. These symptoms suggest that some caregivers are experiencing stress at levels that profoundly affect various aspects of their lives.

Although stress has been documented in caregiving relationships, not all family caregivers report inordinate levels of stress. For example, Noelker and Wallace (1985) found that a sizable portion of caregivers reported little or minimal levels of caregiver stress. The caregiving relationship can be positive to family relationships. Recent studies (Noelker & Townsend, 1987; Townsend & Noelker, 1987) suggest that the effectiveness of caregivers is related to the quality of the family relationships.

Given the potential for stress in the family caregiving situation, what factors contribute to differing levels of stress with these family relationships? What factors contribute to the perception of stress within caregiving families? In the following sections I provide a brief overview of several theoretical approaches to family stress followed by a model describing the particular stressor of caregiving.

THEORETICAL APPROACHES TO UNDERSTANDING STRESS IN FAMILIES

Families respond differently to stressful events and family scholars have devoted considerable energy to understanding how families deal with stress. One of the primary goals of these theorists is to understand how families respond and adapt to a variety of stressful situations. The model presented herein is based on the ABCX model of family stress and the contextual approach to studying family stress.

Hill (1949) developed the ABCX model of family stress to understand families' responses to the return of soldiers from World War II. From Hill's perspective, families establish a level of organization or homeostasis to deal with ordinary life situations. In this model, stress (represented by the letter A) is assumed to create change in the ordinary level of organization and results in some disorganization within the family. The family responds to the disorganization by employing its resources (represented by the letter B) and defining the stressful event (represented by the letter C) in order to return to a level of organization. A crisis (represented by the letter X) is defined as the time between the occurrence of the stressful event and the reorganization of the family. As a reorganized, homeostatic unit, the family can again deal with day-to-day activities.

In Hill's (1949) model, A referred to the event that created the change in the family's organization. Specifically, it referred to "the hardships of the event" (Hill, 1958) that result in change to the family. Burr (1982) noted that a stressor event includes "anything that changes some aspect of the system such as boundaries, structure, goals, processes, roles, or values" (p. 7). The event may be intrafamilial or extrafamilial; it may produce great or little disruption. The key is that the event produces changes within the organization of the family. B refers to the family's resources to deal with the stressful event. Resources have been defined in various ways. For example, Patterson and McCubbin (1983) defined resources as "the psychological, social, interpersonal, and material characteristics of individual family members (e.g., ability to earn an income), of the family (e.g., flexibility, organization) and of the community (e.g., medical services, support groups) which are used to meet family demands and needs" (p. 29). The degree of cohesion and integration within the family is also viewed as a resource (Burr, 1982; Hill, 1949; Olson & McCubbin, 1982).

The family's definition of the event is C in Hill's model. The severity of the stressful event is related to whether the family defines the event as contrary to its goals, values, structure, and overall organization (Hill, 1949). The impact of the stressful event is greater if the family defines it as threatening its ordinary mode of operation and less if it is defined as something the family can deal with in its usual response repertoire. Consequently, similar events may be experienced and, depending on how families define these events, the impact of the events will differ.

The ABCX model of family stress has changed little since its inception (McCubbin et al., 1980), and the basic concepts continue to permeate the literature. More recently, McCubbin & Patterson (1982; Patterson & McCubbin, 1983) proposed an extension of this model to deal with ongoing stressful events (e.g., long-term illness). The Double ABCX model seeks to deal with the "pile-up" of stress that may exacerbate the crisis and influence the family's level of adaptation. The Double ABCX model addresses postcrisis factors and seeks to identify any stress that may result from the family's response to the initial stressful event. This extension provides a framework from which to view family stress as a complicated situation because families' attempts to address one stressful event may lead to additional stressful events, which in turn may increase the level of disorganization within the family.

The contextual approach to the study of stress seeks to include influential characteristics of individual, familial, and extrafamilial systems (Boss, 1987; Walker, 1985). At the same time, the interdependencies of the various levels are emphasized. As Walker (1985) noted, "when stress is present, it is important to note the rippling effect it has on the multiple levels of the social system" (p. 833). The stressful event, the family's identification of resources, and the family's definition of the event develop within a historical, social context. This social network evolved within the framework of the societal (cultural, economic, and religious) system (Boss, 1987). Consequently, an understanding of families' responses to stressful events requires a sensitivity to the interdependencies of the individual family members, the family as a unit, and the social system.

This approach views stress within the context of individuals, family, and society over time. As individuals and families respond to a stressful event, the family unit changes, and these changes need to be monitored over time to yield an understanding of the dynamics of the contextual situation. As Walker (1985) suggested, the contextual approach to the study of stress encourages the examination of individual, dyadic, social network, and societal changes that influence the ways in which individuals, dyads, and families respond to stress. To fully grasp the fluid nature of the contextual situation, the changes in these relationships, and the consequent alteration of the context within which stress occurs, are premised on interactions over time.

A CONTEXTUAL MODEL FOR STUDYING STRESS AMONG CAREGIVERS

The ABCX and contextual approaches can be applied to the study of stress among caregivers within later-life families. Using the ABCX definition of stress, caregiving is an event that causes disorganization in a family and, consequently, stress will inevitably arise within the caregiving situation (Brody, 1985). Thus the issue is not whether family members experience stress in a caregiving situation, rather, the crucial issue is how family members deal with the stress. What familial and extrafamilial resources do they define as available to them? How do they define the stress? To answer these questions, the contextual approach to studying stress in families becomes useful.

Stress experienced by family caregivers of the elderly can be viewed within the context of individual characteristics of the caregivers and the dependent older person, the dyadic relationship between the caregiver and dependent elderly relative, and, finally, the interrelationships with the other family members. Within the caregiving situation, families can identify the events that they perceive as stressful, and they can discuss how they respond to these events. These responses are developed within the context of the structural characteristics of the family as well as the orientations families have developed through patterns of interaction over the years. The way in which the family responds to stress may negatively or positively influence future interactions within the family.

Individuals and families respond differently to the stress in the family caregiving situation. Many times, the stress experienced by caregivers is not related to one event. Rather, the stress results from the cumulative effect of several events or demands: Family caregivers often experience "pile-up" of stress (McCubbin & Patterson, 1982; Patterson & McCubbin, 1983). For many, the daily demands of caregiving, marriage, parenthood, and work present "stressor events" that may be defined as stressful within the structural and familial contexts. As was noted previously, some caregivers experience symptoms that inhibit everyday activity (Crossman et al., 1981; Rabins et al., 1982), whereas others report little or minimal negative effect on their daily lives (Matthews & Rosner, 1988; Noelker, & Wallace, 1985). The situations are complex, and there are many variables that can influence the way in which families define the stress associated with caregiving.

Building on the theoretical approaches to family stress, the contextual model suggests that the perception of stressful caregiving activities is a result of the identification of individual family and extrafamilial resources for dealing with these stressful caregiving activities. Structural characteristics of the caregiver and dependent older person may influence the perception of stress. For some, the structural characteristics are mediated by the relationship between the caregiver and the older dependent person. For example, the influence of gender or age may be mediated by the family history or quality of the relationship. The structural and relationship factors as well as the perception of stress are embedded in the context of other family members and the extrafamilial network. The level of stress develops within the context of structural as well as dyadic and family relationships.

Figure 1 diagrammatically presents the contextual model of stress depicting the special case of caregiving in later-life families. The relationships identified on this diagram are not presented as causal relationships. Rather, the linkages depict key concepts that have been identified in the research. The key components of a contextual model of family caregiving and stress include structural characteristics, dyadic relationship characteristics, and family or social network characteristics.

Gender, age, income, marital status, presence of children and outside employment are structural characteristics that are important determinants within the caregiving situation. Some of these characteristics apply to both the caregivers and the older dependent persons. For example, the gender of the caregiver and older dependent family member may be important. Gender differences in filial obligation for mothers and fathers have been found (Finley et al., 1988). Also, the ages of the caregiver and dependent person are structural characteristics. If both are older (for example, 65 years or older), it is possible that both the caregiver and dependent person have physical difficulty performing caregiving tasks. Another example of a structural component is income. If the caregiver or dependent older person have enough income to hire assistance (according to Stone et. al., 1987, approximately 10% purchase formal services), then, some of the caregiving demands can be transferred outside the family.

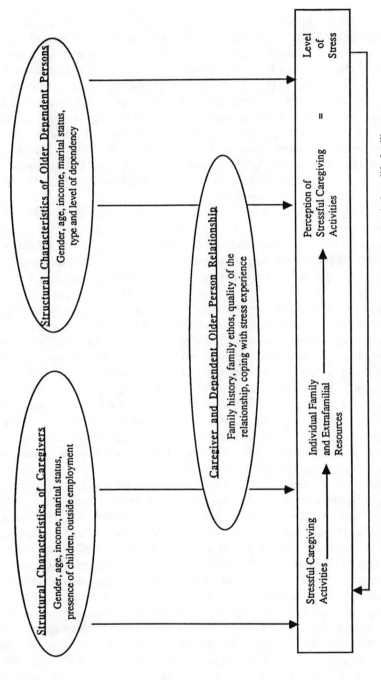

FIGURE 1 A contextual model for studying stress assocaited with caregiving in later-life families.

Structural Characteristics of Older Dependent Persons
Gender, age, income, marital status, type and level of dependency

Structural Characteristics of Caregivers
Gender, age, income, marital status, presence of children, outside employment

Caregiver and Dependent Older Person Relationship
Family history, family ethos, quality of the relationship, coping with stress experience

Level of Stress

Perception of Stressful Caregiving Activities

=

Individual Family and Extrafamilial Resources

Stressful Caregiving Activies

Research has identified the following structural characteristics associated with the caregiver as being influential: gender, age, income, marital status, presence of children in the household, and outside employment. The following structural characteristics have been linked to the older care recipient: gender, age, income, marital status, and level of disability. In a qualitative study of family caregiving, Matthews and Rosner (1988) reported that gender and the older person's level of disability were influential in the way in which families organized to provide for caregiving demands. The structural characteristics of the caregiver and older person may influence familial and extrafamilial resources and the perception of the stressful caregiving events. Thus structural characteristics associated with the caregiver and recipient may affect the level of stress within the caregiving family.

Although the caregiver's and older dependent person's structural characteristics are important, these factors may, in some cases, be mediated by the relationship between the caregiver and older person. For example, Thomas (1988) found that family values about helping one another were related to caregivers' and their older parents' satisfaction with the caregiving situation. Many caregiving families experience multiple demands. Do caregivers and recipients consider these competing demands in the assessment of satisfaction in the caregiving situation? When caregivers had competing demands, they and their parents may have considered these demands in assessing their satisfaction with the situation, or the caregivers may have devoted energy primarily to the caregiving tasks and were satisfied with this distribution of time (Brody, 1985; Thomas, 1988).

Matthews and Rosner's (1988) study of family caregiving suggested that caregivers and their siblings can cooperatively meet the needs of their dependent parents in creative ways. Although the history of family interaction affected the siblings' interactions with one another, they worked together to meet the needs of the older dependent parent. However, strain between siblings can increase the amount of stress experienced in caregiving.

Family history, family ethos, quality of the relationship, and experience in coping with stress are factors that may contribute to the relationship between the caregiver and the older dependent person. As was noted previously, the lengthy family history and family ethos are unique characteristics of later-life families. Caregivers and their parents are familiar with this history and ethos, and the caregiving situation may result in feelings of stress. For example, the caregiver and parent may not have regularly interacted for many years, but in the caregiver situation they are interacting frequently. Their earlier disagreements and hostilities may contribute to the development of stress in the caregiving situation.

Another example of a lengthy family history of interaction relates to the situation in which the caregiver and older person frequently interacted with one another and had a very positive relationship. Now, as a result of the older person's disabilities, they can no longer interact as they did in the past. The remembrance of the vitality in their relationship compared to their frequent, though limited interaction in the caregiving situation may affect the perception of the stressful activities. Gubrium (1988), in a study of families providing care to family members who were experiencing Alzheimer's disease, observed that family history was important because the caregivers initiated caregiving on the basis of past habits, expectations, and interactions.

The quality of the relationship between the caregiver and older dependent person may affect the perception of the caregiving situation. Scharlach (1987) identified a relation between role overload and quality of the relationship between caregiver daughters and dependent mothers. As the strain from the overload increased, the quality of the relationship was negatively affected. There may be a cyclical relationship between role overload and perceptions of stress; for example, as the role overload increases, the quality of the relationship decreases and feelings of stress increase, and with the increased stress, the quality of the relationship may be further affected. Although the relationship between the caregiving role, the quality of the relationship, and the degree of stress is not fully understood, it is likely that the quality of the relationship is an important factor in the development of stress in the caregiving relationship.

The caregiver and older person's experience in coping with stressful situations may influence the perception of the stressful event and, consequently, affect the level of stress within a family caregiving relationship. The literature on family stress (e.g., McCubbin & Patterson, 1982; Patterson & McCubbin, 1983) has noted that families can develop coping strategies based on previous stressful situations. These strategies can become resources with which to deal with stress. Often, caregivers and the older dependent person have dealt with difficult situations and have a knowledge of what has worked for them. Thus, previous coping experience, as a dyadic relationship (caregiver and dependent older person), can affect the definition of stress in caregiving families.

The caregiver's and older person's definitions of stressful caregiving events occurs within the context of relationships with other family members and an extrafamilial social network. Matthews and Rosner (1988) found that caregivers' spouses (sons-in-law or daughters-in-law) had a history of interaction within the family and influenced the caregiver's flexibility to provide assistance. Although these interactions were not necessarily problematic, these spouses had the ability to ease or confound the situation. "The posture of a husband or wife, then, affects how easily an adult child could adapt to the particular style of parent care" (Matthews & Rosner, 1988, p. 192). Other relatives, including siblings of the caregiver as well as the dependent older person, form an informal social network that can affect the perception of stress. These individuals can provide direct caregiving assistance (Matthews & Rosner, 1988; Scott, 1983), or they may provide support to the caregiver.

Extrafamilial support or formal supports contribute to the perception of stress associated with caregiving. Research (Blieszner et al., 1987; Brubaker, 1987; Litwak, 1985; Montgomery & Hatch, 1987) suggests that formal support systems provide assistance to caregiving families. The caregiver's and older dependent person's definitions of stressful events may be affected by the assistance provided by formal organizations. The use of formal support may depend on the type of dependency and the family's perception of who is responsible for helping (Brubaker & Brubaker, 1989). However, the stressful events associated with family caregiving are defined within the context of the formal support system that is a part of the family's social network.

The perception of stress among family members occurs within the context of the caregiver's and older dependent person's structural characteristics, the dyadic relationship between the caregiver and the older person, and the social network including other family members as well as the formal support system. Given differing family contexts, it is not surprising that families experience differing levels of stress from caregiving experiences.

IMPLICATIONS OF THE CONTEXTUAL MODEL

As Walker (1985) suggested, the contextual approach encourages the use of qualitative research. Researchers need to gather information about family caregivers and the interdependencies between the caregiver, older dependent person, and other family members, as well as the extrafamilial support network. The recent studies by Gubrium (1988) and Matthews and Rosner (1988) provide examples of qualitative approaches applied to the care of older dependent persons by their families. Combining quantitative and qualitative research techniques in the study of the stress experienced by caregivers will provide information about structural characteristics and the context of the interrelationships within which caregivers negotiate competing demands.

Often the research designs used in the family caregiving area fail to measure family relationships in terms of history and ethos. Querying caregivers and recipients about who the members of the family are and what they contribute to the caregiving situation is insufficient. The assessment of stress within these situations needs to measure the way in which the family participants interacted in the past and the meanings attached to past interactions. At the same time, the family members' commitment to, and value of, caregiving are crucial factors. The caregiving situation does not begin without a history of social interaction (family history) and a background of definitions associated with caregiving (family ethos). Caregiving is based on families' past experiences, and their perceptions of these experiences can have an influence on who provides care and what care is provided as well as how the care is provided. In some cases, stress associated with the caregiving situation may be a result of past interaction rather than of the demands of the caregiving situation. Research designs need to include the context of the previous family interaction to more fully measure stress in caregiving families.

In many instances, family caregiving research needs to move beyond the description of the caregiving situation and focus on the dynamics of family relationships. The relationship of the caregiver and recipient is complex. Present research provides a description of this relationship, but little is known about why caregivers differ in feelings of stress given similar situations or why care-recipients differ in their feelings of satisfaction when their needs are being met. It is not enough to identify the "who and what" in family caregiving; information about "how and why" caregiving is provided is necessary. Research designs that include the contextual environment of the family caregiving situations are more likely to measure how the care is being provided and why family members associate particular definitions with the provision of care. With the contextual approach, the development of stress in caregiving families is enmeshed in individual, interpersonal, familial, and societal contexts.

Often the context rather than the current behavior is what may be important in understanding the stressful situation. Practitioners are encouraged to develop extensive family histories, including the type of family interactions, the feelings that family members have for one another, and the family definitions about caregiving that were held before the caregiving situation became a reality. Understanding the context within which family caregivers and recipients define the present situation may identify key areas for intervention. Then, intervention can be effectively directed toward reducing stress within caregiving families.

REFERENCES

American Association of Retired Persons. (1988, October). *National survey of caregivers: Summary of findings*. Washington, DC: Author.

Blieszner, R., McAuley, W. J., Newhouse, J. K., & Mancini, J. A. (1987). Rural–urban differences in service use by older adults. In T. H. Brubaker (Ed.), *Aging, health, and family: Long-term care* (pp. 162–174). Newbury Park, CA: Sage.

Borgatta, E. F., & Montgomery, R. J. V. (1987). Aging policy and societal values. In. E. F. Borgatta & R. J. V. Montgomery (Eds.), *Critical issues in aging policy* (pp. 7–27). Newbury Park, CA: Sage.

Boss, P. (1987). Family stress. In M. B. Sussman & S. K. Steinmetz (Eds.), *Handbook of marriage and the family* (pp. 695–723). New York: Plenum Press.

Brody, E. M. (1981). "Women in the middle" and family help to older people. *The Gerontologist, 21,* 471–480.

Brody, E. M. (1985). Parent care as a normative family stress. *The Gerontologist, 25,* 19–29.

Brody, E. M., Poulshock, S. W., & Masciocchi, C. (1978). The family care unit: A major consideration in the long term support system. *The Gerontologist, 18,* 556–561.

Brody, E. M., & Schoonover, C. B. (1986). Patterns of parent-care when adult daughters work and when they do not. *The Gerontologist, 26,* 372–381.

Brubaker, T. H. (Ed.). (1983). *Family relationships in later life.* Beverly Hills, CA: Sage.

Brubaker, T. H. (1985). *Later life families.* Beverly Hills, CA: Sage.

Brubaker, T. H. (Ed.). (1987). *Aging, health, and family: Long-term care.* Newbury Park, CA: Sage.

Brubaker, T. H., & Brubaker, E. (1989). Toward a theory of family caregiving: Dependencies, responsibility and utilization of services. In J. A. Mancini (Ed.), *Aging parents and adult children* (pp. 245–257). Lexington, MA: Lexington Books/D. C. Heath.

Brubaker, T. H., & Michael, C. (1987). Amish families in later life. In D. E. Gelfand & C. M. Barresi (Eds.), *Ethnic dimensions of aging* (pp. 106–117). New York: Springer.

Burr, W. (1982). Families under stress. In H. I. McCubbin, A. E. Cauble, & J. M. Patterson (Eds.), *Family stress, coping, and adaptation* (pp. 5–25). Springfield, IL: Charles C Thomas.

Cantor, M. (1983). Strain among caregivers: A study of experiences in the United States. *The Gerontologist, 23,* 23–43.

Cicirelli, V. G. (1981). *Helping elderly parents: Roles of adult children.* Boston: Auburn House.

Cicirelli, V. G. (1983). Adult children and their elderly parents. In T. H. Brubaker (Ed.), *Family relationships in later life* (pp. 31–46). Beverly Hills, CA: Sage.

Comptroller General of the United States. (1977, April 19). *The well-being of older people in Cleveland, Ohio* (Report No. RD-77-70). Washington, DC: U.S. General Accounting Office.

Crossman, L., London, C., & Barry, C. (1981). Older women caring for disabled spouses: A model for supportive services. *The Gerontologist, 21,* 464–470.

Doty, P., Liu, K., & Wiener, J. (1985). An overview of long-term care. *Health Care Financing Review, 6,* 69–78.

Duvall, E. M. (1977). *Marriage and family development* (5th ed.). Philadelphia: Lippincott.

Fengler, A. P., & Goodrich, N. (1979). Wives of elderly disabled men: The hidden patients. *The Gerontologist, 19,* 175–183.

Finley, N. J., Roberts, M. D., & Banahan, B. F. (1988). Motivators and inhibitors of attitudes of filial obligation toward aging parents. *The Gerontologist, 28,* 73–78.

Fisher, C. B., Reid, J. D., & Melendez, M. (1989). Conflict in families and friendships of later life. *Family Relations, 38,* 83–89.

Grad, J., & Sainsbury, P. (1968). The effects that patients have on their families in a community care and a control psychiatric service: A two-year follow-up. *British Journal of Psychiatry, 114,* 265–278.

Gubrium, J. F. (1988). Family responsibility and caregiving in the qualitative analysis of the Alzheimer's disease experience. *Journal of Marriage and the Family, 50,* 197–207.

Hill, R. (1949). *Families under stress.* New York: Harper & Row.

Hill, R. (1958). Generic features of families under stress. *Social Casework, 39,* 139–150.

Horowitz, A. (1985a). Family caregiving to the frail elderly. In C. Eisdorfer (Ed.), *Annual review of gerontology and geriatrics* (Vol. 5, pp. 194–246). New York: Springer.

Horowitz, A. (1985b). Sons and daughters as caregivers to older parents. *The Gerontologist, 25,* 612–617.

Johnson, E. S. (1978). "Good" relationships between older mothers and their daughters: A causal model. *The Gerontologist, 18,* 301–306.

Kivett, V. R. (1988). Older rural fathers and sons: Patterns of association and helping. *Family Relations, 37,* 62–67.

Lang, A. M., & Brody, E. M. (1983). Characteristics of middle aged daughters and help to their elderly mothers. *Journal of Marriage and the Family, 45,* 193–202.

Lazarus, L., Stafford, B., Copper, K., Cohler, B., & Dyken, M. (1981). A pilot study of an Alzheimer's patient's relatives discussion group. *The Gerontologist, 21,* 353–358.

Litwak, E. (1985). *Helping the elderly: The complementary roles of informal networks and formal systems.* New York: Guilford Press.

Lowy, L. (1985). *Social work with the aging* (2nd Ed.). New York: Harper & Row.

Matthews, S. H., & Rosner, T. T. (1988). Shared filial responsibility: The family as the primary caregiver. *Journal of Marriage and the Family, 50,* 185–195.

Matthews, S. H., & Sprey, J. (1984). The impact of divorce on grandparent-hood: An exploratory study. *The Gerontologist, 24,* 41–47.

McCubbin, H. I., Joy, C. B., Cauble, A. E., Comeau, J. K., Patterson, J. M., & Needle, R. H. (1980). Family stress and coping: A decade review. *Journal of Marriage and the Family, 42,* 855–871.

McCubbin, H. I., & Patterson, J. M. (1982). Family adaptation to crisis. In H. I. McCubbin, A. E. Cauble, & J. M. Patterson (Eds.), *Family stress, coping, and adaptation* (pp. 26–47). New York: Springer.

Miller, B. (1987). Gender and control among spouses of the cognitively impaired: A research note. *The Gerontologist, 27,* 447–453.

Miller, D. A. (1981). The "sandwich" generation: Adult children of the aged. *Social Work, 26,* 419–423.

Montgomery, R. J. V., & Hatch, L. R. (1987). The feasibility of volunteers and families forming a partnership for caregiving. In T. H. Brubaker (Ed.), *Aging, health, and family: Long-term care* (pp. 143–161). Newbury Park, CA: Sage.

Noelker, L. S., & Bass, D. M. (1989). Home care for elderly persons: Linkages between formal and informal caregivers. *Journal of Gerontology, 44,* S63–S70.

Noelker, L. S., & Townsend, A. L. (1987). Perceived caregiving effectiveness: The impact of parental impairment, community resources, and caregiver characteristics. In T. H. Brubaker (Ed.), *Aging, health and family: Long-term care* (pp. 58–79). Newbury Park, CA: Sage.

Noelker, L. S., & Wallace, R. W. (1985). The organization of family care for impaired elderly. *Journal of Family Issues, 6,* 23–44.

Olson, D. H., & McCubbin, H. I. (1982). Circumplex model of marital and family systems: 5. Application to family stress and crisis intervention. In H. I. McCubbin, A. E. Cauble, & J. M. Patterson (Eds.), *Family stress, coping, and social support* (pp. 48–68). Springfield, IL: Charles C Thomas.

Patterson, J. M., & McCubbin, H. I. (1983). Chronic illness: Family stress and coping. In C. R. Figley & H. I. McCubbin (Eds.), *Stress and the family: 2. Coping with catastrophe* (pp. 21–36). New York: Brunner/Mazel.

Patterson, S. L. (1987). Older rural natural helpers: Gender and site differences in the helping process. *The Gerontologist, 27,* 639–644.

Poulshock, S. W., & Deimling, G. T. (1984). Families caring for elders in residence: Issues in measurement of burden. *Journal of Gerontology, 39,* 230–239.

Powers, E. A., & Brubaker, T. H. (1985). Family networks and helping patterns. In E. A. Powers, W. J. Goudy, & P. M. Keith (Eds.), *Later life transitions: Older males in rural America* (pp. 97–110). Boston: Kluwer-Nijhoff.

Rabins, P. V., Mace, N. L., & Lucas, M. J. (1982). The impact of dementia on the family. *Journal of the American Medical Association, 248,* 333–335.

Robertson, J. F. (1977). Grandmotherhood: A study in role conceptions. *Journal of Marriage and the Family, 39,* 165–174.

Scharlach, A. E. (1987). Role strain in mother–daughter relationships in later life. *The Gerontologist, 27,* 627–631.

Scott, J. P. (1983). Siblings and other kin. In T. H. Brubaker (Ed.), *Family relationships in later life* (pp. 47–62). Beverly Hills, CA: Sage.

Seelbach, W. C. (1984). Filial responsibility and the care of aging family members. In W. H. Quinn & G. A. Hughston (Eds.), *Independent aging* (pp. 92–105). Rockville, MD: Aspen.

Shanas, E. (1979). The family as a social support system in old age. *The Gerontologist, 19,* 169–174.

Sheehan, N. W., & Nuttall, P. (1988). Conflict, emotion, and personal strain among family caregivers. *Family Relations, 37,* 92–98.

Smallegan, M. (1985). There was nothing else to do: Needs for care before nursing home admission. *The Gerontologist, 25,* 364–369.

Springer, D., & Brubaker, T. H. (1984). *Family caregivers and dependent elderly: Minimizing stress and maximizing independence.* Beverly Hills, CA: Sage.

Stephens, S. A., & Christianson, J. B. (1986). *Informal care of the elderly.* Lexington, MA: Lexington Books.

Stolar, E., Hill, M. A., & Tomblin, A. (1986). Family disengagement—myth or reality: A follow-up study after geriatric assessment. *Canadian Journal of Aging, 5,* 113–124.

Stoller, E. P. (1983). Parental caregiving by adult children. *Journal of Marriage and the Family, 45,* 851–858.

Stoller, E. P., & Earl, L. L. (1983). Help with activities of everyday living: Sources of support for the noninstitutionalized elderly. *The Gerontologist, 23,* 64–70.

Stone, R., Cafferata, G. L., & Sangl, J. (1987). Caregivers of the frail elderly: A national profile. *The Gerontologist, 27,* 616–626.

Thomas, J. L. (1988). Predictors of satisfaction with children's help for younger and older elderly parents. *Journal of Gerontology, 43,* S9–S14.

Thompson, L., & Walker, A. J. (1987). Mothers as mediators of intimacy between grandmothers and their young adult granddaughters. *Family Relations, 36,* 72–77.

Townsend, A. L., & Noelker, L. S. (1987). The impact of family relationships on perceived caregiving effectiveness. In T. H. Brubaker (Ed.), *Aging, health and family: Long-term care* (pp. 80–99). Newbury Park, CA: Sage.

Walker, A. J. (1985). Reconceptualizing family stress. *Journal of Marriage and the Family, 47,* 827–837.

Wood, V., & Robertson, J. F. (1976). The significance of grandparenthood. In J. F. Gubrium (Ed.), *Time, roles and self in old age.* New York: Human Sciences.

4

THE ELDERS LIFE STRESS INVENTORY: EGOCENTRIC AND NONEGOCENTRIC STRESS

Carolyn M. Aldwin

Normative Aging Study, Veterans Administration Outpatient Clinic, Boston, MA
Boston University School of Public Health

This purpose of this chapter is to present a developmental perspective on stress in later life. The relevance of Erikson's (1953) construct of generativity to stress processes in later life will be explored, utilizing data from the Elders Life Stress Inventory (ELSI). The ELSI is designed specifically for use in older populations, and encompasses both event- and process-based approaches to stress.

This developmental approach to stress in late life is based on two central assumptions. First, stereotypes of the frail elder are simply not applicable to the majority of older individuals, most of whom are between the ages of 60 and 80, are reasonably healthy, and reside in the community. In keeping with negative stereotypes, most studies on stress in late life often focus on the vulnerability of the elderly and the predominance of loss in late life. As an alternative, the proposed developmental schema will focus on what are perceived to be the potential strengths of older adults and their contribution to their families and social milieu. If Erikson is correct and a developmental shift toward generativity occurs in mid- and late life, this shift should be reflected in stress processes. Specifically, stress that occurs to significant others—nonegocentric stress—may

Preparation of this chapter was supported by the Veterans Administration Medical Research Service and two grants from the National Institute on Aging, FIRST Award AG07465 and AG02287. Professors Raymond Bossé, Michael R. Levenson, and Avron Spiro III provided helpful comments on earlier drafts of this chapter; Kathryn Workman-Daniels aided with data analysis, Debra Zand with data management and coding, and Kathleen Culhane and Abigail Seibert with coding.

take on a special salience in late life. Expressing this concern for their family and friends and helping them to cope with their problems may allow older adults to maintain reciprocal relationships and provide important contributions to their communities (cf. James, James, & Smith, 1984).

The second assumption devolves around the assessment of stress. Rather than viewing the life events (Holmes & Rahe, 1967) and process or daily stressors approaches to stress (DeLongis, Coyne, Dakof, Folkman, & Lazarus, 1982) as competing paradigms in the stress field, these can be seen as alternative or complementary means of assessing stress (Kasl, 1987). Event-based approaches provide global information about the major stresses that occurred to individuals over the course of a year, while process approaches provide a more in-depth but narrower perspective on stress by asking individuals to relate minor and major episodes over a shorter time period. Although these assessments overlap to a certain extent, they nevertheless tap different sources of stress that contribute independent variance to mental health status (Aldwin, Levenson, Spiro, & Bossé, 1989). As such, there may be subtle differences in how aging affects these different types of stress, and both levels of assessment are necessary for understanding stress-related developmental processes in late life.

The following sections will review the literature on age and the stress process, including appraisal processes, types of stress experienced, and health effects. I will then describe the development of the Elders Life Stress Inventory and its use in three community surveys, the first in a California retirement community and the other two in a large, longitudinal panel in Boston. Both life events and daily stressors data will be examined for evidence of nonegocentric stress, and the relations of egocentric and nonegocentric stress to health will be contrasted.

AGING AND THE STRESS PROCESS

Aging and Stress Appraisals

It has been widely assumed that elderly individuals are particularly vulnerable to the adverse effects of stress on health. One manifestation of this perceived vulnerability is the belief that, ceteris paribus, negative events will be appraised as more stressful with increasing age. One early study found that older adults tend to rate life events as being more stressful than younger ones and suggested that older individuals are more vulnerable to environmental change (Muhlenkamp, Gress, & Flood, 1975). However, a more recent study using data from the National Health Interview Study found that elderly respondents were less likely than younger ones to report either experiencing stress or that stress had "a lot" of effect on their health (Silverman, Eichler, & Williams, 1987; see also Sands & Parker, 1979–1980). Thus, it is unclear from these studies whether there are developmental differences in stress appraisals. However, severity of stress is only one dimension along which stress can be appraised, and it is likely that other dimensions may be more relevant to developmental processes.

Aging and Life Events

Research on the impact of stressful life events on health among older adults has yielded mixed results. For example, at least two studies have found no relationship between life events and health in older groups (Holahan, Holahan, & Belk, 1984; Kee & Whittington, 1985). However, most stress inventories contain items that occur with higher frequency in younger groups, such as having children, getting married, starting jobs, being arrested, and the like (cf. Teri & Lewinsohn, 1982). The fact that older adults typically report fewer events on these inventories (Paykel, 1983) may reflect only the composition of such scales and not the actual level of stress in their lives. Life event scales with items of greater relevance to older adults may have better success in predicting health (Amstel & Krauss, 1974; Kahana, Kahana, & Young, 1985; Krause, 1986; Norris & Murell, 1987). Life events that appear to be especially harmful for the health of older persons tend to be those that involve disruption of social networks, such as bereavement and relocation (Rowland, 1977).

The Louisville Older Person Events Scale (LOPES; Murrell, Norris, & Hutchins, 1984) represents some of the most comprehensive work done on the types and distributions of stressful life events experienced by older adults. The LOPES consists of 54 items administered in an interview format. For each event that the respondent has experienced in the past six months, five probes were asked, dealing with the following event characteristics: the degree of change required, desirability, preoccupation, date of occurrence, and novelty. In a large, stratified sample of Kentuckians over the age of 55, Murrell et al. (1984) showed, not surprisingly, that the events rated as most undesirable were those involving deaths of family members and loss of a home. The most frequent undesirable events were those that involved health problems of self, friends, and family.

Aging and Daily Stressors

Less is known about the types and distributions of daily stressors or hassles in late life. The Hassles Scale (DeLongis et al., 1982) was originally administered to a middle-aged population, and few correlations with age were found in this sample. However, when they compared the frequency of different types of daily stressors in this sample with college samples, they showed that types of daily stressors did change as a function of age in the expected directions (Lazarus & DeLongis, 1983). Thus, there is reason to suspect that the nature of daily stressors may change in late life. For example, with increasing physical limitations, there may be problems performing routine tasks. Certain roles, such as that of caregiver, may be much more common in late life, especially among older women.

Kinney and Stephens (1989) have recently developed a Caregiving Hassles Scale that consists of five subscales that assess assistance in basic activities of daily living, assistance in instrumental activities, the care-recipient's cognitive status, the care-recipient's behavior, and the caregiver's social network. Interestingly, only the last three hassles subscales correlated with psychological symptoms, especially with anxiety, hostility, depression, and somatization. The most frequently cited hassles were associated with the care-recipient's confused mental state (Kinney & Stephens, in press). However, this scale examines very specialized types of hassles, and more work is needed to investigate the types of daily stressors that older adults typically face. In the Holahan et al. (1984) study cited earlier, general hassles were predictive of health in an older sample, although the age distributions of hassles were not presented.

Egocentric and Nonegocentric Stress

Implicit in both event- and process-based approaches, however, is the assumption that the circumstances that are stressful are primarily those that happen to oneself—that is, those circumstances that threaten or harm the ego (cf., Hobfoll, 1989). Inspection of the types of items on typical stress inventories reveals this assumption of egocentricity; items such as marriage, divorce, job changes, relocations, or car trouble all focus on problems that occur to the self. Items tapping concerns for others, or nonegocentric stress, are relatively rare on stress inventories.

An egocentric approach to stress is incomplete. As so much of the social support literature shows, individuals' lives are intertwined with those in their social networks. Harm, loss, or threat experienced by loved ones is stressful, whether or not it has any direct bearing on our own well-being. For example, older individuals may often dismiss their own problems, but they will extensively discuss problems that their loved ones are experiencing—a child's marital problems or divorce, a grandchild's problems in school, or a spouse's health. A similar phenomenon has been referred to as *network stress* (Eckenrode & Gore, 1981) or the *stress-contagion* process (Riley & Eckenrode, 1986).

In his theory of life span development, Erikson (1953) posited that generativity was central to adult development. In his seminal work, *Childhood and Society,* he stated:

> *In this book the emphasis is on the childhood stages, otherwise the section on*
> *generativity would of necessity be the central one, for this term encompasses the*

evolutionary development which has made man the teaching and instituting as well as the learning animal. The fashionable insistence on dramatizing the dependence of children on adults often blinds us to the dependence of the older generation on the younger one. Mature man needs to be needed, and maturity needs guidance as well as encouragement from what has been produced and must be taken care of. . . Generativity, then, is primarily the concern in establishing and guiding the next generation. (p. 267)

If Eriksonian theories of adult development are correct, and concern with generativity increases in mid- and late life, one would expect that concern for others' problems may become more central. For example, the success of adult children's careers, marriages, and parenting is an important focus of generative concerns. Barring major health crises that might of necessity focus attention on the self, as people age, their perceptions of stress may become less egocentric and more focused on the problems of others.

As Pearlin and Turner (1987) pointed out, relatively little is known about stress processes in later-life families. In the following sections, data will be presented depicting the types of family-related stress experienced by older adults, the perceived severity of the nonegocentric stress as compared to egocentric stress, and the relative relation of these two types of stress to health outcomes, both physical and mental. Exploratory data on the types of daily stressors reported by older adults will also be presented.

THE ELDERS LIFE STRESS INVENTORY

The Elders Life Stress Inventory (ELSI) initially derived from a series of informal interviews conducted during a participant observation study in a southern California retirement community (1982–1985). Because the focus of the study was naturalistic descriptions of the types of problems that older individuals faced, most of the discussions occurred during social visits or at social events.

Three major categories of stressors emerged from these informal discussions. First, health problems were commonly discussed, especially if the respondent had recently experienced a traumatic, crisis situation involving hospitalization. Second, some older people, especially older men, preferred not to talk about their own problems, but rather were much more concerned with larger social issues, namely politics and the state of the society. Although many of these individuals had a long history being politically active, those most pessimistic about the state of society often themselves appeared to be depressed, which may have influenced their perceptions.

The third category, however, was the most striking. Many of the elderly worried, not about their own problems, but about problems faced by their family members. These older adults preferred not to discuss their own health problems, but expressed great concern about their spouses' health. They also worried about their children's careers, marriages, health, and mortgages, and about their grandchildren's struggles with achievement and choice of mates. They also discussed the problems of friends and neighbors and seemed to spend a great deal of time and energy in trying to help others.

At times, their concern for others seemed to involve some denial—it may have been easier to focus on others' problems rather than their own pressing and increasing physical limitations. However, a strong, nonegocentric or generative factor also seemed to be present. They genuinely tried to help their families and each other. They supplied financial assistance to their adult children and their grandchildren and organized collective investments so that those of limited means could participate. Those who could still drive ran errands or took their less fortunate friends shopping. They visited each other in the hospital, and kept a watchful eye on friends who might not be eating adequately.

In sum, many of these elders' concerns and stressors were not, strictly speaking, personal, but rather involved other people's problems. Their concerns seemed more nonegocentric than egocentric, and appeared to accord with Erikson's (1953) theory of generativity. An alternative explanation, however, is that these elderly retirees might have found it easier to discuss others' problems rather than their own, given the social context of the interviews. A more formal test of the prevalence of egocentric and nonegocentric concerns was necessary.

The California Survey

My colleagues and I conducted a pilot study on stress, values, and well-being in older adults (Colby, Aldwin, Price, & Mishra, 1985). We obtained mailing lists from the boards of directors of three voluntary organizations in the same southern California retirement community in which the participant observation study was conducted. Questionnaires were mailed to 862 potential respondents, and reminder postcards were sent two weeks later. A total of 308 questionnaires were returned for a 36% response rate, an acceptable rate for mail surveys, which typically range from 10% to 50% (Selltiz, Wrightsman, & Cook, 1976). A telephone survey conducted with 51 nonrespondents revealed no differences in age, sex, income, education, or self-rated physical health between respondents and nonrespondents. Thus, the sample was representative of older adults who self-select into such organizations, although it is unlikely that it is representative of the general population of older adults.

The respondents ranged in age from 56 to 90, with a mean age of 74. Nearly two-thirds (64%) were female, 59% were married, and 60% had incomes greater than $25,000, even though 85% were retired. This income level reflected the fact that the sample was highly educated, with 38% having had postgraduate training, and 73% having been businessmen or professionals before their retirement (see Colby et al., 1985, for more description of the sample and sampling techniques).

As part of this study, we designed the ELSI with four goals in mind. First, we wanted to identify events that were particularly salient to older populations. Second, we wanted to focus on nonegocentric concerns, that is, problems that other family members may have been facing. Third, we wanted to combine both event-based and process-based approaches to stress. Within the limits of a life events format, we included as much information on stress processes by drawing on items that dealt with gradual changes in the state of older adults' health or their relations to family and friends. Fourth, the scale needed to be reasonably brief and readily applicable in a mail survey, as opposed to an interview, in order to reach as broad an audience as possible.

We created an item pool by drawing on the literature and on the informal interviews mentioned above. We selected 31 items for which respondents were asked to indicate whether or not they had had certain experiences over the past year. The stressfulness of each experience was rated on a scale from 1 (*not at all stressful*) to 5 (*extremely stressful*). Thus, the ELSI can be scored either as a simple count of the number of events experienced (summed items) or as a sum of the ratings (summed ratings). The two health-related items (memory problems and a major illness or injury) are omitted from the overall scales, so as not to confound the stress measures with health outcomes.

The average number of all items checked on the ELSI was 2.64, ranging from 0 to 14. This is similar to the number of items checked on much longer scales designed for older adults, for example, 3.02 on Krause's (1986) 77-item scale and 3.64 on the 54-item LOPES (Norris et al., 1984). On average, two to three items are checked on standard life events scales, but this number can drop to an average of one or less in samples of older adults if items specific to older populations are not included (e.g., Kanner, Coyne, Schaefer, & Lazarus, 1981; Paykel, 1983).

Table 1 lists the items in the ELSI, ordered by frequency of endorsement. The first column and second columns present the total number and valid percent, respectively, of individuals reporting the event (the term "valid percent" indicates that the missing cases on each item were omitted from the denominator). The third and fourth columns present the average stress rating for those reporting the event and the rank order, respectively.

As in the Murrell et al. (1984) study, health concerns for self and others were the most frequently reported items. For example, 79.2% said they had had problems with memory in the past year, 42.9% had experienced the death of a friend or neighbor, and 34.1% witnessed deterioration in the health or behavior of a family member. The least frequently endorsed events in this retired sample were death of a son or daughter and work-related problems, including trouble with the boss or co-workers and change to a less desirable line of work.

The three events that received the highest stress ratings were death of a son or daughter (5.0), institutionalization of spouse (4.82), and death of spouse (4.42). The three least stressful problems were retirement of spouse (1.87),

TABLE 1 Item Frequency and Severity Ratings for the Elders Life Stress Inventory: California Sample ($N = 308$)

Stress occurring in past year	Number	%	Mean stress rating	Rank order
Deterioration of memory	234	79.2	2.12	27
Death of a friend	130	42.9	2.61	20
*Major deterioration in health or behavior of family member	103	34.1	3.35	7
Major decrease in activities that you really enjoy	100	33.0	2.74	18
*Major personal injury or illness	81	26.7	3.33	8
*Death of other close family member	61	11.1	3.18	10
*Child's divorce or marital separation	42	11.9	2.81	15
Decrease in responsibilities or hours at work or where you volunteer	38	12.6	2.55	22
Increase your responsibilities or hours at work or where you volunteer	36	12.0	2.03	29
Loss of a very close friend due to a move or break in friendship	34	11.2	3.26	9
*Death of a spouse	33	10.9	4.42	3
*Worsening relationship with a child	31	10.3	3.03	12
*Worsening relationship with your spouse	29	9.6	2.97	14
Other	27	8.9	3.85	4
Major deterioration in financial state	25	8.3	2.52	23
Retirement	18	6.9	2.00	30
*Spouse retired	15	5.0	1.87	31
Being burglarized or robbed	14	4.6	2.79	16
Loss of prized possessions due to move	12	4.0	2.16	26
*Marriage	11	3.6	2.72	29
*Institutionalization of spouse	10	3.3	4.82	3
*Assuming major responsibility for a parent	8	2.6	3.13	11
*Institutionalization of parent	8	2.6	3.38	6
Move to a less desirable residence	7	2.3	2.57	24
Deterioration in living conditions	5	1.7	2.29	25
*Marital separation	5	1.7	3.40	5
*Divorce	5	1.7	3.00	13
*Death of a grandchild	4	1.3	2.75	17
Change to a less desirable line of work	3	1.0	2.33	24
Troubles with the boss or co-workers	2	0.7	2.29	26
*Death of a son or daughter	1	0.3	5.00	1

Note. The mean stress ratings are for only those individuals reporting the problem. An asterisk (*) denotes a Family item.

retirement of self (2.00), and an increase in hours or responsibility at work or "where you volunteer" (2.03).

For this chapter, two subscales were constructed that contained items relating to the self and the family, respectively, as indicators of egocentric and nonegocentric stress. The 16 family-related or nonegocentric items (indicated by an asterisk on Table 1) included all deaths, health problems, institutionalization, marital problems, disruptions in relationships among family members, and retirement of spouse. The remaining 12 items (excluding the two health items and the "other" item) were considered self-related or egocentric items, and dealt mainly with the individual's own troubles.[1] On average, one egocentric problem (M = 1.41) and one nonegocentric problem (M = 1.19) were reported during the past year. In other words, nonegocentric stresses made up about half of the typical stresses reported in these retired men and women.

Examining the ratings, nonegocentric problems were, on average, rated as being slightly more stressful than egocentric problems (3.92 vs. 3.64), although the standard deviation for nonegocentric problems was much greater (4.96 vs. 3.99). This undoubtedly reflects the fact that deaths and institutionalizations of family members were among the most stressful problems, and other events, such as spouse's retirement, were among the least stressful.

This study also included a self-reported assessment of physical health symptoms, the Health Status Questionnaire (Belloc, Breslow, & Hochstim, 1971), scored as a simple count of symptoms (see Jette, 1980). The total number of health complaints ranged from 0 to 20, with an average of 5.58.

Table 2 presents the correlations between the ELSI subscales, age and physical health symptoms. Age was not correlated with any of the subscales measures. This suggests that the items on the ELSI are generally applicable for an

---

[1]Obviously, a stressor can be both egocentric and nonegocentric. For example, worries about the health of a spouse may reflect concerns for his or her well-being, annoyance at being inconvenienced, and concerns about one's own future. From a survey it is impossible to determine the ratio of egocentric to nonegocentric concerns for each stressor. Thus, the division of items is admittedly arbitrary and done primarily for heuristic reasons.

TABLE 2 Correlations between Age, Physical Symptoms, and Stress Subscales: California Sample (N = 308)

Stress subscales	Age	Physical symptoms
Total number of stressors	−.05	.32*
Nonegocentric stress	.01	.20*
Egocentric stress	−.05	.35*
Total stress ratings	−.05	.35*
Nonegocentric ratings	−.01	.21*
Egocentric ratings	−.04	.34*

*$p < .001$.

older population, for example, the general incidence did not decrease with age, as is seen with other life event scales. Furthermore, nonegocentric problems did not decrease with age, suggesting that generativity-related concerns continue throughout late life. All of the ELSI subscales were significantly correlated with physical symptoms.

Several interesting results emerged from this table. First, corresponding counts and ratings were correlated with health outcomes at about the same level. For example, the correlation between physical symptoms and total count of items was .32, while that between symptoms and the total rating was .35. These correlations are similar to those obtained with life event scales in younger populations. Thus, the ELSI appears to have reasonable validity. It correlates modestly with health outcomes, and endorsement rates are maintained across a wide age range.

Second, egocentric problems were more highly correlated with health than were the nonegocentric problems. Indeed, a hierarchical regression controlling for age revealed that only egocentric problems were significantly related to the number of health problems reported. Age accounted for 2% of the variance, $F(1, 294) = 5.83, p < .05$, while egocentric problems accounted for an additional 13% of the variance, $F(2, 293) = 43.65, p < .001$. In contrast, nonegocentric problems accounted for less than 1% of the variance in the number of health problems reported, $F(3, 292) = 1.73, ns$.

It would be tempting to conclude that, although nonegocentric problems are salient for older adults, their own problems prove more troublesome and perhaps have more adverse effects on their health. However, that conclusion would be premature, given the many problems with assuming causal directionality between stress and health. Thus, replication with other samples is required.

The Boston Surveys

The sample used in these surveys consisted of panel members of a long-term longitudinal study, the Normative Aging Study (NAS). Growing out of a previous study on veterans of the Spanish-American War, the NAS formally began in 1961. Its function is to document the aging process among a large panel of initially healthy men. An initial pool of 6,000 respondents was gathered through advertisements in the newspapers and through soliciting at large corporations, police departments, and fire departments. Between 1963 and 1965, these men were screened for absence of major physical and psychological health problems, using self-report surveys and physical examinations, and also for "geographical stability," operationalized as extensive family ties in the area. A final panel of 2,280 men was selected, ranging in age from 21 to 80, with 80% of the men aged 30 to 50 (see Bossé, Ekerdt, & Silbert, 1984).

The NAS men are reasonably representative of the larger Boston population. Both blue collar and white collar workers are represented, but the average education is slightly higher than the norm. The participants are primarily white; minorities are underrepresentative of the current Boston population, although the distribution reflects the ethnic composition of Boston in the mid-1960's. Mental health appears to be normally distributed (Aldwin, Spiro, Levenson, & Bossé, 1989).

The men receive complete physical examinations every three to five years, depending upon their age. The younger men, up until the age of 52, receive examinations every five years; upon reaching 52, they are examined every three years. Physical examinations and medical histories are done by physicians, and EKGs, chest X-rays, and blood work-ups, are also conducted. Data on anthropometry and pulmonary functioning are also available. Deaths are verified by death certificates and, when available, autopsy reports. The NAS men also complete numerous questionnaires, which now include self-reported physical and psychological symptoms, smoking and alcohol consumption histories, nutritional status, stress, and social support. They have also participated in various studies of personality, cognition, and adaptation to retirement.

The NAS men have been especially loyal to the study. Response rates to mail surveys typically exceed 80%. Assiduous follow-up has resulted in a less than 1% per annum drop out rate due to all causes, including death. Currently, 1,813 men, 80% of the original sample, are still participating in the study.

In 1985 and 1988, surveys on stress and social support were mailed to the men. Both surveys achieved an 83% response rate, for a total of 1,565 and 1,487 questionnaires, respectively. The average ages of the men in the two surveys were 61 and 63, ranging from 40 to 90 years. About half were retired. Nearly all (87%) were married, and about 90% had children.

Both surveys contained the ELSI, as well as five open-ended daily stressor questions (see Aldwin et al., 1989, for further description of these questions). Wording on the ELSI was slightly modified. In addition, one item, death of a grandchild, was replaced by another item, death of a parent. Psychological symptoms occurring during the past three months were assessed using the Hopkins Symptom Checklist (SCL-90-R; Derogatis, 1983). (For more information on the 1985 survey, see Bossé, Aldwin, Levenson, & Ekerdt, 1987).

Table 3 presents item response frequencies on the ELSI for both surveys, along with the average stress rating for those who experienced the event and the rank order of the stress rating. The rank order of the item frequencies is markedly similar to those found in the California sample. As with the California sample, the three items that were most frequently endorsed were deterioration of memory, death of a friend, and major deterioration in health or behavior of family member, although the percentage endorsing each item was slightly smaller.

Compared to the California sample, NAS men reported more work-related stress, including retirement and problems with the boss or co-workers. They were also less likely to report death of a spouse. This was undoubtedly because

TABLE 3 Item Frequency and Severity Ratings for the Elders Life Stress Inventory: Boston Normative Aging Study Sample

Event in past year	1985 (N = 1,565)				1988 (N = 1,487)			
	Number	%	Mean stress	Rank order	Number	%	Mean stress	Rank order
Deterioration of memory	653	42.5	2.26	29	729	50.0	2.09	29
Death of a friend	385	25.2	3.05	23	363	25.2	2.78	13
Major deterioration in health or behavior of family member	340	22.2	3.64	7	375	25.9	3.26	6
Major decrease in activities that you really enjoy	219	14.3	3.12	21	399	27.5	2.63	20
Major personal injury, illness	199	13.0	3.62	8	251	17.3	3.31	5
Death of close family member	221	14.4	3.28	12	234	16.2	3.00	9
Child's divorce or marital separation	109	7.1	3.28	13	84	5.8	2.96	10
Decrease in responsibilities where you work or volunteer	109	7.2	2.56	27	148	10.2	2.32	28
Increase in responsibilities where you work or volunteer	199	13.1	2.60	26	233	15.5	2.35	27
Loss of a very close friend	43	2.8	3.21	15	60	4.1	2.58	22
Death of a spouse	20	1.3	4.42	1	24	1.7	4.00	2
Worsening relationship with child	112	7.3	3.98	5	144	9.9	2.69	14
Worsening relationship with your spouse	99	6.4	3.17	19	160	11.0	2.69	15
Other	29	1.9	4.04	4	34	2.3	3.65	3
Major deterioration in finances	75	4.9	3.33	11	145	10.0	2.44	25
Retirement	200	13.0	1.95	30	160	11.1	1.88	30
Spouse retired	47	3.1	1.63	31	68	4.7	1.24	31
Being burglarized or robbed	55	3.6	3.21	16	54	3.7	2.56	19
Loss of prized possessions	14	0.9	2.54	28	13	0.9	2.38	26
Marriage	42	4.5	2.84	24	12	0.8	2.65	17
Institutionalization of spouse	15	1.0	4.07	3	11	0.8	3.09	8
Assuming major responsibility for a parent	90	5.8	3.15	20	108	7.4	2.64	18
Change to less desirable work	45	2.9	3.17	18	67	4.6	2.84	12
Troubles with boss or co-workers	160	10.4	3.08	22	169	11.6	2.60	21
Institutionalization of parent	30	1.9	3.57	9	38	2.6	2.84	11
Move to less desirable resident	28	1.8	2.70	25	30	2.3	2.47	24
Deterioration in living conditions	30	1.9	3.21	17	65	4.5	2.48	23
Marital separation	21	1.4	3.30	14	17	0.8	2.65	16
Divorce	13	0.8	3.83	6	15	1.0	3.45	4
Death of a son or daughter	5	0.3	4.20	2	14	1.0	4.36	1
Death of a parent	77	5.0	3.42	10	78	5.4	3.23	7

Note. The mean stress ratings are for only those individuals reporting the problem.

the NAS men, being younger, were more likely to be working. Nonetheless, the frequency of event endorsements were markedly similar across samples.

The rank orders of the stress ratings are also similar. Death of a spouse, institutionalization of spouse, and death of a son or daughter were the three most stressful occurrences, as was also the case in the California sample. Similarly, retirement of self or spouse, were the least stressful events.

Similar results were found with the 1988 data. However, nearly twice the number of men reported deterioration in finances (145 vs. 75). Examination of the questionnaires revealed that many of the men had suffered financial losses during the precipitous drop in the stock market the previous year. The other major difference was that the stress ratings uniformly dropped by about one-fourth of a point, reasons for which are not clear.

The various subscale statistics for the Boston sample at both time points were markedly similar to those for the California sample (see Table 4). An average of 1.83 and 2.38 items were checked. Egocentric problems were slightly more likely to be reported (2.81 vs. 2.57), and they tended to be rated as slightly more stressful than nonegocentric problems (3.39 vs. 2.73). Although the average stressfulness of the individual items dropped, the overall number of events experienced increased, resulting in a slight net increase in stress. Unlike the results in the California sample, the egocentric subscale had a slightly higher stress rating than did the nonegocentric subscale.

Table 5 presents the correlations between the ELSI subscales, age, and psychological symptoms. As with the California sample, the egocentric subscale was more strongly correlated with symptoms than was the nonegocentric subscale. In this larger sample, there were modest negative correlations between age and both item counts and ratings. However, the correlation with egocentric subscales, although modest ($-.08$ to $-.16$), were stronger than the correlations with the nonegocentric subscales, which were trivial ($-.05$ and $-.07$), although significant in a sample of this size. When ratios were com-

TABLE 4 Correlations between Age, Physical Symptoms, and Stress Subscales: Boston Normative Aging Study Sample

Stress subscales[a]	1985		1988	
	M	SD	M	SD
Total number of stressors[a]	1.83	1.80	2.38	2.49
Nonegocentric stress	0.80	1.04	0.99	1.29
Egocentric stress	1.02	1.22	1.37	1.59
Total stress ratings[a]	5.40	6.04	6.13	6.77
Nonegocentric ratings	2.57	3.65	2.73	3.67
Egocentric ratings	2.81	3.87	3.39	4.35

[a]Excludes the two health-related items.

TABLE 5   Correlations between Age, Physical Symptoms, and Stress Subscales: Boston Normative Aging Study Sample

	1985		1988	
Stress subscales[a]	Age	Symptoms	Age	Symptoms
Total number of stressors[a]	.09	.36	−.13	.39
Nonegocentric stress	−.05	.23	−.07	.26
Egocentric stress	−.08	.34	−.15	.38
Total stress ratings[a]	−.10	.39	−.14	.42
Nonegocentric ratings	−.05	.23	−.07	.27
Egocentric ratings	−.11	.38	−.16	.44

Note. All correlations are significant beyond the .05 level.
[a]Excludes the two health-related items.

puted, dividing the nonegocentric subscale by the overall score for just those individuals reporting stress, there was no significant correlation with age in 1985 ($r = .00$, $N = 1,140$, *ns*) or 1988 ($r = .02$, $N = 1,121$, *ns*). This suggests that the negative correlations between age and nonegocentric stress were due to a slight decrease in overall stress reporting with age.

Stepwise regression equations controlling for age confirmed that the egocentric subscale was more strongly related to the men's mental health than was the nonegocentric subscale. As Table 6 indicates, the egocentric subscale accounted for 12% to 19% of the variances in psychological symptoms, while the nonegocentric subscale accounted for only 1% to 2% of the variances.

TABLE 6   Regressing Psychological Symptoms on Age and Stress Subscales: Boston Normative Aging Study Sample

	1985			1988		
Indepdent Variables	β	ΔR^2	F	β	ΔR^2	F
Equation 1						
Age	−.02	.00	0.53	−.01	.00	0.04
Egocentric stress	.30	.12	195.84*	.33	.14	239.95*
Nonegocentric stress	.15	.02	35.32*	.12	.01	18.73*
Total equation[a]		.16	114.48*		.16	130.82*
Equation 2						
Age	−.03	.00	1.05	−.01	.00	0.64
Egocentric ratings	.34	.15	253.24*	.40	.19	336.37*
Nonegocentric ratings	.14	.02	30.63*	.11	.01	17.13*
Total equation[a]		.16	114.48*		.20	178.65*

[a]Age was omitted from the final equation for lack of significance.
*$p < .001$.

DAILY STRESSORS

The daily stressors data presented here should be considered preliminary and exploratory. Five open-ended questions were included in both Boston surveys. Respondents were asked to relate information about any problems, whether major or minor, that occurred during the past three months in five areas similar to those used by Pearlin and Schooler (1978), that is health, marital, social, work/retirement, and financial (see Aldwin et al., 1989). Open-ended questions were used because the study was exploratory, and we were reluctant to impose a priori categories. These responses were later content-analyzed (interrater reliability >90%). Respondents rated each stressor on a scale from 0 to 7, with 0 indicating that no problems had occurred, and 7 indicating that it was the most stressful thing ever experienced.

Only information on wife problems and social problems are reported here, as they are most relevant to the construct of nonegocentric stress. The marital question specifically stated that the problems reported could be ones faced by the wife. Social stressors could involve problems with children, other relatives, friends, or formal ties (e.g., landlord, lawyer, or officials). These first three categories were coded to reflect either conflict between the respondent and another person, a proxy in this case for egocentric stress, while concern over another person's problems was a proxy for nonegocentric stress. Problems not dealing with conflict or concern with family members or friends (e.g., formal ties) were omitted from these analyses.

As Table 7 indicates, the majority of the hassles reported in these categories dealt less with conflicts than with concerns for others' problems. At both time points, about one-fourth of the marital stressors dealt with conflicts in marital relations, while the rest addressed concerns about the wife's health, common worries about other family members, and the like. Several of the men mentioned the strain that their wives felt in taking care of elderly parents or babysitting grandchildren for working sons and daughters.

About a third of the reported social stressors dealt with conflicts with chil-

TABLE 7 Percentage of Reported Wife and Social Hassles Reflecting Conflicts and Concerns: Boston Normative Aging Study Sample

Reported hassles	1985		1988	
	Conflicts	Concerns	Conflicts	Concerns
Wife	27.0%	73.0%	28.4%	71.6%
M	4.50	4.63	5.02	4.95
SD	1.63	1.52	1.47	0.48
Social	28.6%	71.4%	37.1%	62.9%
M	4.72	4.55	5.16	4.72
SD	1.52	1.55	1.41	1.39

dren, other family members, and friends; two-thirds were concerned with problems that friends and relatives (mostly children) were facing. The men worried about their childrens' careers and achievement in college, graduations and marriages, their mortgages, and their health.

Given the sparseness of the information we were coding, it may be that we underestimated the amount of conflict in any given situation. Conflicts were coded only when it was clearly indicated that there were arguments or disagreements. More detailed interviews may have revealed more conflict. Nonetheless, even given the likelihood that we underestimated the amount of conflict, the data clearly suggest that a fair amount of stressors are nonegocentric— that is, the NAS men were concerned about the well-being of family and friends.

Turning to the correlations between these types of hassles, age, and psychological symptoms, the data in Table 8 reveal that very few age trends were seen in the stressfulness or types of daily stressors reported. Marital conflicts were slightly more strongly related to symptoms than were marital concerns at both time points. However, no relations emerged between social conflicts and psychological symptoms. Social concerns, however, were moderately related to symptoms at both time points.

DISCUSSION

Erikson and his colleagues (Erikson, Erikson, & Kivnick, 1986) recently expanded on the construct of generativity in late life in a qualitative study of the parents of the participants in the Berkeley Guidance Study. They affirmed that the components of generativity—caring, nurturing, and maintaining—are important throughout the life course, but take on special meaning in mid- and late life. In mid-life, generative responsibility is expressed in

TABLE 8 Correlation between Daily Stressors, Age, and Psychological Symptoms: Boston Normative Aging Study Sample

Reported hassles	1985		1988	
	Age	Psychological symptoms	Age	Psychological symptoms
Wife	27.0%	73.0%	28.4%	71.6%
Conflicts	− .04	.30***	− .08	.24***
Concerns	.11*	.20***	.03	.14*
Social				
Conflicts	.05	.06	.01	.11
Concerns	− .03	.25***	.08	.20**

*p < .05.   ** p < .01.   ***p < .001.

> maintenance of the world. . . . It is . . . the responsibility of each generation
> of adults to bear, nurture, and guide those people who will succeed them as
> adults, as well as to develop and maintain those societal institutions and natural
> resources without which successive generations will not be able to survive. (pp.
> 73–74)

In late life,

> the roles of aging parent, grandparent, old friend, consultant, adviser, and
> mentor all provide the aging adult with essential social opportunities to experi-
> ence grand-generativity in current relationships with people of all ages. . . . The
> capacity for grand-generativity incorporates care for the present with concern for
> the future—for today's younger generations in their futures, for generations not
> yet born, and for the survival of the world as a whole. (pp. 74–75)

The ability to care for and nurture others in integral to the older adult's own development. In this light, it is not surprising that many of the concerns of the California and NAS samples were also focussed on family and friends rather than on the self. Indeed, Erikson's observations on the degree to which these later-life individuals cared about and were involved in the lives of their family and friends were markedly similar to the participant-observation study reported here. One 90-year-old in Erikson's sample stated, "When you get to my age, why, I am willing to die at any time. The only thing that keeps me alive is my obligation to the family" (Erikson et al., 1986, p. 63). Another explained, "I do not have *personal* thoughts about the future, but I do think about my grand-children's future" (p. 66, emphasis in text).

As with the California sample, the older adults Erikson et al. (1986) studied also engaged in communal activities to help their friends and neighbors. They kept an eye on frail neighbors, often participating in telephone networks. One woman delivered "meals on wheels." Another woman in frail health crocheted shawls and afghans for hospital patients. In Erikson's words, "These aged individuals are . . . very much involved in the daily maintenance of one another . . . show[ing] general, communal attitudes toward care" (Erikson et al., 1986, p. 100).

Interestingly, similar themes of older adults' positive involvement in their families and social networks have emerged from the work by other researchers in this volume. For example, DeLongis and O'Brien (Chapter 10) emphasize the importance of empathy in stress processes. Hansson and Carpenter (Chapter 6) focus on the importance of interpersonal competence in late life in maintaining social ties. The ability to provide help to others may be an important way of expressing interpersonal competence and preventing a one-sided dependence on network members. Jackson, Antonucci, and Gibson (Chapter 9) also discussed the important contributions of unpaid labor performed by older adults for their family and community. On the other hand, Rook (Chapter 8) cautions that interpersonal relations are not necessarily completely positive and supportive and may entail stresses of their own.

Although some have argued that network stress or social contagion has harmful effects on health, Riley and Eckenrode (1987) suggested that this is found primarily among those with low social resources. In the California and Boston samples, concern for others' problems tended to be only modestly correlated with health outcomes, suggesting that the relative cost of nonegocentric stress is not that great in these older adults who have relatively high resource levels. The studies reported here did not examine positive outcomes directly, and future work should be directed toward exploring whether such outcomes can be more systematically demonstrated in an older population.

Although stress is generally regarded by researchers as having negative impacts, Lomranz (Chapter 5) argues eloquently that stress, even severe stress, can have positive developmental and social outcomes. Dan Stokols and I reviewed studies demonstrating anomalous or positive outcomes of stress and presented a theoretical framework for the ways in which stress can have positive outcomes (Aldwin & Stokols, 1988). Three particularly relevant positive outcomes of stress are social cohesion (cf. Antonovsky, 1979), altered perspectives or cognitive comparisons (cf. Taylor, 1983), and meaning.

Older adults concern for others' problems can entail similar benefits. As I observed in the California retirement community, concern for others' problems appeared to promote social cohesion. Much of the conversation concerned others' problems and the various arrangements that were made to provide support to them. Helping others also broadened their perspective on their own problems. For example, one older woman's visual impairments prevented her from driving at night, but by helping a legally blind friend run errands during the day, her own problems did not seem quite so bad in comparison. Finally, concern for others' problems and helping others also provided meaning for these older adults' lives. They felt that they had important roles to play and, in some instances, staved off feelings of uselessness by immersing themselves in others' lives.

From a developmental perspective, the ability of older adults to involve themselves in caring and nurturing relations, expressed in nonegocentric concern for others' well-being, is an important component of generativity in later life. Through these concerns, older adults remain involved in the lives of their family and friends, transcend their own physical limitations, and maintain a sense of meaningfulness and usefulness in their lives. Given that generativity is an important step toward the development of personal integrity in late life, nonegocentric stress may be considered a hallmark of successful aging, and certainly merits more investigation. Rather than perceiving older adults primarily as recipients of care, more research should focus on the social support that older adults provide.

REFERENCES

Aldwin, C., Levenson, M. R., Spiro, A. III, & Bossé, R. (1989). Does emotionality predict stress? Findings from the Normative Aging Study. *Journal of Personality and Social Psychology, 56,* 618-624.

Aldwin, C., Spiro, A. III, Levenson, M. R., & Bossé, R. (1989). Longitudinal findings from the Normative Aging Study. I. Does mental health change with age? *Psychology and Aging, 4,* 295-306.

Aldwin, C., & Stokols, D. (1988). The effects of environmental change on individuals and groups: Some neglected issues in stress research. *Journal of Environmental Psychology, 8,* 57-75.

Amster, E., & Krauss, R. (1974). The relationship between life stress and mental deterioration in old age. *International Journal of Aging and Human Development, 5,* 51-55.

Antonovsky, A. (1979). *Health, stress, and coping.* San Francisco: Jossey-Bass.

Belloc, N., Breslow, L., & Hochstim, J. R. (1971). Measurement of physical health in a general population survey. *American Journal of Epidemiology, 109,* 328-336.

Bossé, R., Aldwin, C., Levenson, M. R., & Ekerdt, D. (1987). Mental health differences among retirees and workers: Findings from the Normative Aging Study. *Psychology and Aging, 2,* 383-389.

Bossé, R., Ekerdt, D. J., & Silbert, J. E. (1984). The Veterans Administration Normative Aging Study. In S. A. Mednick, M. Harway, & K. M. Finello (Eds.), *Handbook of longitudinal research: Volume 2. Teenage and adult cohorts* (pp. 273-289). New York: Praeger.

Colby, B. N., Aldwin, C., Price, L., & Mishra, S. (1985). Adaptive potential, stress, and illness in the elderly. *Medical Anthropology, 94,* 283-296.

DeLongis, A., Coyne, J. C., Dakof, G., Folkman, S., & Lazarus, R. S. (1982). Relationship of daily hassles, uplifts, and major life events to health status. *Health Psychology, 1,* 119-136.

Eckenrode, J., & Gore, S. (1981). Stressful events and social supports: The significance of context. In B. Gottlieb (Ed.), *Social networks and social support* (pp. 43-68). Beverly Hills, CA: Sage.

Erikson, E. H. (1953). *Childhood and society.* New York: Norton.

Erikson, E. H., Erikson, J. M., & Kivnick, H. Q. (1986). *Vital involvement in old age.* New York: London.

Hobfoll, S. E. (1989). Conservation of resources: A new attempt at conceptualizing stress. *American Psychologist, 44,* 513-524.

Holahan, C. K., Holahan, C. J., & Belk, S. S. (1984). Adjustment in aging: The role of life stress, hassles, and self-efficacy. *Health Psychology, 3,* 315-328.

Holmes, T. H., & Rahe, R. H. (1967). The Social Readjustment Scale. *Journal of Psychosomatic Research, 11,* 213–218.

James, A., James, W., & Smith, H. L. (1984). Reciprocity as a coping strategy of the elderly: A rural Irish perspective. *The Gerontologist, 24,* 483–489.

Jette, A. (1980). Health status indicators: Their utility in chronic disease evaluation research. *Journal of Chronic Diseases, 33,* 567–579.

Kahana, E., Kahana, B., & Young, R. (1985, November). *Influences of diverse stress on health and well-being in community aged.* Paper presented at the Annual Meeting of the Gerontological Society of America, New Orleans.

Kanner, A. D., Coyne, J. C., Schaefer, C., & Lazarus, R. S. (1981). Comparison of two modes of stress measurement: Daily hassles and uplifts vs. major life events. *Journal of Behavioral Medicine, 4,* 1–39.

Kasl, S. (1987). Methodologies in stress and health: Past difficulties, present dilemmas, future directions. In S. Kasl & C. Cooper (Eds.), *Stress and health: Issues in research methodology* (pp. 307–318). New York: John Wiley.

Kee, C. C., & Whittington, F. J. (1985, November). *Stress, health, and social support.* Paper presented at the Annual Meeting of the Gerontological Society of America, New Orleans.

Kinney, J. M., & Stephens, M. A. P. (1989). Caregiving Hassles Scale: Assessing the daily hassles of caring for a family member with dementia. *The Gerontologist, 29,* 328–335.

Kinney, J. M., & Stephens, M. A. P. (in press). Hassles and uplifts of giving care to a family member with dementia. *Psychology and Aging.*

Krause, N. (1986). Social support, stress, and well-being among older adults. *Journal of Gerontology, 41,* 512–519.

Lazarus, R. S., & DeLongis, A. (1983). Psychological stress and coping in aging. *American Psychologist, 38,* 245–254.

Muhlenkamp, A., Gress, L., & Flood, M. (1975). Perception of life change events by the elderly. *Nursing Research, 24,* 727–731.

Murrell, S., Norris, F. H., & Hutchins, G. L. (1984). Distribution and desirability of life events in older adults: Population and policy implications. *Journal of Community Psychology, 12,* 301–311.

Norris, F. H., & Murrell, S. A. (1987). Transitory impact of life-event stress on psychological symptoms in older adults. *Journal of Health & Social Behavior, 28,* 197–211.

Paykel, E. S. (1983). Methodological aspects of life events research. *Journal of Psychosomatic Research, 27,* 341–352.

Pearlin, L., & Schooler, C. (1978). The structure of coping. *Journal of Health and Social Behavior, 19,* 2–21.

Pearlin, L., & Turner, H. (1987). The family as a context of the stress process. In S. Kasl & C. Cooper (Eds.), *Stress and health: Issues in research methodology* (pp. 143–165). New York: John Wiley.

Riley, D., & Eckenrode, J. (1986). Social ties: Subgroup differences in costs and benefits. *Journal of Personality and Social Psychology, 51,* 770–778.

Rowland, K. (1977). Environmental events predicting death for the elderly. *Psychological Bulletin, 84,* 349–372.

Sands, J. D., & Parker, J. (1979–1980). A cross-sectional study of the perceived stressfulness of several life events. *International Journal of Aging and Human Development, 10,* 335–341.

Selltiz, C., Wrightsman, L. S., & Cook, S. W. (1976). *Research methods in social relations* (3rd ed.). New York: Holt, Rinehart, & Winston.

Silverman, M., Eichler, A., & Williams, G. (1987). Self-reported stress: Findings from the 1985 National Health Interview Survey. *Public Health Reports, 102,* 47–53.

Teri, L., & Lewinsohn, P. (1982). Modification of the pleasant and unpleasant event schedules for use with the elderly. *Journal of Consulting and Clinical Psychology, 50,* 444–445.

5

STRESS, SUPPORT, AND WELL-BEING IN LATER LIFE: FOCUSING ON SALIENT SOCIAL ROLES

Neal Krause

University of Michigan

There has been a phenomenal growth in the number of studies on the impact of stressful life events on psychological well-being. Vingerhoets and Marcelissen (1988) have reported that there are now well over 1,000 articles in the literature that examine some facet of the stress process. Moreover, several journals have appeared that are devoted solely to the study of life stress (e.g., *Stress Medicine* and *Behavioral Medicine*). It is gratifying to see that a significant number of the studies in this literature have been concerned with the effects of life stress on older adults (see George, in press, for a review of this research).

Many researchers expected stress to be a major determinant of well-being. Empirical research findings, however, indicate that stressful events have only a limited impact on well-being (see Murrell, Norris, & Grote, 1988, for a critique if these studies). The modest effects of stress on well-being are especially apparent in longitudinal studies (e.g., Norris & Murrell, 1984). These discouraging results have led investigators to argue that models that merely examine the direct effects of stress on well-being are inadequate, and that the role played by social psychological resources in the stress process must be taken into consideration (e.g., Barrera, 1988; Hobfoll, 1989).

Perhaps the most frequently examined coping resource is social support (see Cohen & Wills, 1985, for a review of this research). Although empirical evidence is far from conclusive, the general consensus is that the deleterious effects of life stress appear to be reduced for those people who have strong social support systems. As the literature has evolved, however, it has become increasingly clear that the nature of the stress-buffering role played by social support is by no means simple, and that supportive social relations may function in complex ways (see Krause, in press a, for a detailed discussion of this issue). For example, some researchers have argued that greater insight into the stress process can be obtained by examining specific types of supportive behaviors, such as tangible assistance or emotional support (e.g., Cohen et al., 1982). Building on this observation, other investigators have suggested that we need to abandon the use of global life-event checklists and focus instead on how specific types of social support buffer or reduce the effects of specific types of stressful life events, such as bereavement or events that occur to significant others (e.g., Kessler, 1983; Krause, 1986).

Although the research of Kessler (1983) and others has allowed investigators to make significant strides toward understanding the stress process more fully, researchers have generally failed to address a basic but critically important question: *How* does social support reduce the negative effects of life stress? Existing research has largely involved refinements in the measurement of stress and social support, but these measurement strategies are not based on a theoretical foundation that has been articulated fully. Moreover, few attempts have been made to identify and measure the specific mechanisms that intervene between the provision of supportive behaviors and the subsequent restoration or maintenance of a sense of well-being.

The purpose of this chapter is to introduce a conceptual framework that seeks to identify the specific mechanisms in the stress process. Throughout, my emphasis is on developing a model that can actually be tested in the field. Accordingly, the discussion that follows is divided into three sections. First, a conceptual framework or model is presented, which may be used to explain how stress and social support affect the psychological well-being of older adults. Next I identify key measurement issues and propose procedures for evaluating the model empirically. Finally, I present theoretical elaborations that involve potentially important limitations of the beneficial effects of social support.

THEORETICAL RATIONALE
FOR A MODEL OF THE STRESS PROCESS

In order to understand how social support might buffer the effects of stressful life experiences in elderly populations, it may be helpful to first examine how life events affect older adults. The work of Caplan is especially helpful in this regard. According to Caplan (1981), stressful life events affect people primarily by diminishing their feelings of self-worth and by eroding their sense of mastery or personal control. Pearlin and his associates captured the essence of this perspective when they stated that stress "can confront people with dogged evidence of their own failures—or lack of success—and with inescapable proof of their inability to alter the unwanted circumstances in their lives" (Pearlin, Menaghan, Lieberman, & Mullan, p. 340).

If stress affects individuals by diminishing their feelings of self-worth and personal control, then social support may help to maintain or restore a sense of well-being by bolstering these important resources. Caplan (1981) provided a convincing theoretical rationale for the linkage between social support and feelings of personal control. He suggested that an effective social support group helps to replenish feelings of perceived control by providing stressed individuals with concrete help in dealing with their problems. Significant others help to evaluate the situation, formulate a plan of action, assist in implementing this plan, and provide feedback and guidance while the plan is being executed. Given this support, stressed individuals come to feel as though the problem situation can be controlled and overcome.

The rationale for linking social support with self-esteem is based on a rich theoretical tradition in the social and behavioral science literature. Kaplan's research represents an important point of departure for understanding this perspective. According to Kaplan (1975), feelings of self-worth and positive self-regard are essential for the maintenance of psychological well-being. Consequently, he regarded the maintenance of positive self-feelings as a primary motivational factor in social behavior.

If stress operates by eroding feelings of positive self-esteem, and if people are motivated to maintain or enhance their feelings of self-worth, then perhaps individuals turn to supportive others in times of stress in order to replenish this important personal resource. This view is supported by Thoits (1985), who observed that an evaluation of one's sense of worth, importance, and competence arises from the perceived appraisal of one's significant others. In short, she maintained that social support is a primary source of reflected self-esteem (see also Cooley, 1902, for an early discussion of this viewpoint). Knowing this, individuals who are experiencing stress may actively seek the support of others in order to enhance their depleted feelings of self-worth.

Empirical support for the linkages between social support, self-esteem, and feelings of personal control can be found in the gerontological literature. For example, I found that social support buffers the effects of life stress on depressive symptoms in older adults by bolstering feelings of self-worth (Krause, 1987a). Moreover, I found in a subsequent study that, under certain circumstances, social support tends to increase feelings of personal control in elderly people (Krause, 1987b).

Despite the intuitive appeal of the theoretical linkages proposed by Caplan (1981) and Thoits (1985), progress in the empirical assessment of this perspective has been hampered by an overly simplistic view of the nature of both personal control and self-esteem. In their recent review of the literature, Rodin, Timko, and Harris (1985) argued convincingly that the construct of control is not a unidimensional phenomenon and that researchers should begin to examine domain-specific measures of control. Essentially, these researchers maintain that feelings of personal control are not consistent across all areas of life and that older adults may feel that they can exercise more control in some areas than in others. For example, elderly people may feel that they have more control over their interpersonal relationships than over their personal financial circumstances.

When an event arises in a given life area, it seems reasonable to look for the impact of that stressor on feelings of control over the same life domain. For example, financial difficulty may have the greatest impact on feelings of control over personal finances. In contrast, the use of a generalized measure of control, such as the Rotter I-E Scale (Rotter, 1966), may produce less dramatic effects because these global evaluations are based on experiences in a broad range of life areas that may not be affected by the stressor confronting the individual. A thorough review of the literature reveals that there have been only a few limited attempts to measure domain-specific feelings of personal control (see, e.g., Lachman, 1986) and that no one has assessed the effects of stress on these more focused measures of control in a population of older adults.

Similar conceptual difficulties are encountered with respect to self-esteem. Gerontologists in the life stress field have focused exclusively on global measures of self-worth without examining the impact of life events on more specific dimensions of the self-concept. This is somewhat surprising because for some time, social psychologists have argued that it is important to move beyond global conceptualizations of self-esteem to a view of the self as being composed of domain or role-specific identities (see Bengtson, Reedy, & Gordon, 1985, for a review of this research). Essentially, social psychologists maintain that there are multiple selves or identities and that there is a specific identity for each major role that people play. It is important to point out, however, that although older people arrive at a self-evaluation of their performance in each of these roles, these identity-specific evaluations may contribute differentially to overall feelings of self-worth, because some identities are more important or salient than others. More specifically, Stryker (1987) and others have suggested that individual identities forming the self are organized into a salience hierarchy that reflects varying levels of commitment to the roles underlying these identities.

The theoretical contributions of Stryker (1987) and Rodin et al. (1985) are important because they allow us to take advantage of recent developments in the conceptualization of life stress. In a study of respondents drawn from the general population, Thoits (1987) makes a forceful case for studying life events that threaten those roles that are the most salient to the respondent. A personal example may help to clarify the logic that underlies this perspective. I am not an artist, nor have I spent much time attempting to draw or paint. Should I attempt to do so and fail, it is unlikely that there would be a noticeable change in my sense of well-being because being an artist is not important to me—it does not represent a highly salient role. In contrast, failure as a researcher would have a much more devastating effect because I am deeply committed to that role and, as a consequence, it is a core element in my self-identity.

By focusing on salient roles, the unit of analysis shifts from a stressful event per se to the extent to which highly cherished roles are threatened by a stressor. If a role is not important to an older adult, then an event arising in that domain is less likely to create psychological distress. Undoubtedly, a given event can affect a number of areas of life, but the crux of the argument presented here is that the resulting deleterious effects will be greatest when the stressor involves a highly valued role.

Assume, for example, that an older person values the parental role highly. Under these circumstances, the death of a child is likely to increase the risk of psychological disorder. To be sure, the death of a child may create difficulties in other areas of life. It is possible that funeral costs may create financial difficulties. However, this is less likely to be a source of distress if the role of provider is not highly salient. According to the theoretical rationale presented here, the critical factor in the genesis of psychological distress is the fact that an event threatened a highly valued role (i.e., the parental role).

I have argued recently that social roles have figured prominently in past conceptualizations of stressful life events, but that feasible strategies for operationalizing and implementing measures that test these views have been fraught with difficulty (Krause, in press c). One of the most comprehensive examinations of social roles within a life-event measurement perspective has been proposed by Aneshensal and Pearlin (1987). Beginning with the observation that individuals occupy multiple roles, these investigators suggested that a top priority in stress research should be to focus on the points where multiple roles intersect. Presumably, conflicts arising at these junctures are a key factor in the etiology of psychological disorder. This means, for example, that women may feel that employment outside the home is stressful not because of conditions on the job, but because work responsibilities must be performed in conjunction with homemaking tasks or because working creates conflict with a spouse.

Although the theoretical orientation proposed by Aneshensal and Pearlin (1987) is thought-provoking, it is not clear how this perspective can be operationalized and implemented practically in the field. In effect, researchers would have to identify combinations of stressors that arise at the juncture of all possible social roles in order to test this viewpoint. The survey instrument needed to perform such a task would clearly be quite lengthy and time-consuming, especially if a researcher must also gather data on social support, self-esteem, feelings of personal control, and psychological well-being. Perhaps more important, statistical tests for evaluating this perspective would involve complicated statistical interaction effects that could quickly become unwieldy when joint effects of three or more roles are considered simultaneously.

One advantage of the theoretical rationale provided in this chapter is that it provides a theoretically driven basis for simplifying this task. Instead of focusing on stressors arising at the juncture of every role that is occupied by each study participant, it is necessary to focus only on those roles that are the most salient. Moreover, concentrating on salient roles makes it possible to incorporate recent developments in the literature on self-esteem and personal control into the conceptual model.

A CONCEPTUAL MODEL
OF THE STRESS PROCESS

In the discussion that follows, the theoretical linkages that were specified in the previous section are depicted graphically. There were two reasons for developing a conceptual model in this manner. First, it makes the theoretical underpinnings explicit, and, second, it provides a framework for subjecting these assumptions to rigorous empirical evaluation (see Campbell, 1988, for a recent discussion of these advantages).

The notation used in Figure 1 is consistent with the notation developed by Joreskog and Sorbom (1988). More specifically, η_1 denotes latent or unobserved constructs, whereas ζ_i represents disturbance terms in the structural equations. The observable indicators associated with each latent construct are not shown in Figure 1 in order to simplify the presentation of this model. However, precise measurement model specifications are provided in the next section.

Based on the discussion provided by Thoits (1987), it is assumed in Figure 1 that the most threatening life events are those stressors that arise in highly salient roles (η_1). Following the theoretical rationale developed in the previous section, it is predicted that stressors arising in salient roles (η_1) affect psychological distress (η_5) primarily by eroding feelings of personal control over salient roles (i.e., role-specific personal control—η_3) and by diminishing self-evaluations of one's performance in those roles (i.e., role-specific self-esteem—η_4). Because feelings of self-worth and personal control are assumed to play a major role in the stress process, it is anticipated that the direct effects of stress (η_1) on psychological disorder (η_5) will be smaller than the indirect effects operating through role-specific personal control (η_3) and role-specific self-esteem (η_4). This means that if personal control and self-esteem are in fact the key intervening links in the stress process, then the inclusion of these resources in the model should serve to reduce the direct effects of stress on well-being. According to this theoretical framework, social support is also assumed to be an important factor in the stress process. According to this rationale, supportive social relations (η_2) offset or buffer the deleterious effects of life stress (η_1) by increasing feelings of role-specific personal control (η_3) and by bolstering feelings of role-specific self-esteem (η_4).

In his cogent discussion of stress-buffering models, Wheaton (1985) identified a series of conceptual schemes that are designed to explain how social support and stress affect psychological well-being (see Barrera, 1986; Dohrenwend & Dohrenwend, 1981; and Lin, Dean, & Engel, 1986, for additional stress-buffering models). The specifications involving stress, support,

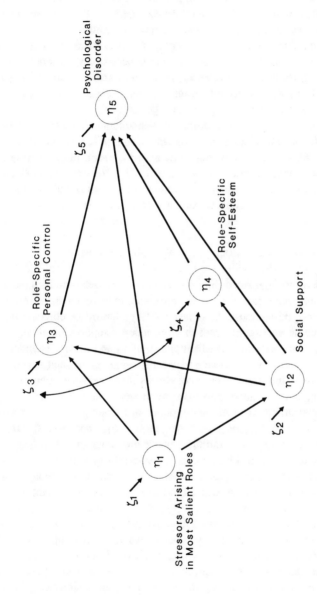

FIGURE 1 A basic model of the stress process.

and well-being that are presented in Figure 1 constitute an extension of what Wheaton (1985) referred to as the suppressor model of the stress process. It is assumed in this model that the relationships among stress, support, and well-being are additive and linear. The key characteristic of this theoretical formulation is that the amount of support that is provided is contingent upon the amount of stress that is present. More specifically, this perspective assumes a resource mobilization approach that suggests that as stress increases, individuals seek out (or mobilize) support from significant others (see Alloway & Bebbington, 1987, for a recent review of this crisis-support model).

Another major characteristic of the suppressor model becomes evident when the direct, indirect, and total effects of stress (η_1) on psychological disorder (η_5) are assessed. According to this view, stress (η_1) exerts a direct (and negative) effect on well-being (η_5). However, the direct effects of stress (η_1) are offset or diminished by the indirect effects that operate through social support (η_2). More specifically, stress (η_1) increases social support (η_2), and support in turn tends to reduce psychological distress (η_5), thereby suppressing or limiting the total effects of life stress.

The suppressor model proposed by Wheaton (1985) is extended or elaborated in Figure 1 by the addition of role-specific personal control (η_3) and role-specific self-esteem (η_4). According to these theoretical elaborations, stress (η_1) diminishes these important self-evaluations, but these detrimental effects are offset or suppressed by the support provided by significant others (η_2). In effect, this formulation suggests that the presence of suppressor effects will be more evident when self-conceptualizations (i.e., η_3 and η_4) are included in the model than when the analyses focus only on stress, support, and psychological disorder. By including the causal mechanisms that intervene between support and well-being, the predictive power of the model should be enhanced.

As is shown in Figure 1, no assumptions are made about the direction of causality between role-specific personal control (η_3) and role-specific self-esteem (η_4). Instead, the structural disturbance terms associated with these constructs are merely correlated (ζ_3 and ζ_4). This specification makes it possible to take the correlation between control and self-esteem into account when the model is estimated, without making any assumptions about the temporal ordering of these constructs.

The model depicted in Figure 1 is a simple or basic model that can be elaborated upon or improved in a number of ways. For example, it would be advisable to control for the effects of stressors arising in less salient roles when estimating the model shown in Figure 1. In this way it would be possible to determine whether stressors arising in salient roles exert a significant impact on well-being above and beyond the effects of more general life stress measures. Similarly, global measures of personal control and self-esteem should also be included in order to evaluate explicitly the relative contributions of their role-specific counterparts.

There were two reasons why the model depicted in Figure 1 was specified in a relatively simple way. First, the intent was to provide a conceptual scheme that could actually be tested in the field. All too often researchers propose far-reaching models of the stress process that encompass a bewildering array of constructs that are extremely difficult to operationalize or measure explicitly. Even if adequate measures are available, these conceptual schemes frequently contain so many constructs that any attempt to actually estimate them in their entirety would prove to be extremely difficult in practice (see, e.g., the family stress model devised by McCubbin & Patterson, 1983).

The second reason for developing a relatively simple conceptual model has to do with issues in the measurement of role-specific life events, feelings of control, and self-esteem. As the discussion in the next section shows, the measurement models for these constructs are quite complex. Such complicated measurement specifications limit the size and scope of structural equation models that can be estimated realistically.

MEASURING KEY CONSTRUCTS

The model depicted in Figure 1 is based on the premise that researchers should focus on those social roles that are the most salient. Two issues must be addressed if this framework is to be adapted successfully in the field. First, a mechanism must be devised for identifying the roles that are the most important to older adults. Second, a data analytic approach must be outlined for aggregating and comparing data when respondents have identified a diverse array of roles as being the most salient. Although Thoits' (1987) discussion of role-specific stressors is stimulating, she does not provide a satisfactory resolution to the dilemma that arises when stressors associated with one role must be compared with stressors arising in an entirely different role. In fact, Thoits (1987) suggested that because some stressors are unique to certain roles, it may be impossible to conduct direct comparisons of persons who occupy different social roles. As the following discussion provided will reveal, this is an unnecessarily restrictive assumption.

At the broadest level, the purpose of this section is to provide practical resolutions to the measurement dilemma already described. First, I outline procedures for identifying salient social roles. Following this, I propose measurement strategies for assessing life events, feelings of personal control, and feelings of self-esteem that are associated with salient social roles. Finally, I examine in detail issues that may arise when developing an appropriate measure of social support.

In the discussion that follows, the measurement of key study constructs is presented within a latent variable framework. Those who are less familiar with this data analytic approach may wish to read the next few sections more casually. It must be emphasized, however, that a major contribution of this chapter lies in the expression of complex theoretical issues in explicit measurement models. The interested reader is referred to Alwin (1988) for a comprehensive review of the techniques described.

Identifying Salient Social Roles

An obvious first step in evaluating the theoretical rationale provided in the previous section is to develop procedures for identifying salient social roles. Hoelter (1985) gave some useful suggestions for obtaining this information. He recommended that respondents be given a deck of eight cards, each of which contains the name of a major role. A deck that might be used for older adults may contain the following major roles: (1) spouse; (2) parent; (3) grandparent; (4) sister, brother, or other relative; (5) friend or neighbor; (6) homemaker; (7) provider; and (8) voluntary worker or club, church, or professional association member.

Study participants may then be asked to keep those cards that they feel best describe them and return those cards that do not reflect how they tend to view themselves. Ideally, it would be best to identify the one role that is the most important for each person. However, it is likely that people may feel as though two or more roles are equally important to them, such as the role of spouse and parent. Under these circumstances, it may be too restrictive to focus exclusively on those stressors that are associated with the parental role while ignoring those arising in the role of spouse. Instead, greater insight into the stress process may be obtained if events arising in *both* the spouse and parent roles are taken into consideration.

In order to confront this problem, study participants could be asked to identify the three most important roles they occupy. If possible, these roles should be rank-ordered according to their degree of importance. By following this alternative procedure, it will be possible to contrast the effects of stress in the single most important role with the impact of events arising in three roles that are clustered at the top of the salience hierarchy.

Identifying Role-Specific Stressful Events

Having identified the roles that are the most salient for study participants, the next step is to determine whether any stressful events arose in these roles. I discuss two issues in this section. First I provide specific procedures for assessing life events that are associated with salient roles. Following this, I review techniques for aggregating these stressors into a useful life event index. The information provided in this section relies heavily on my earlier work (Krause, in press b).

I have previously devised a stressful life event index that provides a useful point of departure for developing measures of role-specific life events (Krause, 1986). An important feature of this scale is that life events are organized into sections according to the following major life areas: events involving a respondent's children, spouse, other relatives, friends, neighbors, finances, and crime. With a few simple modifications, this scale could be used to cover events arising in all of the salient social roles identified.

It is virtually impossible to assemble check lists that contain every possible stressor that can arise in every social role. However, I have recently devised a strategy for confronting this problem (Krause, 1986). It is possible to determine whether any additional events have occurred in a given domain by placing an open-ended item at the end of each list of role-related stressors. For example, the section dealing with stressors that involve a respondent's children would conclude with an open-ended item that asks if anything else had happened to their children in addition to those events contained in the scale.

Although identifying stressors that arise in salient roles is a relatively straightforward task, aggregating these events into a measure that can be used to compare people who experience stressors in highly diverse roles represents a much more formidable undertaking. Figure 2 contains a measurement model that attempts to take this kind of diversity into account. As in Figure 1, the notation system used in Figure 2 is consistent with that developed by Joreskog and Sorbom (1988). The x_1 in Figure 2 represents the stressors that are associated with the three most salient roles identified by study participants. Based on literature reviewed by Thoits (1983), it may be best to compute the simple unweighted sum of the undesirable or negative events that arise in each role. However, it should be emphasized that the model depicted in Figure 2 can accommodate measures that focus on other dimensions of life events, such as events that are uncontrollable or unanticipated.

The χ_1 denotes latent or unobserved exogenous constructs that are associated with the χ_1, η_1 is a latent higher-order construct representing life stress, and δ_1 stands for random measurement error in the χ_1. Finally, ζ_1 is a structural disturbance term that stands for the effects of stressful events that have not been measured explicitly in the model. In order to understand how events arising in diverse social roles can be compared, it is important to reiterate a basic point that was made earlier: The unit of analysis is not a specific event or even a particular role per se. Instead, an emphasis is placed on assessing the amount of stress that was experienced in a highly valued role, whatever that role may happen to be.

As is shown in Figure 2, the higher-order stressful life event (η_1) construct is a linear composite of three first-order factors: stressors arising within the first-mentioned salient role (χ_1), life events associated with the second-mentioned salient role (χ_2), and stressful events occurring within the third-mentioned salient role (χ_3). The proposed specification of stressful life events (η_1) is unique because the three first-order factors (χ_1, χ_2, and χ_3) are considered to be cause indicators rather than effect indicators (see Bollen, 1984, for a detailed discussion of this distinction). The use of cause indicators is justified because the life events arising within each salient role should be relatively independent (i.e., the correlation among the χ_1 should be low). This interpretation is consistent with the work of

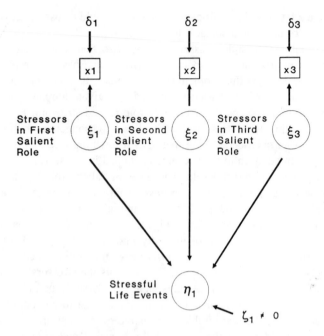

FIGURE 2   A measurement model of role-specific stressful life events.

Cleary (1980), who observed that life events should be independent of each other and that there is no reason to believe that people who experience one life event will necessarily experience other stressors as well.

An alternative strategy is to develop a measurement model in which events in the three salient roles are considered to be effect indicators (i.e., the direction of the arrows linking η_1 with the χ_1 would be reversed). This represents the classic approach to latent variable modeling and assumes that each stress indicator is a function of some latent construct plus measurement error. Perhaps more important, it is assumed that cause indicators are at least moderately intercorrelated because they are mutually dependent (i.e., caused by) the same underlying or latent construct (η_1). It follows from this measurement specification that stress indicators that have low correlations with the remaining stress indicators should be excluded from the model. However, it would be a mistake to exclude events on the basis of low item intercorrelations because this may result in the elimination of rare but potentially quite damaging events from subsequent analyses.

Two options are available for specifying the value of the structural disturbance term (ζ_1) in Figure 2: This construct could assume either a zero or a nonzero value. The distinction between these options has important implications for the way in which life events arising in salient roles are conceptualized. As has been mentioned, the structural disturbance term (ζ_1) stands for the effects of variables that are not specifically included in the model but that have a significant impact on the latent construct (η_1). A large nonzero value of ζ_1 would suggest that the latent life stress construct is determined by events other than those that arise within the three most salient roles (i.e., the χ_1 in Figure 2). Consequently, the estimation of ζ_1 provides further information that is useful for determining whether it is important to focus exclusively on stressors that arise in salient roles.

As Hoelter (1986) and others have observed, cause indicator models have a troublesome property that must be addressed. When developing measurement models such as the one shown in Figure 2, researchers typically assume that the observable indicators (i.e., the specific life events—χ_1) have been measured without error. However, findings from studies of the reliability of life stress measures suggest that this may be an unrealistic assumption. For example, Tennant, Bebbington, and Murry (1981) reported that the test–retest reliability of life stress measures generally ranges from .50 to .75, indicating that these indices contain a sizable amount of measurement error. As Bollen (in press) and others have demonstrated convincingly, such error can bias resulting parameter estimates substantially.

Fortunately, a partial resolution to this problem is available in the literature. Based on the work of Munck (1979) and others, it is possible to use the information on the test–retest reliability reported by Tennant et al. (1981) to take the effects of measurement error into account when the impact of stress is being assessed. More specifically, this approach involves (a) constraining (i.e., fixing) the respective factor loadings (i.e., the paths from the χ_1 to the x_1) to the validity coefficient (i.e., the square root of the reliability) and (b) setting the corresponding elements in the measurement error vector (i.e., the δ_1) to (1.0 reliability) times the variance of the observed indicators (i.e., the χ_1). Based on research reviewed by Tennant et al. (1981), a reasonable estimate to use in this formula might be .70 or .75.

The procedure developed by Munck (1979) is useful because it allows investigators to account for known measurement error, thereby providing more accurate parameter estimates. However, it should be emphasized that the reliability estimates used in conjunction with this formula are obtained from the literature, and not from the sample that is used in a given study. Consequently, the reliability estimates are not precise. Nevertheless, it is preferable to use these estimates instead of making the more unrealistic assumption that the stress measures (i.e., the x_1) have been measured without error (see Anderson & Gerbing, 1988, for a discussion of a similar statistical procedure).

Developing Role-Specific Measures of Self-Esteem

Once the three most salient roles have been identified and stressors associated with these roles have been assessed, the next task is to devise measures that gauge respondents' feelings of self-worth and personal control within each life domain. Once again, the work of Hoelter is especially helpful for developing items to assess these constructs. Hoelter (1985) developed a series of brief rating scales to measure eight dimensions of the self-concept. The indices assessing role-specific self-evaluations and power are especially relevant for operationalizing the constructs in Figure 1. These items are cast in a semantic differential format. More specifically, Hoelter (1985) asked respondents to rate their performance in specific roles along a five-point continuum that was bounded by the following adjective pairs: successful/unsuccessful, important/ unimportant, and good/bad.

Hoelter's (1985) strategy can be easily adapted to assess feelings of self-worth that are associated with the salient roles that have been identified by older study participants. An example may help to clarify this measurement strategy. Assume that respondents indicate that the role of provider is very important to them. Based on this information, the following qualifying statement and response formats could be used to assess self-worth in the provider role: "As a provide, I am successful/unsuccessful, or important/unimportant, or good/ bad." Comparable items could be developed to measure feelings of self-worth in the two remaining salient roles as well.

Figure 3 contains a second-order measurement model of role-specific self-esteem that can be developed from responses to these items. As shown in this conceptual scheme, x_1, x_2, and x_3 denote response to three semantic differential items that assess feelings of self-worth in the first-mentioned salient role (χ_1), whereas x_4, x_5, and x_6 and x_7, x_8, and x_9 represent role-specific measures of self-esteem in the second- (χ_2) and third- (χ_3) mentioned salient roles respectively.

Consistent with the procedures used to develop a measurement model of life stress, the higher-order self-esteem construct (η_1) shown in Figure 3 is a linear composite of the self-evaluations made in each of the salient roles $(\chi_1, \chi_2,$ and $\chi_3)$. It is important to identify clearly the underlying rationale for relying on a cause indicator approach because there may be alternative ways of specifying this model. Earlier, based on the work of Caplan (1981), it was predicted that role-specific feelings of self-worth are influenced primarily by life stressors arising within each salient role. Because events arising in salient roles are thought to be relatively independent, then self-evaluations of performance in salient roles may be differentially determined. If constructs have different determinants, then the intercorrelations among them should be relatively low, and, as a consequence, a cause indicator approach may be the most appropriate specification.

Despite the intuitive appeal of this argument, some researchers might argue that role-specific self-evaluations are in fact highly correlated. More specifically, based on cognitive consistency theory (e.g., Heider, 1958), one might maintain that individuals have a tendency to develop and maintain self-views that are consistent across all areas of life. According to this view, when noncompatible or

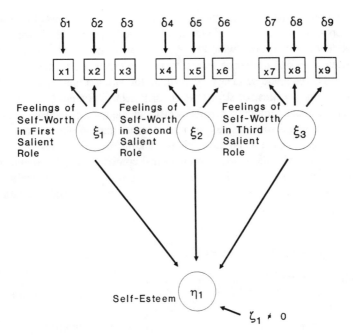

FIGURE 3   A measurement model of role-specific self-esteem.

contradictory self-evaluations emerge, individuals strive to reconcile the inconsistencies and restore a balanced view of the self (see Jones, 1973; for a discussion set in a gerontological context, see Fillip & Klauer, 1986).

Because the notion of independent role-specific self-evaluations forms the cornerstone of the conceptual model developed in this chapter, it is essential that these competing views be assessed empirically. Fortunately, this can be accomplished with a relatively straightforward two-step process. In the first step, the model depicted in Figure 3 would be estimated exactly as it is shown. Following this, the model could then be respecified in an effect indicator format. More specifically, the direction of the causal arrows linking the first-order self-evaluations (χ_1, χ_2, and χ_3) with the higher-order self-esteem (η_1) construct would be reversed. After estimating this respecified model, the goodness-of-fit indices for the competing specifications could be compared. The model with the best fit to the data would indicate which conceptual orientation is most likely to be correct.

Developing Role-Specific Measures of Control

Hoelter's (1985) work is also useful for developing measures of role-specific perceptions of personal control. As was discussed earlier, he constructed measures of eight dimensions of the self-concept, including power. Because the constructs of power and control are closely related, it is possible to assess role-specific feelings of control with a modified version of the indicators developed by Hoelter (1985). Continuing with the example presented earlier, control over the provider role could be measured with the following items: "As a provider, I am powerful/powerless, or strong/weak, or potent/impotent."

A measurement model of role-specific feelings of personal control that could be developed with this data is presented in Figure 4. Once again, a cause indicator approach has been adopted for linking the role-specific evaluations (χ_1, χ_2, and χ_3) with the second-order control construct (η_1). However, following the procedures described in the previous section, it is possible to derive empirical estimates of the extent to which these domain-specific evaluations are developed independently.

Measuring Supportive Social Relations

The purpose of the following discussion is to propose a strategy for measuring social support that flows logically from the theoretical framework that has been developed in this chapter. In describing this measurement approach I will show how it confronts a major problem that is inherent in many existing social sup-

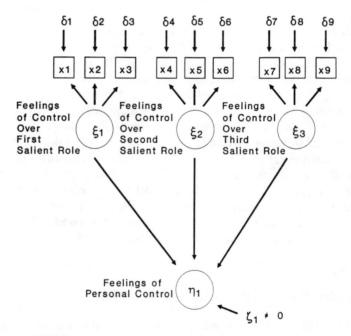

FIGURE 4 A measurement model of role-specific personal control.

port indices. In order to highlight the unique aspects of the measurement strategy used here, it is useful to first examine how social support is frequently assessed in existing studies. Although researchers have devised a bewildering array of ways to conceptualize and measure social support, a large number of studies have relied on scales that attempt to assess received or enacted support (see Krause, in press a, for a detailed discussion of social support measures). Essentially, scales of enacted support are designed to determine the amount of support that has actually been provided to a study participant. Frequently an attempt is made to assess specific types of helping behaviors within this context, such as emotional support, tangible help, and informational assistance.

An obvious difficulty with this strategy is that information on enacted support as well as data on stressful life events can only be gathered retrospectively. In conducting such studies, respondents are typically asked about the stressors they have experienced during a certain period of time (e.g., during six months or one year) as well as the amount of support they have received during the same time period. However, it is important to think carefully about the kind of information that is actually being obtained. Investigators using this approach assume that the stressors identified by respondents arose first and that any support that was provided was subsequently given in response to these stressful events. Unfortunately, this may not necessarily be true. It is possible, for example, that a respondent may receive a significant amount of emotional support for a reason totally unrelated to a given stressful event. Moreover, this emotional support may have even been received prior to the occurrence of that stressor. Should we conclude that emotional support has buffered the effects of stress in this instance?

It seems that a much more focused picture of the stress process will emerge if efforts are made to gather information about supportive behaviors that were given in response to particular stressful events. Within the context of the theoretical framework developed in this chapter, a researcher would first identify stressors that have arisen in salient social roles and then ask about the supportive behaviors that were given specifically in response to those events. So, for example, if respondents indicate that they have experienced a financial stressor in the past year (i.e., a threat to the provider role), they would subsequently be asked about specific things that significant others might have done to help them confront that particular event. More specifically, study participants might be asked whether anyone loaned or gave them money when the financial stressor occurred (tangible support), or told them where to go to get help with this financial difficulty (informational support), or whether anyone just listened to them talk about this financial problem (emotional support).

At first, it might appear that asking about support that was provided in response to each stressor would be an overwhelming task that would create a redundant and excessively long questionnaire. However, the perspective developed in this chapter serves to limit the extent of this problem in two important ways. First, it is not necessary to ask about support given in response to all stressful events that confront a study participant. Instead, information is gathered only on events arising in salient roles. The literature suggests that in general, older adults do not experience a large number of stressful life events. For example, the elderly respondents in one of my recent studies experienced an average of only three undesirable stressful events in a 12-month period (Krause, 1986). Moreover, it should be emphasized that the scale used in that study attempted to identify events in all areas of life, not just those associated with salient roles. Clearly, the number of events arising solely in salient roles must be even lower.

The procedure recommended here is also not likely to become unwieldy because an extensive number of items are not needed to measure received social support. Because the data can be analyzed in a latent variable framework, it is necessary to develop only three observable indicators for each latent construct (see Bentler & Chou, 1988, for a detailed discussion of this issue). Consequently, a carefully crafted scale consisting of only nine items would probably be adequate for assessing the amount of emotional, tangible, and informational support given in response to each salient event. If older adults experience an average of 3 undesirable events in roles that are salient to them, then the amount of social support given in response to these events could be assessed in total with an average of 27 items.

Figure 5 contains a preliminary measurement model of social support given in response to stressors arising in salient roles. Based on the discussion provided earlier, it was assumed in developing this model that emotional, tangible, and informational support were each assessed with three items, and that the resulting nine-item measure was administered (with appropriate modifications) for each event experienced in each of three salient roles. Consequently, the y_i in Figure 5 represents composite measures that were computed by summing the responses to the support items across all salient life events. This means, for example, that y_1 denotes the responses to the first emotional support item summed across all salient stressors.

The composite scores (i.e., the y_i) shown in Figure 5 are thought to be determined by three latent constructs: received emotional support (η_2), tangible assistance provided to study participants (η_3), and enacted informational assistance (η_4). The existence of a second-order factor, received social support (η_1), is hypothesized to account for the intercorrelations among the specific types of enacted support (i.e., η_2, η_3, and η_4). Consequently, a cause indicator approach is proposed to link the first- and second-order factors. This specification is justified because research indicates that specific types of enacted social support are highly intercorrelated (see Barrera, 1988, for a recent review of this research).

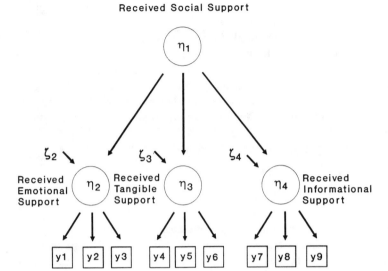

Received Social Support

FIGURE 5 A measurement model of received social support.

THEORETICAL ELABORATIONS

Although the conceptual model depicted in Figure 1 is fairly simplistic, the measurement of the key constructs depicted in this scheme has proven to be quite complex (see Figures 2–5). Given the amount of work that must be done, there is a temptation to strive for closure and to be satisfied with the existing model specifications. However, recent developments in the life stress literature make it imperative that additional theoretical possibilities be considered.

As was discussed earlier, life stress was predicted to affect well-being primarily by eroding feelings of personal control and self-worth. However, it was also hypothesized that these deleterious effects would be offset because assistance from others can replenish or restore these important self-evaluations. As the model depicted in Figure 1 currently stands, the relationships among support, control, and self-esteem are additive and linear. This means that a unit increase in support is associated with an increase in feelings of control or self-worth that is constant across *all* levels of support. In essence, this specification implies that there are no limits to the beneficial effects of supportive social relations and that older adults will continue to experience increased feelings of control and self-worth even when they are receiving exceptionally high amounts of support from significant others.

Recently, research by Rook (1984), as well as my own work (Krause, 1987b) has begun to point up questions about this assumption. More specifically, these studies suggest that the effects of support are not always beneficial and that, under certain circumstances, interaction with significant others may even tend to diminish self-evaluations and feelings of well-being. The purpose of the final section in this chapter is twofold: to discuss these compelling theoretical developments in greater detail and to examine procedures for evaluating these alternative specifications within a latent variable framework.

Exploring the Limitations of Supportive Social Relations

Gerontologists are becoming increasingly aware that interactions with others is not always beneficial and that contact with important persons in our social networks can have negative or undesirable effects as well (see Chapter 8, this volume). Recently, I discussed one way in which this might occur (Krause, 1987b). As Lee (1985) and others have observed, independence is valued highly by older adults in American culture, whereas being dependent on significant others, especially kin, is considered to be a negative attribute. Consequently, relationships in which older adults rely heavily on others may engender feelings of dependence and enmeshment that may in turn erode feelings of personal control.

Based on this rationale, I proposed that support from significant others may exert beneficial effects on feelings of control initially, but that beyond a certain threshold, increased support would tend to diminish perceptions of personal control (Krause, 1987b). Findings from an initial attempt to confirm this hypothesis among older adults provided some support for this rationale (Krause, 1987b).

Additional insights into the stress process can also be obtained if we recognize that there may be limits in the extent to which supportive social relations can bolster feelings of self-worth. The literature suggests that there are several ways in which excessively high levels of social support can reduce or diminish feelings of self-worth. Research indicates that prolonged help-giving can lead to a deterioration in the relationships between older adults and their significant others (e.g., O'Brien, 1980). Perhaps as their resources become depleted, significant others begin to withdraw or avoid contact with overly dependent people. As the work of Rodin and Langer (1980) suggests, such avoidance behavior can in turn diminish feelings of self-worth among the aged. However, avoidance or withdrawal may not always be possible. Under these circumstances, significant others may become resentful and begin to interact with elders in ways that are patronizing, condescending, or even derogatory. Such negative messages may encourage older adults to view themselves as dependent, incapable, and aged, thereby diminishing their feelings of self-worth (see Krause, in press b, for a discussion of this issue). Although the theoretical rationale provided here appears to be plausible, a thorough review of the literature fails to reveal any studies that have examined this issue empirically.

Modeling Limitations in the Effects of Social Support

Taken as a whole, the preceding discussion specifies that there is a nonlinear (i.e., curvilinear) effect of social support on feelings of personal control as well as on feelings of self-worth. Stated more explicitly, increases in social support will be associated initially with increased feelings of self-worth and control, but beyond a certain threshold, additional increments in support will tend to erode or decrease these self-evaluations.

There is considerable controversy in the literature on how to estimate nonlinear effects (see Kenny & Judd, 1984, for a detailed discussion of this problem). Unfortunately, there is presently no solution that is entirely satisfactory. However, some options are less problematic than others. In the discussion that follows, the nature of these data analytic problems will be examined briefly. Following this discussion, a partial resolution to these difficulties will be proposed.

An example may help to illustrate more clearly the kinds of problems that researchers encounter when they attempt to estimate nonlinear effects. Virtually all tests for nonlinear effects in the current literature have been performed with ordinary least squares multiple regression analysis (OLS). If a researcher were interested in estimating the nonlinear effects of social support on self-esteem, then he or she might use some form of the following OLS equation (referred to hereinafter as Equation 1):

$$SE = a + b_1 SS + b_2 SS^2 + e$$

where SE stands for self-esteem, SS represents social support, SS^2 is a quadratic term formed by squaring social support scores (this captures the nonlinear effect of support), and e is a disturbance term. Finally, a is the intercept in Equation 1 and b_1 denotes unstandardized regression coefficients.

Two specific problems arise when equations such as the one described here are used to estimate nonlinear effects. In both instances, these problems can produce biased estimates of b_1 and b_2. The first problem arises when social support (SS) has been measured with error and the resulting reliability of this scale is low. Unfortunately, this is all too often the case in the literature, where internal consistency estimates can be as low as .31 (see O'Reilly, 1988, for a recent review of this research). Under these circumstances, the reliability of the quadratic term (SS^2) will be even lower than the reliability of the original social support composite (SS) (see Busemeyer & Jones, 1983, for a detailed discussion of how this problem arises). As a consequence, estimates of b_1 and b_2 can be biased substantially.

Other difficulties arise in estimating Equation 1 that may also be attributed to error in the measurement of social support. More specifically, error in the social support measure (SS) is correlated with error in the quadratic term (SS^2) because the quadratic term is formed by multiplying the social support measure by itself. As the size of the correlation of these error terms increases, estimates of b_1 and b_2 will become increasingly biased.

At the present time, perhaps the best way to avoid these problems is to rely on subgroup comparisons within a latent variable structural equation framework (see Sorbom, 1979, for a detailed discussion of this procedure). In the context of the present example, this would involve partitioning the sample into two groups: those older adults with high social support and those with low social support. The model depicted in Figure 1 could then be estimated separately within each group, and systematic tests could be performed to determine whether the impact of support on self-esteem is significantly different across the two groups. If the nonlinear hypothesis is correct, social support should have a positive effect on self-esteem in the low-support group. This would suggest that, initially, support from others tends to maintain or bolster feelings of self-worth. In contrast, social support should be negatively related to self-esteem in the high-support group, indicating that excessive amounts of support tend to diminish feelings of self-esteem.

There is, however, one difficulty that is associated with the use of subgroup analyses: It is difficult to identify the appropriate cut-point score for dividing the sample into groups consisting of people who have received either high or low amounts of social support (see Blalock, 1982, for a discussion of the difficulties encountered in performing subgroup analyses). This problem may be attributed in part to the fact that norms have not been established for social support scales, and, as a consequence, we have no empirical basis for selecting a support score that correctly differentiates high from low social support.

At present, it may be best to simply partition the groups at the median social support value for a given sample. Analyses based on this cut-point can subsequently be compared to analyses using slightly different cut-points that fall above and below the median value. By probing for the appropriate cut-point in this manner, it may be possible to identify precisely that score at which increments in support cease to be beneficial and being to erode feelings of personal control.

SUMMARY

The purpose of this chapter was to present a model that may provide a means for better understanding the relationships among stress, social support, and psychological well-being among older adults. This model expands the existing knowledge base by encouraging researchers to evaluate three specific hypotheses. First, it was proposed that the deleterious effects of stress would be especially noxious if stressors threaten salient social roles. Second, it was proposed that support tends to diminish these effects by bolstering feelings of personal control and self-worth that are associated with the salient roles that are being threatened. Finally, it was hypothesized that there were limits to the beneficial effects of supportive social relations and that as older adults become dependent on others, high levels of support tend to erode feelings of self-worth and personal control.

In the process of developing this theoretical framework, a deliberate attempt was made to outline explicit procedures and to provide guidance that could be used to estimate this model in the field. In order to achieve this goal, an effort was made to avoid developing a highly complicated model that included a broad range of constructs. However, there are drawbacks associated with taking this approach because a number of relevant constructs had to be excluded from the model. For example, social support was hypothesized to erode feelings of control by engendering a sense of dependence and to diminish feelings of self-worth by promoting negative interaction with significant others. Neither feelings of dependence nor negative interaction was included specifically in the model. Clearly, these as well as a host of other constructs should eventually be measured and incorporated explicitly into the model; but for now, the present specifications should prove to be sufficiently complex.

At the present time, there is a certain intuitive appeal in studying stressors that arise in salient roles, but the theoretical foundations of such research have not been explicated fully in the current literature, nor has this perspective been subjected to careful empirical scrutiny. The ideas in this chapter were largely derived from discussion sections in existing empirical studies as well as other off-the-cuff remarks that have been made in the literature. Perhaps the major contribution of this chapter lies in the attempt to specify the underlying theoretical rationale more clearly and the development of a specific blueprint for subjecting the resulting assumptions to rigorous empirical testing.

REFERENCES

Alloway, R., & Bebbington, P. (1987). The buffer theory of social support. *Psychological Medicine, 17,* 91–108.

Alwin, D. (1988). Structural equation models in research on human development and aging. In K. Schaie, R. Campbell, W. Meredith, & S. Rawlings (Eds.), *Methodological issues in aging research* (pp. 71–170). New York: Springer.

Anderson, J., & Gerbing, D. (1988). Structural equation modeling in practice:

A review and recommended two-step approach. *Psychological Bulletin, 103,* 411–423.

Aneshensal, C., & Pearlin, L. (1987). Structural contexts of sex differences in stress. In R. C. Barnett, L. Biener, & G. K. Baruch (Eds.), *Gender and stress* (pp. 75–95). New York: Free Press.

Barrera, M. (1986). Distinctions between social support concepts, measures, and models. *American Journal of Community Psychology, 14,* 413–445.

Barrera, M. (1988). Models of social support and life stress: Beyond the buffering hypothesis. In L. Cohen (Ed.), *Life events and psychological functioning: Theoretical and methodological issues* (pp. 211–236). Beverly Hills, CA: Sage.

Bengtson, V., Reedy, M., & Gordon, C. (1985). Aging and self-conceptions, personality processes and social contexts. In J. E. Birren & K. W. Schaie (Eds.), *Handbook of psychology of aging* (pp. 544–593). New York: Van Nostrand Reinhold.

Bentler, P., & Chou, C. P. (1988). Practical issues in structural modeling. In S. C. Long (Ed.), *Common problems/proper solutions: Avoiding error in quantitative research* (pp. 161–192). Beverly Hills, CA: Sage.

Blalock, H. M. (1982). *Conceptualization and measurement in the social sciences.* Beverly Hills, CA: Sage.

Bollen, K. (1984). Multiple indicators: Internal consistency or no necessary relationship? *Quality and Quantity, 18,* 377–385.

Bollen, K. (in press). *Structural equations with latent variables.* New York: Wiley.

Busemeyer, J., & Jones, L. (1983). Analysis of multiplicative combination rules when the causal variables are measured with error. *Psychological Bulletin, 93,* 549–562.

Campbell, R. (1988). Integrating conceptualization, design, and analysis in panel studies of the life course. In K. W. Schaie, R. Campbell, W. Meredith, & S. Rawlings (Eds.), *Methodological issues in aging research* (pp. 43–69). New York: Springer.

Caplan, G. (1981). Mastery of stress: Psychosocial aspects. *American Journal of Psychiatry, 138,* 413–420.

Cleary, P. (1980). Problems of internal consistency and scaling of life events schedules. *Journal of Psychosomatic Research, 25,* 309–320.

Cohen, F., Horowitz, M., Lazarus, R., Roos, R., Robins, L., Rose, R., & Rutter, M. (1982). Panel report on psychosocial aspects and modifiers of stress. In G. Elliott & C. Eisdorfer (Eds.), *Stress and human health: Analysis and implications for research* (pp. 147–188). New York: Springer.

Cohen, S., & Wills, T. (1985). Stress, social support, and the buffering hypothesis. *Psychological Bulletin, 98,* 310–357.

Cooley, C. (1902). *Human nature and the social order.* New York: Scribner's.

Dohrenwend, B. S., & Dohrenwend, B. P. (1981). Life stress and illness:

Formulation of the issues. In B. S. Dohrenwend & B. P. Dohrenwend (Eds.), *Stressful life events and their contexts* (pp. 1–27). New York: Prodist.

Fillipp, S. H., & Klauer, T. (1986). Conceptions of self over the life span: Reflections on the dialectics of change. In M. M. Baltes & P. B. Baltes (Eds.), *The psychology of control and aging* (pp. 167–205). Hillsdale, NJ: Erlbaum.

George, L. K. (in press). Stress, social support, and depression over the life course. In K. Markides & C. Cooper (Eds.), *Aging, stress, social support, and health.* New York: Wiley.

Heider, F. (1958). *The psychology of interpersonal relations.* New York: Wiley.

Hobfoll, S. (1989). Conservation of resources: A new attempt at conceptualizing stress. *American Psychologist, 44,* 513–524.

Hoelter, J. (1985). The structure of self-conception: Conceptualization and measurement. *Journal of Personality and Social Psychology, 49,* 1392–1407.

Hoelter, J. (1986). The relationship between specific and global evaluations of self: A comparison of several models. *Social Psychology Quarterly, 49,* 129–141.

Jones, S. C. (1973). Self and interpersonal evaluations: Esteem theories versus consistency theories. *Psychological Bulletin, 79,* 185–199.

Joreskog, K., & Sorbom, D. (1988). *LISREL 7: A guide to the program and applications.* Chicago, IL: SPSS, Inc.

Kaplan, H. (1975). *Self-attitudes and deviant behavior.* Pacific Palisades, CA: Goodyear.

Kenny, D., & Judd, C. (1984). Estimating the nonlinear and interactive effects of latent variables. *Psychological Bulletin, 96,* 201–210.

Kessler, R. (1983). Methodological issues in the study of psychosocial stress. In H. Kaplan (Ed.), *Psychosocial stress: Trends in theory and research* (pp. 267–341). New York: Academic Press.

Krause, N. (1986). Social support, stress, and well-being among older adults. *Journal of Gerontology, 41,* 512–519.

Krause, N. (1987a). Life stress, social support, and self-esteem in an elderly population. *Psychology and Aging, 2,* 349–356.

Krause, N. (1987b). Understanding the stress process: Linking social support with locus of control beliefs. *Journal of Gerontology, 42,* 589–593.

Krause, N. (in press a). The measurement of social support in studies on aging and health. In K. Markides & C. Cooper (Eds.), *Aging, stress, social support, and health.* New York: Wiley.

Krause, N. (in press b). Satisfaction with social support and changes in functional disability through time. In N. Coupland, H. Giles, & J. Weiman (Eds.), *Communication, health, and the elderly: Proceedings from the 1988 Fullbright Colloquium Series.* Washington, DC: Hemisphere.

Krause, N. (in press c). Stress measurement. *Stress Medicine.*

Lachman, M. (1986). Personal control in later life: Stability, change, and cognitive correlates. In M. Baltes & P. Baltes (Eds.), *Aging and the psychology of control* (pp. 207–236). Hillsdale, NJ: Erlbaum.

Lee, G. (1985). Kinship and social support of the elderly: The case of the United States. *Ageing and Society, 5,* 19–38.

Lin, N., Dean, A., & Engel, W. (1986). Modeling the effects of social support. In N. Lin, A. Dean, & W. Engel (Eds.), *Social support, life events, and depression* (pp. 173–209). New York: Academic Press.

McCubbin, H., & Patterson, J. (1983). Family stress and adaption to crisis: A double ABCX model of family behavior. In D. Olson & B. Miller (Eds.), *Family studies review yearbook* (pp. 87–106). Beverly Hills, CA: Sage.

Munck, I. (1979). *Model building in comparative education: Applications of the LISREL method to cross-national survey data.* Stockholm: Almqvist & Wiksell International.

Murrell, S., Norris, F., & Grote, C. (1988). Life events in older adults. In L. Cohen (Ed.), *Life events and psychological functioning: Theoretical and methodological issues* (pp. 96–122). Beverly Hills, CA: Sage.

Norris, F., & Murrell, S. (1984). Protective function of resources related to life events, global stress, and depression in older adults. *Journal of Health and Social Behavior, 25,* 424–437.

O'Brien, M. (1980). Effective social environment and hemodialysis adaptation: A panel analysis. *Journal of Health and Social Behavior, 21,* 360–370.

O'Reilly, P. (1988). Methodological issues in social support and social network research. *Social Science and Medicine, 26,* 863–873.

Pearlin, L., Menaghan, E., Lieberman, M., & Mullan, J. (1981). The stress process. *Journal of Health and Social Behavior, 22,* 337–356.

Rodin, J., & Langer, E. (1980). Aging labels: The decline of control and the fall of self-esteem. *Journal of Social Issues, 36,* 12–29.

Rodin, J., Timko, C., & Harris, S. (1985). The construct of control: Biological and psychosocial correlates. In M. P. Lawton & G. Maddox (Eds.), *Annual review of gerontology and geriatrics* (Vol. 5, pp. 3–55). New York: Springer.

Rook, K. (1984). The negative side of social interaction: Impact on psychological well-being. *Journal of Personality and Social Psychology, 46,* 1097–1108.

Rotter, J. (1966). Generalized expectancies for internal versus external control of reinforcement. *Psychological Monographs: General and Applied, 80*(Whole No. 609), 1–28.

Sorbom, D. (1979). An alternative methodology for the analysis of covariance. In K. Joreskog & D. Sorbom (Eds.), *Advances in factor analysis and structural equation models* (pp. 219–234). Cambridge, MA: Abt Books.

Stryker, S. (1987). Identity theory. Developments and extensions. In K. Yradly

& T. Honess (Eds.), *Self and identity: Psychosocial perspectives* (pp. 89–104). New York: Wiley.

Tennant, C., Bebbington, P., & Murry, J. (1981). The role of life events in depressive illness: Is there a substantial causal relation? *Psychological Medicine, 11*, 379–389.

Thoits, P. (1983). Dimensions of life stress that influence psychological distress: An evaluation and synthesis of the literature. In H. Kaplan (Ed.), *Psychosocial stress: Trends in theory and research* (pp. 33–103). New York: Academic Press.

Thoits, P. (1985). Social support and psychological well-being: Theoretical possibilities. In I. Sarason & B. Sarason (Eds.), *Social support: Theory, research and applications* (pp. 51–72). The Hague, The Netherlands: Martinus Nijhoff.

Thoits, P. (1987). Gender and marital status differences in control and distress: Common versus unique stress explanations. *Journal of Health and Social Behavior, 28*, 7–22.

Vingerhoets, A., & Marcelissen, F. (1988). Stress research: Its present status and issues for future developments. *Social Science and Medicine, 26*, 279–291.

Wheaton, B. (1985). Models of the stress-buffering functions of coping resources. *Journal of Health and Social Behavior, 26*, 352–364.

6

LONG-TERM ADAPTATION TO TRAUMATIC STRESS IN LIGHT OF ADULT DEVELOPMENT AND AGING PERSPECTIVES

Jacob Lomranz

Tel Aviv University

How can we best comprehend the long-term effects of traumatic stress on the life course and aging process? In this chapter I integrate the concepts of aging; interpersonal, familial, and cultural processes; and coping with traumatic stress through a review of the literature and of an ongoing narrative research project with aging Holocaust survivors. First I outline the orientation of the chapter and introduce the focus on traumatic stress experienced by survivors of the Holocaust. Next I propose a multidimensional, integrative framework that includes the relationship between developmental stages and historical and cultural contexts, on the one hand, and the patterns of traumatic stress on the other. I discuss long-term adaptation to traumatic stress in light of the personal, interpersonal, and familial aspects of adult development and aging. I conclude the chapter with a discourse on the conceptual and methodological implications of my work.

Different scientists hold different images of humankind. These and cultural factors determine, to a great extent, the nature of their scientific products (Polanyi, 1964). Catastrophes, and certainly national traumas such as wars or the Holocaust, can have particularly overpowering intellectual effects on investigators. The most common approach to stress has focused on pathology; the *Diagnostic and Statistical Manual of Mental Disorders,* third edition (DSM-III; American Psychiatric Association, 1980) has reinforced an association between

The author is grateful to N. Eyal and M. Gush-Chalav for their valuable assistance in the preparation of this chapter.

postraumatic stress and disorder in its classification of posttraumatic stress disorder (PTSD). Because the result of a traumatic event is not necessarily a disorder, I prefer to use the term *posttraumatic stress reaction* (PTSR).

According to the orientation reflected by this term, it is essential to abandon the notion that trauma causes only irreparable damage. I have attempted to supplement the deficit-oriented approach with a view that PTSR may also be a positive, health-promoting, and adjustive process. This approach focuses upon efficacy and health resourcefulness (Rosenbaum, in press) and wellness models (Antonovsky, 1979; Recker & Wong, 1985). It emphasizes coping as a compromising concept that derives from competence and growth (White, 1974). Also integral to this orientation are individually initiated coping (see Chapter 7, this volume) and variations in coping (Lazarus & Folkman, 1984), which are often overlooked in the research on trauma. Additionally, I conceptualize PTSR in terms of aging in a life-span perspective, whereby the concepts of life stages, developmental tasks, transitions, change, history, and multidisciplinary issues receive special attention (Baltes & Brim, 1985). These notions are not exclusive to this approach, and it can be seen that gerontology, too, now concentrates on adaptation and successful aging.

TRAUMATIC STRESS AND COPING

Whereas the concept of stress has many different meanings and referents, and some writers have suggested that the term be abandoned altogether (e.g., Goldberger & Breznitz, 1982; Monat & Lazarus, 1985), the concept of trauma is more easily agreed upon. *Trauma* (used interchangeably with *catastrophe*) refers to unusual events, or series of continuous events, that subject people to extreme, intensive, overwhelming bombardment of threat to themselves or to significant others. Human-inflicted trauma encompasses a variety of disastrous events or situations such as death row, terrorism, battle fatigue, and wartime casualties (Figley, 1985; Milgram, 1982). The trauma I focus on in this chapter is the Nazi Holocaust, as experienced by death camp survivors.

Coping is a multifaceted, mediating operation aimed at reestablishing homeostasis in a disequilibrated organism. Coping with long-term PTSR involves behavior that reduces, to tolerable limits, the physiological and psychological manifestations of cognitively and emotionally disturbing arousals. Coping modes, categorizations, strategies, and effects have been researched extensively (e.g., Lazarus & Folkman, 1984; Lieberman & Tobin, 1983; Pearlin & Schooler, 1978; Wilson, Harel, & Kahana, 1988). The holistic aspects of coping and the tendency toward growth have been emphasized (Hobfoll, 1988).

The investigation of PTSR introduces some basic questions. For example, what is the effect of posttraumatic stress on one's ability to subsequently cope with day-to-day hassles? What is the effect of prior stress on a person's reaction to a new crisis? Is it possible for stress to have a positive, strengthening immune effect? All of these questions await further exploration. Another unclarified question is whether it is possible to predict proneness to PTSD. According to one study, fewer than half of the populations that experienced severe natural disasters (e.g., tornadoes, floods, and volcanic eruptions) revealed any symptoms of PTSD; a far smaller segment displayed intense symptoms (Figley, 1985). Enduring or recurring responses to past traumas may exaggerate responses to new stressors or reactivate unresolved conflicts. Consequently, some individuals may be extremely vulnerable to catastrophic events.

PTSR comprises the consequent behaviors and emotions expressed during and after a stressful state. Traditionally, two reaction phases have been defined: an initial state of shock, characterized by blocking and depersonalization defenses, and a later, more prolonged, instrumental but symptomatically defined, coping phase. My examination of long-term adaptation emphasizes a third characteristic. I have observed idiosyncratic modes of adjustment that are a product of personal, familial, and historical and cultural factors and life-course coping. Trauma always has a permanent impact; how trauma affects daily coping has been the focus of my work. Such coping may have intrapsychic and interpersonal consequences that in various developmental periods and situations may be either alien and destructive to the organism or integrated into its personality structure. Depending on multiple factors, the behavior of survivors may be adaptive or nonadaptive; it may vary in kind, in intensity, in delay of onset, and in duration.

Traumatic Stress and the Holocaust

The colossal impact of the Holocaust created a tremendous challenge to the ability of its victims to make lifelong adjustments. An extensive amount of literature describes the unimaginably inhuman circumstances in the concentration camps, the continuous traumatic stressors, and the various methods of coping used during and after the Holocaust. These conditions included the cumulative effects of prolonged physical abuse, degradation, hunger, exposure to unbearable weather, lethal labor, repeated losses, and, above all, the constant threat of extermination and death—all in the absence of normative civilized laws and principles.

Under such dreadful conditions, people experience massive trauma leading to the collapse of bodily, cognitive, and emotional functions and a feeling of total helplessness. Because survival demands coping, the modes used by the Holocaust victims were physical, intrapsychic, cognitive, emotional, interpersonal, and social. These modes of coping include numbness, detachment, isolation of affects, depersonalization, blocking of emotionality, splitting, submissiveness, denial, fatalism, robotization, identification with aggressors, mistrust, guilt, intrusive thoughts, constrictions in intellectual functioning, sexual difficulties, a depressive style of existence, anhedonia, development of psychosomatic disorders, acting (risking, suicidal attempts), hope, finding meaning and purpose, identity diffusion, and interpersonal affiliation and companionship (e.g., Dimsdale, 1980; Kahana, Kahana, Harel, & Rosner, 1988; Krystal, 1968, 1987; Levi, 1961). Many of these have been incorporated in what has come to be called the concentration camp survivor syndrome. Even if coping were successful, it was always partial and limited. One camp inmate explained how he was able to obtain a wooden shoe that relieved some of the pain he felt while marching in the snow. But his basic fear and hunger were so great that his relief was extremely short-lived. The overall effect of the Holocaust on survivors has been physically and mentally damaging. Research, although not definitive (Orenstein, 1985), indicates that the impact has carried over to the second and third generations.

The research approach taken by my colleagues and I reinforces two positions. First, the term *survivor* also has a positive connotation: It implies endurance, resourcefulness, mastery, and strength that most survivors reflect. Second, our interest is not in the symptomatic effects of the Holocaust, but in how most of the survivors have adjusted and lead constructive lives despite their Holocaust experience. The findings that I have just described have led to my present focus on the interactions of the sequelae of posttraumatic, developmental, personal, familial, and historical stressors.

A MULTIDIMENSIONAL INTEGRATIVE EXAMINATION OF ADAPTATION TO LONG-TERM STRESS

Traumas are multifaceted, and long-term stressors and coping occur in multiple contexts. Therefore, it is useful to investigate how stress, coping, and integration take place, on various levels at different times, from a temporal, life-course perspective. Figure 1 incorporates these components and presents a multidimensional, integrative framework. Three separate time lines represent different contextual courses and their resultant stressors. The framework also encompasses the self and the resources that help the survivor cope with these stressors.

Developmental Time-Line

The extensive body of knowledge on human development enables us to anticipate stages and resultant developmental stressors (Lazarus & DeLongis, 1983; Rosow, 1976). The stages may be biological, psychological, or culturally determined, operating in various temporal and social zones (Markson, 1973; Neugarten, 1968). There may be critical times for accomplishing certain tasks. Traumatic effects depend, in part, on the developmental stage at which the trauma occurred (Davidson, 1980).

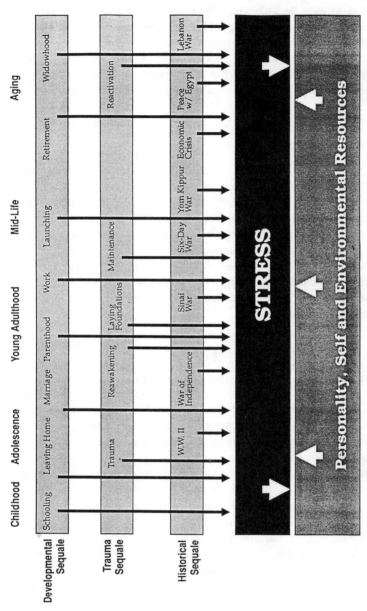

FIGURE 1 A multidimensional, integrative framework for understanding the adaptation of Holocaust survivors to long-term stress.

Questions to ask when investigating survivors in light of a developmental time line include the following. What are the developmental consequences when a prolonged period of normal life is denied to a person who is forced to undergo an extremely different, traumatic, inhuman experience? What if certain expected life tasks or roles are unobtainable? What if the ability to anticipate one's life course in hindered? What are the effects at different points in the life course, especially for the person who has undergone trauma earlier in their life?

Historical–Cultural Line

The historical–cultural time line comprises historical and cultural events and cohort effects. It reflects the complex interplay between personal development and culture. In this depiction of the framework, the major traumatic events are wars—starting with World War II and the Nazi Holocaust and continuing through Israel's successive wars with its Arab neighbors—and milestone economic events. The personal/historical dialectics take on additional complexity when victimization is socially and culturally based, as in genocide or persecution on ethnic or political grounds. That is, the concentration camp experience is unlike other war experiences because it is personally directed and aims at extinction, not defeat.

Sequelae of Traumatic Stress

Lifelong effects of severe stress may be conceived within a formulated pattern. In this framework, five temporal periods, which represent the sequelae of trauma, are interwoven with the processes in the developmental and historical–cultural dimensions. The horizontal movement of the Trauma-Sequelae may be seen as depicting survivors coping in various interactive contexts throughout their developmental life.

The first entry on the trauma sequelae line indicates the onset of trauma, in this case which includes the horrible experiences of WWII and the Holocaust. It should be noted that even at the onset of trauma, differences in response style and coping exist and have post-war adaptational consequences (Danieli, 1981). *Reawakening* refers to the first posttraumatic coping period as survivors attempt to find themselves and their families and reenter normal society, and to the alternative outlets for actions that survivors find (Levi, 1987). Eventually, many survivors of the Holocaust left the European continent in search of places more conducive to building new lives. My research has concentrated on those who emigrated to Israel.

During the *laying foundations* period, which lasts for a number of years, foundations are laid in various domains of life for constructive adaptation. Survivors invest a great deal of effort in migration, acquiring new languages, mastering new occupations, and creating relationships and families. The conditions under which these processes take place largely determine their subsequent courses. For example, the initial meetings between Holocaust survivors and host cultures produced tremendous strain. A schism between the two cultures became apparent, and they maintained a "conspiracy of silence." However, although the literature on survivors condemns these negative characteristics of the host culture, the Israeli culture also contained may positive factors for the survivors. Silence in itself, in the aftermath of severe trauma, may at times be constructive. Furthermore, the needs of the country and those of the survivors were synchronized. Both had to secure their existence, rebuild, and establish themselves.

The longest period of the survivor's life course, up to his or her early old age, is called *maintenance*. During these years, PTSR is controlled while the survivor is occupied with the important matters of day-to-day living, committing and investing energy accordingly. In the case of Holocaust survivors who emigrated to Israel, the survivors now live in a country that is concerned with problems of existence and is involved in wars and economic struggles. Their sensitivity to threatened annihilation is not always an obstacle; in fact, it may even be conducive to coping with realistic threats. In the meantime, the Israeli culture has taken a more compassionate approach toward the survivors, revealed also in cultural rituals reflecting bonding and solidarity.

During old age survivors may experience the *reactivation* of traumatic effects. Both PTSR and cultural discord can more easily interfere with their aging process. Biological and developmental aging may weaken their sense of control (Perlmuter & Langen, 1982) and their coping strategies, thereby reactivating the posttraumatic stress. Mass traumas require cultural support for the victimized as a group, especially if the survivors are elderly. Israel's current existential and cultural strains as well as its power- and youth-oriented value systems, increase the burden and stress of elderly survivors without offering them constructive channels for coping or support. It was reported recently, for example, that the aged have reacted to war-related events with extremely high levels of depression (Hobfoll, Lomranz, Eyal, Bridges, & Tzemach, 1989).

The processes that survivors of prolonged mass catastrophes undergo, which are symbolized by the interplay of the three time lines of the framework, may be described as follows.

1. The posttraumatized person needs appropriate conditions for reawakening personally and reentering culturally.
2. The first meeting between the survivor and the culture is mutually difficult; however, the encounter may also provide the needed moratorium for both parties to reorganize.
3. In time, the culture becomes more accepting of the survivors' experience (e.g., as happened toward Holocaust survivors and Vietnam veterans).

4. Long-term adaptation integrates PTSR, cultural components, and the developmental life stages. Whereas adulthood and mid-life may be conducive to adjustment, in old age traumatic stress may be reactivated—leading to adaptational difficulties.

Other Dimensions

The framework also includes the dimensions of *personality, self,* and *resources*. The self presents a posttraumatized personality configuration, including specific coping strategies, the management of stress, adaptation, and growth. Resources are entities that provide assistance to the person under stress. They include a wide range of physical, financial, personal, interpersonal, and environmental resources. The focus of this chapter is on specific aspects of personal, familial, and cultural resources.

Each component in this framework represents an existential area that comes together in a person's dynamic and changing life-span construction (Whitebourne, 1985). The lines in the framework should be viewed as interactional and dialectic. A multidimensional perspective should help answer such as questions the following: Why do people react differently to severe trauma? How can we understand the constructive or nonconstructive adaptation of posttraumatized people? How can vulnerability of PTSR be conceived? Do delayed reactions to trauma have a time limit? When are they likely to appear and reappear? These questions lead to a focus on the individual.

LONG-TERM ADAPTATION OF TRAUMATIZED AGED IN LIGHT OF ADULT PERSONAL AND INTERPERSONAL DEVELOPMENTAL ISSUES

Personality and the Self

A boundary-balanced self and coping mechanism appears to be the most integrative concept that can explain long-term adaptation to traumatic experiences. The concept is based on ego psychology, dynamic cognitive psychology (Giora, 1975), developmental life-span personality theory (Bengston, Reedy, & Gordon, 1985; Lomranz, 1986), and especially Lewinian structural properties (Lewin, 1935). Taken in combination these different viewpoints emphasize (a) a growth orientation, (b) the evolution of the self in the face of social relations, (c) a life-span approach to development, and (d) a configuration of life-space, the regions of which are differentiated and modified according to permeable or nonpermeable boundaries.

According to this perspective the self strives for balance; absorbs internal, age-related, and environmental demands and stress; and has enough elasticity to incorporate these demands as well as to change continuously. Coping mechanisms should include clinical defense. However, especially in the long-term adaptive period, it is appropriate to focus on mechanisms for competence and growth. Defense mechanisms are not functionally absolute. The same defense may be constructive in one situation, and destructive in another. Defenses operate at different levels of intensity; they intermingle and function simultaneously. For example, a concentration camp inmate may be cognitively numb to the humiliation he is being forced to endure yet be extremely alert in his attempt to steal a piece of bread.

The indicated personality approach is in line with the cognitive appraisal approaches to coping with stress. In addition, it takes into account the external situation and preserves idiosyncrasy. Continuous homeostasis, split existence, stability or instability, intrusive thoughts and vulnerable selves are all ideas that can be incorporated. Such a process-oriented approach can explain life-span changes that occur in a survivor's coping period—changes that may be disturbed during the next period by reactivated traumatic stress to which the aging process may have made the survivor more vulnerable. The self is conceived as a delicate configuration of checks and balances, in which the forces of stability and growth are offset against vulnerability. As a result, the aging of a traumatized person is an extremely precarious, sensitive, and balanced process, as is indicated in the following list of developmental issues that are pertinent to the ability of elderly Holocaust survivors.

Health and the body. In the death camps, bodily well-being was a main index of survival. The issue of health harbors potential difficulties for the survivor. These include concerns about changes in body image and loss of bodily control, operations that lead to the denial of illness, procrastination about getting treatment, rejection of medical care, and preoccupation with bodily complaints and medicine. Little is known about survivors who stay healthy, or about the positive effects of avoiding or procrastinating about bodily concerns.

Regulation and mastery of affect. The handling of affect was an important key to survival in the concentration camps. During their adult years, survivors of traumatic and posttraumatic affective experiences molded their emotional behavior patterns. Do such patterns remain adaptive in old age? Affective processes may become more complex and threatening for elderly survivors. They now need to regulate affect so that the requirements and losses of aging can be assimilated and adaptation maintained.

Aggression. Anger over shame and loss that were suppressed during the traumatic experience are often expressed later through aggressive behavioral patterns. Although aggressive behavior can result in behavioral problems, there is evidence that it is conducive to survival in old age—especially in institutions (Lieberman & Tobin, 1983).

Continuity. Continuity is considered to be crucial in adult development and integration in late life (Bengtson et al., 1985). For many victims, the Holocaust destroyed their personal sense of continuity as well as their sense of belonging to society and humanity. However, the capacity for dealing with discontinuity appears to depend on the survivor's developmental stage. Although it was feasible during mid-life, it became a problem and a source of stress for many in old age, as the feeling that one's life cycle is not continuous can be painful and limiting. Is continuity a necessary condition to long-term adaptation? My conclusion is that even when there is a break in continuity, it is still possible to maintain a coherent self-image. This is congruent with the structure and dynamics of the boundary-balanced self system noted earlier.

Temporality. Temporality is another major component of adjustment to old age (Hazan, 1980). A positive orientation toward the future is related to physical and mental health, satisfaction with life, and successful aging (Recker & Wong, 1985). Holocaust survivors are considered to be low in future orientation. When survivors were asked to compartmentalize their life-lines, they perceived the Holocaust period as being extended in time—usually because they perceived the pre-Holocaust period as being shrunken (Lomranz, Shmotkin, Zchovoi, & Rosenberg, 1985). Although survivors were pessimistic about the future in general, they had concrete future-oriented expectations and plans for their children and grandchildren.

Narcissism. Narcissism is a core issue in the dynamics of the self (Kohut, 1971), in the aging process, and in PTSR. Losses during aging constitute narcissistic blows and can lower self-esteem and cause identity confusion. For vulnerable survivors, these are additional obstacles to adaptational efforts. For many survivors, the Holocaust shattered their illusion of omnipotence and made them cautious, fearful, and superstitious. For others, the Holocaust increased their sense of omnipotence, which resulted in an increased sense of power. This supported their posttraumatic efforts in laying new foundations.

Loss, death, and dying. During their traumatic state, survivors were exposed to constant death and destruction. This caused a disruption in their formative psychological processes and an identification with death and dying—one manifestation of which is the "dead to the world" response (Lifton, 1979). After the Holocaust the survivor reconstructed a self with nonpermeable boundaries around the region containing death imagery. However, questions arise as to whether in old age and in the light of death, these boundaries may become permeable and cause intrusive trauma-related thoughts and stress. If mourning is possible it may enable a constructive integration of pre-Holocaust memories. For elderly survivors, trauma-related losses, present losses, and their own forthcoming death are interrelated.

Adaptation Through Narrative and Life Review

Coping with trauma involves reorganizing cognitive maps that were ruptured by the catastrophe. Survivors are expected to assimilate the trauma, rebuild an integral, stable assumptive world (Janoff-Bulman, 1988), find personal meaning, and regain a view of the world as meaningful. Finally, especially in old age, they are expected to engage in the integrative function of these processes, which find expression in the life review. The life review constitutes one's life history—a universal prerequisite to aging successfully that includes coming to terms with death (Wolf, 1985). All of these processes are also developmental tasks that elderly survivors cannot always deal with, as our theories would expect. It may well be that in some assumptive worlds, the acceptance of vulnerability is an asset. Survivors may be thankful for whatever they may have achieved, may not fear finitude, and may accept losses as a natural part of human vulnerability.

Many survivors publicly "bear witness," publish memories, and engage in educational missions and Holocaust-related activities, whereas for many others, present losses and past vulnerability are a constant source of fear and stress. Many cope with the sense of vulnerability through political action. Still others have developed a feeling that because they survived, nothing can destroy them. They believe themselves to be untouchable. The required life review can cause extreme stress. The bleaching away of childhood memories, the painful years of the Holocaust, the inability to mourn, the availability of guilt and shame, and the trauma-related fears (Horowitz, 1986), all render the life review a complicated and perhaps, for some, impossible task. The decades-long primacy of denial cannot easily be undone. For those elderly survivors who have been successful in building a new assumptive world, the life review may be constructive, freeing energies for later-life alternatives. For many survivors, the life review may be only partial, not meeting the standards of integrating all experiences or confirming the life course. Still, even in this form it may bear positive results.

In summary, traumatization causes severe stress and unique changes in the realm of personality and the self. There appears to be a contrast between required emotional demands in middle age, that were structured in the traumatic and posttraumatic periods, and those of old age. Thus developmental stage processes in a posttraumatic configuration may bring about disequilibrium and stress. However, personality structures may be flexible enough to absorb disturbing and contradictory experiences. Cognitive restructuring, such as basic assumptions or life review, seem to be central, as do the mastery of emotionality and defenses.

LONG-TERM ADAPTATIONAL PROCESSES IN THE FAMILIES OF POST-TRAUMATIZED ELDERLY

The family is a major vehicle for adaptation. At the same time, it is also an arena for conflict, the absorber of PTSR and the transmitter of intergenerational conflict (Bowen, 1978). Survivors may be more prone to trauma-derived familial difficulties, especially in the later-life family. Dependence, guilt, communication, blurring of boundaries, separation difficulties, management of emotionality, grandparenthood, intergenerational obstacles, widowhood, and mourning all may cause complex (and sometimes difficult) behaviors in the last stages of the family. Nevertheless, the value of the family in long-term adaptation cannot be overemphasized. The potential difficulties should be seen as a bearable price to pay for survival and adjustment.

The data presented here come from an ongoing study of families who have at least one member who survived being in a Nazi concentration camp. Many of the families were established later than normal. This influenced the family culture and the timing of the family life cycle tasks. Most of the families were formed during the reawakening period, after the survivors had searched in vain for their original families. Disillusioned, alienated, lonely, and unable to comprehend the tragedy, they yearned to unite with another human being. Under such conditions, "marriages of despair" and "marriages of convenience" (Danieli, 1981) took place. Most of these families were limited in their "extendedness." Survivors often had no parents or siblings (Bank & Kahn, 1982; Kahn & Lewis, 1988) and later had only one or two children.

Potential Stressors

At different times in the family life cycle, PTSRs are incorporated constructively or destructively in various family tasks. The typical patterns of survivors' families—in structure, processes, and temporality—have not been found to coincide with those in normative families. Role positions, role sequence, interpersonal processes, and change are all more complex in survivors' families, and role strain is higher. This may be partly explained by the fact that the behavior in these families revolved around two core characteristics: (a) a commitment to build and maintain the family as the most important entity, which was more important than the relationships between its members, and (b) a preoccupation with developing behavioral patterns that would give no access to PTSR. Although both of these characteristics were adaptive in the younger family, they became a source of increased stress in the postparental family.

Different kinds of family cultures were created, depending on the survivors' personalities, histories, perceptions of the Holocaust, assumptive worlds, and resources. Difficulty in managing aggression and guilt had damaging, inhibiting effects, especially on the men who were trying to serve as family authority figures. Some families exhibited a somewhat forced happy atmosphere, emphasizing the importance of external appearance. Others were pervaded by a more solemn mood, and the atmosphere at times resembled continuous mourning. Boundaries and privacy were discouraged, and it was often a complicated matter to develop intimacy. Nutrition, body care, and material support often substituted for emotional closeness or expressiveness. Many survivors considered crying to be a weakness. One man who had built up a gratifying family system reported that tears and crying were absolutely unbearable to him—to the extent that he avoided visiting his newborn grandchild.

Coping with PTSR led many of the families to develop a traditional, authoritarian, constricted atmosphere. There was little delegation of responsibility. Many families dreaded passivity, emphasized active coping, valued stoicism, praised control and achievement, and projected a false sense of cohesion. There was an underlying fear of catastrophe and a general mistrust of the authorities (Danieli, 1981; Dimsdale, 1980).

The postparental years are potentially troublesome in many families of survivors, especially in those involving marriages of despair. Yet, divorce in such families is extremely threatening and an infrequent occurrence. Proper involvement with children may however lead to positive familial change (Muller & Yahav, 1989). It should be emphasized that most of the survivors that my colleagues and I interviewed led satisfying family lives and enjoyed intergenerational relationships.

Communication in the Post-Traumatic Family

Communication among family members was determined to a great extent by the quality of the survivor's posttraumatic coping. Although many survivors were able to communicate about their pre-Holocaust world (Gample, 1989), two major patterns emerge. Some survivors became enmeshed in their families—violating boundaries and turning their spouses and children into captive audiences. However, the majority held back, believing that their silence and avoidance were protecting their dear ones. In many families, however, children became the confidants of one of the parents. This led to family coalitions and interfered with the flow of communication.

Silence is used as a tool for withholding information and avoiding sharing. Spouses who lived with survivors for decades knew that they had been in concentration camps—but not when, where, or anything else. Some were unaware that a member of their extended family was a Holocaust survivor. One cheerful woman—very successful in her career, and a devoted mother—said that no one in her family knew that most nights, alone in bed, she became sad, remembered Auschwitz, and smothered her sobs with her pillow. Silences here are usually not the result of denial, but of a conscious effort to withhold memories and a desire for privacy and solitude. As such, they may be conceived of as part of the survivors' coping strategy.

Narratives of survivors indicate that at least four communication patterns among families of survivors are amazingly similar to those found between psychiatrists and survivors in therapeutic relationships (Hoppe, 1969). First, when survivors were complainers and exhibited symptomatic, trauma-related behavior, the family members were often retreating and unresponsive. Second, when survivors were relatively open about their experiences, yet dependent on their families, the members showed strong support through overidentification and exaggerated caretaking—but did not necessarily talk about the Holocaust. Third, when survivors were authoritarian and rational, the family members communicated generally well—except about the Holocaust, which was a taboo subject. Finally, survivors often expressed feelings of guilt about their communication or lack of it, declaring that they were exploiting or hurting their spouses.

Despite the stress and the difficulties in communication, the importance of the family as an adjustive anchor and support system, cannot be overemphasized. For survivors, the family is a holding and containing environment. The family absorbs the doubts of survivors, satisfies their affiliative needs (which increase under stress), tolerates their discomfort, and lives with their PTSR. It serves as the arena for their identity formation and for regaining their meaning and hope. Whereas the death camps taught survivors to be apathetic and docile, the family reeducates them to strive, to invest, to demand, and to anticipate. Families enable survivors to overcome the past and build a future. Despite overt and covert conflict in these marriages, they compensate for losses, fill emptiness, provide offspring, counter the massive disruption in continuity, and make rehumanization possible.

Survivors and Their Adult Children

The quality of the relationship between the adult child and the elderly parent is a basic factor in the well-being of both. For Holocaust survivors, children may play an imperative role. They serve as a symbol of survivors' victory over the Nazis, a replacement for agonizing losses and lost opportunities, or an affirmation of life and the dawning of a better world. Many survivors achieved long-term adaptation mainly through the presence and functions of their children. However, the price was high. There is an increasing amount of literature on the complex existences of the second and third generations of survivors (Davidson, 1980). It should be emphasized, however, that this literature is seriously criticized (Orenstein, 1985; Peskin, 1981).

As children become the vehicle for the survivors' adaptation, their parents expectations soar. Stress, frustrations, and conflicts are bound to appear. Intense involvement in their children's lives (symbolized by doors always being left open around the home) enabled the survivors to live vicariously through their children. At times, the offspring of survivors were driven into the position of replacing lost relatives or being engaged by the survivors' desire that the children internalize some of the death camp experience. Some children were given the names of lost relatives. Some survivors reported dreams in which their children appeared in concentration camps. As a result of the conspiracy of silence, many children could not understand the inexplicable torment within their families. They became adults, feeling guilty without knowing about what, and feeling rejected without knowing why. In some families, the perception of the survivor as a supernatural giant who had survived hell may have elicited support from the children—but it also distanced them from the parent and made them feel inferior.

Separation and individuation seem to be troublesome issues in the families of survivors. The launching of children is more difficult than in other families. The children of victims leave their parents' home later and stay in closer contact (Danieli, 1981). These characteristics weigh heavily on the later relationships between adult children and elderly parents. The separation issue comes full circle when adult children have difficulty launching their parents into homes for the aged.

The survivors' longstanding emotional dependency on their children becomes even more intense in old age and may result in complications. Filial maturity requires emotional interaction between adult children and their parents. Given their intergenerational history, this is extremely difficult for both sides. After years of familial processes involving guilt, aggression, and control, the children are afraid of causing additional harm to their survivor parents, and they find it hard to be assertive. The aged parent finds it hard to accept support—because survival in the family context depended on giving to others, not taking from them. Survivors fear that the distance, privacy, and independence, which at times sheltered them during their long-term adaptation, are now being invaded.

Grandparenthood

Grandparenthood is receiving growing attention. It is important because it endows the elderly with special roles (Bengston & Robertson, 1985; Rosow, 1976). The constructive resources in grandparenthood constitute a major adaptational source for survivors in later life. One main fear of survivors is that they will perish as individuals and as an ethnic and national group. The presence of grandchildren lessens this fear by creating a sense of continuity. In addition, elderly survivors now perform a sustaining function for the family. However, grandparenthood and intergenerational relationships are also a source of friction and stress—derived from the combined effects of relational history, personality development, and the difficulties between the first and second generations.

Many Holocaust survivors grew old without having had grandparenting models—and their children, too, never had grandparents. Familial bonds develop on the basis of accumulated and shared experiences. Because survivors lack such experiences with grandparents, the quality of the bonds with their grandchildren may be affected and their own grandparenting behavior may be unrealistic or inappropriate. The unfinished business and tensions that exist between the first two generations, stemming from Holocaust-related issues, may cause survivors to exhibit behaviors such as displacement, splitting, guilt, or overcompensation toward their grandchildren. Survivors' values may be foreign to their grandchildren, especially because their home culture has been wiped out. For the same reason, the usual role of grandparents as "wardens of culture" could be regarded as superfluous.

Traditionally grandparents fill the symbolic role of "just being there" for their grandchildren, which counters a child's feelings of vulnerability and fear of death (Bengston & Robertson, 1985). However, elderly survivors are often a weak representation of life and vitality—particularly if they complain often of physical ailments and make frequent visits to doctors. Another common role of grandparents is that of family mediator. Due to the intergenerational complexities, and the fact that survivors had limited opportunities to perform this function in their original family, this role may not be in the behavioral repertoire of Holocaust survivors.

Grandparenthood has an emotional context that requires expressions of love, warmth, physical closeness, and softness. At this stage of life, these behaviors are also demanded developmentally (Gutmann, 1987). However, after decades of denying their emotions or fearing to display them, elderly survivors can now find it extremely difficult to express them. This is another instance in which survivors' PTSR was appropriate during mid-life but interferes with later developmental processes such as grandparenthood.

Widowhood and Mourning

Widowhood or the loss of another close significant other has been viewed as the most stressful normative event. Mourning has been elaborated as a model for coping with stress (Horowitz, 1986). Reconciliation with losses is part of the life review, and appropriate mourning is considered to be a condition for the well-being of the survivor. Uncompleted mourning may cause maladaptation and distress in the future. An elderly person's reaction to loss has been perceived as a test of whether the aging process has been liberating and successful or binding and unsuccessful (Pollock, 1987).

Many survivors find it extremely difficult, if not impossible, to mourn. Mourning is interwoven with various object losses from the past and present. Such a multifaceted mourning process may be too painful for survivors to endure. The avoidance of past mourning may prevent their present mourning. Mourning presently means another separation or abandonment, which may cause suppressed memories to return. Survivors may fear the return of the trauma and be unable to manage the affective processes involved in mourning. It may mean a break-up of the family that was the survivor's main long-term adaptational foundation. This may shatter the survivor's illusion of being "untouchable."

One major difficulty in mourning is not being emancipated from bondage to the deceased. Most Holocaust survivors started new lives and developed deep loyalties to their spouses and children. The strength of these loyalties may be correlated to the repression of pre-traumatic family ties. In old age, present mourning for a lost significant other and thoughts of one's own approaching death can arouse guilt-associated struggles that involve feelings of loyalty and fidelity to the pre-traumatic lost person. These can constitute an additional source of stress for the elderly survivor.

Even though appropriate mourning is considered a superhuman task (Krystal, 1987), most elderly Holocaust survivors have performed it. Although old age increases coping difficulties for the survivors as a group, most of them have gone through mourning without any special problems. Ironically, it appears that for some survivors, the Holocaust experience helped prepare them to respond appropriately to future losses. Such responses seem to be related to their personality structures as well as to their death camp and posttraumatic histories. The ability to predict these responses awaits further research.

THEORETICAL IMPLICATIONS

The lack of a comprehensive theory makes it extremely difficult to comprehend and predict long-term adaptation to trauma. In this chapter I have cross-referenced various disciplines and concepts so that new theoretical propositions can be developed. I now emphasize a number of points concerning the status of theory, specifically as it applies to the long-term adaptation of Holocaust survivors. The field lacks theoretical models and conceptualizations. In addition, long-term adaptation to trauma has not yet produced a conclusive evaluation of the impact of continuous stress on the human organism: the "wear-and-tear" conception or the immune effect.

Culture and Historical Events

Culture and history may facilitate or hinder people's attempts to cope. The case of Holocaust survivors lends itself to modified versions of the anthropological principles of "parallelism" and "synchronization" (Honigman, 1959). The parallelism is not between cultures, but between individual and national or cultural needs. In the case of Holocaust survivors, the coping process contributes to cultural change as well as to individual adaptation of survivors. So as Israel emerged out of the post-Holocaust era, so did those who emerged from the death camps.

The findings on Holocaust survivors indicate a need for major revisions in these areas. Personality theory (Lomranz, 1986) is unable to explain long-term adaptive processes to trauma, perhaps because of the influence of psychoanalytically oriented principles. There has been emphasis on the relevance of a structurally conceived, balanced self; an ego-oriented psychology (Greenfield

& Mitchell, 1983); and a positive approach to defense mechanisms. In light of the psychology of aging, the theoretical implications of other major concepts should also be emphasized.

Major theorists in adult development and psychic trauma emphasize the importance of the integrated self. Erikson stated that to achieve integrity in old age, "one must achieve acceptance of one's own and only life cycle and of the people who have become significant to it *as something that had to be and that, by necessity, permitted no substitution* [italics added]" (1963, p. 98). However, it seems that such conceptions are based on a pathogenic approach or refer to total consciousness as an aspired value (Fromm & Xirau, 1968). The elderly person's ability to live integratively with guilt, despite the Eriksonian approach, should be reconsidered. Denial and repression reflected, for instance, in the extent of not remembering dreams (Kaminer, 1989) appear to be more conducive to posttraumatic adaptation.

Affirmation of one's past in Eriksonian terms is virtually impossible for the aged survivor. Personality theorists may have overemphasized the principles of congruence and harmony. The conditions for an Eriksonian integration do not always prevail with people experiencing posttraumatic stress. The sense of continuity may have breaks in it. Many experiences may be inaccessible to consciousness, whereas others may be totally unacceptable. Nevertheless, the person may have high levels of self-esteem and a relatively strong sense of well-being.

We should be more lenient with these concepts, and allow more variability, partiality, and incompleteness in processes. Even with opposing tendencies, a person may live constructively. A life review may be achieved only partly, if at all. Encapsulated regions in the self surrounded by impermeable barriers may be very conducive to a sense of integrity in the aged.

Family Processes

The characteristics of healthy family systems, such as open communication, expressiveness and "on-time" role functioning, may be inapplicable in comprehending adaptive processes in many families of survivors. The latter families may have no function as if under siege, and their features may include emotional constriction, circumscribed communication patterns, and a preference for instrumentalism. Cognitive and empathic coping (see Chapter 10, this volume) with stress may be hindered. By themselves, such structural features may be judged negatively according to total standards of happy, well-functioning families. However, in the total context of posttrauma survival, these features may facilitate adaptation, enable continuity, and promote growth. Further investigation of posttrauma systems may also enrich our understanding of how nontraumatized families cope with stress.

METHODOLOGICAL IMPLICATIONS

Most studies on long-term adaptation to trauma are retrospective. Although this does not diminish their importance in present-oriented investigations such as on the impact of life reviews, they have limited power when it comes to causal explanations and prediction. Because of the difficulty in obtaining information on the pre-traumatized person, most efforts have, unfortunately, been abandoned rather than pursued with more sophisticated methodologies.

Most researchers report that the physical well-being of Holocaust survivors is below average, but most studies have focused on help-seeking populations. These studies have led to a deficit-oriented concept of adaptation and should not be the basis for generalizations. More controlled studies should be performed on representative samples of the population. Control groups pose another difficulty. Because victims who are investigated are people who have already been changed by a trauma, it is impossible to determine what was changed and how. Finally, we are dealing with people who are survivors of old age as well as survivors of trauma. This makes controlled differentiation extremely complicated.

Most research does not distinguish among the different situational determinants of trauma (e.g., death camps, work camps, hiding places, and partisan groups). This point is emphasized by the question "Can miners trapped underground be compared with seamen trapped on a mid-ocean shipwreck?" This applies also to the nature of trauma. There is a danger in labeling many divergent events as a single construct (e.g., can the effects of battle fatigue be compared with those of rape?). Similarly, a single determinant of stress, such as battle fatigue or floods, is an insufficient basis for research into an all-encompassing and ongoing traumatic situation.

A multidimensional research framework is needed to encompass the broad array of stress characteristics encountered during prolonged traumatic situations in extended posttraumatic adaptational decades. Many domains must be addressed, including the numerous coping modes, the survivors' predispositions, personality structures and dynamics, cogent issues of the self, and the environmental and cultural influences. Severe trauma has a lifelong but varied influence on the survivor. Therefore, research should not dismiss individual differences, but rather should be life-span oriented, developmental, longitudinal, interactive, and multivariate. I consider the narrative method as being conducive to this orientation (Cohler, 1982).

CONCLUSION

Comparative investigations and integrative attempts have begun (Figley, 1985; Goldberger & Breznitz, 1982; Wilson et al., 1988), and more are needed. However, these studies should be planned cautiously. For example, apparent similarities in responses to traumas may actually be limited in time (e.g., only the initial reactions may be similar). PTSR may differ in intensity at different levels (cognitive, emotional, and behavioral); in their long-term impact on the total organism (e.g., the effect of denial on other personality configurations in later life); or in levels of specification and explanation.

Most research on severe stress has assumed a steamroller effect—that is, that the colossal impact of extreme trauma suppresses all individual differences in coping. This assumption does not stand up in light of the individual narratives of Holocaust survivors, and it is certainly inappropriate in regard to long-term reactions. Both the nomothetic and idiographic assumptions are still relevant to the assessment of elderly people (Zarit, Eiler, & Hassinger, 1985) and can help us comprehend posttraumatic effects on the aged. Extensive observations can be the basis for summative generalizations, so both methods are essential.

In this chapter I have tried to shed light on long-term adaptation to severe trauma, exemplified by survivors of the Nazi Holocaust. Most posttraumatized people have succeeded in coping constructively and achieving long-term adaptation. What made this possible, and at what cost? The gains and their price were viewed as coping and examined in the various dimensions. My approach complements the prevailing clinical approach with a health approach. I also examined the multidimensionality of historical, cultural, personal, interpersonal, social, and familial factors that bear on the victims during their life spans and as they are especially reflected in old age. The interfaces and cross-references among the conceptual worlds of (a) adulthood and aging in a developmental perspective, (b) traumatic stress, (c) the Holocaust experience, (d) personal and familial processes, and (e) long-term adaptation have been exemplified.

New propositions and hypotheses should be derived, developed, and tested. Research should produce appropriate policies for dealing with stress on a massive scale. To overcome the mentioned theoretical and methodological obstacles, researchers should integrate multidimensional variables into their conceptual schemes. More work is needed to integrate theories of development, family systems, aging, and adaptation with national catastrophes and stress reactions. Stress and family researchers, life-span developmentalists, and gerontologists should cooperate in interdisciplinary, longitudinal research to advance theory and methodology and to develop appropriate intervention programs in this area.

REFERENCES

American Psychiatric Association. (1980). *Diagnostic and statistical manual of mental disorders* (3rd ed.). Washington, DC: Author.

Antonovsky, A. (1979). *Health, stress, and coping* (p. 100). San Francisco: Jossey-Bass.

Baltes, P. B., & Brim, O. G. (Eds.). (1985). *Life-span development and behavior.* New York: Academic Press.

Bank, S. P., & Kahn, M. D. (1982). *The sibling bond.* New York: Basic Books.

Bengston, V. L., Reedy, M. N., & Gordon, C. (1985). Aging self-conceptions. In J. E. Birren & K. W. Schaie (Eds.), *Handbook of the psychology of aging* (pp. 544–593). New York: Van Nostrand Reinhold.

Bengston, V. L., & Robertson, J. F. (Eds.). (1985). *Grandparenthood.* London: Sage.

Bowen, M. (1978). *Family therapy in clinical practice.* New York: Aronson.

Cohler, B. J. (1982). Personal narrative and life-course. In P. B. Baltes & O. J. Brim (Eds.), *Life-span development and behavior* (pp. 206–243). New York: Academic Press.

Danieli, Y. (1981). Families of survivors of the Nazi Holocaust: Some short- and long-term effects. In C. Spielberger, N. Sarason, & N. Milgram (Eds.), *Stress and anxiety* (Vol. 8, pp. 405–421). Washington, DC: Hemisphere.

Davidson, S. (1980). Effects of massive psychic trauma in families of Holocaust survivors. *Journal of Marital and Family Therapy, 6,* 11–21.

Dimsdale, J. E. (Ed.). (1980). *Survivors, victims and perpetrators.* Washington, DC: Hemisphere.

Erikson, E. (1963). *Childhood and society* (2nd ed.). New York: Norton.

Figley, C. R. (Ed.). (1985). *Trauma and its wake: The study and treatment of post-traumatic stress disorder.* New York: Brunner/Mazel.

Fromm, E., & Xirau, R. (1968). *The nature of man.* New York: Macmillan.

Gample, J. (January, 1989). *Patterns of communication between survivors.* Paper presented in the 4th International Conference on Psychology in Time of War and Peace, Tel Aviv, Israel.

Giora, Z. (1975). *Psychopathology: A cognitive view.* New York: Gardner Press.

Goldberger, L., & Breznitz, S. (Eds.). (1982). *Handbook of stress: Theoretical and clinical aspects.* New York: Free Press.

Greenfield, J., & Mitchell, S. (1983). *Object relations in psychoanalytic theory.* Cambridge, MA: Harvard University Press.

Gutmann, D. (1987). *Reclaimed powers.* New York: Basic Books.

Hazan, H. (1980). *The limbo people.* London: Routledge & Kegan Paul.

Hobfoll, S. E. (1988). *The ecology of stress.* Washington, DC: Hemisphere.

Hobfoll, S., Lomranz, J., Eyal, N., Bridges, A., & Tzemach, M. (1989). Pulse of a nation: Depressive mood reactions of Israelis to the Israel-Lebanon war. *Journal of Personality and Social Psychology, 56,* 1002–1012.

Honigman, J. J. (1959). *The world of man.* New York: Harper & Row.

Hoppe, K. D. (1969). Reactions of psychiatrists to examination of survivors of Nazi persecution. *Psychoanalysis Forum, 3,* 182–211.

Horowitz, M. J. (1986). *Stress response syndromes*. New York: Aronson.

Janoff-Bulman, R. (1988). Victim of violence. In S. Fisher & J. Reason (Eds.), *Handbook of life stress, cognition and health* (pp. 101–113). New York: Wiley.

Kahana, E., Kahana, B., Harel, Z., & Rosner, T. (1988). Coping with extreme stress. In J. Wilson, Z. Harel, & B. Kahan (Eds.), *Human adaptation to extreme stress* (pp. 55–79) New York: Plenum Press.

Kahn, M. D., & Lewis, K. G. (Eds.). (1988). *Siblings in therapy*. New York: Norton.

Kaminer, H. (1989). *Long-term coping of Holocaust survivors as revealed in sleep and dreams*. Paper presented at the meeting of the Israeli Psychological Association, Haifa, Israel.

Kohut, H. (1971). *The analysis of the self*. New York: International University Press.

Krystal, H. (Ed.). (1968). *Massive psychic trauma*. New York: International University Press.

Krystal, H. (1987). The impact of massive psychic trauma and the capacity to grieve effectively: Later life sequelae. In J. Sadavoy & M. Leszez (Eds.), *Treating the elderly with psychotherapy* (pp. 95–156). Madison, WI: International University Press.

Lazarus, R. S., & DeLongis, A. (1983). Psychological stress and coping in aging. *American Psychologist, 38*, 245–254.

Lazarus, R. S., & Folkman, S. (1984). *Stress appraisal and coping*. New York: Springer.

Levi, P. (1961). *Survival in Auschwitz*. New York: Collier Books.

Levi, P. (1987). *The reawakening*. New York: Collier Books.

Lewin, K. (1935). *A dynamic theory of personality*. New York: McGraw-Hill.

Lieberman, M. A., & Tobin, S. (1983). *The experience of old age*. New York: Basic Books.

Lifton, R. J. (1979). *The broken connection. On death and the continuity of life*. New York: Simon & Schuster.

Lomranz, J. (1986). Personality theory: A position and derived teaching implications in clinical psychology. *Professional Psychology: Research and Practice, 17*, 551–559.

Lomranz, J., Shmotkin, D., Zchovoi, A., & Rosenberg, E. (1985). Time orientation in Nazi concentration camp survivors: Forty years after. *American Journal of Orthopsychiatry, 55*, 230–236.

Markson, E. (1973). Readjustment in old age. *Psychiatry, 36*, 37–48.

Milgram, N. A. (1982). *Stress and anxiety* (Vol. 8). Washington, DC: Hemisphere.

Monat, A., & Lazarus, R. S. (1985). *Stress and coping*. New York: Columbia University Press.

Muller, U. F., & Yahav, A. (1989). Object relations, Holocaust survival and family therapy. *British Journal of Medical Psychology, 62*, 13–21.

Neugarten, B. L. (Ed.). (1968). *Middle age and aging.* Chicago: University of Chicago Press.

Orenstein, A. (1985). Survival and recovery. *Psychoanalytic Inquiry, 14,* 99–130.

Pearlin, L. I., & Schooler, C. (1978). The structure of coping. *Journal of Health and Social Behavior, 19,* 2–21.

Perlmuter, L., & Langer, E. (1982). The effects of behavioral monitoring on the perception of control. *Clinical Gerontologist, 1,* 37–43.

Peskin, H. (1981). Observations on the first international conference of children of Holocaust survivors. *Family Process, 20,* 391–394.

Polanyi, M. (1964). *Personal knowledge.* New York: Harper Touchbooks.

Pollock, G. H. (1987). The mourning-liberation process. In J. Sadavoy & M. Leszez (Eds.), *Treating the elderly with psychotherapy* (pp. 3–30). Madison, CT: International Universities Press.

Recker, G. T., & Wong, T. P. (1985). Personal optimism, physical and mental health. In J. Birren & J. Livingston (Eds.), *Cognition, stress, and aging* (pp. 134–173). New York: Prentice-Hall.

Rosenbaum, M. (in press). *Learned resourcefulness: On coping skills, self control and adaptive behavior.* New York: Springer.

Rosow, I. (1976). Status and role change through the life-span. In R. E. Binstock & E. Shanas (Eds.), *Handbook of aging and the social sciences.* New York: Van Nostrand Reinhold.

White, R. W. (1974). Strategies of adaptation: An attempt at systematic description. In G. V. Coelho, D. A. Hamburg, & J. E. Adams (Eds.), *Coping and adaptation.* New York: Basic Books.

Whitebourne, S. K. (1985). The psychological construction of the life-span. In J. E. Birren & K. W. Schaie (Eds.), *Handbook of the psychology of aging* (pp. 594–618). New York: Van Nostrand Reinhold.

Wilson, J. P., Harel, Z., & Kahana, B. (Eds.). (1988). *Human adaptation to extreme stress: From the Holocaust to Vietnam.* New York: Plenum Press.

Wolf, M. A. (1985). The meaning of education in later life: An exploration in life review. *Gerontology and Geriatrics Education, 5,* 51–59.

Zarit, S. H., Eiler, J., & Hassinger, M. (1985). Clinical assessment. In J. E. Birren & K. W. Schaie (Eds.). *Handbook of the psychology of aging* (pp. 725–789). New York: Van Nostrand Reinhold.

II

SOCIAL RESOURCES FOR COPING WITH STRESS IN LATER-LIFE FAMILIES

7

OVERVIEW

Virginia Kline Norris

Kent State University

In Part I of this volume the nature and effects of stressful events for both older adults and their families were documented. The reactions of older adults to stressful events are not uniform. Some older adults are quite resilient in the face of serious threats and challenges to their physical health or emotional well-being. The chapters in Part II focus on one of several potential coping resources, social support. Social support is the provision of emotional, instrumental, or informational resources to individuals by members of their social networks. A broad and comprehensive literature has established the effectiveness of social support as a protector of psychological, physical, and social well-being. The authors in this section, however, move our understanding of social support beyond the question of effectiveness.

Both the chapter by Hansson and Carpenter and the chapter by Felton focus on the processes by which social networks are established, maintained, and mobilized. A common thread among all four chapters in Part II is the recognition that social support is only one element of interpersonal relationships, and that these relationships may contain negative elements as well as positive ones. Rook focuses directly on this issue and evaluates the effects of disruptive social relationships on the psychological well-being of older adults. Jackson, Antonucci, and Gibson examine a specific linkage between social support and the well-being process by focusing on the integration of older adults into productive activity.

Why should social support be studied in special reference to later-life families? First, older adults may have needs that are specific to later life. For example, older adults are susceptible to chronic illnesses that present major life crises. Thus their needs for resources to cope effectively with health crises may occur more frequently than they do for younger generations. In addition, the need for help in procuring tangible resources may increase with age, owing to conditions such as immobility or financial strain. Furthermore, older adults may also experience increased difficulty in maintaining a sense of self-worth. In later life, older adults may find themselves isolated from some of the sources of emotional support that once affirmed their usefulness to society. A second reason for studying social support in later-life families is that these families often assume the responsibility of supplying social support to their older family members. Thus the stress of providing support may affect the quality of this support, which, in turn, affects the quality of life that the older adult experiences.

Unlike many other theorists who have examined personal characteristics as an alternative explanation for social support, Hansson and Carpenter examine personal characteristics as a precursor to social network structure. Because interpersonal relationships form the pool from which social support is drawn, the presence and structure of these relationships should be an important factor in determining whether social support occurs. Their chapter has two major theses: that interpersonal relationships are important for dealing with the demands of old age and that the individual's ability to secure and to maintain interpersonal relationships determines the presence and the effectiveness of a supportive social structure. Thus the major focus of this chapter is not on whether social support is needed but on who will enter old age with either the necessary social structure or the ability to assemble a needed structure.

Hansson and Carpenter suggest that the availability and accessibility of support is determined by a constellation of personal characteristics that they refer to as relational competence. When relational competence causes smoother interpersonal relationships and easier functioning in social situations, the individual is more effective in entering into and benefiting from personal and supportive ties. Hansson and Carpenter present evidence that some personal characteristics are effective for establishing and mobilizing social networks, whereas others are effective for maintaining social networks.

Hansson and Carpenter's conceptualization and measurement of relational competence and its effects on interpersonal relationships differs from ideas explored in previous research that relates social networks to personal characteristics. Hansson and Carpenter examine a variety of personal characteristics in conjunction with several aspects of social networks (e.g., structure and accessibility). Thus they have begun to specify the relational competence skills needed to combat the unique stressors faced by older adults. Other applications of this model to older adults include prediction of success at various phases of a stressful situation and clarification of how particular types of support networks best serve particular functions.

Felton reviews the research on the coping and support processes that are used to manage a specific stressor in later life, chronic illness. She concludes that chronic illness, regardless of its intensity, is managed most often by emotion-focused coping strategies and by realignment of social relationships. Although others have noted the change in social relationships resulting from chronic illness, Felton deals with the issue of why these changes occur. The more typical approach to this problem is to examine how much social support chronically ill people receive. Occasionally researchers examine these changes in social support in terms of tangible and expressive exchanges. Felton goes further and provides a finer grained analysis of the content of social exchanges. A model of the effects of chronic illness and social network structure on older adults' social relationships and, ultimately, on their psychological well-being, is proposed.

Felton suggests that the contents of social relationships, or "provisions," vary on two dimensions: the complexity of the skills needed to maintain the relationship and the externality of the focus. Furthermore, she argues that social provisions occupy a hierarchy. The higher-order provisions involve focusing on and responding to external stimuli (e.g., one's partner in the dyad or the larger social group) and, thus, require greater skills than do the lower-order provisions, which involve focusing on and responding to internal stimuli (e.g., one's own needs). By narrowing one's focus and energy to internal rather than external stimuli, chronic illness may restrict access to upper-level provisions. Felton's unique contribution is that she attempts to explain (a) why the chronically ill tend to use emotion- rather than problem-focused coping strategies and (b) the dynamics by which illness disrupts social relationships.

Rook deals with the negative elements of older adults' social relationships. Her major contribution is linking social psychological theory to empirical findings. She defines negative social exchanges as actions that are regarded by the recipient as misdeeds and that cause the recipient emotional distress. Three theoretical explanations for the potency of these negative reactions are presented. The first is based on a frequency–saliency explanation whereby acts that occur infrequently are more salient to the individual. The second is derived from attribution theory. Because positive behaviors are normative, they do not provide information about the quality of a relationship. However, negative behaviors, being counternormative, stimulate attributional activity. The third comes from an adaptive significance approach. It has been adaptive for humans to be more aware of potential threats than of potential benefits and, thus, we are more reactive to negative behaviors than to positive ones.

In addition to these theoretical perspectives, Rook draws our attention to two other issues that have not previously been addressed. First, she points out that the threshold for effects may be different for positive and negative social exchanges, and that these effects may be diminished once exchanges exceed a critical threshold. Second, she examines the association between older people's sensitivity to negative exchanges and their psychosocial vulnerability to such exchanges. That social relationships contain negative elements, and that these negative elements are potent predictors of poor outcomes has been amply validated in the empirical literature. Rook has begun the search to understand the process by which this transpires.

Integrating social support into a life-span perspective, Jackson, Antonucci, and Gibson examine the links between social relationships and the macro-social environment. They explore how social exchanges are productive for the individual and how they benefit society. This chapter links the larger social environment to the functioning of primary networks and the effects of those networks on individuals. Their use of the concept of productivity is similar to many of the societal indices that are called *social indicators,* but instead of valuation in monetary terms, the valuation is that of worthwhileness to the individual. Basic to their argument is the premise that productive activities occur in three different economic networks: regular, irregular, and social. These economic networks provide resources that are of primary importance in coping with stress.

Assessing factors that influence participation in the three economies (e.g., age, race, class, and economic necessity), Antonucci and her associates conclude that different economies are optimal at different points in the life course. Two of these economic networks, the irregular (e.g., productive activity exchanged for unreported monetary currency) and the social (e.g., productive activity performed or exchanged without monetary pay), may be particularly important for meeting the needs of older adults. Proponents of ecological models of social support have long argued that such links between social systems are needed, but the social support literature has not previously moved beyond linking the individual with the primary group level. Antonucci and her colleagues carry this one step further by linking the larger social context to the primary group and individual levels.

The chapters in this section offer several insights on social support. First, they emphasize that social support is multidetermined. Taken in combination, the ideas presented by Hansson and Carpenter and by Felton indicate that it is both the characteristics of the person (e.g., relational competence) and the changing demands created by situational factors (e.g., chronic illness) that determine whether an individual will establish, maintain, and mobilize a social network and close personal ties that are adequate for meeting their needs. The life-span, convoy model presented by Antonucci and her colleagues indicates that both personal (e.g., life-stage) and environmental (e.g., presence of attachment figures) factors contribute to the size and character of one's social network. Theoretical and empirical evidence presented by Rook indicates that both personal (e.g., sensitivity to negative exchanges) and environmental (e.g., exposure to negative exchanges) factors affect the perception that a social exchange is negative.

Second, social support both is affected by and affects the health of older adults. All of the authors focus on the effects of social support in managing illness. However, Antonucci and her associates and Felton address the question of how health affects social support. Both of these chapters address the contents of social exchanges—Antonucci and her colleagues in terms of the worthwhileness of socioeconomic exchanges and Felton in terms of provisions.

Third, social relationships both enhance provision of social support and expose individuals to social costs. Rook focuses directly on this issue, but all of the authors in this section both acknowledge and accommodate this concept in their theoretical presentations. Although these chapters generally regard social problems as failures in the social network, Hansson and Carpenter's ideas about relational competence suggest that social problems arise, at least in part, from poorly developed personal skills. They also imply that the very act of maintaining social ties involves certain costs to individuals.

Finally, these chapters suggest that social support serves well-being in two ways. As Antonucci and her colleagues argue, integration within a social network can provide protection in psychological, health, and economic realms. Social support also can serve as a buffer that intervenes between the experience of a stressful life event and decreased well-being by providing coping resources or, as Felton suggests, by increasing the efficacy of the social provisions provided by the social network. Rook, too, concludes that the effects of negative social exchanges are most evident when they occur after an individual has experienced a stressful life event, and that these experiences heighten the effects of the stressful event.

This section confirms that the study of social support in the context of later-life families is important. The study of social support in later-life families provides answers to questions of high priority to gerontologists as well as answers to questions relevant to the more general social support literature.

8

RELATIONAL COMPETENCE AND ADJUSTMENT IN OLDER ADULTS: IMPLICATIONS FOR THE DEMANDS OF AGING

Robert O. Hansson
Bruce N. Carpenter

University of Tulsa

Interpersonal functioning is particularly important during later life because relationship problems constitute a significant portion of the difficulties facing older adults, and because this important coping resource is especially needed. The later years are often marked by a clustering of difficult social events that may include bereavement and widowhood, retirement, a diminishing number of functional roles in society, and isolation owing to chronic illness, reduced sensory competence, or reduced income. Simultaneously, older individuals often cope for the first time with reduced physical capacity, with age stereotyping or discrimination, and with those institutions and bureaucracies that administer health care, social security entitlements, and the like.

Many of these events are interpersonal, as they directly involve the loss of important relationships, changing social roles, or the attitudes of others. Even demands that are not themselves interpersonal, such as an increasing need for health care, are often most effectively met in a positive interpersonal environment. The extensive literature on social support has shown how others can contribute to the adjustment process. Yet social support networks are themselves sometimes problematic, reflecting the personal relationships on which they are formed. In old age, one's demands on the network may also change in response to new stressors at the same time that relationship dilemmas may be increasing because of diminishing resources. We view relationships as being important for coping with the demands of old age in at least three ways: (a) relationships themselves are an important source of stress; (b) many coping options are best exercised in an interpersonal context; and (c) relationships constitute an important coping resource for addressing a wide variety of problems.

We believe that an older adult's success in adjusting to stressful life change will in part reflect that individual's ability to actively construe, construct, access, and maintain social relationships. These abilities are important for coping with interpersonal stressors and for establishing a social environment that can be useful and supportive in time of need. In this connection we have for some time been studying the construct of *relational competence* in both younger and older populations.

We have three general goals in this chapter. First, we explore the problematic nature of social relationships, including social support networks, that become important in old age. Second, we outline our thinking about the construct of relational competence as it might mediate success in such relations and describe our related research on the topic. Third, we introduce a model for more formally conceptualizing and measuring relational competence.

PROBLEMATIC RELATIONSHIPS IN LATER YEARS

That interpersonal competencies should help in solving interpersonal problems is a relatively straightforward idea. The ways in which relational competence contributes to a supportive environment, however, are more complex. The analysis of relevant interpersonal process might best be conducted within a systems perspective. For example, in a caregiving relationship the support felt by the recipient often occurs at the expense of the caregiver. We should not simply assess older adults as individuals, but rather we should also evaluate the implications of caregiving for family, friends, and others. The stress and coping dynamics that affect older people also affect the people with whom they have relationships. In an effort to address these concerns we review the literature across a number of domains in an attempt to demonstrate the potential value of the relational competencies an older adult might bring to the situation. We have divided these discussions into four categories of particular interest: family issues, interactions with health care systems, housing-related issues, and the implications of bereavement and widowhood.

Family and Caregiving Issues

Gerontologists have to date been most interested in family-centered relationships, and with good reason: The family is the primary source of support for its older members. A wealth of studies have detailed the family's continuing role in the provision of emotional, logistical, and caregiving support as an older adult's abilities, needs, and personal resources change (cf. Brody, 1985; Mitchell & Register, 1984; Stone, Cafferata, & Sangl, 1987; Chapters 2, 7, and 11, this volume). This research establishes a picture of the ongoing process within families, of who turns to whom for what, of who provides resources, and at what cost. It has also begun to identify some of the barriers to continued, effective support, especially the strain or burden caregivers experience.

Research consistently demonstrates the willingness of families to assume the care of their older relatives. The availability of a family support network is a major factor in deferring institutionalization in old age. However, a family's resources are not unlimited, and as Brody (1985) noted recently, parent care is perhaps best characterized as a "normative family stress" experience. The nature of a parent's dependency has in this century been altered, now involving more chronic illness and disability, and chronically ill people live longer. The family's caregiving responsibilities thus extend over longer periods of time than ever before, perhaps further complicated by society's shift away from a structure built around the extended family.

Concerns over family burdens have prompted numerous attempts to objectively assess the degree and categories of strain caused by caregiving and to identify its antecedents and consequences (e.g., Poulshock & Deimling, 1984; Zarit, Reever, & Bach-Peterson, 1980; Chapter 12, this volume). Attempts to measure burden have tended to focus on experienced (or anticipated) negative changes in the relationship between caregiver and recipient, stressful constraints on the caregiver's (or family's) activities, time, or freedoms, emotional strain, and economic hardship.

A review of the research provides a context for evaluating such concerns. In one study, for example, 35% of the caregivers of noninstitutionalized older people were age 65 or older, more than 30% were poor to near poor, 33% were themselves in fair to poor health, 20% had felt a conflict between the demands of caregiving and a job, and 20% had been caring for a disabled older adult for as long as five years (Stone et al., 1987). Such figures are consistent with other studies of this type, although some variance is seen across diagnosis categories (e.g., among stroke, dementia, and heart patients).

It is also noteworthy that a single individual often emerges as the primary caregiver, rather than the entire family acting as a sharing, integrated support network. Indeed, Johnson (1983) found that additional family members generally become available for such responsibilities only when the primary caregiver has burned out or become unable to continue. In such cases, then, the older family member may experience periodic, involuntary changes of residence, and have to renegotiate interpersonal and living arrangements each time. Under such pressures, the personal relationships on which support depends may become more vulnerable to conflict. Such conflict could result in an older person's experiencing loss of control, invasions of privacy, broken promises, and overprotectiveness, or attempts to trivialize their complaints or to encourage a more "graceful" progression to the next life stage (Rook, 1984; Stephens, Kinney, Norris, & Ritchie, 1987). Thus the costs of the relationship to the care-recipient might often outweigh its benefits (Rook, 1984; Chapter 8, this volume).

A number of recent studies reveal in substantial detail the normative experience of the caregiving burden and the kinds of individual and relationship factors that appear to influence its variations. For example, Cantor (1983) assessed several aspects of worry or strain experienced by several types of caregivers of older people (spouse, child, relative, and friend or neighbor). She found that of all types of caregivers, approximately 70% felt quite close to the recipient and felt well treated by the recipient. However, they were less likely to get along every day. Only 53% of the involved children felt that they got along with the recipient, compared to 60% of the caregiver-spouses, 86% of the other relatives, and 92% of friends or neighbors involved in caregiving. Children in such relationships thus appeared to fare worse relationally, with only 48% feeling that they understood their parent well, and only 28% feeling that the parent understood them.

An important conclusion from this study was that the closer the relational bond and, hence, the greater the "normative role of responsibility," the more strain experienced. Elderly spouse caregivers frequently report experiencing loneliness and depression and difficulty in asking for help. Many also feel that other people fail to understand what their life is like. Often, they seek help from family or professionals. However, this has not been found to yield the most effective coping outcome (Barusch, 1988).

Caregiving for older people is a process and not a single event. Schultz, Tompkins, and Rau (1988) found that the percentage of patients at risk for depression decreased from 34% at several weeks after a stroke to 25% six months later. However, the percentage of caregivers at risk remained constant at about 34%. Schultz et al. suggested that the caregiver's earlier depression is a consequence of acute caregiving, whereas later it arises from the caregiver's sense of the long-term nature of the burden. The interpersonal ramifications become more evident from two findings. First, caregiver's level of depression at the second assessment interval, after controlling for initial depression level, was associated with disruption in the quality of reciprocal confiding relationships and of satisfying social contacts. Second, friends and relatives of the caregiver began, over time, to avoid contact or discussion, perhaps on the premise that communication might further burden the caregiver. Consistent with these findings, better outcomes for caregivers, especially in terms of health and reported life satisfaction, have been found to occur when the caregiver has a larger social support network, more shared activity with members of the network, and more satisfaction with the social provisions of the network (Haley, Levine, Brown & Bartolucci, 1987).

These findings are consistent with those of a recent study of family caregivers for demented, older adults (George & Gwyther, 1986). Caregivers experienced nearly three times the stress symptoms seen in comparison samples. However, the well-being of caregivers was not strongly related to the actual nature or severity of the patient's impairment, but instead was more likely to reflect the nature of the caregiving context (e.g., living arrangements) and the availability of social support for the caregiver. Those who reported a relative lack of social support (59% of the respondents) had more negative scores on self-rated health, stress symptoms, life satisfaction, usage of psychotropic drugs, and income. They also reported fewer meaningful outside social activities (contacts with friends, visits with family and friends, and attendance at church and clubs) and less satisfaction with their social activities. Unfortunately, the need to devote continuously increasing amounts of one's personal and social resources to the caregiving relationship may eventually result in the social isolation of the pair from others and distancing of potentially supportive others from the dyad (Johnson & Catalano, 1983).

The preceding discussion then suggests a number of potential risks likely to be associated with the strain of caregiving. Whereas the support needs of an older person are likely to be long-term, support network resources could be stressed, discontinuous, and unpredictable. Such risks among the frail elderly would be expected to affect the quality of care and lead to premature institutionalization. An additional risk in many families is the potential for intensification of conflict and for the abuse of elders. Two recent papers have placed this concern in perspective and relate to the issues we have been discussing. Pillemer & Finkelhor (1988) recently found the overall rate of reported abuse of people aged 65 or older to be 32 in 1,000. Older people in poor health were three times more likely to become victims, and spouses were more likely to be the abuser than were adult children.

Interpersonal factors also play a principal role in determining risk of abuse (Kosberg, 1988). The characteristics of older adults at high risk include the presence of intergenerational conflict, with intensifying family conflict over time; provocative behavior, such as being unpleasant, ungrateful, or overdemanding; and social isolation, permitting conflict or abuse to continue unnoticed by others. There are also a number of interpersonal characteristics of caregivers at high risk. They are dispositionally unsympathetic and neglectful, lack understanding of the consequences of age-related events, and may be impatient with an older adult's diminished physical, cognitive, or social competencies. Moreover, they may be uninvolved outside the home, thus having fewer social or formal contacts and less access to social support or to community-centered monitoring of the family caregiving situation. Finally, there are a number of characteristics of the family system at high risk for abuse, including an overload of support burdens, marital conflicts that spill over into relationships with dependent older people, and disharmony among family members regarding the availability and form of potential assistance to be provided.

Interactions with Health Care Systems

Interpersonal concerns also pervade older adults' interactions with formal health care systems. A number of special difficulties experienced by older adults in health care settings underscore the importance of their ability to assert their needs and assure the timely and effective response of others. The rights and competence of older persons may simply be discounted in the medical encounter. For example, physical rehabilitation therapists, especially those with negative attitudes toward the elderly, have been found to recommend less aggressive goals for rehabilitation therapy for older patients (Barta Kvitek, Shaver, Blood, & Shepard, 1986).

The experience of illness in older people is not always simply physiological. Psychological and social factors can play an important role in onset, access to support, caregiving, adherence to regimen, modulation of the immune and cardiovascular systems, and shaping patterns of coping (e.g., excess use of medications or alcohol). However, older patients often do not raise psychosocial concerns with their physicians (Greene, Hoffman, Charon, & Adelman, 1987). In addition, physicians may be less likely to raise psychosocial issues with older patients and less responsive to such issues raised by these patients (Greene et al., 1987).

Another problematic aspect of the doctor–patient relationship involving older patients is the presence of a third party. Unlike younger adults, some 20% of older patients are accompanied to doctor visits by a relative or friend (Adelman, Greene, & Charon, 1987). This third person usually acts in the role of supportive advocate, or as a passive participant. In some cases, however, these participants have a personal agenda for the visit. They may misattribute the patient's health complaints to age, they may wish to assert personal preferences for treatment options or for patient behavior, or they may wish to involve themselves in decision making regarding housing or institutionalization options for the older patient. The presence of a third party at the interview also might alter the content of the patient's disclosures regarding symptoms, problems in living, distressed feelings, sexuality, or other embarrassing concerns. The third party's presence might also inhibit the development of a trusting relationship between the patient and health care provider.

These concerns have implications for the patient's satisfaction, for informed consent, and for adherence to prescribed regimens, and here again it would probably be beneficial if the older patient were able to assert some ground rules and personal control over how the health interview is conducted (Adelman et al., 1987). However, such actions may be more difficult for older individuals, as is suggested by findings that they are less likely than younger individuals to change doctors after an upsetting experience in a physician's office (Hansson, Remondet, Obrochta, & Bell, 1988).

Many community outreach programs of the American health care system may also have interpersonal barriers that hinder access to the system. Such programs could play an important role in early detection and monitoring of health status in the older population (Rubenstein, Josephson, Nichol-Seamons, & Robbins, 1986). However, few such programs actively search out all of the older people in a community. Instead programs often are held in a local community center or nutrition center to which older persons must travel on a voluntary basis. Consequently, such programs typically will not reach all in need.

Indeed, age-segregated community centers appear to serve only a small minority of the older population. One reason may be the attitudes of many older people and their lack of identification with the spirit and charter of such entities. Another reason may be that America has evolved into a voluntaristic society, wherein social interaction and its many benefits depend in great part on the willingness or ability of the individual to actively seek aid (Lopata, 1988). This pattern seems particularly relevant to the circumstances of older women in America, who in their later years are more likely to be widowed, to live alone, to have limited financial resources, and to live in social isolation (National Institute on Aging, 1978). Negotiating services with formal health care systems, then, often appears to involve potentially difficult interpersonal interactions. It can be expected that those older people with greater interpersonal competence will fare better in the process.

Housing-Related Interpersonal Issues

Much of the publicly assisted housing in the United States is now devoted to older adults. The widespread development of planned senior housing in part reflects two assumptions: (a) that close proximity to similar others will facilitate social interaction and serve as a buffer against loneliness in old age, and (b) that close proximity will provide easier access to networks for potential support. Unfortunately, proximity to other older residents does not always serve these functions. For example, most of the support received by residents of senior housing still comes from family members and from nonresident friends, rather than from fellow residents (Stephens & Bernstein, 1984). This is perhaps understandable. Deep relationships do not usually form quickly, and old, established relationships are often safer and more predictable. Moreover, other residents are relatively similar in terms of resources, and one may accurately realize that others have few tangible support resources to share. An important result, however, is that those residents in the greatest need of support are the least likely to be in relationships that might provide it. That is, those with chronic health conditions, sensory impairment, and long-term illness become more socially isolated (Stephens & Bernstein, 1984).

It is of interest to examine why those most in need of support are more isolated. Older and frailer residents report several reasons for their low social involvement. Sheehan (1986) noted, for example, that these individuals want to avoid conflict with social cliques or gossipy neighbors, feel unable to keep up with their healthier, more active neighbors, and believe that some activities are too expensive. Other reasons offered included their reluctance to ask for help, anticipation of social discrimination on the basis of health status, and their beliefs that previous, long-term relationships could not be replaced with new ones of appropriate quality. In contrast, the younger, healthier, and still independent residents express the following kinds of reasons for their reluctance to become involved with frailer neighbors: interactions with the less healthy residents often serve as reminders of their own aging and of their own limited emotional and tangible resources. In addition, the healthier residents want to avoid interfering with ongoing family or formal support relationships involving the less healthy residents. Finally, they are sensitive to unilateral costs that could become too high in a nonreciprocal support relationship. Thus both frail and independent residents appear in their own way to want to avoid high-cost relationships (Sheehan, 1986).

We therefore conclude that age similarity and planned proximity does not necessarily translate into reciprocal support or social relationships among older adults. In fact, they may instead isolate those with the greatest needs from others who have the greatest potential for providing needed help. We should be sensitive to the importance of identifying ways to reduce the costs of forming potentially supportive relationships.

Bereavement and Widowhood

The early clinical investigations of bereavement were generally intrapersonal in nature, viewing the event as one to be worked through alone and focusing primarily on mental and physical health consequences, psychologically at-risk groups, and the potential for clinical intervention. More recently, theory and research have adopted an interpersonal perspective, acknowledging the social consequences of the loss, the importance of supportive interactions with others in resolving one's grief, and the context of societal constraints on the process of recovery (cf. Hansson, Stroebe, & Stroebe, 1988). We describe a variety of these social-contextual concerns, to illustrate the ways in which individual differences in relational competence might facilitate the adjustment and well-being of older, bereaved, and long-term widowed individuals.

Among older people, the stress of bereavement is likely to be compounded by the occurrence of multiple stressors related to the loss of the loved one. These include economic decline, loss of independence, and loss of social status. Moreover, with the death of a spouse, not only do people usually lose the person to whom they are most likely to turn in time of stress, but also the death is likely to distress the entire family system. This, in turn, diminishes the family's ability to come to the aid of the most immediately affected person. Older bereaved people, especially women, may also experience social constraints on the range of options they are encouraged to pursue in establishing an independent life style. Such constraints might, for example, reflect traditional sex role patterns that encourage dependency on a husband and inhibit a widow's options to seek new occupational, social, or sexual outlets after the spouse's death (Lopata, 1988).

Moreover, age-related factors may also socially isolate bereaved people from community support resources. Lopata (1988) has described a particularly interesting mechanism of such isolation in her analysis of older urban widows. She noted that most older people spent their childhoods in smaller, more tightly woven social communities with highly attentive and effective support systems. Following a half century of industrial modernization and urbanization, however, society has changed substantially. An important change, she argued, is that older adults must now depend for the most part on their own initiative to become and remain involved in social relationships, because today's loosely woven communities no longer attempt to reach out to people undergoing disrupting events such as widowhood. She further proposed that a volunteristic society can be particularly problematic for older women, who were not socialized in their youth to assertively initiate social contact and new relationships. Lopata concluded from her research that, "The most friendless widows were the ones who either had moved into a new neighborhood and lacked skills at friendship making, or were the remnants of their own ethnic group in a neighborhood now occupied by another group" (1988, p. 122).

THE CONSTRUCT OF RELATIONAL COMPETENCE

In the preceding section we attempted to show that many important problems facing older adults are interpersonal, that much of their coping activity takes place an interpersonal context, and that supportive relationships are often problematic. We have come to believe, however, that individual difference variables often mediate such difficulties. Some individuals possess the skill to readily solve or soothe interpersonal difficulties, to function in social situations so that their coping options are greater, and to more effectively enter into and benefit from personal and supportive relationships in time of need. In this context, we initially proposed the construct of relational competence, comprising individual characteristics likely to facilitate the acquisition, development, maintenance, and utilization of successful relationships (Carpenter, Hansson, Rountree, & Jones, 1983; Hansson, Jones, & Carpenter, 1984).

We originally described the construct of relational competence within the limited context of the social support literature, and the potential difficulties and strains inherent in support relationships. It is clear, however, that the construct can be viewed more broadly. For example, to the extent that relational competence enhances older adults' success in building and maintaining a diverse network of social resources, it may foster their personal control and independence (Hansson & Remondet, 1988). Similarly, because relational competence facilitates a reliable and diverse network of social coping resources, it may contribute to stress resistance, enhancing the likelihood of access to the coping resources most appropriate to the demands of the current situation (Hobfoll, 1985, 1988).

We initially anticipated that relational competence would involve a mix of temperamental, cognitive, and emotional characteristics, and we proposed a four-part model with which to explore how such characteristics might influence important support relationships (see Hansson et al., 1984, for a review of previous personality research relevant to the model). The four elements of the model are as follows:

1. Personality should affect one's likelihood of both approaching others for support and evaluating relational status by shaping the way we *construe* our relationships and interpersonal environments. Thus people would be expected to vary in their expectations that interactions will be welcomed and rewarding, that they will not be evaluated negatively or rejected, that others can be trusted, and so on. Furthermore, within the context of secondary appraisal of stress (the evaluation of one's resources to meet a stressful demand; Lazarus & Folkman, 1984), the way one thinks about relationships and their functions should strongly affect subsequent coping responses and stress reactions.

2. People are frequently required to actively *construct* their support networks. Such networks are in part a function of opportunity and the skills of significant others, but initially they depend to a large extent on one's own social skills and instrumental traits and resources. Support networks typically depend heavily on intimate, long-lasting relationships; therefore, these networks often have longevity. Consequently, relationship-constructing skills will typically be important only periodically when the network is disrupted or lost, as in geographic relocation or following divorce or death of a family member. We expected, therefore, that traits such as assertiveness, internality, perseverance, instrumentality, and extraversion would be of great value, whereas shyness would be inhibitive.

3. We have shown in the previous section that even those people who are members of potentially supportive networks may encounter difficulty in *accessing* these support systems. We anticipated that a variety of traits might inhibit such help-seeking. For example, people who are shy or socially anxious and those with low self-esteem might fear negative evaluations or feel stigmatized in seeking help. Highly independent people might see help-seeking as a sign of weakness, and those with minimal social skills might simply be less effective when they do ask for help. A lack of forcefulness

and perseverance would also minimize one's chances of getting the attention of members of an already overburdened network.

4. Finally, relational competence should help in *maintaining* relationships and support networks. After all, support networks comprise people, each with their own needs and burdens. In a long-term caregiving relationship particularly, the caregiver's needs and burdens become more salient, and it is in the recipient's best interests to contribute whatever possible to the relationship to ensure its maintenance, health, and continued availability. For example, we anticipated that traits such as empathy would influence such efforts. Empathy enables the recipient to understand the other's perspective, feelings, and needs, and to know how to nurture the personal relationship on which the support depends by showing appropriate gratitude and by finding ways to benefit the caregiver. Similarly, by being flexible regarding one's care demands and by assuming greater personal responsibility and control over one's own care, one might minimize the costs of the relationship to the caregiver.

RESEARCH ON RELATIONAL COMPETENCE

We have in the last few years conducted a number of studies with older adults to assess the role of relational competence variables in facilitating successful transitions and well-being in old age. The results of this research, bolstered by the parallel findings of others, demonstrate the potential scope of the construct's utility. We first offer a few examples of the impact of individual differences in social functioning on outcomes that are important to older people.

The manner in which one responds to care is critical to the maintenance of caregiving relationships. Impaired sociability and social skills in an older care-recipient have been found to be related negatively to the caregiver's mental health and to negatively affect the caregiver's family (Poulshock & Deimling, 1984). Personality appears also to be important to adjustment in congregate living situations. Carp (1985) assessed older adults in such a setting to determine the relative predictive value of (a) competence and social status variables and (b) personality on adjustment. Competence assessments included cognitive status on the WAIS (Wechsler, 1958), a composite health assessment, and sensory–motor status. Social status indices included age, education, marital status, income, and socioeconomic status prior to retirement. Personality indices were staff ratings of the resident's extraversion, congeniality, neuroticism, culture, conscientiousness, and nosiness/gossip tendencies. Adjustment was assessed as self-reported happiness, peer ratings of sociometric status, and ratings by housing staff of one's adjustment to the housing setting.

Across the three adjustment criteria, competence and social status (together) accounted for 3% to 13% of the variance when personality had been statistically controlled. In contrast, personality accounted for 17% to 63% of the variance in rated adjustment when competence and status had been statistically controlled. Three of the personality variables were consistently important across all three criteria, with extraversion and congeniality positively correlated and neuroticism negatively correlated with all adjustment variables. Acknowledging the possibility of error variance across staff ratings of personality and adjustment ratings, it is nevertheless interesting that such staff perceptions of personality were more important than were objective assessments of cognitive, health, and sensory–motor function across all three adjustment criteria.

Our own research has focused on independently living older adults and on stressors and transitions characteristic of the later years. One such stressor involves a deteriorating living environment. Lawton and Simon (1968) hypothesized that older adults who are less competent, in terms of health and social or psychological status, will have a more limited range of adaptability to environmental stress. Previous research confirms that older people who are less competent in health, social status, and even cognitive status experience more immediate stress when their housing and neighborhoods become less safe or supportive (cf. Lawton, 1980).

Our research supported such findings but has also demonstrated similar relationships for personality (Morgan et al., 1984). We classified older adults as "high-competent" or "low-competent" on the basis of four dispositional variables commonly associated with successful coping (internality, assertiveness, self-esteem, and willingness to accept marginal levels of assistance in order to continue to live independently). Among high-competent individuals (on each of the four dispositional variables), correlations between assessed level of environmental stress and psychological adjustment and well-being were very low in magnitude. However, among low-competent individuals all correlations were significant. Interpersonal skills and dispositions thus appear to be important resources in coping with environmental stress.

A related stressor among older adults is fear of crime. Older adults appear to be more likely to fear crime, although they are not substantially more likely to be victimized. Nevertheless, the fear itself may be maladaptive if it prevents older people from freely interacting within their communities. We wondered whether fear of crime also might be as much related to one's personality as to situational variables (Hansson & Carpenter, 1986). Our study thus focused on two personality–temperament characteristics (shyness and emotional stability), and on two situational variables (the older person's own or family experience with victimization, and his or her ratings of the safety of the neighborhood). We anticipated that shy people, who find social interaction more intimidating in general, would be less likely to have developed friendships and supportive relationships in the neighborhood. Shy people, then, should be less likely to view their community as a safe haven from street crime. Similarly, more emotional individuals should have lower thresholds for potentially threatening events and situations. Of the 128 elderly respondents in this study (median age of 73 years), 17% had been criminally victimized in recent years, and 46% had a friend or neighbor who had been victimized. Results indicated, however, that both personality variables significantly predicted fear of crime, whereas neither of the situational variables did so.

We have also studied the relative contributions of personality and situational characteristics to adjustment among chronically unemployed older adults (Hansson, Briggs, & Rule, in press). Older adults are especially vulnerable to the consequences of unemployment, and many simply become discouraged and either drop out of the work force or take early retirement. We anticipated that individual differences in personality would be important in job seeking, a fundamentally social process requiring social competence and perseverance in evaluative interactions with those who control hiring. Participants in the study (average age equals 56 years) had been unemployed for an average of 22 weeks and were recruited from a state unemployment office for a nominal fee. They completed an employment/unemployment history, three outcome measures (perceived control in the employment situation, depression, and loneliness), and measures of assertiveness, shyness, and perspective-taking. We assumed that assertive and non-shy people would continue to persevere in an increasingly difficult social situation and that people who were able to take another's perspective would be less likely to overpersonalize any setbacks or to unnecessarily attribute continued failures to obtain work to oneself rather than to a difficult economy.

Results indicated that, as expected, the outcome variables were somewhat related to one's unemployment experience, including previous job instability, duration of current unemployment, and remaining unemployment benefits. However, supporting our thesis, the three relational competence variables generally predicted the outcome variables at least as consistently as did the experience variables. Moreover, a regression analysis showed that the personality variables contributed more to explained variance in both personal control and loneliness than did experience factors. Only in the case of depression did experience contribute more unique variance than did personality factors.

We have also pursued the broader role of personality variables in the experience of loneliness in old age. Loneliness is a common but unpleasant psychological state, usually defined in terms of level of dissatisfaction with social relationships and networks. Loneliness in many instances results from a disruption of established networks or relational loss, such as in widowhood or divorce, loss of friends through death, or because of a variety of structural barriers to satisfying social contact, such as low income. Such socially disruptive events are especially relevant to the experience of older people, because they are more characteristic of the later years. Here again, we assumed that relational competence would enhance one's efforts to replenish disrupted relationships. Pursuing this line of reasoning, we found that anxiety, shyness, and assertiveness significantly predicted loneliness among older, independently living people (Hansson, Jones, Carpenter, & Remondet, 1986–1987). These findings were independent of the effects of health, frequency of illness, income, and education.

How adult children are drawn into the caregiving process for older parents, and the characteristics of parents that elicit support, are now being studied. Specifically, researchers are interested in how adult children's perceptions of their elderly parents with respect to dispositional characteristics might influence the likelihood, timing, and nature of intervention in caregiving or decision making (Hansson, Nelson, Carver, NeeSmith, & Dowling, 1988). The Hansson et al. (1988) study suggests that adult children do acquire a sense of their parent's psychological status, in terms of loneliness and in terms of personality variables that might influence continued coping and the likelihood of remaining independent. Such impressions were at least moderately related to the extent to which children become aware of and involved in their parents' concerns in later life. Two outcome variables were examined: (a) the extent to which the adult child had begun to think seriously about a parent's changing needs and problems, to learn about these issues, and to more consciously monitor the parent's status; and (b) the extent to which the adult child and family members other than the spouse were already involved in caregiving for the parent. Results indicated that increased consciousness of the issues and family involvement were associated with perceptions that one's parent was shy, lonely, or depressed, or lacked self-esteem, internality, or instrumentality.

An analysis in which the data from "young-old" (age 60–75) and "old-old" (mid-70s and older) individuals were analyzed separately suggests an important parameter on the role of relational competence and of satisfying personal relationships in psychological adjustment and well-being. In several such analyses, for the young-old, positive outcomes were clearly related to relational competence, but for the old-old, adjustment and well-being were less predictable from relational competence variables, or from satisfactory social involvements (Hansson, 1986). These findings are consistent with a role-theoretical interpretation that personality traits assume meaning only when they have important interpersonal consequences. That is, the old-old may experience a less evaluative social environment, with fewer role functions in which they are responsible to the cultural group for their performance. They may therefore feel less pressure to continue to rise to the occasion. Thus many relational competence variables and the kinds of relationships they are likely to foster may simply diminish in importance. Research to date, then, suggests that relational competence can facilitate successful transitions and well-being in one's later years. What one brings to the situation can play an important role in coping situations in which other people are either a part of the problem, or a potential coping resource.

A MODEL FOR CONCEPTUALIZING
AND MEASURING RELATIONAL COMPETENCE

Studies of older populations, to date, have focused on the relational competence variables in which researchers had greatest interest. One researcher, however, has recently proposed a unified model for conceptualizing and measuring the construct. Carpenter's (1987) model of relational competence proposes two components, Initiation and Enhancement. Initiation skills are those that facilitate meeting people, developing relationships, and drawing on relationships in time of need. These skills are socially valued and associated with status, and so are closely associated with self-esteem. In contrast, enhancement skills are critical for meeting the needs of relational partners, and for maintaining and strengthening existing relationships so that the functions of close relationships can occur. Although enhancement skills are also socially valued, they are used primarily within the context of close relationships, thus having a more limited sphere of influence. A wide variety of attributes might easily be subsumed under each of these components. Also, the ability to construe, construct, and access support systems (the first three elements of the initial model) are nicely incorporated into Initiation (Hansson, Jones, & Carpenter, 1984), and the ability to maintain such relationships (the fourth element of that model) generally matches Carpenter's Enhancement component.

The two-component model derives from several sources, including other models of relational functioning and our own work on interpersonal factors in adjustment. In a study of interpersonal correlates of loneliness (Jones, Carpenter, & Quintana, 1985), factor analysis revealed that the largest factor included variables such as assertiveness, masculinity, and shyness. However, several other social competence variables, such as love, trust, and altruism, strongly correlated with loneliness, but did not load on this factor. A similar distinction is found in many theories of interpersonal functioning. Although not focusing on competencies, these theories (e.g., Horowitz & Vitkus, 1986; Wiggins, 1982) commonly propose two, usually orthogonal dimensions, with names such as Affiliation versus Control or Love /Hate versus Autonomy/Dependence.

Measure of Relational Competence

The Relational Competence Scale (Carpenter, 1989) was developed from this two-component model. This scale samples broadly from both domains, focusing on personal attributes that have been empirically demonstrated to be relevant to the development, nurturance, and maintenance of relationships. Using a rational-theoretical approach to scale construction, five subscales were constructed for each component to sample from the possible domain. Each subscale contains 10 Likert-format items with balanced keying for an overall total of 100 items. The Initiation subscales include Assertiveness, Dominance, Instrumental Competence, Shyness, and Social Anxiety (the last two loading negatively). The Enhancement subscales include Intimacy, Trust, Interpersonal Sensitivity, Altruism, and Perspective Taking.

The initial psychometric and validity studies on the scale have been conducted with college and non-college adult populations. In spite of the relatively brief length, each of the subscales has rather high internal consistency and test–retest reliability. Coefficient alpha for each component score is about .95, and the component scores are essentially uncorrelated with one another. Gender differences are relatively modest, occurring primarily between Enhancement subscales for non-college men and women. Exploratory factor analysis reproduces the two-factor model, with each of the subscales loading on the proper factor and altogether accounting for about two-thirds of the variance. Confirmatory factor analysis also suggests that the two-factor model provides a good fit for the data.

A number of studies have been completed to evaluate the validity of the scale and model. The subscales correlate quite substantially with existing criterion measures of the attributes involved. Self-ratings were strongly correlated with peer ratings. Ratings of oneself and one's spouse yield a meaningful pattern of relationships with marital satisfaction and with measures of marital conflict. Frequency of use of various coping strategies is differentially related to initiation and enhancement skills. In addition, both components are highly correlated with appraisal, coping activities, and emotional outcomes for subjects placed in a controlled, stressful, interpersonal situation with the pattern of correlates differentially predicting components of the coping process. Thus, data collected so far strongly support the two-component model and the value of relational competence for examining interpersonal functioning and coping processes.

Applications to the Elderly

With emerging evidence that a two-component model of relational competence is useful for understanding relational functioning and coping in a general population, we speculate briefly on how the model might be useful for thinking about the special relational situations of older adults. First, it is likely that some of the relational difficulties that the elderly encounter require different skills. For example, taking advantage of available community resources probably requires initiation skills but has little to do with enhancement skills. In contrast, those with enhancement skills might provide greater payoffs to caregivers, minimizing caregiver burnout.

Relational skills might also differentially predict success at various phases of the relationship process. For example, initiation skills might predict short-term recovery from widowhood in that alternative relationships are more readily begun or were more likely to have already existed. Enhancement skills, in contrast, may be a better predictor of long-term adjustment by helping people to reestablish the intimacy and closeness that was lost with the spouse's death.

Finally, as research progresses on the processes involved in social support, we are likely to clarify how particular types of support networks best serve particular functions. We might then anticipate that differences in social competencies would enhance the development of those different types of support networks. Thus an assessment of a given older adult could help to determine that individual's ability to initiate and enhance support relationships that best match his or her support needs.

A wide range of practical applications for the model and measurement strategy are also evident in the research discussed earlier in this chapter. For example, at a number of points in the later years, major health events (e.g., lengthy hospitalization, heart attack, disabling injury, or onset of diabetes) or life events (e.g., bereavement or children moving to another region of the country) may require that a decision be made regarding new living arrangements or required levels of care. In such cases, a hospital discharge planner, physician, or family member often attempts to assess the caregiving support network to which an older adult must turn, with respect to the network's availability, stability, diversity, and adaptability. If the informal caregiving network is insufficient, this usually affects decisions regarding level of placement, that is, whether to also consider visiting caregiver services, more formal congregate living, or institutional arrangements (Kane & Kane, 1981).

Such an analysis, however, addresses only one side of the equation in predicting an older person's well-being within a given network. We believe that it is also critical to consider individual differences in the ability of older adults to work with available support systems, to improve and solidify their functioning, thus deferring the need for higher level interventions or placements. An assessment of the profiles of one's relational competencies in this context could provide important insights into this potential.

CONCLUSION

We have shown that many of the demands and stressors associated with aging are interpersonal. Moreover, the relationships on which support depends cannot be taken for granted. Stressful life events tend to cluster in old age, and illness and disability become more chronic in nature, requiring commitments from caregivers that are progressive and long-term. The needs of elderly people often may be stereotyped and discounted, and support relationships are built on personal relationships that can themselves become problematic.

Families often fail to organize their support resources into shared-function, effectively integrated networks, instead leaving primary responsibility to a single individual, who may not have volunteered, and who may experience considerable burden in the enterprise. Even planned, supportive environments such as congregate senior housing may be vulnerable to unintended social barriers to supportive interaction when the "costs" of nonreciprocal support relationships with frail elderly are viewed as prohibitive.

However, we have come to believe that relational competence can be an important factor in mediating such difficulties, permitting some individuals to more effectively interact with those who can provide support or coping resources. Relational competence, however, would appear to embody a complex weave of personal qualities, dispositions, and skills. Thus we have found it useful to conceptualize it in terms of one's ability to positively construe, construct, access, and maintain relationships. The more precise two-component model and measurement strategy should now permit us to begin to systematically assess the utility of the construct overall among older adults, and to discover those of its elements that have greatest relevance across differing situations.

REFERENCES

Adelman, R. D., Greene, M. G., & Charon, R. (1987). The physician-elderly patient-companion triad in the medical encounter: The development of a conceptual framework and research agenda. *The Gerontologist, 27,* 729–734.

Barta Kvitek, S. D., Shaver, B. J., Blood, H., & Shepard, K. F. (1986). Age bias: Physical therapists and older patients. *Journal of Gerontology, 41,* 706–709.

Barusch, A. S. (1988). Problems and coping strategies of elderly spouse caregivers. *The Gerontologist, 28,* 677–685.

Brody, E. M. (1985). Parent care as a normative family stress. *The Gerontologist, 25,* 19–29.

Cantor, M. H. (1983). Strain among caregivers: A study of experience in the United States. *The Gerontologist, 23,* 597–604.

Carp, F. M. (1985). Relevance of personality traits to adjustment in group living situations. *Journal of Gerontology, 40,* 544–551.

Carpenter, B. N. (1987, August). *Development, structure, and concurrent validity of the Relational Competence Scale.* Paper presented at the meeting of the American Psychological Association, Washington, DC.

Carpenter, B. N. (1989). *Relational competence: Conceptualization and measurement.* Unpublished manuscript, The University of Tulsa, OK.

Carpenter, B. N., Hansson, R. O., Rountree, R., & Jones, W. H. (1983). Relational competence and adjustment in diabetic patients. *Journal of Social and Clinical Psychology, 1,* 359–369.

George, L. K., & Gwyther, L. P. (1986). Caregiver well-being: A multidimensional examination of family caregivers and demented adults. *The Geron-tologist, 2,* 253–259.

Greene, M. G., Hoffman, S., Charon, R., & Adelman, R. (1987). Psychoso-cial concerns in the medical encounter: A comparison of the interactions of doctors with their old and young patients. *The Gerontologist, 27,* 164–168.

Haley, W. E., Levine, E. G., Brown, S. L., & Bartolucci, A. A. (1987). Stress, appraisal, coping, and social support as predictors of adaptational outcome among dementia caregivers. *Psychology and Aging, 2,* 323–330.

Hansson, R. O. (1986). Relational competence, relationships, and adjustment in old age. *Journal of Personality and Social Psychology, 50,* 1050–1058.

Hansson, R. O., Briggs, S. R., & Rule, B. (in press). Old age and unemploy-ment: Predictors of perceived control, depression, and loneliness. *Journal of Applied Gerontology.*

Hansson, R. O., & Carpenter, B. N. (1986). Coping with fear of crime among the elderly. *Clinical Gerontologist, 4,* 38–39.

Hansson, R. O., Jones, W. H., & Carpenter, B. N. (1984). Relational compe-tence and social support. In P. Shaver (Ed.), *Review of personality and social psychology* (Vol. 5, pp. 265–284). Beverly Hills: Sage.

Hansson, R. O., Jones, W. H., Carpenter, B. N., & Remondet, J. H. (1986–1987). Loneliness and adjustment to old age. *International Journal of Ag-ing and Human Development, 24,* 41–53.

Hansson, R. O., Nelson, R. E., Carver, M. D., NeeSmith, D. H., & Dowling, E. M. (1988, July). *Adult children with frail elderly parents: When to intervene?* Paper presented at the Fourth International Conference on Per-sonal Relationships, Vancouver, Canada.

Hansson, R. O., & Remondet, J. H. (1988). Old age and widowhood: Issues of personal control and independence. *Journal of Social Issues, 44,* 159–174.

Hansson, R. O., Remondet, J. H., Obrochta, D., & Bell, L. (1988). The dissatisfied medical patient: Predictors of intent to change doctors. *Medical Times, 116,* 97–101.

Hansson, R. O., Stroebe, M. S., & Stroebe, W. (1988). Bereavement and widowhood. *Journal of Social Issues, 44*(3).

Hobfoll, S. E. (1985). Personal and social resources and the ecology of stress resistance. In P. Shaver (Ed.), *Review of personality and social psychology* (Vol. 6, pp. 265–290). Beverly Hills: Sage.

Hobfoll, S. E. (1988). *The ecology of stress.* Washington, DC: Hemisphere.

Horowitz, L. M., & Vitkus, J. (1986). The interpersonal basis of psychiatric symptoms. *Clinical Psychology Review, 6,* 443–469.

Johnson, C. L. (1983). Dyadic family relations and social support. *The Geron-tologist, 23,* 377–383.

Johnson, C. J., & Catalano, D. J. (1983). A longitudinal study of family sup-ports to impaired elderly. *The Gerontologist, 23,* 612–618.

Jones, W. H., Carpenter, B. N., & Quintana, D. (1985). Personality and interpersonal predictors of loneliness in two cultures. *Journal of Personality and Social Psychology, 48,* 1503–1511.

Kane, R. A., & Kane, R. L. (1981). *Assessing the elderly.* Lexington, MA: Lexington Books.

Kosberg, J. I. (1988). Preventing elder abuse: Identification of high risk factors prior to placement decisions. *The Gerontologist, 28,* 43–50.

Lawton, M. P. (1980). *Environment and aging.* Monterey: Brooks/Cole.

Lawton, M. P., & Simon, B. B. (1968). The ecology of social relationships in housing for the elderly. *The Gerontologist, 8,* 110–115.

Lazarus, R. S., & Folkman, S. (1984). *Stress, appraisal, and coping.* New York: Springer.

Lopata, H. Z. (1988). Support systems of American urban widowhood. *Journal of Social Issues, 44,* 113–128.

Mitchell, J., & Register, J. C. (1984). An exploration of family interaction with the elderly by race, socioeconomic status and residence. *The Gerontologist, 24,* 48–54.

Morgan, T. J., Hansson, R. O., Indart, M. J., Austin, D. M., Crutcher, M., Hampton, P. W., Oppegard, K. M., & O'Daffer, V. E. (1984). Old age and environmental docility: The roles of health, support, and personality. *The Journal of Gerontology, 39,* 240–242.

National Institute on Aging. (1978). *The older woman: Continuities and discontinuities* (NIH Publication No. 80-1897). Bethesda, MD: U.S. Department of Health and Human Services.

Pillemer, K., & Finkelhor, D. (1988). The prevalence of elder abuse: A random sample survey. *The Gerontologist, 28,* 51–57.

Poulshock, S. W., & Deimling, G. T. (1984). Families caring for elders in residence: Issues in the measurement of burden. *Journal of Gerontology, 39,* 230–239.

Rook, K. S. (1984). The negative side of social interaction: Impact on psychological well-being. *Journal of Personality and Social Psychology, 46,* 1097–1108.

Rubenstein, L. Z., Josephson, K. R., Nichol-Seamons, M., & Robbins, A. S. (1986). Comprehensive health screening of well elderly adults: An analysis of a community program. *Journal of Gerontology, 41,* 342–352.

Schultz, R., Tompkins, C. A., & Rau, M. T. (1988). A longitudinal study of the psychosocial impact of stroke on primary support persons. *Psychology and Aging, 3,* 131–141.

Sheehan, N. W. (1986). Informal support among the elderly in public senior housing. *The Gerontologist, 26,* 171–175.

Stephens, M. A. P., & Bernstein, M. D. (1984). Social support and well-being among residents of planned housing. *The Gerontologist, 24,* 144–148.

Stephens, M. A. P., Kinney, J. M., Norris, V. K., & Ritchie, S. W. (1987).

Social networks as assets and liabilities in recovery from stroke by geriatric patients. *Psychology and Aging, 2,* 125–129.

Stone, R., Cafferata, G. L., & Sangl, J. (1987). Caregivers of the frail elderly: A national profile. *The Gerontologist, 27,* 616–626.

Wechsler, D. (1958). *The measurement and appraisal of adult intelligence.* Baltimore, MD: Williams & Wilkins.

Wiggins, J. S. (1982). Circumplex models of interpersonal behavior in clinical psychology. In P. C. Kendall & J. N. Butcher (Eds.), *Handbook of research methods in clinical psychology.* New York: Wiley.

Zarit, S. H., Reever, K. E., & Bach-Peterson, J. (1980). Relatives of the impaired elderly: Correlates of feelings of burden. *The Gerontologist, 20,* 649–655.

9

COPING AND SOCIAL SUPPORT IN OLDER PEOPLE'S EXPERIENCES OF CHRONIC ILLNESS

Barbara J. Felton

New York University

Chronic illness may well be the most prevalent of all of the major stressors facing the aged. Of the most devastating stressors on lists of life events (e.g., Dohrenwend, Kransoff, & Dohrenwend, 1978), widowhood happens only to those who have married and survived their spouses, and other social losses are equally dependent on other interpersonal relationships. Illness, however, can befall almost anyone, and very few older adults, in fact, escape health problems of some degree of seriousness. About 85% of people over 65 in the United States have at least one chronic health condition (Shanas & Maddox, 1985), and almost 46% of people aged 65 and over in the United States report having some kind of activity limitation (U. S. Department of Health, Education and Welfare, 1976). These figures suggest that chronic illnesses are quite common among the aged and that most of them have tangible, negative consequences in people's everyday lives. If we think of illness as a stressor that strikes people (for many purposes, a wholly reasonable way to think of the process of illness onset), then it is useful to ask what kinds of individual coping efforts and interpersonal support processes shape people's experiences of chronic illness. Knowing what kinds of responses to illness and disability are successful in fending off the pessimism, psychologically based inactivity, and loss of morale that frequently accompany chronic illness has great practical value.

The first task of this chapter is to identify the coping strategies, both individual and interpersonal, that enable people to deal successfully with the stresses of chronic illness. Studies of coping are presented in the first section, followed by a review of investigations of the consequences of social support in late-life illness. These reviews consider whether or not the coping and support processes that are used successfully in dealing with chronic illness are different from those that are used successfully in meeting the demands of other stressors.

The second major task of this chapter is to offer a model of social relationships that is designed to explain the coincident influences of disability and social network configuration on social relationships and resultant psychological well-being. A hierarchy of social provisions is proposed as an alternative way of understanding social support in the special conditions imposed by chronic illness and disability. This hierarchy, seen as an outgrowth of social network arrangements, should lead to better predictions of older people's psychological adjustment to the stressors of chronic illness.

CHRONIC ILLNESS AND COPING AMONG OLDER ADULTS

Studies of middle-aged and older adults' efforts to contend with illness suggest that illness prompts reactions of forbearance and the use of wishful thinking— forms of coping, overall, that can be called "meaning manipulation" or "stress management" strategies. The predominance of these forms of coping leads to the conclusion that illness tends to promote the use of particular kinds of coping strategies. Such emotion-focused coping strategies are aimed at reducing the emotional distress aroused by the stressful situation rather than altering the stressful situation itself.

Evidence for the predominance of emotion-focused coping strategies in older adults' reactions to illness has appeared in several studies of specific illnesses or medical conditions. Lambert (1985) found that avoidance and "attention deployment" were more prevalent than direct action strategies among older women with rheumatoid arthritis. Similar findings emerged in a study of cancer patients (Weisman & Worden, 1976); these researchers used different techniques and a sample of both men and women spanning a wider age range. In a study of four different chronic illnesses (Felton, Revenson, & Hinrichsen, 1984) a few illness-to-illness differences were found in the use of coping strategies but most middle-aged and older adults met the stresses of illness with a cognitive stance aimed at minimizing the threat of illness, a cognitive stance aimed at looking on the bright side, or wish-fulfilling fantasy. Conway (1985–1986) found both action-oriented and cognitive-oriented strategies among older women's responses to medical problems. It seems, overall, however, that people with chronic illness are especially likely to use the emotion-focused strategies of attention deployment or avoidance, and strategies that redefine the meaning of the illness into a more tolerable condition.

Based on these findings, one can fruitfully ask how distinctive chronic illness is among stressors in prompting the use of these coping strategies. In theory, coping reactions are specific to the nature of the stressor (Lazarus &

Folkman, 1984). In fact, commonsensical views of illness as an uncontrollable and undesirable condition fit well with its observed tendency to produce the noninstrumental coping reactions just described. Pearlin and Schooler (1978) found that stressors in life domains that were minimally changeable through the efforts of an individual prompted more meaning manipulation and stress management strategies than did stressors in more tractable life domains. Folkman and Lazarus (1980) found that, among stressors named by middle-aged adults, health problems prompted more emotion-focused coping than did stressors in life domains such as work and family. Quayhagen and Quayhagen (1982) compared the coping strategies used by middle-aged and older adults contending with serious interpersonal conflict with information on the coping strategies of chronically ill adults (Felton et al., 1984). They concluded that conflict prompted much greater use of problem solving and existential growth than did chronic illness. Furthermore, minimization of threat was the least used strategy in contending with interpersonal conflict and the most frequently used strategy among adults with chronic illness.

In contrast to physical illness, other diverse life stressors (Aldwin & Revenson, 1987; Billings & Moos, 1984; Foster & Gallagher, 1986) such as marital problems (Menaghan, 1982), and interpersonally based life transitions (Chiriboga, 1984) typically do not lead to coping reactions so thoroughly dominated by emotion-focused coping. Comparisons among investigations of coping strategies elicited by various stressors are difficult to make, especially when different types of coping strategies measured differently among different samples are used. Such comparisons are further complicated in that life stressors are not randomly distributed, and people's likelihood of experiencing one or another stressor (or particular combinations of stressors) is almost certainly related to factors that are also related to coping. However, consistent with the view that threatening stressors provoke more palliative coping than do challenging stressors (Irion & Blanchard-Fields, 1987; McCrae, 1982, 1984), it is reasonable to conclude that emotion-focused coping is a more characteristic response to illness than to some other life stressors.

Given the evidence that coping reactions are fairly specific to the nature of the stressor, we might expect reasonable variation in the ways in which people cope with different kinds of illnesses. Medical diagnoses can vary quite dramatically in the types of demands they make on the people who experience them. Life-threatening illnesses, for example, would seem to prompt different coping strategies than those prompted by more benign illnesses. Illness with complicated treatment regimens might well be expected to elicit coping approaches that are different from those elicited by easily treated or virtually untreatable illnesses. The evidence available, however, shows a tendency toward uniformity across diagnoses in people's reactions to illnesses (Cassileth et al., 1984; Pearlman & Uhlmann, 1988).

In one investigation, coping proved to be remarkably similar across a group of illnesses that were selected to represent a wide continuum of controllability (Felton et al., 1984). Even more important, the psychological consequences of emotion-focused and problem-focused coping did not differ across illnesses in that study. More specifically, information-seeking was beneficial and wish-fulfilling fantasy was deleterious to emotional well-being regardless of illness controllability (Felton & Revenson, 1984). The demand characteristics of illness seem surprisingly uniform, regardless of the severity, life threat, and medical treatment demands that characterize the illnesses of late life.

The onset of chronic illness appears to be met differently by younger and older adults. Although the range of coping strategies showing age differences is generally small (McCrae, 1982), studies of reactions to illness have shown older patients to be less active in seeking detailed information about their conditions (Cassileth, Zupkis, Sutton-Smith, & March, 1980), more accepting or resigned, less anxious (Westbrook & Winey, 1983), and less likely to pursue active behavioral coping (Keyes, Bisno, Richardson, & Marston, 1987), and interactions between age and stress have been found to be significant in explaining coping (Felton & Revenson, 1987). Thus it is possible that older age potentiates the effects of illness and perceptions of illness (Levkoff, Cleary, & Wetle, 1987), by eroding the optimistic or resigned stance that has proven valuable for emotional well-being.

What do we know about the emotional and psychological consequences of people's strategies of coping with illness, beyond the inferences drawn from the research just reviewed? Investigations of the effects on emotional well-being of different strategies for coping with illness suggest that cognitive coping strategies (especially those consisting of optimistic comparisons and other active cognitive efforts to construe the illness as meaningful or manageable) seem to be particularly beneficial. Using positive affect, negative affect, self-esteem, and a measure of acceptance of illness as criterion variables, my colleagues and I (Felton et al., 1984) found that two distinct patterns in the relationship between adjustment and coping among chronically ill adults. Emotion-based coping, including wish-fulfilling fantasy, emotional expression, and self-blame, was related to poorer adjustment and unrelated to positive affect. Two cognitive strategies, information seeking and cognitive restructuring, in contrast, were related to positive affect but not to the other criterion variables. This distinction between the beneficial impact of cognitive strategies and the deleterious effect of emotional strategies was confirmed in a longitudinal evaluation. Over a seven-month period, information-seeking reduced negative affect whereas wish-fulfilling fantasy reduced adults' acceptance of their own illness (Felton & Revenson, 1984). These findings echo cross-sectional descriptions of the negative effects of emotional forms of coping on older women's adjustment to arthritis (Lambert, 1985; Revenson & Felton, 1989).

Cognitive coping strategies were related to life satisfaction among women in a community-based sample studied by Lohr, Essex, and Klein (1988). Cross-sectional analyses showed that cognitive coping strategies mediated the impact of objective measures of health on subjective health assessments, making them relatively more positive. Positive cognitive strategies (similar to those evaluated by Felton et al., 1984) increased life satisfaction among women who had the most severe physical conditions and greatest functional impairment. Passive cognitive coping, including avoidance and resignation, decreased life satisfaction for women with the most positive subjective health assessments but, interestingly, increased life satisfaction for women who subjectively assessed their health as poor.

Similar kinds of cognitive coping strategies have proven beneficial to some forms of mental health in studies of other age groups and other stressors (e.g., Aldwin & Revenson, 1987; Billings & Moos, 1984). Cognitive appraisal strategies seem to be most valuable in meeting stressors that are not subject to an individual's control, as is the case in chronic illness or other life domains such as occupation and household finance (Pearlin & Schooler, 1978). When impairment is great, even cognitive strategies cross-sectionally associated with poor adjustment (e.g., Felton et al., 1985; Lambert, 1985) can prove beneficial (Lohr et al., 1988). For many older adults, however, the onset of illness forces them to focus inward, toward the emotions aroused by illness. For many, this marks the beginning of a vicious cycle of inward focus, poor emotional adjustment, and greater reliance on emotion-focused coping.

In all of this research, the amounts of variance accounted for in all outcome measures have been quite small, often explaining less than 5% of dependent variable variance. Self-report data may be largely to blame because much of what occurs as coping probably goes unrecognized by respondents because of its familiarity. Older people and middle-aged people rehearse their reactions to illness for many years (Leventhal, 1984), since illness is the prototypically dreaded condition of old age. Reliance on dependent variables describing overall well-being may also be too limiting. People's evaluations of their overall well-being are the end products of many complex processes in many arenas of life (Andrews & Withey, 1976). Insight into the process of coping might be better gained by examining concrete behaviors people undertake in reaction to illness. In the following section I propose, in effect, that the kinds of changes people make in their social worlds may enlighten our understanding of how people cope with the stresses of illness.

SOCIAL RELATIONSHIPS AND OLDER ADULTS' ADJUSTMENT TO CHRONIC ILLNESS

The seeking of social support has been conceptualized by many as a coping strategy, that is, as an action undertaken by an individual in an effort to resolve a problematic situation or alleviate the emotional distress aroused by that situation. The stress-buffering hypothesis of social support parallels the coping theory prediction that coping is differentially effective depending on the types and level of stress. This hypothesis suggests that stressors will have their most deleterious impact on people who lack social supports. The stress-buffering view encompasses social supports that arise through individual requests for help (like the coping strategy of "social support seeking") as well as those that arise through others' spontaneous offers of help, or through some other more interactive process. In either case, the explanation of the effects of social support lies in the interaction between stress and social support.

The quality of social support available to ill older adults seems to make a difference in their emotional adjustment to illness. The amount of impact, however, seems to be small and fairly specific to the types of stress associated with illness, and findings have not been consistent. Snow and Crapo (1982) found that morale among elderly medical patients could be explained by emotional bondedness, a measure of closeness somewhat akin to intimacy. In another study researchers (Revenson, Wollman, & Felton, 1983) studied middle-aged and older cancer patients' reports of emotional support and found, unexpectedly, that the effects of social support were either nonexistent or deleterious to individuals' emotional well-being. The negative consequences of emotional support did not emerge among the minimally disabled but were pronounced among the most severely disabled. Somewhat more compatible with stress-buffering predictions, emotional support had negative consequences among those who were not undergoing chemotherapy or radiotherapy at the time, but had no ill effects among those in active treatment. These findings suggest the importance of qualitative features of the stressful context in determining the consequences of social support.

Arling (1987) found limited evidence for stress-buffering in his study of the impact of health problems, activities of daily living impairment, and economic deprivation on psychosomatic symptoms and emotional distress among a state-wide sample of noninstitutionalized older people. An assistance measure of social support (but not measures of the size of social network or amount of social contact) interacted with impairment in activities of daily living to explain psychosomatic symptoms. Stephens, Kinney, Norris, and Ritchie's (1987) study of older adults' recovery from stroke documented the importance of distinguishing between positive and negative social interactions. Negative interactions, not positive ones, proved to be significant predictors of morale and psychiatric symptoms, although positive interactions were significant in predicting cognitive functioning.

Working from the proposition that the effects of social support are dependent on both the type and severity of stressor faced (Krause, 1987) and from the literature available, it seems reasonable to suggest that it is the provision of emotional support and instrumental aid that are most critical in older adults' adjustment to illness. Maintaining emotionally gratifying social relationships seems to be an adjustment demand with particular relevance to the stresses of illness (Wortman, 1984; Wortman & Dunkel-Schetter, 1979), and the studies cited testify to the importance of emotional support to chronically ill older adults.

The importance of emotional social support in psychological adjustment is not, of course, exclusive to illness (e.g., House & Kahn, 1985). All studies that show emotional well-being to be related to the availability of confidants (e.g., Lowenthal & Haven, 1968) and to participation in satisfying social relationships (e.g., Liang, Dvorkin, Kahana, & Mazian, 1980) point to the importance of emotional support in these relationships. House and Kahn (1985), in fact, have argued that emotional support is the common denominator in measures of social support shown to be effective in predicting adjustment. Although there seem to be stressors in which emotional support plays no role in older adults' psychological adjustment (e.g., Krause, 1987), illness does not seem to be one of them.

The importance of instrumental aid for older people's psychological adjustment to illness is less well documented. For the most part, the conclusion that instrumental aid has psychological benefits for the ill is an inference from correlations between health status and social network features. Cross-sectional analyses of the social networks of older adults living in the community reveal that higher levels of disability are associated with the use of more help from family members (Branch & Jette, 1983; Stoller & Earl, 1983; see Chatters, Taylor, & Jackson, 1985, for different findings). Recently, longitudinal data have shown that older adults' moves into the households of others tend to be prompted by declines in health rather than vice versa (Magaziner, Cadigan, Hebel, & Parry, 1988), supporting the view that illness onset causes notable changes in social networks.

Our knowledge of the consequences of receiving instrumental aid for assistance with illness is limited. We know that having kin, especially a spouse or children, prevents or forestalls institutionalization (Tobin & Kulys, 1981), but we know less about the emotional meaning of receiving aid from these people. Arling's (1987) data provide direct evidence of the emotional benefits of assistance to the functionally impaired elderly. Furthermore, Johnson and Catalano's (1983) study of family contact following hospital discharge showed that declines in morale were associated with decreasing family contact, although the provision of assistance per se was not assessed.

We might expect the psychological benefits of assistance to be limited, because kin are the most likely providers of help (Cantor, 1979; Kivett, 1985; Shanas, 1979), and relationships with family have been shown to contribute less to, or detract from, psychological morale compared to nonkin relationships (e.g., Seccombe, 1987). Most studies showing kin relationships to have less psychological benefit, however, have been cross-sectional and thus incapable of allowing for the possibility that high levels of contact with family are the consequence of ill health, a well-known cause of decreased well-being. Family and friends often play very different roles in the lives of older people, evidenced recently in data by Larson, Mannell, and Zuzanek (1986) demonstrating major differences in the kinds of activities that older adults engage in with family and friends. Differences in the emotional consequences of the different types of activities may at least partly account for the divergence in the emotional meaning of relationships with friends and family. The possibility that family relations offset the negative emotional consequences of illness but do not increase positive mood states is a proposition that remains untested.

How much change occurs in older adults' social relationships as a consequence of illness and disability is largely unknown. We have no prospective data on the quality of social relations before and after illness onset. In addition, little longitudinal data on amounts of contact, size of network, and network composition are available to determine the role that illness plays in social relationships (cf. Berkman, 1985).

Longitudinal analyses of social relations in adulthood (Palmore, 1981) have documented the robustness of family relations. Other longitudinal data have shown continuity in social relations to be quite pronounced in older adults' relationships with their children even when social support beyond the family was characterized by considerably more change (Field & Minkler, 1988). The role of health and illness in these studies, as well as in other longitudinal analyses of older adults' social relations (e.g., Adams, 1987), is largely unstudied. However, Johnson and Catalano (1983) showed that the frequency of family contact declined over an eight-month period following elderly patients' discharge from a hospital; contact with friends remained the same, but at a lower level than family's.

Learning about the shifts in social relations occasioned by illness and the psychological consequences of those shifts, can improve our understanding of coping processes in adjustment to illness as well as be valuable in illuminating important social dynamics in late life. Another important issue is understanding the content of social exchanges, or what resources are provided in social relationships. The next section offers a perspective on these social provisions and how they may be influenced by chronic illness and disability.

A HIERARCHY OF SOCIAL PROVISIONS APPROACH

One of the most frequently made proposals for improving our understanding of the impact of social support is the recommendation that we redefine, or further refine, distinctions among the types of social support offered and received (House & Kahn, 1985; Wortman & Conway, 1985). Specific types of social support can be quite different in their consequences, and distinctions among informational, tangible, and emotional support, among others, have proved useful in predicting different aspects of psychological well-being (e.g., Baldassare, Rosenfield, & Rook, 1984). Such distinctions are appealing in their utility for designing social network interventions (Gottlieb, 1985) and are valuable in helping us specify the mechanisms through which support works (Umberson, 1987).

Attending to the content of social support seems well advised. The notion of support itself, however, may be too narrow and may place too severe a limitation on our view of the process through which people adjust to stress (Morgan, 1988). For example, measures of social support that directly ask respondents about the "help", "assistance", or "support" they receive, are especially limiting as they exclude relationships that are not recognized by respondents as helpful even though those relationships may well contribute to some aspect of a person's emotional or physical well-being. Many characteristics of the larger social environment affect us without being recognized (Shinn, in press). Many of the kinds of social relationships that epidemiological data indicate are related to longevity and morbidity (e.g., Berkman, 1984, 1985; Blazer, 1982), consist of social relationships with organized groups and other forms of social participation that respondents would not necessarily perceive as supportive.

One approach to widening the range of thinking about social support and possibly of improving our understanding of the particular processes set into motion by chronic illness, is to focus on the content of social relationships, regardless of their ostensible support. Weiss (1974) outlined six provisions that social relationships potentially make and suggested that social relationships are important to us because they provide us with the essential offerings of these provisions. People have adequate social resources, in Weiss's (1974) view, regardless of the number of people with whom they interact or can claim as network members, to the extent that each of these six social provisions is made by the people who are part of their networks.

In striving to understand the role of social relationships in older adults' adjustment to illness, it may be useful to think of social provisions, including but not limited to Weiss's list, as forming a sort of hierarchy. This hierarchy reflects the relative difficulty in maintaining different social provisions, and in this regard is similar to notions of social competence (see Chapter 6, this volume). Higher-order provisions are more difficult to maintain. For example, the task of providing nurturance to others, one of Weiss's proposed provisions, is a relatively complex task, requiring the emotional capacity for empathy, knowledge of the other person, and skills in caregiving, among other things. Attachment, in contrast, is a social provision that requires relatively less skill and knowledge; according to many, attachment arises almost biologically (Bowlby, 1969; Weiss, 1975) and persists quite readily. Being the recipient of aid, yet another kind of social provision, may be least taxing. Although there are costs to receiving aid (Fisher, Nadler, & Whitcher-Alagna, 1982), the efforts and skills needed to maintain a relationship based on the receipt of instrumental aid are minimal.

This hierarchy also reflects the degree to which one's social relationships deal with concerns, events, and issues beyond the self or the dyad directly involved in an interaction. As such, higher-order provisions are those whose exchanges include events and issues in the world beyond the pair of people involved and thus move the participants, at least psychologically, into a world beyond their own (Larsen et al., 1986). Middle-level social provisions are those whose content involves the smaller world consisting of the pair of people interacting. Exchanges at this level of the hierarchy are about the needs of the pair of actors and about their relationship to each other. Thus, companionship, social integration, and attachment are characteristic provisions in this middle level. Lowest-level social provisions are those in which the exchanges center on a single recipient of aid; social exchanges at this level tend to be unilateral and to focus on the needs and well-being of the receiving member of the dyad.

Although ordering social provisions along this hierarchy is a speculative undertaking at this point, some data on older adults' receipt of social provisions is available to assist hypothesizing. Cutrona, Russell, and Rose (1986) found the provisions of reassurance of worth and opportunity for nurturance to improve older adults' physical health over a six-month period, a finding that suggests placing these provisions at the highest level of the hierarchy. The health-promoting quality of these provisions presumably derives from the demands they make on people's energies and the resultant exercise of psychological and physical abilities.

Guidance and reliable alliance seemed to serve a largely compensatory role in Cutrona et al.'s (1986) findings. These two provisions proved effective in reducing symptoms of psychological distress among those most severely stressed but had little effect on those under less stress. Because guidance and reliable alliance involve explicit helping and function in a compensatory fashion, we could assume target individuals' involvements to be relatively passive. These two provisions would thus understandably occupy lowest ranks on the hierarchy.

Any relationship between two people might include exchanges at all three levels of social provision, with higher-level provisions more likely to coexist with lower-level positions than vice versa. Levels of social provision may vary over time, as the foundations for relationships shift and the demands on the relationship alter. The hierarchy can describe, overall, the various levels at which people operate in social relationships and the range of provisions available to any individual.

Illness, ultimately, taxes the individual's capacities and, for longer or shorter periods of time, saps the individual's attentions and efforts. Pennebacker (1982) proposed that the symptoms an individual experiences depend on the ratio of internal to external stimuli. In a similar fashion, it seems that when internal stimuli, namely physical symptoms and the worry, anxiety, and anger that can accompany them predominate, one may attend less to external stimuli and thus learn less about others, less often practice empathy, let one's mind turn to outside interests and concerns less frequently, and thus effectively limit the scope of possible social relationship forms. Illness can force a kind of egocentrism upon people. For example, physical disability (requiring that people use much of their energy to plan and execute the tasks of daily living) can place a cap on the breadth of concerns they can encompass, and this will be reflected in their social relationships. Thus, in the view proposed here, higher-order social provisions would be retained by those with emotional, physical, and psychic capacity to retain them. These particular provisions would be too luxurious for those whose attentions and efforts would be forced, by illness or disability, to be devoted to more everyday concerns. Lower-level social provisions, however, would be rather easily obtained even by those with limited physical capacity.

Although increasing disability is assumed to erode the level of social provisions characteristic of the individual's social relationships, disability's impact depends on several features of the individual's social network (see Figure 1). People with specialized, or "uniplex" social relationships (Fischer, 1982), for example, are more likely to have social relationships making higher-level provisions. But multiplex social networks may be better able to resist erosion by illness. If the people in one's social network who provide attachment and reliable alliance are the same people who provide reassurance of worth, receiving more help from these people may not atrophy one's sense of worth as quickly or as severely as in the case when the former provisions are made by others. The increasing commitment felt toward children in old age (Field & Minkler, 1988) may well reflect the increasing multiplexity of social networks based on an efficiency that illness prompts in the use of social relationships; more provisions must be packed into fewer interactions or relationships.

Consideration of the psychological consequences of the range of social provisions that an individual receives must include both positive affect (or psychological well-being) and negative affect (or psychological distress), because social provisions differ in their impact on these outcome variables. Positive affect, we have reason to believe, is boosted by relationships that move the individual beyond his or her own world. As an illustration, Bradburn (1969) found social roles to be the major predictor of positive, not negative, affect. Differences in the emotional consequences of contact with friends and with family (e.g., Larson et al., 1986; Seccombe, 1987), along with Weiss's (1974) notions about the likely providers of each social provision, suggest that higher-order provisions are both more likely to be made by friends than family and more likely to boost positive affect than to suppress negative affect. Family relationships, however, are likely to occupy lower levels on the hierarchy than are nonkin relationships, and family relationships are more likely than nonkin relationships to counter negative affect than to boost positive affect (Lawton, 1983).

Some tentative hypotheses linking disability and social network characteristics with the social provisions hierarchy and emotional well-being follow:

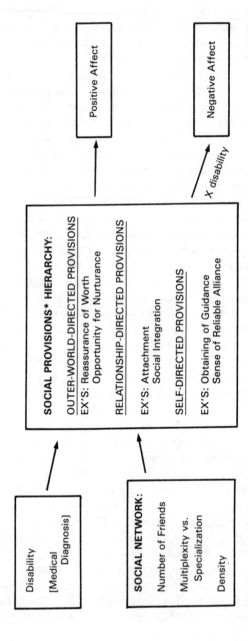

FIGURE 1 A model describing the impact of disability and social network characteristics on the older adult's receipt of social provisions, and the impact of receiving those social provisions on emotional well-being. *Note.* The social provisions named as examples are those identified by Weiss (1974); the list, in fact, need not be limited to these provisions.

1. Disability will tend to limit the range of provisions received and lower the level at which one's social relationships are transacted. The content of social exchanges will become increasingly focused on the self and will involve fewer events, concerns, and issues stemming from the larger world.
2. Social networks with larger numbers of friends (i.e., nonkin) are more likely to include exchanges at high levels in the hierarchy of social provisions. Friendships, almost of necessity, involve some content beyond the mere fact of association (e.g., a shared occupation, a common social position, a mutually enjoyed activity), and thus they readily involve worlds beyond the individual or the relationship itself. Kin-based networks, in contrast, are likely to prevail where the range of social provisions is limited to the lower levels of the hierarchy.
3. Specialized social networks are more likely to include exchanges at high levels of the social provisions hierarchy than are multiplex social networks. Social relationships at different levels tend to develop in different social circumstances. High specialization of function, accordingly, will tend to reflect a greater range of social involvements, including those extending beyond individually based concerns.
4. Under conditions of high disability, multiplex rather than specialized networks will ensure maintenance of higher-level social provisions. Reliance on social relationships that encompass many different functions may permit a higher level of social provisions to be maintained when illness forces a reduction in the number of social relationships than when the division of labor across one's social network members is more specialized.
5. Dense social networks, or those in which most members know each other, will tend to occupy the middle level of the social provisions hierarchy, because mutual knowledge may tend to promote a focus on the commonly held relationships themselves.
6. Positive affect will result from the higher-order social provisions. It is the individual's psychological removal to different worlds and the condition of being pressed somewhat beyond one's level of adaptation (Lawton, 1977) that contributes to positive affect.
7. Under conditions of high disability, middle-level provisions will boost positive affect as well. The foundations of self-esteem will change with increasing disability. With standards for one's self-esteem lowered by expectations of continuing disability, participation in middle-level relationships will be the occasion for increased positive affect.
8. The reduction of negative affect will result from having lower-level social provisions, particularly under conditions of high disability. The inward focus forced upon ill adults by disability will threaten emotional well-being, but receiving assistance can offset potentially damaging negative affect. Those social provisions capable of countering the negative consequences of stressors seem to be those that are unilaterally offered rather than fully

dyadic. Such relationships can be sustained with little active effort on the part of the individual.

Although coping is not directly measured in this model, we can assume that the forms of social relationships that emerge reflect, in part, coping efforts made by the ill individual. In the face of chronic illness, older people almost certainly put some amount of coping effort into rethinking and rearranging the social relationships that will be altered if a state of dependency ensues. Direct action aimed at changing the illness itself may be futile, but direct action aimed at arranging a physical and social location for getting one's needs met if impaired, is a coping strategy probably used with some regularity by older adults. Regardless of what practical or physical changes they might make, ill older adults almost certainly renegotiate the terms of their relationships with others when their capacities change. The cognitive stance that emerges from the ill adult's appraisal-focused coping efforts will almost certainly shape the content of one's social relationships.

Greater knowledge of the dynamics that alter older adults' social networks (e.g., Field & Minkler, 1988) and of the forces that shape social networks early in adulthood (e.g., Perl & Trickett, 1988) may help us further articulate the links among social network, social provisions, and illness. In any event, this hierarchical view offers a means of understanding the content of social relationships and the changes imposed by illness. This model offers a stress-specific conception of social support and of coping and, to the extent that specificity increases our comprehension, ought to improve our predictions of psychological adjustment among the chronically ill elderly.

REFERENCES

Adams, R. G. (1987). Patterns of network change: A longitudinal study of friendships of elderly women. *The Gerontologist, 27*, 222–227.

Aldwin, C. A., & Revenson, T. A. (1987). Does coping help? A reexamination of the relation between coping and mental health. *Journal of Personality and Social Psychology, 53*, 337–348.

Andrews, F. M., & Withey, S. B. (1976). *Social indicators of well-being.* New York: Plenum Press.

Arling, G. (1987). Strain, social support, and distress in old age. *Journal of Gerontology, 42*, 107–113.

Baldassare, M., Rosenfield, S., & Rook, K. (1984). The types of social relations predicting elderly well-being. *Research on Aging, 6*, 549–559.

Berkman, L. F. (1984). Assessing the physical health effects of social networks and social support. *Annual Review of Public Health, 5*, 413–432.

Berkman, L. F. (1985). The relationship of social networks and social support to morbidity and mortality. In S. Cohen & S. L. Syme (Eds.), *Social support and health* (pp. 241–262). New York: Academic Press.

Billings, A. G., & Moos, R. H. (1984). Coping, stress, and social resources among adults with unipolar depression. *Journal of Personality and Social Psychology, 46,* 877–891.

Blazer, D. (1982). Social support and mortality in an elderly community population. *American Journal of Epidemiology, 165,* 684–694.

Bowlby, J. (1969). *Attachment and loss* (Vol. 1). New York: Basic Books.

Bradburn, N. (1969). *The structure of psychological well-being.* Chicago: Aldine.

Branch, L. G., & Jette, A. M. (1983). Elders' use of informal assistance. *The Gerontologist, 23,* 51–56.

Cantor, M. H. (1979). Neighbors and friends: An overlooked resource in the informal support system. *Research on Aging, 1,* 434–463.

Cassileth, B. R., Zupkis, R. V., Sutton-Smith, K., & March, V. (1980). Information and participation preferences among cancer patients. *Annals of Internal Medicine, 92,* 832–836.

Cassileth, B. R., Lusk, E. J., Strouse, T. B., Miller, D. S., Brown, L. L., Cross, P. A., & Tenaglia, A. N. (1984). Psychosocial status in chronic illness: A comparative analysis of six diagnostic groups. *New England Journal of Medicine, 311,* 506–511.

Chatters, L. M., Taylor, R. J., & Jackson, J. S. (1985). Size and composition of the informal helper networks of elderly blacks. *Journal of Gerontology, 40,* 605–614.

Chiriboga, D. A. (1984). Social stressors as antecedents of change. *Journal of Gerontology, 39,* 468–477.

Conway, K. (1985–1986). Coping with the stress of medical problems among black and white elderly. *International Journal of Aging and Human Development, 21,* 39–48.

Cutrona, C., Russell, D., & Rose, J. (1986). Social support and adaptation to stress by the elderly. *Psychology and Aging, 1,* 47–54.

Dohrenwend, B. S., Kransoff, L., Askenasy, A. R., & Dohrenwend, B. P. (1978). Exemplification of a method for scaling life events: The PERI life events scale. *Journal of Health and Social Behavior, 19,* 205–229.

Felton, B. J., & Revenson, T. A. (1984). Coping with chronic illness: A study of illness controllability and the influence of coping strategies on psychological adjustment. *Journal of Consulting and Clinical Psychology, 52,* 343–353.

Felton, B. J., & Revenson, T. A. (1987). Age differences in coping with chronic illness. *Psychology and Aging, 2*(2), 164–170.

Felton, B. J., Revenson, T. A., & Hinrichsen, G. A. (1984). Stress and coping in the explanation of psychological adjustment among chronically ill adults. *Social Science and Medicine, 18,* 889–898.

Field, D., & Minkler, M. (1988). Continuity and change in social support between young-old and old-old or very-old aged. *Journal of Gerontology, 43,* P100-P106.

Fischer, C. S. (1982). *To dwell among friends.* Chicago: University of Chicago Press.

Fisher, J. D., Nadler, A., & Whitcher-Alagna, S. (1982). Recipient reactions to aid. *Psychological Bulletin, 91,* 27-54.

Folkman, S., & Lazarus, R. S. (1980). An analysis of coping in a middle-aged community sample. *Journal of Health and Social Behavior, 21,* 219-139.

Folkman, S., Lazarus, R. S., Pimley, S., & Novacek, J. (1987). Age differences in stress and coping processes. *Psychology and Aging, 2*(2), 171-184.

Foster, J. M., & Gallagher, D. (1986). An exploratory study comparing depressed and nondepressed elders' coping strategies. *Journal of Gerontology, 41,* 91-93.

Gottlieb, B. H. (1985). Social support and community mental health. In S. Cohen & S. L. Syme (Eds.), *Social support and health* (pp. 306-326). New York: Academic Press.

House, J. S., & Kahn, R. L. (1985). Measures and concepts of social support. In S. Cohen & S. L. Syme (Eds.), *Social support and health* (pp. 83-108). New York: Academic Press.

Irion, J. C., & Blanchard-Fields, F. (1987). A cross-sectional comparison of adaptive coping in adulthood. *Journal of Gerontology, 41,* 502-504.

Johnson, C., & Catalano, D. (1983). A longitudinal study of family support to impaired elderly. *The Gerontologist, 23,* 612-618.

Keyes, K., Bisno, B., Richardson, J., & Marston, A. (1987). Age differences in coping, behavioral dysfunction and depression following colostomy surgery. *The Gerontologist, 27,* 182-184.

Kivett, V. R. (1985). Consanguinity and kin level: Their relative importance to the helping networks of older adults. *Journal of Gerontology, 40,* 228-234.

Krause, N. (1987). Chronic financial strain, social support, and depressive symptoms in older adults. *Psychology and Aging, 2,* 185-192.

Lambert, V. (1985). Study of factors associated with psychological well-being in rheumatoid arthritic women. *Journal of Nursing Scholarship, 17,* 50-53.

Larson, R., Mannell, R., & Zuzanek, J. (1986). Daily well-being of older adults with friends and family. *Psychology and Aging, 1,* 117-126.

Lawton, M. P. (1983). The varieties of well-being. *Experimental Aging Research, 9,* 65-72.

Lawton, M. P. (1977). The impact of the environment on aging and behavior. In J. E. Birren & K. W. Schaie (Eds.), *Handbook of the Psychology of Aging* (pp. 276-301). New York: Van Nostrand Reinhold.

Lazarus, R. S., & Folkman, S. (1984). *Stress, appraisal and coping.* New York: Springer.

Leventhal, E. A. (1984). Aging and the perception of illness. *Research on Aging, 6,* 119–135.

Levkoff, S., Cleary, P. D., & Wetle, T. (1987). Differences in the appraisal of health between aged and middle-aged adults. *Journal of Gerontology, 42,* 114–120.

Liang, J., Dvorkin, L., Kahana, E., & Mazian, F. (1980). Social integration and morale: A re-examination. *Journal of Gerontology, 35,* 746–757.

Lohr, M. J., Essex, M. J., & Klein, M. H. (1988). The relationship of coping responses to physical health status and life satisfaction among older women. *Journal of Gerontology, 43,* P54–P60.

Lowenthal, M. F., & Haven, C. (1968). Interaction and adaptation: Intimacy as a critical variable. *American Sociological Review, 33,* 20–30.

Magaziner, J., Cadigan, D. A., Hebel, J. R., & Parry, R. E. (1988). Health and living arrangements among older women: Does living alone increase the risk of illness? *Journal of Gerontology, 42,* M127–M133.

McCrae, R. R. (1982). Age differences in the use of coping mechanisms. *Journal of Gerontology, 37,* 454–460.

McCrae, R. R. (1984). Situational determinants of coping responses: Loss, threat, and challenge. *Journal of Personality and Social Psychology, 46,* 919–928.

Menaghan, E. (1982). Measuring coping effectiveness: A panel analysis of marital problems and coping efforts. *Journal of Health and Social Behavior, 23,* 220–234.

Morgan, D. L. (1988). Age differences in social network participation. *Journal of Gerontology, 43,* S129–S137.

Palmore, E. B. (1981). *Social patterns in normal aging.* Durham, NC: Duke University Press.

Pearlin, L. I., & Schooler, C. (1978). The structure of coping. *Journal of Health and Social Behavior, 19,* 2–21.

Pearlman, R. A., & Uhlmann, R. F. (1988). Quality of life in chronic diseases: Perceptions of elderly patients. *Journal of Gerontology, 43,* M25–M30.

Pennebaker, J. W. (1982). *The psychology of physical symptoms.* New York: Springer-Verlag.

Perl, H. I., & Trickett, E. J. (1988). Social network formation of college freshmen: Personal and environmental determinants. *American Journal of Community Psychology, 16,* 207–224.

Quayhagen, M. P., & Quayhagen, M. (1982). Coping with conflict: Measurement of age-related patterns. *Research on Aging, 4,* 364–377.

Revenson, T. A., & Felton, B. J. (1989). Disability and coping as predictors of psychological adjustment to rheumatoid arthritis. *Journal of Consulting and Clinical Psychology, 57,* 344–348.

Revenson, T. A., Wollman, C. A., & Felton, B. J. (1983). Social supports as stress buffers for adult cancer patients. *Psychosomatic Medicine, 45,* 321–331.

Seccombe, K. (1987). Children: Their impact on the elderly in declining health. *Research on Aging, 9,* 312–326.

Shanas, E. (1979). The family as a social support system in old age. *The Gerontologist, 19,* 169–174.

Shanas, E., & Maddox, G. L. (1985). Health, health resources and the utilization of care. In R. H. Binstock & E. Shanas (Eds.), *Handbook of aging and the social sciences* (2nd ed., pp. 696–726). New York: Van Nostrand Reinhold.

Shinn, M. (in press). Mixing and matching levels of conceptualization, measurement, and statistical analysis in community research. In P. C. Keyes, F. Shertok, & L. Jason (Eds.), *Researching community psychology: Integrating theories and methods.* Washington, DC: American Psychological Association.

Snow, R., & Crapo, L. (1982). Emotional bondedness, subjective well-being, and health in elderly medical patients. *Journal of Gerontology, 37,* 609–615.

Stephens, M. A., Kinney, J. M., Norris, V. K., & Ritchie, S. W. (1987). Social networks as assets and liabilities in recovery from stroke by geriatric patients. *Psychology and Aging, 2*(2), 125–129.

Stoller, E. P., & Earl, L. L. (1983). Help with activities of everyday life: Sources of support for the noninstitutionalized elderly. *The Gerontologist, 23,* 64–70.

Tobin, S. S., & Kulys, R. (1981). The family in the institutionalization of the elderly. *Journal of Social Issues, 37,* 145–157.

U.S. Department of Health, Education and Welfare. (1976). *Health characteristics of persons with chronic activity limitation: United States–1974* (Publication No. PHS-77-1539). Rockville, MD: National Center for Health Statistics.

Umberson, D. (1987). Family status and health behaviors: Social control as a dimension of social integration. *Journal of Health and Social Behavior, 28,* 306–319.

Weisman, A. D., & Worden, J. (1976). The existential plight in cancer: Significance of the first 100 days. *International Journal of Psychiatry in Medicine, 7,* 1–15.

Weiss, R. S. (1974). The provisions of social relationships. In Z. Rubin (Ed.), *Doing unto others* (pp. 17–26). Englewood Cliffs, NJ: Prentice-Hall.

Weiss, R. S. (1975). *Marital separation.* New York: Basic Books.

Westbrook, M. T., & Viney, L. L. (1983). Age and sex differences in patients' reactions to illness. *Journal of Health and Social Behavior, 24*(4), 313–324.

Wortman, C. (1984). Social support and the cancer patient: Conceptual and methodological issues. *Cancer, 53,* 2339–2360.

Wortman, C., & Conway, T. L. (1985). The role of social support in adaptation and recovery from physical illness. In S. Cohen & S. L. Syme (Eds.), *Social support and health* (pp. 281–302). New York: Academic Press.

Wortman, C., & Dunkel-Schetter, C. (1979). Interpersonal relationships and cancer: A theoretical analysis. *Journal of Social Issues, 35,* 120–155.

10

STRESSFUL ASPECTS OF OLDER ADULTS' SOCIAL RELATIONSHIPS: CURRENT THEORY AND RESEARCH

Karen S. Rook

University of California, Irvine

In the past two decades numerous researchers have examined the health-protective effects of social relationships, and many studies have demonstrated that supportive relationships contribute to psychological health by ameliorating the adverse effects of life stress (see reviews by Cohen & Wills, 1985; Kessler & McLeod, 1985; Vaux, 1988). Yet research has also demonstrated that attempts to provide support sometimes backfire, increasing rather than decreasing the distress of the intended support recipients (Wortman & Dunkel-Schetter, 1979; Wortman & Lehman, 1985). In addition, social scientists have long recognized that social relationships can be a source of considerable frustration as well as support (e.g., Croog, 1970; Thibaut & Kelley, 1959) and, in some cases, may contribute to serious disturbances in functioning (e.g., Jacob, 1975; Leff & Vaughn, 1981).

Despite recurring references to the negative side of social relationships, however, most researchers have continued to emphasize the positive aspects of relationships. This emphasis appears in research on older adults as well as in work on other age groups. This neglect of the negative aspects of older adults' social ties is unfortunate, particularly in light of a small but growing body of evidence that suggests that negative social exchanges have quite potent effects on older adults' emotional well-being (Fiore, Becker, & Coppel, 1983; Pagel, Erdly, & Becker, 1987; Rook, 1984; Stephens, Kinney, Norris, & Ritchie,

Preparation of this chapter was supported in part by National Institute on Aging Grant AG03975-03.

1987). For most older adults, negative encounters occur much less often than do positive encounters (Antonucci, 1985; Pagel et al., 1987; Rook, 1984; Stephens et al., 1987), but to overlook such negative encounters yields an incomplete picture of the impact of social ties on older adults' psychological health and functioning.

The purpose of this chapter is to assess our current state of knowledge regarding the negative aspects of older adults' social relationships and to suggest directions for further research. The chapter is organized in four sections. The first section provides an overview of previous empirical work on the association between negative social exchanges and older adults' psychological health. Theoretical explanations for the potent effects of negative exchanges are discussed in the second section. The third section addresses the question of which older adults are most vulnerable to negative exchanges with members of their social networks. Two aspects of vulnerability are considered—sheer exposure to negative exchanges and sensitivity (or reactivity) to such exchanges. In the final section I briefly discuss parallels between the theoretical and methodological puzzles that have challenged social support researchers and the puzzles that await researchers interested in the problematic aspects of social relationships. I also urge a balanced perspective on the dual aspects of older adults' social relationships, one that exaggerates neither the supportive nor the problematic aspects of these relationships.

Before turning to the first section, I should clarify what I mean by negative or problematic exchanges. In this chapter I emphasize actions by a member of an older person's social network that cause the older person to experience psychological distress (e.g., resentment, shame, or sadness) and at least some reservations about the relationship itself (cf. Rook, 1989). This emphasis excludes the conventional costs of social relationships that have been discussed by social exchange theorists (Homans, 1974; Thibaut & Kelley, 1959), such as the time, money, and material goods that may be required to maintain a relationship or the displacement of opportunities to engage in other kinds of activities. This emphasis also excludes actions by network members that may be irritating but that do not cause lingering distress because they can be attributed to benign motives, such as an adult child's recurring efforts to persuade an elderly parent to stop smoking for the sake of the parent's health. Instead, I wish to emphasize those actions by others that older adults specifically regard as misdeeds or transgressions and that cause emotional distress. This definition includes acts of omission (e.g., failing to repay a loan from a friend or forgetting a friend's birthday) as well as acts of commission (e.g., criticizing a friend or betraying a confidence).

Finally, I should acknowledge that a long tradition of research exists on pathogenic aspects of family relationships, emphasizing differences in the family functioning of psychiatrically impaired versus nonimpaired populations (e.g., Jacob, 1975; Leff & Vaughn, 1981). I do not discuss this work in the current chapter because my primary goal is to examine the significance of negative interpersonal encounters in the everyday lives of normal, community-residing older adults, rather than to compare psychiatrically impaired versus nonimpaired older adults.

RESEARCH ON THE STRESSFUL ASPECTS OF SOCIAL RELATIONSHIPS

Researchers have pursued two primary strategies in their efforts to understand how negative social exchanges affect psychological well-being. The more common strategy has involved explicitly contrasting the effects of positive and negative exchanges on various aspects of emotional health and functioning (Fiore et al., 1983; Pagel et al., 1987; Rook, 1984; Stephens et al., 1987). Studies that have taken this approach and that focus on the elderly are reviewed in this section. A somewhat less common strategy has involved conceptualizing these negative exchanges as stressors (Eckenrode & Gore, 1981; Shinn, Lehmann, & Wong, 1984; Chapter 6, this volume) and comparing the impact of interpersonal versus noninterpersonal stressors (Bolger, DeLongis, Kessler, & Schilling, 1989). Studies of this sort have not focused specifically on the elderly but nonetheless are discussed briefly because they illustrate a useful approach to evaluating the significance of aversive interpersonal events.

Given the current interest in factors that moderate older adults' adaptation to stressful events, another approach to gauging the effects of negative social exchanges entails contrasting the stress-alleviating effects of social support with the stress-exacerbating effects of social conflict (cf. Shinn et al., 1984). Important insights about the health-protective or health-damaging consequences of social relationships may be gained by investigating how older adults' efforts to cope with financial difficulties, relocation, or other stressors are aided versus hindered by supportive and aversive social interaction, respectively. Such research must, of course, avoid confounding the measure of life stress with measures of support and conflict (cf. Thoits, 1982; Monroe, Bromet, Connell, & Steiner, 1986). Few published studies have taken this approach, but a handful do provide indirect evidence about the effects of support and conflict in moderating adaptation to stress (e.g., Fiore et al., 1983; Pagel et al., 1987; Stephens et al., 1987).

The Relative Effects of Positive Versus Negative Exchanges

The results of three recent studies that contrasted the effects of positive and negative social exchanges on older adults' psychological functioning suggest that negative exchanges have consistently detrimental effects (Fiore et al., 1983; Pagel et al., 1987; Rook, 1984). Although the studies differed with respect to the specific populations sampled and the manner in which supportive and problematic exchanges were operationalized, the findings nonetheless converged in suggesting that the detrimental impact of negative social exchanges exceeds the beneficial impact of positive social exchanges (see Rook & Pietromonaco, 1987, for a review of similar findings from studies of other age groups, and Gottman, 1979, for a discussion of the significance of negative interaction as a determinant of marital satisfaction). The results converged further in demonstrating that positive social exchanges generally made weak contributions to the emotional health of the individuals studied.

The findings of Pagel et al. (1987) are especially persuasive because the researchers made use of a short-term longitudinal design that permitted statistical controls for respondents' initial levels of depression. Changes in the level of negative social exchanges predicted changes in depression, controlling for initial depression levels as well as for age, sex, and health status. Additional analyses indicated that respondents' initial depression status did not predict their subsequent exposure to negative social exchanges. These findings address the concern that the "negativity effect" documented in the three studies could have been a mere artifact of respondents' state of psychological adjustment. Moreover, the negativity effect did not appear merely to reflect restricted variability or lower test–retest reliability of the measures of positive interactions (Pagel et al., 1987).

The results of a study of older adults recovering from a stroke (Stephens et al., 1987) departed somewhat from the pattern just described because both positive and negative social exchanges proved to be important but for different aspects of respondents' psychological health. Controlling for respondents' status upon discharge from the hospital, negative interactions were associated with lower morale and more psychiatric symptoms, whereas positive interactions were unrelated to these two outcomes. In contrast, positive interactions were related to better cognitive functioning (e.g, fewer memory problems, less disorientation and confusion), but negative exchanges were unrelated to this index of recovery. Although these results did not demonstrate that negative social exchanges always outweigh positive exchanges in impact, they did provide further evidence of the adverse impact of negative exchanges on the emotional health of older adults, particularly those who are frail.

One methodological issue that must be considered in attempting to evaluate the results of these studies concerns the possibility of threshold effects. Social support researchers have often argued that the benefits of social support may be most apparent when individuals who have little or no support are compared with those who have at least a modest level of support (House, 1981; Kahn & Antonucci, 1980). That is, a critical threshold may exist beyond which increased levels of support contribute little to a person's psychological well-being. The same prediction could be made about the effects of negative social exchanges. Differences in emotional health between those with low versus moderate or higher levels of problematic interaction may be quite pronounced, whereas differences between those with moderate versus high levels of problematic interaction may be comparatively modest.

The studies discussed in this section, as well as comparable studies that have focused on other age groups (reviewed in Rook & Pietromonaco, 1987), rarely have included tests for such nonlinear patterns. Moreover, researchers (myself included) generally have not discussed the distributions of positive and negative exchanges in the samples studied. In my own work (e.g., Rook, 1984) I have found that as many as 25% to 30% of the elderly respondents report having no problematic interactions with members of their social networks. Very few respondents, in contrast, report having no supportive interactions with members of their networks. Nearly half of the recovering stoke patients that Stephens et al. (1987) studied reported no problematic social interactions with others, whereas only a small fraction reported no supportive interactions. Other studies likewise may have tended to underrepresent individuals with quite deficient levels of support because such individuals are often difficult to locate or, once located, are often reluctant to participate in research. These differences in the clustering of respondents at the low end of the distributions of positive and negative exchanges could partly account for the apparently greater impact of negative exchanges on psychological functioning. That is, the data collected in these studies may have included the critical threshold for negative exchanges but may have excluded the critical threshold for positive exchanges.

If this were so, it would not disconfirm the importance of conflictual social exchanges, but it would cast doubt on the conclusion emerging from this work that conflictual exchanges have more potent effects than do supportive exchanges. In future studies that compare the effects of supportive and problematic exchanges, researchers may wish to include specific tests for possible threshold effects (see Viel, 1987, for a discussion of statistical procedures for detecting threshold effects).

Social Versus Nonsocial Stressors

Few studies have explicitly contrasted interpersonal and noninterpersonal stressors, but those that have testify to the uniquely upsetting effects of interpersonal stressors (see Thoits, 1982). For example, Bolger et al. (1989) examined 10 different categories of daily stress in a sample of married couples, including several kinds of stressful interpersonal events (family demands; demands from other individuals; and interpersonal conflicts or tensions with one's spouse, child, another person, or multiple persons at the same time). Respondents kept daily diaries for six weeks in which they recorded the occurrence of these stressors as well as their mood. Regression analyses were designed to analyze within-person covariation in daily stressors and mood. These analyses clearly revealed that interpersonal conflicts had the most serious consequences for emotional health. Indeed, interpersonal conflicts accounted for more than 80% of the explained variance in respondents' moods. Additional analyses of multi-day stress episodes indicated that the adverse effects of interpersonal stressors tended to persist over several days, whereas the effects of other stressors dissipated more quickly.

Although these data did not address the relative impact of negative and positive social events in people's everyday experiences, they do indicate that, among daily stressors, those of an interpersonal nature have the greatest significance for psychological well-being. Bolger et al. (1989) concluded from their research that future investigations of daily stressors should concentrate intensively on the interpersonal domain.

Positive Versus Negative Social Exchanges as Moderators of Adaptation to Stress

As was noted earlier, a logical extension of the current stress and coping paradigm is to consider the role of problematic social exchanges in sustaining or aggravating reactions to stress, but few empirical studies have explored this role. Some researchers have examined how exposure to upsetting or hurtful social exchanges affects adaptation to a specific type of life stress, such as chronic illness (e.g., Dunkel-Schetter, 1984; Manne & Zautra, 1989; Revenson, Woolman, & Felton, 1983; Stephens et al., 1987; Chapter 7, this volume) or caring for a family member with Alzheimer's disease (Fiore et al., 1983; Pagel et al., 1987). Although such studies yield important insights about the effects of negative exchanges on the course of adaptation to or recovery from a specific stressor, they do not indicate whether negative exchanges have distinctive effects on stressed individuals as compared with nonstressed individuals. Studies that treat stress as a constant rather than a variable do not permit clear differentiation of main effects and moderator effects of negative exchanges (Dooley, 1985). Thus existing research provides little basis for determining whether negative social encounters primarily have direct effects on older adults' lives (e.g., lowered mood or self-esteem) or indirect effects (e.g., aggravation of reactions to stressful events).

Without duplicating the either/or debate regarding main effects and interaction effects that preoccupied social support researchers for many years, researchers interested in negative social exchanges may wish to devote some attention to comparisons of main effects and stress-exacerbation effects of such exchanges. The sophistication of this work may be enhanced by drawing on the conceptual distinctions that social support researchers have emphasized, such as the need to distinguish among different kinds of problematic interactions or among the sources of problematic interactions. For example, certain kinds of negative exchanges might be expected to have main effects on psychological health, whereas other kinds of negative exchanges may be influential primarily in the context of stress (Rook & Pietromonaco, 1987). Similarly, negative exchanges involving certain categories of social actors may be more potent than those involving other categories of actors (Abbey, Abramis, & Caplan, 1985; Schuster, Kessler, & Aseltine, 1989).

In addition to comparing main effects and interaction effects of problematic social interactions, more work should contrast the stress-exacerbation and stress-alleviation effects of problematic and supportive exchanges, respectively. Such work would provide another means of gauging the relative significance of negative and positive social encounters and, ideally, would also shed light on the specific processes that account for stress-exacerbation versus stress-alleviation effects.

Social support researchers have proposed a number of different ways in which support may function to reduce the adverse effects of stressful events, including altering support recipients' appraisal of the degree of threat posed by the stressor, increasing recipients' motivation to engage in coping efforts, elevating their mood and self-esteem, and altering their psychophysiological responses (see reviews by Cohen, 1988; Wills, 1985; Vaux, 1988). Much current research on social support is aimed at identifying which of these processes actually plays a significant role in stress reduction. Important advances in our understanding of the stress-exacerbating role of social conflict would stem from similar attempts to formulate and test predictions about the specific affective, cognitive, physiological, and behavioral reactions that are triggered by social conflict.

In the foregoing discussion I have highlighted several different strategies for analyzing the effects of negative social exchanges on older adults' functioning and reviewed preliminary evidence that suggests that these effects can be fairly potent. Of course, readers who are familiar with the literature on social support will recognize that many of the methodological problems that characterize research on support also characterize research on social conflict, including reliance on self-reports of conflict and adjustment, failure to control systematically for personality factors and other potential confounds, derivation of causal inferences from cross-sectional data, and so forth. Nevertheless, the effects of negative social exchanges have survived controls for health, sex, marital status, and education (e.g., Pagel et al., 1987; Rook, 1984; Stephens et al., 1987) and have emerged in some well-controlled prospective analyses (e.g., Pagel et al., 1987). Thus further research on the negative aspects of older adults' social relationships clearly seems warranted, and this work should include efforts to explain *why* negative exchanges appear to cause substantial emotional distress.

THEORETICAL EXPLANATIONS FOR POTENT EFFECTS OF NEGATIVE EXCHANGES

Several theoretical accounts have been developed to explain why negative social exchanges appear to have such strong effects and, indeed, why they often appear to have substantially stronger effects than do positive social exchanges (Rook & Pietromonaco, 1987). The explanations discussed here do not focus specifically on the elderly, but few a priori reasons exist for doubting their applicability to older people.

Frequency–Salience Explanation

This explanation traces the powerful impact of negative social exchanges to their comparative rareness and, as a result, to their greater salience. Studies have shown that positive social interactions occur much more frequently than do negative social interactions (e.g., Abbey et al., 1985; Pagel et al., 1987; Rook, 1984; Stephens et al., 1987; see also studies of marital interaction, e.g., Jacobson, Follette, & McDonald, 1982). For example, in my study of older women (Rook, 1984), supportive relations outnumbered problematic relations 6 to 1. Positive exchanges accordingly may form a general backdrop against which the comparatively infrequent negative exchanges appear quite salient. Indeed, the substantially greater frequency of positive events may allow people to take them for granted to some extent (Berscheid, 1983). Positive exchanges with others appear to be assimilated to a mere baseline level of expectation. Wiseman (1986) argued that people tend to develop expectations that their close associates will exhibit desired behaviors stably and predictably. Behaviors that confirm such expectations arouse little excitement; behaviors that disconfirm such expectations, in contrast, appear puzzling or even shocking and may prompt ruminative scrutiny.

Indirect evidence that the comparative rareness of negative interactions helps to account for their disproportionate impact comes from studies of relationship satisfaction. Jacobson et al. (1982), for example, had married couples keep daily records of positive, negative, and neutral actions by their spouses as well as daily ratings of their satisfaction with the marital relationship. Reactivity to negative behaviors of a spouse was inversely related to the frequency of the behaviors. The rarer the negative behaviors, the more they were associated with marital dissatisfaction. Reactivity to positive behaviors of the spouse, in contrast, was unrelated to the frequency of such behaviors. Pagel et al. (1987) found a similar pattern when they tested interactions between network members' helpful and upsetting behaviors in predicting elderly respondents' overall network satisfaction. Among respondents whose networks were characterized by a generally high level of helpfulness, upsetting behaviors strongly predicted lower network satisfaction. Among respondents whose networks were characterized by a generally low level of helpfulness, upsetting behaviors exhibited only a weak association with network satisfaction. Thus, consistent with the frequency–salience argument, a pattern of predominantly positive interactions with network members appeared to be a precondition for negative interactions to have much impact. As was noted earlier, this pattern characterizes the social networks of many older adults.

Attributional Explanation

A second explanation for the often disproportionate impact of unpleasant social exchanges emphasizes the cognitive processing that follows positive versus negative encounters with others (Pagel et al., 1987; Rook & Pietromonaco, 1987; Suls, 1982). Attribution theorists have argued that only counternormative behavior permits confident inferences about other people's motives (Jones & Davis, 1965; Kelley, 1967). To the extent that positive actions stimulate attributional processing at all, people may question whether the actions reflect genuine caring or merely feelings of obligation to behave supportively. Negative behaviors of friends, in contrast, present no such attributional ambiguity (Suls, 1982). It is counternormative to withhold help from friends, to insult or exploit them, or to upset them in other ways. People may readily attribute such behaviors to malice or at least insufficient caring, which would help to explain their strong adverse effects.

Adaptive Significance Explanation

A third reason why negative and positive social exchanges often have dissimilar consequences stems from the idea that they differ in adaptive significance. In trying to interpret negativity effects that have appeared in studies of diverse topics, Kanouse and Hanson (1972) argued that humans may have an innate tendency to be more vigilant toward potential threats or risks than toward potential pleasures or benefits. Berscheid (1983) commented in this regard that the human "emotional system appears to be a 'trouble-shooting' system" (p. 145). Such vigilance makes people quite reactive to negative events. In a provocative paper on stress, Hobfoll (1989) similarly argued that the threat of loss motivates people more than does the possibility of gain and that stress should be conceptualized in terms of people's efforts to guard against the loss of valued resources.

A variant of this adaptive significance explanation suggests that many negative experiences have the power to spoil the pleasure of positive events, whereas comparatively few positive experiences can cancel the misery of negative events (Kanouse & Hanson, 1972). For example, a single heated exchange during the course of an otherwise pleasant dinner party may spoil the experience; in contrast, a single pleasant experience in the midst of an evening marred with strife has little power to restore tranquility (Rook & Pietromonaco, 1987). Because of such differences in reversibility, along with potential differences in adaptive significance, it is not surprising that people appear to be more sensitive to negative interpersonal exchanges than to positive ones, even though such an orientation at times takes an emotional toll.

The explanations considered in this section trace the potent effects of negative interpersonal encounters to their greater salience, their greater tendency to elicit suspicious attributional accounts, and their greater adaptive significance (or greater irreversibility). These explanations are neither exhaustive nor mutually exclusive. Indeed, efforts to understand the reasons why negative interpersonal encounters have such potent effects on psychological well-being may well reveal multiple processes to operate simultaneously. Further theoretical work is needed to identify plausible explanations for the seemingly asymmetrical effects of positive and negative social exchanges. In addition, few empirical tests of these explanations have been undertaken and, such tests accordingly represent a high priority for further work. Efforts to investigate why negative social exchanges cause so much distress may also help to shed light on the important question of which older adults are most vulnerable to negative exchanges.

VULNERABILITY TO NEGATIVE EXCHANGES

Older adults might differ in their vulnerability to negative exchanges in at least two different ways. First, some older adults may experience a large number of problematic interactions with members of their social networks, whereas other older adults may experience comparatively few such problematic interactions. Thus they may differ in their exposure to problematic exchanges. Second, older adults may differ in their sensitivity or reactivity to any given interaction. That is, some older adults may be relatively impervious to unkind comments or misdeeds by their associates, whereas other older adults may be highly distressed by the same actions. This kind of vulnerability thus reflects the individual's sensitivity (or reactivity) to problematic social exchanges. These two different types of vulnerability may have somewhat different origins; the sections that follow consider several factors that may affect each of these kinds of vulnerability in older adults' social lives.

Unfortunately, very little published research exists on this topic and it is not legitimate simply to infer from research on social support that the same factors that lead to a low level of social support also lead to a high level of problematic interaction. Attempting to draw such parallels is unwarranted in light of research that suggests that positive and negative social exchanges represent independent phenomena rather than opposite ends of a single continuum. Measures of positive and negative interaction have been found to be virtually unrelated rather than inversely related, as one might intuitively expect (e.g., Fiore et al., 1983; Manne & Zautra, 1989; Pagel et al., 1987; Rook, 1984; Stephens et al., 1987). Indeed, in my own research, I found correlations approaching zero between measures of positive and negative social interaction. These near-zero correlations emerged with measures that assessed the frequency of contact with supportive versus problematic network members, the number of supportive versus problematic network members, and the number of positive versus negative functions performed by respondents' network members (Rook, 1984). Stephens et al. (1987) similarly reported a near-zero correlation between the frequency of positive interactions and frequency of negative interactions in their sample of recovering stroke patients. Thus different dynamics may underlie positive and negative social exchanges, necessitating separate analyses of the predisposing factors for each kind of exchange.

Factors that Affect Exposure to Negative Exchanges

Only a few published studies have provided detailed information about factors that affect one's exposure to problematic exchanges with others. Fortunately, several of these studies have focused on older adults (Pagel et al., 1987; Rook, 1984; Stephens et al., 1987). The researchers approached this issue in the same way by comparing groups of respondents who differed in the quantity of negative exchanges that they experienced with members of their social networks. For example, I contrasted three groups of elderly widows (those with low, medium, and high levels of problematic exchanges) and found that the groups did not differ in major background characteristics, such as age, education, income, religion, perceived health, length of residence in the local area, or the length of widowhood (Rood, 1984). Stephens et al. (1987) similarly contrasted two groups of recovering stroke patients—those who reported no problematic interactions with others and those who reported one or more problematic interactions. These researchers found no differences between the two groups with respect to sex, education, ethnicity, marital status, or health status assessed at several different points in time. However, they did find a significant association with age. Respondents who reported negative interactions were younger (mean age of 68.9 years) than respondents who reported no such interactions (mean age of 73.6 years). Pagel et al. (1987) found a similar association with age, as well as a greater tendency for women to report that they experienced upsetting interactions with members of their social networks.

In each of these studies researchers also attempted to make group comparisons on measures that could be considered indicative of interpersonal competence. Pagel et al. (1987) found that elderly respondents who reported a greater number of upsetting interactions had neither larger nor smaller social networks than did respondents who reported fewer upsetting interactions. In addition, these two groups interacted equally often with members of their social networks. The two groups of stroke patients compared by Stephens et al. (1987) did not differ on a measure of positive interaction with others. Similarly, the three groups of widows that I studied did not differ in the size of their social networks, their frequency of contact with others, or the number of supportive functions that others performed. The groups also reported comparable levels of intimacy and comfort with others, as well as comparable involvement in social organizations, such as senior citizen centers (Rook, 1984).

These findings do not portray older adults who report at least some strained relationships in their social networks as people who have inadequate social skills or severely limited relational competence (Chapter 6, this volume). If their social skills were deficient or if they otherwise tended to alienate people, they would be expected to have few supportive relationships or to have infrequent contact with supporters. These studies yielded little evidence of such social marginality. However, some clues did emerge regarding the role of assertion skills in affecting vulnerability to stressful interactions with others. The older women in my study were asked a series of questions about their patterns of decision making with their friends. Women who had a greater number of problematic social ties were more likely to characterize their friendships as unequal with respect to decision making. Specifically, they were more likely to report that their friends decided (rather than they themselves or both parties equally) when they would get together and how they would spend their time when they got together (Rook, 1984). Thus the women's problematic interactions with their friends appeared to be linked more to difficulties with assertion than to globally deficient social skills or alienating personality characteristics.

The only other clues that have emerged from these studies about factors that may increase older adults' vulnerability to negative social exchanges concern the unique role that kin may play in such exchanges. Pagel et al. (1987) reported a suggestive but nonsignificant tendency for networks characterized by a high degree of negativity to contain more kin relations than did networks characterized by a low degree of negativity. Similarly, I found that elderly women who had problematic social ties were significantly more likely than other elderly women to volunteer negative comments about their children, siblings, and other family members in response to open-ended questions about desirable and undesirable aspects of their social relationships. These groups of women did not differ, however, in expression of negative comments about their friends (Rook, 1984).

In a study that was not designed explicitly to examine the antecedents or consequences of problematic social exchanges, Kahn and Antonucci (1984, reported in Crohan & Antonucci, 1989) nonetheless found similar evidence that kin ties may figure prominently in the problematic interactions that older adults experience. Specifically, they found in a large sample of older adults that perceiving one's social network as demanding was associated with lower satisfaction with family members but was unrelated to satisfaction with friends. One interpretation of this finding is that interactions of a demanding nature occurred more often with family members than with friends. In my study (Rook, 1984), roughly equal percentages of the elderly women's friends (38%) and family members (36%) were involved in problematic exchanges, but the evidence I have discussed here suggests that problematic exchanges with family members may cause greater irritation.

The results of a study of married couples departed from this general pattern (Bolger et al., 1989). In this nonelderly sample, conflicts with family members were found to be less distressing than were conflicts with other people, such as friends or neighbors. Why the results of this study differ from those discussed here is unclear, although it is possible that older adults experience particularly pernicious family conflicts or disappointments. As this review indicates, a great deal remains to be learned about the factors that affect older adults' exposure to negative exchanges with members of their social networks. Further research is needed that examines individual characteristics, network properties, and properties of dyads as antecedents of conflictual interaction.

With respect to individual characteristics, more needs to be learned about the influence of characteristics such as sex, age, education, and health. In addition, greater attention should be given to older adults' relational competence (Chapter 6, this volume) and cognitive appraisal processes. For example, Lazarus and Folkman (1984) have argued that how a person evaluates a life event determines whether or not the event triggers a stress reaction, and the appraisal of interpersonal events similarly may influence their stressfulness. We know very little about the way that older adults perceive social exchanges that have the potential to cause distress. Some older adults may be quick to perceive others' questionable actions in negative terms, whereas other older adults may tend to shrug off such negative interpretations or to generate benign alternatives. Similarly, certain kinds of social skills may afford some older adults a degree of protection from conflict and disappointments with others, but we know little at present about how older adults attempt to regulate their contact with others so as to minimize problematic interaction.

The investigation of social network properties that influence exposure to negative social exchanges obviously cannot be divorced completely from the investigation of individual difference factors, because social networks are shaped to some extent by personality characteristics and other individual difference factors. Nevertheless, some network properties may influence the occurrence of negative exchanges in a manner that is relatively independent of such individual difference factors. For example, older adults who live a considerable distance from their kin may be forced to turn to friends for instrumental support that kin normally would provide, thereby increasing the possibility of friction with their friends (cf. Rook, 1987). Similarly, factors such as the density of a social network may affect the ease with which matters that one would prefer to keep private become publicized, or the ease with which social network members can exert coordinated pressure to influence one's behavior (Hirsch, 1980).

Research on social network properties that influence older adults' exposure to conflictual interaction should be complemented by research on the properties of dyadic relationships that may similarly influence exposure to conflict. Of the few studies that have examined the role of negative social exchanges in older adults' lives, most have tended to aggregate reports of positive and negative exchanges across older adults' entire networks; few have analyzed negative exchanges that occur within key dyadic relationships, such as marital relationships or relationships with specific adult children or with best friends. The aggregate approach is valuable in determining the overall level of negative interaction that older people experience, but it may obscure important variations among dyadic relationships in the significance of negative exchanges or the factors that trigger conflict. Factors such as the frequency of interaction or degree of similarity between the two individuals and the extent to which the resources and sentiments they exchange are characterized by reciprocity may influence the potential for tension within a dyadic relationship. Additionally, people sometimes provoke conflicts with their partners precisely because of the emotional intensity that conflicts afford (cf. Berscheid, 1983). As Hobfoll (personal communication, May, 1989) put it, a "good fight can be hard to leave." Thus, the dyadic determinants of negative exchanges merit investigation from a variety of different perspectives.

Factors that Affect Reactivity to Negative Exchanges

Apart from differences in their sheer exposure to negative exchanges, older adults may differ in how strongly they react to negative exchanges. Reactivity undoubtedly has several dimensions, including the consistency, intensity, and duration of distress aroused by negative social encounters. It might be important to assess, for example, not only how much anger is aroused by a family member's critical remarks but also how long it takes for the anger to dissipate (cf. Schuster et al., 1989). Knowledge about individual differences in these aspects of reactivity would be useful in efforts to identify older adults who are particularly vulnerable to negative social encounters.

Unfortunately, few have examined this aspect of vulnerability among older adults, although research conducted with younger age groups may provide clues about factors that could influence older adults' reactivity to negative exchanges. Personality factors such as a depressive style, introversion, and self-consciousness have been found to be associated with greater sensitivity to aversive interpersonal experiences in studies of young adults (e.g., Fenigstein, 1979; Gray, 1972; Graziano, Feldesman, & Rahe, 1985). These factors similarly might influence sensitivity among the elderly. Because negative interpersonal encounters can be conceptualized as stressors, older adults' reactivity to such encounters may be affected by their coping skills, willingness to draw upon social support, and other factors that have been widely investigated as moderators of stress reactions. These factors may influence older adults' efforts to manage specific episodes of interpersonal conflict as well as their efforts to manage their emotional responses to such episodes.

Only scant information currently exists about the factors that influence older adults' vulnerability to negative social encounters. Gerontological researchers who wish to investigate this topic might be advised to follow the lead of stress researchers who have distinguished factors that influence the occurrence of stressful events from factors that influence the impact of stressful events. Moreover, the search for such "vulnerability factors" should include attention not only to older adults' personal characteristics (such as sex, health status, or personality) but also to properties of their social networks and significant dyadic relationships. Ideally, such research would include longitudinal studies that shed light on how older adults attempt to protect themselves from aversive encounters with others and, when such efforts fail, how their reactions evolve over time.

CONCLUSION

Social relationships in late life, as in other life stages, provide a complex mix of supportive and problematic experiences. Until recently, researchers have focused primarily on the positive aspects of older adults' social networks, while ignoring the negative aspects. Clearly, more work is needed that examines how supportive and problematic interpersonal encounters combine to influence older adults' psychological health and functioning.

Not surprisingly, many of the unresolved theoretical and methodological issues that confront researchers who are interested in the problematic aspects of social relationships mirror the issues that have confronted researchers who are interested in the supportive aspects of these relationships. Indeed, an extensive agenda for further research on negative social interaction may be derived by posing parallel versions of the questions that have been raised by social support researchers (Rook, in press). For example, many questions remain about the prevalence of main effects versus interaction effects of negative social exchanges, the distinctive effects of negative exchanges that involve different categories of social actors (such as kin versus friends), the distinctive effects of different kinds of negative exchanges (such as invasion of privacy versus criticism or behavioral omissions versus commissions), the specific processes that underlie the adverse effects of negative exchanges, the factors that affect exposure or reactivity to negative exchanges, and the implications for intervention that stem from research on negative exchanges. Methodological issues that must be addressed in studies of problematic interaction also have parallels in the literature on social support, including the reliability and validity of self-reports of negative exchanges, the need to control for the effects of factors that may be confounded with negative exchanges, the evaluation of threshold effects or other curvilinear patterns, and the use of research designs that permit legitimate inferences about causal associations.

Beyond these questions that have direct parallels in the social support literature, unique questions arise in attempting to consider how supportive and problematic social exchanges combine to affect older adults' psychological health. For example, do positive and negative aspects of social interaction represent truly independent domains of experience, as previous research has suggested, or do positive and negative interactions covary systematically in certain kinds of relationships (cf. Abbey et al., 1985) or in specific subgroups of older adults? What implications stem from viewing positive and negative interpersonal events as independent rather than interdependent phenomena? What theoretical models best characterize the additive and interactive effects of positive and negative exchanges? What theoretical explanations most effectively account for the apparently dissimilar effects of positive and negative exchanges? Should positive and negative exchanges be expected to influence the same or different dimensions of older adults' psychological health (cf. Rook & Pietromonaco, 1987; Stephens et al., 1987)? This list of questions is by no means exhaustive but illustrates the kind of thinking that will be required of researchers as they shift from a preoccupation with either supportive or problematic aspects of social relationships to consideration of the complex, joint effects of these dual aspects of social relationships.

Finally, readers should not take the focus of this chapter to imply that older adults are particularly susceptible to troubled relationships. Indeed, evidence suggests that the elderly may be more satisfied with their social relationships than are other age groups. For example, as compared with younger age groups, the elderly generally report higher levels of friendship satisfaction, are less likely to wish that they had more friends, and report fewer negative feelings about members of their social networks (Antonucci, 1985). In cross-national studies conducted in this country and Europe, the elderly have been found to report lower levels of loneliness than have other age groups (Peplau, Bikson, Rook, & Goodchilds, 1982; Revenson, 1986). Only after age 80 does loneliness appear to represent a significant problem for older adults (Peplau et al., 1982).

A balanced perspective on older adults' social relationships requires acknowledgment of the enormous benefits provided by their relationships as well as recognition that problems can arise in their relationships. Neither the positive nor the negative aspects of older adults' social relationships should be exaggerated, nor should we overstate the significance of social relationships for older adults' emotional health. Most older adults undoubtedly welcome opportunities for solitude as well as for social interaction (Lowenthal & Robinson, 1976), and researchers need to attend to such fluctuating preferences for social contact as they seek to understand the meaning of positive and negative interpersonal experiences in older adults' lives.

REFERENCES

Abbey, A., Abramis, D. J., & Caplan, R. D. (1985). Effects of different sources of social support and social conflict on emotional well-being. *Basic and Applied Social Psychology, 6,* 111–129.

Antonucci, T. C. (1985). Personal characteristics, social support, and social behavior. In R. H. Binstock & E. Shanas (Eds.), *Handbook of aging and the social sciences* (2nd ed., pp. 94–128). New York: Van Nostrand Reinhold.

Berscheid, E. (1983). Emotion. In H. Kelley, E. Berscheid, A. Christensen, J. H. Harvey, T. L. Huston, G. Levinger, E. McClintock, L. A. Peplau, & D. Peterson (Eds.), *Close relationships* (pp. 110–168). New York: Freeman.

Bolger, N., DeLongis, A., Kessler, R. C., & Schilling, E. A. (1989). Effects of daily stress on negative mood. *Journal of Personality and Social Psychology, 57,* 808–818.

Cohen, S. (1988). Psychosocial models of the role of social support in the etiology of physical disease. *Health Psychology, 7,* 269–297.

Cohen, S., & Wills, T. A. (1985). Stress, social support, and the buffering hypothesis. *Psychological Bulletin, 98,* 310–357.

Crohan, S. E., & Antonucci, T. C. (1989). Friends as a source of social support in old age. In R. G. Adams & R. Blieszner (Eds.), *Older adult friendship* (pp. 129–146). Newbury Park, CA: Sage.

Croog, S. H. (1970). The family as a source of stress. In S. Levine & N. A. Scotch (Eds.), *Social stress* (pp. 19–53). Chicago: Aldine.

Dooley, D. (1985). Causal inference in the study of social support. In S. Cohen & L. Syme (Eds.), *Social support and health* (pp. 109–125). Orlando, FL: Academic Press.

Dunkel-Schetter, C. (1984). Social support and cancer: Findings based on patient interviews and their implications. *Journal of Social Issues, 40,* 77–98.

Eckenrode, J., & Gore, S. (1981). Stressful life events and social supports: The significance of context. In B. H. Gottlieb (Ed.), *Social networks and social support* (pp. 43–68). Beverly Hills, CA: Sage.

Fenigstein, A. (1979). Self-consciousness, self-attention, and social interaction. *Journal of Personality and Social Psychology, 37,* 75–86.

Fiore, J., Becker, J., & Coppel, D. (1983). Social network interactions: A buffer or a stress? *American Journal of Community Psychology, 11,* 423–439.

Gottman, J. M. (1979). *Marital interaction: Experimental investigations.* New York: Academic Press.

Gray, J. (1972). The psychophysiological nature of introversion-extroversion: A modification of Eysenck's theory. In V. O. Nebylitsyn & J. A. Gray (Eds.), *Biological basis of individual behavior* (pp. 182–205). London: Academic Press.

Graziano, W. G., Feldesman, A. B., & Rahe, D. F. (1985). Extraversion, social cognition, and the salience of aversion in social encounters. *Journal of Personality and Social Psychology, 49,* 971–980.

Hirsch, B. J. (1980). Natural support systems and coping with major life changes. *American Journal of Community Psychology, 8,* 159–172.

Hobfoll, S. E. (1989). Conservation of resources: A new attempt at conceptualizing stress. *American Psychologist, 44,* 513–524.

Homans, G. G. (1974). *Social behavior* (2nd ed.). New York: Harcourt Brace Jovanovich.

House, J. S. (1981). *Work stress and social support.* Reading, MA: Addison-Wesley.

Jacob, T. (1975). Family interaction in disturbed and normal families: A methodological and substantive analysis. *Psychological Bulletin, 18,* 35–65.

Jacobson, N. S., Follette, W. C., & McDonald, D. W. (1982). Reactivity to positive and negative behavior in distressed and nondistressed married couples. *Journal of Consulting and Clinical Psychology, 50,* 706–714.

Jones, E. E., & Davis, K. E. (1965). From acts to dispositions: The attribution process in person perception. In L. Berkowitz (Ed.), *Advances in experimental social psychology* (Vol. 2, pp. 219–266). New York: Academic Press.

Kahn, R. L., & Antonucci, T. (1980). Convoys over the life course: Attachment, roles, and social support. In P. B. Baltes & O. Brim (Eds.), *Lifespan development and behavior* (Vol. 3, pp. 253–286). Boston: Lexington.

Kanouse, D. E., & Hanson, L. R. (1972). Negativity in evaluations. In E. E. Jones, D. E. Kanouse, H. H. Kelley, R. E. Nisbett, S. Valins, & B. Weiner (Eds.), *Attribution: Perceiving the causes of behavior* (pp. 47–62). Morristown, NJ: General Learning Press.

Kelley, H. H. (1967). Attribution theory in social psychology. In D. Levine (Ed.), *Nebraska symposium on motivation* (Vol. 2, pp. 192–238). Lincoln: University of Nebraska Press.

Kessler, R. C., & McLeod, J. D. (1985). Social support and mental health in community samples. In S. Cohen & L. Syme (Eds.), *Social support and health* (pp. 109–125). Orlando, FL: Academic Press.

Lazarus, R. S., & Folkman, S. (1984). *Stress, appraisal, and coping.* New York: Springer.

Leff, J., & Vaughn, C. (1981). The role of maintenance therapy and relatives' expressed emotion in relapse of schizophrenia. *British Journal of Psychiatry, 139,* 102–104.

Lowenthal, M. F., & Robinson, B. (1976). Social networks and isolation. In R. H. Binstock & E. Shanas (Eds.), *Handbook of aging and the social sciences* (pp. 432–482). New York: Van Nostrand Reinhold.

Manne, S. L., & Zautra, A. J. (1989). Spouse criticism and support: Their association with coping and psychological adjustment among women with rheumatoid arthritis. *Journal of Personality and Social Psychology, 56,* 608–617.

Monroe, S. M., Bromet, E. J., Connell, M. M., & Steiner, S. C. (1986). Social support, life events, and depressive symptoms: A one-year prospective study. *Journal of Abnormal Psychology, 95,* 423–431.

Pagel, M. D., Erdly, W. W., & Becker, J. (1987). Social networks: We get by with (and in spite of) a little help from our friends. *Journal of Personality and Social Psychology, 53,* 793–804.

Peplau, L. A., Bikson, T. K., Rook, K. S., & Goodchilds, J. (1982). Being old and living alone. In L. A. Peplau & D. Perlman (Eds.), *Loneliness: A sourcebook of current theory, research and therapy* (pp. 327–347). New York: Wiley.

Revenson, T. A. (1986). Debunking the myth of loneliness in late life. In E. Seidman & J. Rappaport (Eds.), *Redefining social problems* (pp. 115–135). New York: Plenum Press.

Revenson, T. A., Woolman, C. A., & Felton, B. J. (1983). Social supports as stress buffers for adult cancer patients. *Psychosomatic Medicine, 45,* 321–331.

Rook, K. S. (1984). The negative side of social interaction. *Journal of Personality and Social Psychology, 46,* 1097–1108.

Rook, K. S. (1987). Reciprocity of social exchange and social satisfaction among older women. *Journal of Personality and Social Psychology, 52,* 145–154.

Rook, K. S. (1989). Strains in older adults' friendships. In R. G. Adams & R. Blieszner (Eds.), *Older adult friendship* (pp. 166–194). Newbury Park, CA: Sage.

Rook, K. S. (in press). Parallels in the study of social support and social strain. *Journal of Social and Clinical Psychology.*

Rook, K. S., & Pietromonaco, P. (1987). Close relationships: Ties that heal or ties that bind? In W. H. Jones & D. Perlman (Eds.), *Advances in personal relationships* (Vol. 1, pp. 1–35). Greenwich, CT: JAI Press.

Schuster, T. L., Kessler, R. C., & Aseltine, R. H., Jr. (1989). Positive interactions, negative interactions, and depressed mood. Unpublished manuscript, University of Michigan, Institute for Social Research.

Shinn, M., Lehmann, S., & Wong, N. W. (1984). Social interaction and social support. *Journal of Social Issues, 40,* 55–76.

Stephens, M. A. P., Kinney, J. M., Norris, V. K., & Ritchie, S. W. (1987). Social networks as assets and liabilities in recovery from stroke by geriatric patients. *Psychology and Aging, 2,* 125–129.

Suls, J. (1982). Social support, interpersonal relations, and health: Benefits and liabilities. In G. S. Sanders & J. Suls (Eds.), *Social psychology of health and illness* (pp. 255–277). Hillsdale, NJ: Erlbaum.

Thibaut, J. W., & Kelley, H. H. (1959). *The social psychology of groups.* New York: Wiley.

Thoits, P. A. (1982). Conceptual, methodological, and theoretical problems in studying social support as a buffer against life stress. *Journal of Health and Social Behavior, 23,* 145–159.

Wills, T. A. (1985). Supportive functions of interpersonal relationships. In S. Cohen & S. L. Syme (Eds.), *Social support and health* (pp. 61–82). Orlando, FL: Academic Press.

Wiseman, J. P. (1986). Friendship: Bonds and binds in a voluntary relationship. *Journal of Social and Personal Relationships, 3,* 191–211.

Wortman, C., & Dunkel-Schetter, C. (1979). Interpersonal relationships and cancer: A theoretical analysis. *Journal of Social Issues, 35,* 120–155.

Wortman, C., & Lehman, D. R. (1985). Reactions to victims of life crises: Support attempts that fail. In I. G. Sarason & B. R. Sarason (Eds.), *Social support: Theory, research, and application* (pp. 463–489). The Hague, The Netherlands: Martinus Nijhof.

Vaux, A. (1988). *Social support: Theory, research, and intervention.* New York: Praeger.

Veiel, H. O. F. (1987). Buffer effects and threshold effects: An alternative interpretation of nonlinearities in the relationship between social support, stress, and depression. *American Journal of Community Psychology, 15,* 717–740.

11

SOCIAL RELATIONS, PRODUCTIVE ACTIVITIES, AND COPING WITH STRESS IN LATE LIFE

James S. Jackson
Toni C. Antonucci
Rose C. Gibson

University of Michigan

We propose that social relations serve an important function by linking the individual to economic networks, thereby providing a context for productive activities and a conduit for social, physical, and psychological well-being. Among the multiple effects of this linkage is the provision of resources that can enable the individual to cope with stressful life situations. This is a particularly useful tie for older adults who often are retired from the paid labor force but have longstanding and extensive social relations. In the following section the literatures on social relations, stress, and well-being over the life span are briefly reviewed. In subsequent sections we present a theoretical framework that places the conceptualization and assessment of individual productivity within the context of economic and primary social relationship networks, and we speculate on the nature and implications of productive activities within these networks for individual stress and well-being over the life course. We conclude the chapter with a brief discussion of the advantages of a network model of individual productivity and the implications of this model for studies of stress and well-being in older adults.

SOCIAL RELATIONS, STRESS, AND WELL-BEING OVER THE LIFE COURSE

In recent years there has been a tremendous surge in the amount of research being conducted concerning social relations, especially social support. The social support research was initially inspired by social epidemiologists and physicians who, based primarily on clinical intuition, proposed that there was a positive association between good social relations with important others and the ability to resist and recover from illness. Social support research focuses on the relationship between a target individual and single or multiple significant others. The research suggests that these social relationships have far-reaching effects on the individual. This influence is not merely on the specific social relationship but often has implications for other contemporaneous and long-term or yet-to-be-developed relationships.

For example, research on mother–infant attachment has been extended to fathers, grandparents, teachers, and peers (cf. Emde & Harmon, 1982). In adult social relationships, similar patterns of social relations are being explored (see, e.g., research on the family, social networks, or ethnic interactive styles— Kreppner & Lerner, 1989; Stack, 1974). Early social relationships have been related to later ego-resiliency and competent performance in pre- and grade-school children (Arend, Grove, & Sroufe, 1979). Among adults, social relationships have been shown to influence an individual's ability to perform competently on the job, to withstand stress and crises and to influence both susceptibility to and recovery from disease (Cohen & Syme, 1985; Kasl & Cooper, 1987).

The majority of research in the social support area has been conducted by sociologists, social psychologists, and social epidemiologists. Their interests have stemmed from a view that social relationships are important as coping mechanisms. Social support has been viewed by these researchers as primarily a means of helping the individual cope with stressful life events. Social support also has a more direct effect as a longitudinal, developmental basis for a wide range of social and nonsocial activities (Antonucci & Jackson, 1987; Pearlin & Turner, 1987). It is this more fundamental or main effect view of social support that lends itself best to a life-span developmental framework.

A LIFE-SPAN APPROACH
TO SOCIAL RELATIONSHIPS

Social relationships are hierarchical, developmental, and causally related to antecedent and consequent events. Interpersonal relationships have been shown to be hierarchical. Both the infant attachment literature and the adult social support literature has shown that some people and relationships are closer and more important than others. Research on infants often focuses on the mother or the attachment figure; among older children or adults, one is more likely to speak of best friend, significant other, or confident. Empirical evidence has demonstrated a hierarchical preference for these closer, intimate figures in times of stress. It is also clear that these relationships develop over time. As children gain more advanced cognitive and social abilities, the nature of their social relationships also develops, becoming, for example, more complex, more multifaceted, and more intricate. Empirical investigations have also shown that social relationships are affected by antecedent or a priori conditions (e.g., the presence or absence of attachment figures, contingent interactive styles, extended family, and enriched environments) and that social relationships affect consequent events or outcomes (e.g., other social relationships, health, feelings of well-being).

At the individual level, researchers have become interested in, and have noted our lack of understanding concerning the processes and mechanisms by which social relationships have beneficial effects on health and well-being (Heller, Swindle, & Dusenbury, 1986; Jemmott, 1987; Knipscheer & Antonucci, in press; Sarason, Sarason, & Pierce, in press). One line of research suggests that social relationships are continuous, life-span developmental processes, emerging from early social relationships of infants with their mothers and eventuating in family and friendship relationships among the elderly (Antonucci, 1985; Blieszner, 1989; Hazan & Shaver, 1987; Kingson, Hirshorn, & Cornman, 1986; Levitt, in press; Pearlin & Turner, 1987; Schultz & Rau, 1985). This approach emphasizes both the individual's developmental stage and the parallel level of interindividual development. Relationships with other people, that is, interindividual relationships, develop both with specific other people and in a more generalized way across people. Thus one's relationships with one's children change as they grow and mature from infancy through adulthood.

However, relationships also change with other people more generally, for example, as one matures from an entry level co-worker to senior vice president, then to retirement. These developmental stages also influence the nature of social relationships, of individuals' opinions of themselves and others and, in turn, affects well-being across many domains (e.g., coping with stressful life events or maintaining physical and mental health).

Several studies indicate that personality characteristics such as efficacy, social competence, mastery, and locus of control are related to social support—as antecedents, consequences, or both (Bandura, 1986; Costa & McCrae, in press; Dunkel-Schetter, Folkman, & Lazarus, 1987; Holahan & Holahan, 1987; Lawton, Moss, & Kleban, 1989; Sarason et al., in press). Research on social relations has also focused on social integration and social isolation. Much of this work has come from sociological and epidemiological studies in which health (morbidity and mortality) and coping are outcomes. Social relationships are viewed as static and unchanging. Focus in this type of research is on the existence of relationships and contacts rather than on the context and content of interactions. Nevertheless, a consistent and significant association has been demonstrated between social relations measured in this way and both morbidity and mortality (e.g., Dean, Kolody, & Wood, in press; Goldberg, Van Natta, & Comstock, 1985; Orth-Gomer & Johnson, 1987; Schoenbach, Kaplan, Freman, & Kleinbaum, 1986; Seeman & Syme, 1987).

Another area of research, motivated in part by the desire to understand these epidemiological findings, focuses on the buffering effects of social support. This work suggests that social support mitigates the negative effects of stressors. This view has been contrasted with one of social support as having main effects on health and well-being; that is, social relationships have a generalized and positive influence, and individuals come to feel better about themselves because of their (positive) interactions with others. Cohen and Wills (1985) provided an extensive review of evidence concerning buffering effects and concluded that buffering is more likely if the support provided is specific to the crisis. The main idea that we propose in this chapter is that social relations have far-reaching effects on the individual, one of which is the individual's tie to productivity and access to economic networks.

NETWORKS AND PRODUCTIVITY

A great deal of research points to the need to examine individual social behavior within family and friendship networks (Kreppner & Lerner, 1989; Wellman, 1981; Wentowski, 1981). These networks have often been studied within the social support paradigm. The social support literature, however, has not systematically related larger macrosocial and economic opportunity factors to the functioning and effects of these primary networks. Much of the research on social support networks has focused on either the descriptive characteristics of primary groups and principal caregivers or on the ability of social relations to buffer or insulate individuals from the deleterious effects of stress (Conners, Power, & Bultena, 1979; Fischer, 1982; Kahn, Wethington, & Ingersoll, 1987; LaRocco, House, & French, 1980; Noelker & Harel, 1983; Pearlin & Schooler, 1978; Thoits, 1982; Wellman, 1981).

The literature on the networks of older adults suggests that they serve an important function in both providing a context for productive activities and contributing generally to the well-being of the family itself (Chatters, Taylor, & Jackson, 1985; McAdoo, 1981). It is hypothesized that three distinct economic networks—regular, irregular, and social—provide the larger context for the functioning of primary group relationships. These economic networks are assumed to affect and interact with primary group networks to influence individual functioning (Ferman, Berndt, & Selo, 1978). Participation in these economic networks are hypothesized to be differentially and reciprocally related to interactions within smaller primary group networks. These relationships are critical, as indicated in the social support literature, which clearly points to the mediating role of primary group ties to individual productive activities and social, physical, and psychological well-being (Herzog, Kahn, Morgan, Jackson, & Antonucci, 1987).

It has been recently proposed that the definition of productivity be expanded to include inputs from labor that reflect paid work, unpaid work, voluntary organizational work, mutual help, and self-care (Kahn, 1986; Morgan, 1986; Myers, Manton, & Bacellar, 1986; National Institute on Aging, 1982). Most attention has focused on understanding the effects of productive activity on individual well-being, particularly in the latter stages of the life course (Kahn, 1986; Morgan, 1986; National Research Council, 1986). The traditional definition of individual productive activities and individual productivity has been activities that generate valued goods and services. The magnitude of this productivity has been defined by the actual or attributed market dollar value, minus the nonlabor cost involved in their production (Kahn, 1986). This definition is derived from and emphasizes the input of labor into measures of national productivity accounting (Rosen, 1984).

Two criteria are commonly used in the definition of productive activities: their monetary value in actual or attributed dollars or the amount of time engaged in the activity (Kahn, 1986; Morgan, 1986). A third criterion, although less uniformly accepted, involves the individual's subjective ratings of the value or "worthwhileness" of the activity (Kahn, 1986). Recent work by Juster and his colleagues (Dow & Juster, 1985; Juster, 1985; Juster, Courant, & Dow, 1981) may provide a useful empirical approach to combining the objective and subjective dimensions of productive activity. Juster et al. (1981) suggested that the subjective evaluation of engaging in some activities to the exclusion of others be called "process benefits" that are independent of the tangible outcomes of the activities.

Juster et al. (1981) were concerned with assessing process benefits related to household activities. We believe that their theoretical model and approach is useful in obtaining measures of individual productivity. Essentially, it is argued that above and beyond the objective indicators of productive activities (i.e., amount of time spent or pay received), the subjective dimensions of worthwhileness—satisfaction, enjoyment, and benefit to others—may be additional, critical factors in individual productivity. In the following section we present a framework that illustrates how the social relations of older people are linked to the objective and subjective assessment of productivity and to their engagement in three economic networks.

THEORETICAL FRAMEWORK OF PRODUCTIVE ACTIVITIES

The productive activities of all adults occur within the larger context of three separate economic exchange networks. The existence of these networks has been documented by a small but growing body of literature (Ferman et al., 1978; Lowenthal, 1975; Smith, 1982). These networks are the regular economy, which refers to formal economic exchanges of goods and services for money payments; the irregular economy, which refers to economic exchanges that are informal and not subject to normal societal oversight and taxation; and the social economy, in which goods and services are exchanged reciprocally, independent of money payments. It is hypothesized that involvement in the same productive activity, whether paid or unpaid, may have different outcomes and consequences for the individual if performed in the different economic networks.

It has been suggested that activities in the three types of economic networks interact to help meet individual and family economic needs. Among well-educated young and middle-aged adults the formal, regular economic network may be sufficient for addressing subsistence and objective needs. For more subjective needs and among other less advantaged groups including many older adults, however, the irregular and social economy network may offer important coping, survival, and adaptation strategies (Ferman et al., 1978; Stack, 1974). In order to comprehend the nature, correlates, and consequences of productive activities among adults, each of these three different but interrelated networks need to be examined.

For example, social and irregular economy exchanges may be of particular importance in the productive behavior of economically disadvantaged groups because they provide an alternative context for economic participation (Ferman et al., 1978; Lowenthal, 1975). Economic necessity and relatively stable life opportunity restrictions may result in extensive intraindividual continuity across the life span in network participation and productive activities. It might be expected that because of differences in the past and immediate social environments, members of socially and economically disadvantaged groups may have distinctly different experiences across the life span than do others in the nature, course, and consequences of productive activities (Kalleberg & Sorenson, 1979). Similarly, older adults who find their access to the regular economic network blocked might develop or enlarge participation in the irregular and social economic networks.

The broader theoretical framework within which to view these economic exchanges is presented in Figure 1. Properties of the situation (A) and the individual (B) jointly determine economic incentives (C). These incentives, in combination with properties of the person and the situation, predict involvement in the regular, irregular, and social economic networks (D). Involvement in these networks both influences and is influenced by relationships in primary group networks (E) and can be viewed within various domains of productive activities (paid employment, unpaid activities, voluntary activities, mutual help, and self-help). Productive behaviors influence individual primary group, community, and societal level outcomes (F). These outcomes, especially those at the individual and group levels feed back to influence network involvement through noneconomic incentives (G).

Regular Economy Network

The regular economy network refers to the traditional market economy in which the majority of the adult population participates (Cook, 1973; Godelier,

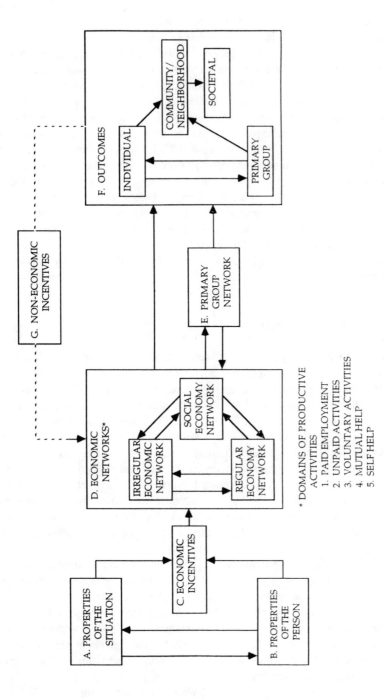

FIGURE 1 Antecedents and consequences of productive activities.

* DOMAINS OF PRODUCTIVE ACTIVITIES
1. PAID EMPLOYMENT
2. UNPAID ACTIVITIES
3. VOLUNTARY ACTIVITIES
4. MUTUAL HELP
5. SELF HELP

A. PROPERTIES OF THE SITUATION

B. PROPERTIES OF THE PERSON

C. ECONOMIC INCENTIVES

D. ECONOMIC NETWORKS*

IRREGULAR ECONOMIC NETWORK

SOCIAL ECONOMY NETWORK

REGULAR ECONOMY NETWORK

E. PRIMARY GROUP NETWORK

G. NON-ECONOMIC INCENTIVES

F. OUTCOMES

INDIVIDUAL

COMMUNITY/ NEIGHBORHOOD

SOCIETAL

PRIMARY GROUP

1980). Cook (1973) defined economic behaviors as the production, transfer, or use of material goods with use or exchange value, performances that involve the transfer or use of services and remuneration in cash or kind, for the purpose of satisfying wants or contributing to subsistence. In the traditional market economy most Americans sell their labor (Cook, 1973; Godelier, 1980; Kalleberg & Sorenson, 1979; Lowenthal, 1975). The available literature reveals that many social groups, including older adults generally, have been and continue to be blocked from full participation in regular economic activities (Anderson & Cottingham, 1981; Hill, 1981; Montagna, 1977). Numerous articles and aggregate data (Current Population Reports, 1980) document the disadvantaged economic position of different social groups in American society. Statistics show that the individual and family needs of many Americans are not met through participation in the regular market economy (Anderson & Cottingham, 1981; Cain, 1976; Hill, 1981). For purposes of economic survival as well as to fulfill meaningful social roles, it is hypothesized that individuals create alternative access to benefits if their full participation in the regular economic network is restricted.

Irregular Economy Network

Many authors have pointed to the existence of other networks that may serve a subsistence function. Although most have focused on the social, friendship, and kin networks as being of paramount importance (e.g., Stack, 1974), others have proposed that a separate market economy operates parallel to the regular market economy (Ferman et al., 1978; Gutmann, 1977; Smith, 1982; Witte & Simon, 1983). This network has been given a variety of names—for example, underground economy, subterranean economy, or hidden economy. Ferman et al. (1978) described the irregular economy as the sector of the economy that exists outside of or apart from the conventional structures and market relationships of the regular economy but that still uses a cash base. He defined irregular economic activities involving monetary payment for services or goods that are not produced, distributed, or provided formally through regularly established enterprises.

The basic notion of involvement within the irregular economic network concerns the receipt of pay for activities that are not recorded or monitored within the regular apparatus of the economy (Ferman et al., 1978). It is proposed that a sizable proportion of what older people do might fall into this category. Behaviors such as caregiving, transporting, and providing services may be performed in exchange for some other valued goods or services or for cash. Although the difficulties of obtaining reports on activities within the nonmarket irregular economy involving the sales of goods and services has been noted previously (Ferman et al., 1978), we found in an earlier study (Jackson,

Tucker, & Bowman, 1982) that individuals were willing to report activities involving the sales of goods and services within the nonmarket economy. Thirty-nine percent of this national probability sample of Blacks reported receiving services of this type, and approximately 33% who received them indicated that they paid for that service. When asked whether the respondent did things for others, approximately 45% responded affirmatively, and 17% of those individuals indicated that they were paid. Similarly, Smith (1982) found that approximately one-fifth of a national probability sample of the United States population reported that they had ways of earning extra money by providing goods and services outside of the regular economy. In a recent set of analyses on productive activities (Herzog, Kahn, Morgan, Jackson, & Antonucci, 1987, 1989) it was reported that 15.3% of a national probability sample of the United States reported engaging in irregular economic activities.

One of the few empirical studies of the social and psychological aspects of the irregular economy drew the following general conclusions regarding the nature of the irregular economic network (Ferman et al., 1978). First, the irregular economy exists and is widespread throughout various levels of society. The range of services and goods represented within the irregular economy were classified in the following seven broad categories: sale or production of goods, home-related services provided to consumers, personal services provided to consumers, "off the books" employment by a regular establishment, rental of property, provision of entertainment, and criminal activities.

Second, the irregular economy stands as an arbitrator between the regular economy network and the social economy network. It is a distributor, maintainer, and producer of materials manufactured or sold in the regular economy. The social economy network provides the link between individuals and the underlying feelings of trust and stability that are necessary for the operation of irregular economic activities. Third, the irregular economy network seems to be most widely used for services that are usually not provided by regular firms or businesses. Ferman et al. (1978) also indicated that reasons other than price (e.g., previous contact, social reasons, and convenience) might enter in the decision to use the irregular economy network.

Fourth, although individuals seem to prefer to work within the regular economic network, blocked opportunities as well as positive benefits other than economic ones may play a role in why people participate in irregular activities. Participants in the irregular economy range from people who are also employed in the regular economy to people who never have worked in the regular economy. Fifth, older adults appear to participate in the irregular economic network for reasons in addition to the actual economic value, namely because they could provide needed services that give them much satisfaction and enjoyment, keep them occupied, and keep them involved in the life of the community.

Social Economy Network

The social economy network encompasses economic activities that are not registered by the economic measuring techniques of society and that do not require money as a medium of exchange (Ferman et al., 1978; Lowenthal, 1975). Additionally, the economic exchanges are often embedded in and based on the networks of social relationships that people maintain over time (Lowenthal, 1975; Stack, 1974). The provision of goods and services within the social, friendship, and kin networks has been the subject of much research on the types of exchanges and activities that we include under productive behaviors (Cantor, 1979; Martineau, 1977; McAdoo, 1981; Stack, 1974). Although the majority of these studies have been conducted for a variety of different reasons, almost uniformly they point to the importance of the informal friend, neighbor, and kin networks in providing both economic and social support for their members.

A number of studies point to the importance of community activities that are embedded within these social networks in the economic and social survival of their members. Although there have been very few systematic studies of the social economy network (Lowenthal, 1975), Herzog et al. (1987, 1989) reported recently that approximately 83% of all respondents in a national study indicated participating in activities that would be included under this rubric. Of special importance to elderly people is the provision of care for both acute and chronic conditions (Herzog et al., 1987). This care, particularly for frail elderly people, is becoming increasingly important as growing numbers of older people require more intensive and longer-term care (Soldo & Manton, 1986).

A distinction between social economy network and primary group relationships should be emphasized. The former refers to relationships that involve the explicit exchange of goods and services, albeit without a monetary component. Primary group relationships refer to the social, emotional, evaluative, or informational aspects of support frequently associated with the concept of social support (Antonucci, 1985; House & Kahn, 1985).

FACTORS EXPLAINING INVOLVEMENT IN ECONOMIC NETWORKS

Central to the proposed process of economic network involvement is the fact that individuals, because of economic necessity, participate in a variety of different types of economic networks for individual and family survival (Hill, 1981). Socioeconomic position may play an important role in the qualitative and quantitative aspects of participation in the three economic networks (Cantor & Little, 1985). Other socio-cultural distinctions, however, may also contribute to important differences between social groups (e.g., age, gender, and race) in the rates, frequency, and type of participation. For example, differences between Blacks and Whites, young and old, and men and women have often been reported for attachment to the labor force (Anderson & Cottingham, 1981), level of involvement in subjective experiences in regular economic participation (Ferman et al., 1978), and rates and types of participation in social or barter economies (Stack, 1974).

Involvement in productive activities begins early in pre-adult life in the irregular and social economic networks. This early participation may be dictated by a variety of motivating factors, but the overriding condition is that of economic necessity. This participation strengthens over the years; by mid-adulthood and old age, participation has become well entrenched and the individual has played a variety of key roles in the operation of the irregular economy and the social economy networks. Similar types of parallel activities may have also transpired in the regular market economy, although for many disadvantaged Americans this is not necessarily the case (Hamilton, 1975; Kalleberg & Sorenson, 1979; Montagna, 1977). For many groups (e.g., Blacks and older adults) participation in the regular economy is less than satisfactory, particularly in terms of economic subsistence, as well as the noneconomic incentives and rewards gained from market employment (Montagna, 1977). Thus there are clear economic and noneconomic reasons for participating in these other economic networks (Ferman et al., 1978; Lowenthal, 1975).

Among the importance noneconomic factors may be religious values and church participation, family attachment and intergenerational relationships, perceptions and experiences with the opportunity structure, social identity and group consciousness, and differences in basic values regarding the role and importance of individual versus family and group achievement. It is expected that these factors contribute to participation in the economic networks and both influence and are influenced by primary group affiliations, resulting in subsequent differences in behaviors as well as other social, psychological, and health outcomes.

The major, but not sole, motivating factor for entry into any of these networks is economic necessity. This motivation, however, may be tempered by several important factors. Personal characteristics such as age and gender may play an important role in regulating entry into economic networks. Similarly, economic necessity may be conditioned by the nature of the social environment. The neighborhood where an individual is raised as well as family structure may affect the extent to which economic necessity functions as a motivator of behavior.

Economic necessity and blocked access are predicted to have the strongest influence on involvement in irregular and social economic network activity. For example, economic necessity is predicted to be stronger among Blacks than Whites, and thus Blacks should show greater involvement in the social and irregular economy networks than do Whites. Of course, older people with similar economic needs would also fall into this category. It is predicted that socioeconomic status variables such as education and occupation will reduce the relationship between demographic categories like race and age and participation in social and irregular network economies. However, participation in the irregular and social economic networks for reasons other than economic necessity (e.g., enjoyment or benefit to others) may also be more likely among adults.

Participative patterns within the social, irregular, and regular economic networks are viewed as interrelated. A person may participate in all three simultaneously, two, or only one. Similarly, participation may be sequential or periodic. For example, a person with an episodic, formal employment history may maintain an adequate level of individual productivity by moving between the regular and irregular economy networks as a function of general economic conditions but consistently maintain relationships and position within the social economy network. As was indicated earlier, however, the nature and interpretation of participation in these economic networks may affect and be affected by the primary group relationships in which the individual is enmeshed (Moen, Kain, & Elder, 1983). This proposed connection emphasizes our concern with the effects of participation within the economy networks on primary group relationships and how these relationships may affect productive activities and in turn social, psychological, and health outcomes.

Some productive behaviors will be more or less likely to occur as a function of the type of networks in which an individual participates. Thus, if an individual's network relationships are in the regular economy, the productive activity of prime importance is likely to be paid work. The person may also be engaged, however, in the full range of other activities. Whether these other activities are related to the regular economy network or not may be a function of the degree of connectedness to the irregular economy and social economy networks.

One of the major outcomes is conceptualizing productive behaviors as occurring within the nexus of these three different types of networks is the fact that the same productive behavior performed within different networks may differ qualitatively and quantitatively. For example, paid employment within the regular economic network may be important for securing a salary to help meet monthly bills and provide for the basic standard of living. Engaging in the same activities within the irregular network (even for less pay, perhaps) may be viewed as more enjoyable and self-satisfying because it occurs within a milieu of friends, neighbors, and kin.

One set of the major outcomes of productive activities will probably be at the individual level. Some of the outcomes that may occur as a function of participating in these activities are in the areas of coping, self-esteem, perception of control, and general well-being (Ferman et al., 1978). Furthermore, it is assumed that positive outcomes derived from engaging in these productive activities will affect noneconomic incentives for further participating in these networks. One of the most common observations has been that involvement in the social, irregular, or even the regular economy network is dictated by noneconomic considerations (Ferman et al., 1978; Lowenthal, 1975; Sarason, 1977; Stack, 1974). Although economic necessity is usually the overriding consideration for participation in these networks, at least initially (Oppenheimer, 1981), other incentives gain importance over time as a function of these individual outcomes.

Participation in the social economy network, and to some extent the irregular economy network, is pervasive in some communities. In addition, this involvement may have direct beneficial effects on the community itself by providing work and income. Several authors have reported on the importance of networks in maintaining the viability and integrity of the community (Ferman et al., 1978; Stack, 1974). In fact Lowenthal (1975) suggested that reciprocal arrangements are important for the community and help cement the social relationships themselves. She argued that this type of interaction helps people feel secure and lends a permanence to their connectedness beyond what involvement based on regular paid work offers. Although life-course continuity of participation in the irregular and social economy networks is likely, it is expected that involvement may demonstrate qualitative or quantitative differences at different points in the life span. Similarly, noneconomic incentives may gain importance across the life span in relationship to economic ones, especially if basic economic needs are met.

Changes in status within the regular economic network should have less impact on the total individual productivity of social and economically disadvantaged group members than it will for others. This prediction is based on the belief that the former groups are much more likely to be involved in the other two networks and that more of their individual productivity is derived from these networks. It is predicted that total productivity for all social groups should be reduced with changes in regular economy network participation over time. This reduction should be greater and more debilitating for advantaged groups because of the disproportionate contribution of regular economic network participation to total individual productivity in comparison to less advantaged groups. Thus, loss of jobs, retirement, or disability should have the effect of disproportionately reducing individual productivity in advantaged groups subsequently leading to greater reductions in well-being and health outcomes than for less advantaged groups, especially if participation in alternative economic networks is not substituted.

The viability and integration of communities may also have some direct relationship to the well-being of the larger society. Obviously, activities within the regular economy network have direct and measurable effects on the society through estimates of national income and the Gross National Product (Ferman et al., 1978; Institute of Medicine/National Research Council, 1986; Leichter, 1984; National Research Council, 1979; Rosen, 1984). The contributions of productive behaviors in other economic networks, however, may have gone largely unrecognized in terms of their implications for individual well-being, and community survival and viability, which in turn have direct effects on the larger society.

CONCLUSION

The framework provided in this chapter should aid in the study of productive behaviors, primary social relationships, and well-being in older age. This life-course model highlights the importance of these networks for productive behaviors at all life stages (Herzog et al., 1987). As McAdoo (1981) and others (Ferman et al., 1978; Hamilton, 1975) have indicated, however, these networks gain particular value for older adults in providing an avenue for engaging in activities that are of value to the community and also to themselves. Commenting on the function of the irregular economy network, Ferman et al. (1978) noted that for the elderly who are on fixed incomes, participation in these alternative economic networks could be very critical for monetary reasons, but other motivational factors were also often operating, especially when financial necessity was not. For some, feeling useful, enjoying the work, and keeping active and busy were of equal or more importance.

The very nature of what is considered to be productive behaviors may show significant shifts with advancing age. While declining physical abilities may severely limit some forms of productive behaviors, others may become more prominent. For example, counseling and advice for younger family members and friends may assume greater importance as productive activities in older rather than in younger adults (Herzog et al., 1987, 1989).

Social relations may be viewed as dynamic, ongoing, and interactive, and the implications are far-reaching. For example, in this chapter we speculated on the role of social relationships in the maintenance of productive activity through adult life. At the macro level, some research has demonstrated differences in patterns of social relationships among different ethnic, racial, and cultural groups. We know little about the role of these macro-level environmental variables on the individual's development of, and expectations for, social relationships.

In addition to direct cultural influences, other differences may be due to differential access to resources. Thus a group with scarce resources is not likely to have the same expectation of the receipt of resources as a group with plentiful resources. At a more evaluative level, it is possible that macro-level environmental influences affect the individual in a manner contrary to the prevailing norms of most of the society. Such influences may operate when, for example, a religious group prevents access to certain forms of care, or an individual feels bound by honor (culture) to commit suicide once a certain level of disability is achieved. Finally, future research should be based on cohesive, comprehensive models of social relations and productive activities. Because these areas encompass many fields, the specific types of models likely to be developed will differ by discipline. However, it is critical that researchers test hypotheses designed to understand not only whether, but how and why social relations and productive activities intersect and their influences on stress, coping, and well-being.

The framework presented in this chapter attempts to account for relationships among position in, and openness of, the opportunity structure of society, productive activities, primary group relationships, stress, health, and well-being across the individual life course. Previous work on productive activities has not developed a theoretically meaningful definition of productive activities at the individual level. The proposed definition is an attempt to combine objective and subjective factors in conceptualizing individual productivity. This conceptual approach links individual indices of productivity to measures used in national accounting schemes (Rosen, 1984) and permits comparable measures across all forms of activities.

By placing the relationship between individual productivity and well-being within an economic network context, differential predictions are possible regarding the same behaviors across settings and situations that may differ both qualitatively and quantitatively, that is, regular market, irregular paid, and social barter situations. This aspect of the model also provides for a theoretical linkage to personal and friend networks that have been shown to have positive effects on stress and individual well-being. Finally, the model is important for providing independent assessments of productive activities separate from their predicted effects on individual well-being (Moss, 1979). This life-course framework provides an accounting of current findings, links opportunity structure factors with primary social relationships, and leads to specific predictions regarding the nature of nonmarket activities and socially supportive relationships and their hypothesized effects over the adult life-course.

REFERENCES

Anderson, B. E., & Cottingham, D. H. (1981). The elusive quest for economic equality. *Daedalus, 110,* 257–274.

Antonucci, T. C. (1985). Personal characteristics, social support, and social behavior. In E. Shanas & R. H. Binstock (Eds.), *Handbook of aging and the social sciences* (2nd ed.) (pp. 94–128). New York: Van Nostrand Reinhold.

Antonucci, T. C., & Jackson, J. S. (1987). Social support, interpersonal efficacy, and health. In L. Carstensen & B. A. Edelstein (Eds.), *Handbook of clinical gerontology* (pp. 291–311). New York: Pergamon Press.

Arend, K., Grove, F. I., & Stroufe, L. A. (1979). Continuity of individual adaptation from infancy to kindergarten: A predictive study of ego-resiliency and curiosity in preschoolers. *Child Development, 58,* 958–959.

Bandura, A. (1986). *Social foundations of thought and action.* Englewood Cliffs, NJ: Prentice-Hall.

Blieszner, R. (1989). Developmental processes of friendship. In R. G. Adams & R. Blieszner (Eds.), *Older adult friendship: Structure and process.* Newbery Park, CA: Sage.

Cain, G. G. (1976). The challenge of segmented labor market theories to orthodox theory: A survey. *Journal of Economic Literature, 14,* 1215–1257.

Cantor, M. H. (1979). The informal support system of New York's inner city elderly: Is ethnicity a factor? In D. E. Gelfand & A. J. Kutzik (Eds.), *Ethnicity and aging: Theory, research and policy* (pp. 153–174). New York: Springer.

Cantor, M. H., & Little, J. K. (1985). Aging and social services. In E. Shanas & R. H. Binstock (Eds.), *Handbook of aging and the social sciences* (2nd ed.) (pp. 745–781). New York: Van Nostrand Reinhold.

Chatters, L. M., Taylor, R. J., & Jackson, J. S. (1985). Aged Blacks' nominations to an informal helper network. *Journal of Gerontology, 41,* 94–100.

Cohen, S., & Syme, L. (Eds.). (1985). *Social support and health.* New York: Academic Press.

Cohen, S., & Wills, T. A. (1985). Stress, social support, and the buffering hypothesis. *Psychology Bulletin, 98*(2), 310–357.

Conners, K. A., Power, E. A., & Bultena, G. L. (1979). Social interaction and life satisfaction: An empirical assessment of late-life patterns. *Journal of Gerontology, 34,* 116–121.

Cook, S. (1973). Economic anthropology: Problems in theory, method, and analysis. In J. J. Honigman (Ed.), *Handbook of social and cultural anthropology.* Chicago: Rand McNally.

Costa, P. T., Jr., & McCrae, R. R. (in press). Personality, stress, and coping: Some lessons from a decade of research. In K. S. Markides & C. L. Cooper (Eds.), *Aging, stress, social support, and health.* New York: Wiley.

Current Population Reports. (1980). *The social and economic status of the Black populations in the United States: An historical view, 1790–1978* (Special studies series P-23, No. 80). Washington, DC: U.S. Department of Commerce, Bureau of the Census.

Dean, A., Kolody, B., & Wood, P. (in press). The effects of types of social support from adult children on depression in elderly persons. *The Journal of Community Psychology.*

Dow, G., & Juster, F. T. (1985). Goods, time and well-being: The joint dependence problem. In F. T. Juster & F. P. Stafford (Eds.), *Time, goods and well-being* (pp. 397–413). Ann Arbor, MI: Institute for Social Research.

Dunkel-Schetter, C., Folkman, S., & Lazarus, R. S. (1987). Correlates of social support receipt. *Journal of Personality and Social Psychology, 53,* 71–80.

Emde, R. N., & Harmon, R. J. (Eds.). (1982). *The development of attachment and affiliative systems.* New York: Plenum Press.

Ferman, L. A., Berndt, L., & Selo, E. (1978). *Analysis of the irregular econ-*

omy: Cash flow in the informal sector (Report to the Michigan Department of Labor, Bureau of Employment and Training). Ann Arbor: University of Michigan-Wayne State University, Institute of Labor and Industrial Relations.

Fischer, C. S. (1982). *To dwell among friends.* Chicago: University of Chicago Press.

Gutmann, P. M. (1977). The subterranean economy. *Financial Analysts Journal, 34,* 26–27.

Godelier, M. (1980). Anthropology and economics: The analysis of production, circulation, and consumption in economic goods. In I. Rossi (Ed.), *People in culture: A survey of cultural anthropology* (pp. 256–284). New York: Praeger.

Goldberg, E. L., Van Natta, P., & Comstock, G. W. (1985). Depressive symptoms, social networks and social support of elderly women. *American Journal of Epidemiology, 121*(3), 448–456.

Hamilton, R. N. (1975). *Employment needs and programs for older workers: Especially Blacks.* Washington, DC: National Center on Black Aged.

Hazan, C., & Shaver, P. (1987). Romantic love conceptualized as an attachment process. *Journal of Consulting and Clinical Psychology, 54*(4), 446–470.

Heller, K., Swindle, R. W., & Dusenbury, L. (1986). Component social support processes: Comments and Integration. *Journal of Consulting and Clinical Psychology, 54*(4), 466–470.

Herzog, A. R., Kahn, R. L., Morgan, J. N., Jackson, J. S., & Antonucci, T. C. (1987). *Productive activities and health over the life course.* Paper presented at the meeting of the American Association for the Advancement of Science, Chicago, IL.

Herzog, A. R., Kahn, R. L., Morgan, J. N., Jackson, J. S., & Antonucci, T. C. (1989). Age differences in productive activities. *Journal of Gerontology, 44,* 5129–5138.

Hill, R. B. (1981). *Economic policies and Black progress: Myth and realities.* New York: National Urban League.

Holahan, C. K., & Holahan, C. J. (1987). Self-efficacy, social support, and depression in aging: A longitudinal analysis. *Journal of Gerontology, 42*(1), 65–68.

House, J. S., & Kahn, R. L. (1985). Measures and concepts of social support. In S. Cohen & L. Syme (Eds.), *Social support and health* (pp. 83–108). New York: Academic Press.

Institute of Medicine/National Research Council. (1986). *America's aging: Productive roles in an older society.* Washington, DC: National Academy Press.

Jackson, J. S., Tucker, M. B., & Bowman, P. J. (1982). Conceptual and methodological problems in survey research on Black Americans. In W. T. Liu

(Ed.), *Methodological problems in minority research* (pp. 11–39). Chicago: Pacific/Asian American Mental Health Research Center.

Jemmott, J. B. III. (1987). Social motives and susceptibility to disease: Stalking individual differences in health risks. *Journal of Personality, 55,* 267–298.

Juster, F. T. (1985). Preferences for work and leisure. In F. T. Juster & F. P. Stafford (Eds.), *Time, goods and well-being* (pp. 333–351). Ann Arbor, MI: Institute for Social Research.

Juster, F. T., Courant, P. N., & Dow, G. K. (1981). The theory and measurement of well-being: A suggested framework for accounting and analysis. In F. T. Juster & K. C. Land (Eds.), *Social accounting systems* (pp. 23–94). New York: Academic Press.

Kahn, R. L. (1986). *Productive activities and well-being.* Paper presented at the meeting of the Gerontological Society of America, Chicago, IL.

Kahn, R. L., Wethington, E., & Ingersoll, B. N. (1987). Social networks: Determinants and effects. In R. Abeles (Ed.), *Implications of the life-span perspective for social psychology* (pp. 139–165). Hillsdale, NJ: Erlbaum.

Kalleberg, A. L., & Sorenson, A. B. (1979). The sociology of labor markets. *Annual Review of Sociology, 5,* 351–379.

Kasl, S., & Cooper, C. L. (Eds.). (1987). *Stress and health issues in research methodology* (pp. 143–165). New York: Wiley.

Kingson, E. R., Hirshorn, B. A., & Cornman, J. M. (1986). *Ties that bind.* Washington, DC: Seven Locks Press.

Knipscheer, K., & Antonucci, T. C. (Eds.). (in press). *Social network research: Methodological questions and substantive issues.* Amsterdam, The Netherlands: Swets & Zeitlinger.

Kreppner, K., & Lerner, R. M. (1989). *Family systems and life-span development.* Hillsdale, NJ: Erlbaum.

LaRocco, J. M., House, J. S., & French, J. R. P., Jr. (1980). Social support, occupational stress, and health. *Journal of Health and Social Behavior, 21,* 202–218.

Lawton, M. P., Moss, M., & Kleban, M. H. (1989). *Psychological well-being, mastery, and the social relationships of older people.* Manuscript submitted for publication.

Leichter, H. M. (1984). National productivity: A comparative perspective. In M. Holzer, & S. S. Nagel (Eds.), *Productivity and public policy* (pp. 45–68). Beverly Hills, CA: Sage.

Levitt, M. J. (in press). Attachment and close relationships: A life span perspective. In J. L. Gewirtz & W. F. Kurtines (Eds.), *Intersections with attachment.* Hillsdale, NJ: Erlbaum.

Lowenthal, M. F. (1975). The social economy in urban-working class communities. In G. Gappert & H. M. Rose (Eds.), *The social economy of cities* (pp. 447–469). Beverly Hills, CA: Sage.

Martineau, W. (1977). Informal social ties among urban Black Americans. *Journal of Black Studies, 8,* 83–104.

McAdoo, H. P. (1981). *Black families.* Beverly Hills, CA: Sage.

Moen, P., Kain, E. L., & Elder, G. H., Jr. (1983). Economic conditions and family life: Contemporary and historical perspectives. In R. R. Nelson & F. Skidmore (Eds.), *American families and the economy* (pp. 213–259). Washington, DC: National Academy Press.

Montagna, P. D. (1977). *Occupations and society: Toward a sociology of the labor market.* New York: Wiley.

Morgan, J. N. (1986). Unpaid productive activity over the life course. In Institute of Medicine/National Research Council (Eds.), *America's aging: Productive roles in an older society* (pp. 73–109). Washington, DC: National Academy Press.

Moss, M. (1979). Welfare dimensions of productivity measurement. In National Research Council (Ed.), *Measurement and interpretation of productivity* (pp. 276–308). Washington, DC: National Academy Press.

Myers, G. C., Manton, K. G., & Bacellar, H. (1986). Sociodemographic aspects of future unpaid productive roles. In Institute of Medicine/National Research Council (Ed.), *America's aging: Productive roles in an older society* (pp. 110–147). Washington, DC: National Academy Press.

National Institute on Aging. (1982). *A national plan for research on aging: Report of the National Research on Aging Planning Panel.* Washington, DC: U.S. Government Printing Office.

National Research Council. (Ed.). (1979). *Measurement and interpretation of productivity.* Washington, DC: National Academy Press.

Noelker, L., & Harel, Z. (1983). The integration of environment and network theories in explaining the aged's functioning and well-being. *Interdisciplinary Topics in Gerontology, 17,* 84–95.

Oppenheimer, V. K. (1981). The changing nature of life-cycle squeezes: Implications for the socioeconomic position of the elderly. In R. W. Fogel, E. Hatfiled, S. B. Kiesler & E. Shanas (Eds.) *Aging: Stability and change in the family* (pp. 47–81). New York: Academic Press.

Orth-Gomer, K., & Johnson, J. B. (1987). Social network interaction and mortality. A six year follow-up study of a random sample of the Swedish population. *Journal of Chronic Disease, 40,* 949–957.

Pearlin, L., & Schooler, C. (1978). The structure of coping. *Journal of Health and Social Behavior, 19,* 2–21.

Pearlin, L. I., & Turner, H. A. (1987). The family as a context of the stress process. In S. Kasl & C. L. Cooper (Eds.), *Stress and health issues in research methodology* (pp. 143–165). New York: Wiley.

Rosen, B. (1984). Productivity: Concepts and measurement. In M. Holzer & S. S. Nagel (Eds.), *Productivity and public policy*(pp. 19–43). Beverly Hills, CA: Sage.

Sarason, S. B. (1977). *Work, aging and social change: Professionals and the one life one career imperative.* New York: The Free Press.

Sarason, I. G., Sarason, B., & Pierce, G. R. (Eds.). (in press). *Social support: An interactional view.* New York: Wiley.

Schulz, R., & Rau, M. T. (1985). Social support through the life course. In S. Cohen & S. L. Syme (Eds.), *Social support and health* (pp. 129–149). New York: Academic Press.

Schoenbach, V. J., Kaplan, B. H., Fredman, L., & Kleinbaum, D. G. (1986). Social ties and mortality in Evans County, Georgia. *American Journal of Epidemiology, 123,* 577–591.

Seeman, T. E., & Syme, S. L. (1987). Social networks and coronary artery disease: A comparison of the structure and function of social relations as predictors of disease. *Psychosomatic Medicine, 49,* 340–353.

Smith, J. D. (1982). *The measurement of selected income flows in informal markets* (Final report no. TIR 81-28 to the Internal Revenue Service). Ann Arbor, MI: Institute for Social Research.

Soldo, B., & Manton, K. G. (1985). Changes in the health status and service needs of the oldest old: Current patterns and future trends. *Milbank Memorial Fund Quarterly, 63,* 286–323.

Stack, C. B. (1974). *All our kin: Strategies for survival in the Black community.* New York: Harper & Row.

Thoits, P. A. (1982). Conceptual methodological and theoretical problems in studying social support as a buffer against life stress. *Journal of Health and Social Behavior, 23,* 145–149.

Wellman, B. (1981). Applying network analysis to the study of support. In B. H. Gottlieb (Ed.), *Social networks and social support* (pp. 171–200). Beverly Hills, CA: Sage.

Wentowski, G. J. (1981). Reciprocity and the coping strategies of older people: Cultural dimensions of network building. *Gertontologist, 21,* 600–609.

Witte, A. D., & Simon, C. D. (1983). The impact of unrecorded economic activity on American families. In R. R. Nelson & F. Skidmore (Eds.), *American families and the economy* (pp. 145–182). Washington, DC: National Academy Press.

III

THE IMPACT OF PROVIDING CARE IN LATER-LIFE FAMILIES

12

OVERVIEW

Paula K. Ogrocki

Kent State University

The authors of the foregoing chapters of this volume have documented the nature and effects of stressful events for both older adults and their families and have discussed social support as a factor that may mediate the effects of stress. A broad and comprehensive literature has been established on the stressful nature of providing care to an impaired older adult. However, there is a great amount of variability in the reactions of families to the caregiving role and the stress experienced as a result of this role. It appears that some families adapt well whereas others do not, although the reasons for why this is so are not clear. It is likely that the coping responses of caregivers play a significant role in determining how these families adapt. The three chapters in this section examine caregiving stress and a variety of factors that could possibly alleviate this stress. In particular, these chapters explore the ways caregivers can and do cope with their stressful role and factors that can be employed to enhance effective coping.

The authors of these three chapters examine caregiving stress and coping from different perspectives. DeLongis and O'Brien focus on individual caregivers and their relationships to others in the family, especially relationships with the care-recipient. They introduce us to the concept of dyadic coping, whereby coping efforts of the caregiver and care-recipient are considered to be interactive. In particular, they emphasize the importance of one form of relationship-focused coping—empathy. Zarit focuses on interventions that have been developed to enhance the coping skills of caregivers and discusses several methodological issues involved in evaluating the effectiveness of these interventions. Additionally, he offers a new conceptualization of burden, which is a caregiving-specific measurement of stress. Townsend focuses on institutionalization as both an attempt to cope with caregiving stress and as a source of stress itself. Like Zarit, Townsend also addresses several methodological issues in the caregiving literature.

DeLongis and O'Brien introduce stress and coping as not only an individual cognitive process, but as an interpersonal process as well. They offer a cognitive interpersonal formulation of stress and coping, which integrates the cognitive factors of an individual within that individual's social context. These authors pinpoint the need for theory in the area of cognitive and interpersonal events in stress and coping among caregivers, asserting that because caregiving stress strongly involves interpersonal events, current models that do not consider the social context may be incomplete.

DeLongis and O'Brien apply this formulation of coping to the situation of providing care to a family member afflicted with Alzheimer's disease. As part of this interpersonal perspective, they introduce the concept of relationship-focused coping. As a third type of coping (in addition to emotion-focused and problem-focused coping), relationship-focused coping is described as involving the regulation of social relationships. One type of relationship-focused coping emphasized by DeLongis and O'Brien is empathic coping. As the name implies, this form of coping includes the concept of empathy, which involves making another person's experience one's own and, on this basis, expressing caring and understanding to that person. The role of empathy is discussed in terms of families caring for a person who has Alzheimer's disease. They suggest that empathic coping can help caregivers understand the emotions underlying the patient's cognitive and behavioral problems and that this understanding may help caregivers to circumvent some of the stress that they experience.

The concept of empathic coping is a unique contribution to the caregiving literature. Although the concept of empathy has been the focus of substantial work within the general helping literature, and despite the obvious helping nature of caregiving, empathy has tended to be overlooked in research. Throughout the literature the focus tends to be on the care-recipient as the direct cause of the stress that caregivers experience. However, DeLongis and O'Brien suggest that the stress and coping experienced in the caregiving situation occurs within a dyad, and thus is bidirectional. Thus, caregivers may inadvertently influence the levels of stress experienced in the caregiving situation because their attempts to cope have an impact on the care-recipient, as well as on themselves. The use of empathy may not only facilitate more effective coping among caregivers, but also may have the potential to improve the quality of the relationship between the caregiver and care-recipient.

Zarit discusses two basic types of interventions designed to enhance the coping skills of caregivers: (a) psychoeducational interventions aimed at improving and enhancing the personal resources of caregivers by modifying coping patterns and facilitating supportive relationships and (b) respite programs, which are interventions aimed at providing resources to relieve caregivers. The major goal of these interventions is to enhance the caregivers' skills in coping with the stressors of the caregiving situation. Such behavioral changes are designed to buffer stress not only through the acquisition of new coping skills, but also by facilitating supportive relationships.

The major focus of Zarit's chapter is on the effectiveness of these interventions. He points out that there is an abundance of programs and interventions that are designed to alleviate the stress of caregiving. However, little evidence for the effectiveness of these interventions has been reported. Because it is unlikely that the interventions and programs offered to caregivers to help them cope with the stress of their role are wholly ineffective, Zarit suggests that the studies examining these effects may not be adequately designed. He offers a careful analysis of the methodological limitations in research evaluating the effectiveness of psychoeducational and respite interventions, and offers a number of suggestions for improving the methodology. The value of Zarit's chapter is that it forces us to examine more carefully possible reasons why studies are not detecting effects rather than leading us to automatically conclude that these programs are ineffective.

Given the nature of burden as a construct specific to caregiving stress, the conceptualization and measurement of burden is a major issue in caregiving research. Zarit suggests that there are many limitations to burden as it has been previously defined, and he offers a new framework for conceptualizing burden. He goes beyond previous definitions of burden involving primary appraisal or the perception that caregiving is stressful, and focuses on secondary appraisal processes. According to this approach, caregivers evaluate whether their own resources (e.g., time, money, effort, social network, and emotions), are adequate to meet the demands of caregiving. Caregivers are thought to experience burden when they have to do more than they are willing, or if they perceive the situation as exceeding the resources they have available. Thus, the experience of burden varies widely across individuals. When planning and evaluating interventions for caregivers, Zarit argues that attention to this individual variation in the experience of caregiving burden must be considered because objective indicators of stress alone may not reflect the actual caregiving experience.

Townsend discusses institutionalization as both a stressor and as a means for coping. Her chapter is valuable in that she brings together two literatures that have been virtually autonomous: one that focuses on the precursors of institutional placement, and another that focuses on the consequences for the family following this placement. What her review makes clear is that nursing home placement may be an attempt to cope with the stress of caregiving, but the institutionalization of a loved one may pose new stressors with which families must cope.

Townsend raises important questions about factors that may be related to institutionalization. She discusses the dearth of research about the predisposing conditions leading to nursing home placement. Her review reveals that institutionalization is the result of a breakdown in the balance between the older adult's care needs and self-care abilities, and the primary caregiver's resources, motivation, and other larger support networks. Townsend conceptualizes burden in a manner similar to Zarit, speculating that nursing home placement occurs when the burden of caregiving becomes too great, that is, when caregivers perceive themselves as no longer having the ability or willingness to continue with the provision of resources.

It is further suggested that institutionalization of an older relative, which is meant as a means of coping, may actually become a source of caregiving stress. Although the relative's placement in a nursing home may liberate family caregivers from some of the time-consuming and physically demanding caregiving tasks, not all family caregivers appear to experience relief, and some may experience a negative impact on their time and their well-being. In regard to the social realm, some families experience improvement or continued closeness after institutionalization, whereas others suffer deterioration or continued conflict. Townsend also elucidates several important limitations of research on caregiving families and institutional placement and offers insightful suggestions for their solution.

The authors in this section go beyond the well-established fact that caregiving can be stressful and emphasize a variety of stress management strategies. Each delineates possible factors involved in the facilitation of effective coping, focusing on different aspects of the caregiving situation. Their perspectives and the interventions they suggest can be viewed in terms of primary, secondary, and tertiary prevention, with each differing in terms of the extensiveness and timing of the intervention relative to the caregiving process.

Primary prevention refers to interventions that are aimed at reducing the incidence of a problem. The concept of empathic coping offered by DeLongis and O'Brien has the potential to be used as a means of primary prevention. Empathy can be used to build a more positive relationship within the caregiver–care-recipient dyad by fostering awareness and understanding of the care-recipient's limitations and facilitating more effective coping. Secondary prevention refers to those interventions applied to people who are at risk for a particular problem, and those aimed at curtailing the duration of this problem through early detection and prompt action. Psychoeducational interventions, as discussed by Zarit, have the potential to reduce the stress experienced not only by enhancing the caregiver's understanding of the care-recipient's situation but also by facilitating actual behavior change that may relieve stress. Tertiary prevention refers to treatment given at a point when the manifestation of a problem is most severe. Institutionalization, as discussed by Townsend, can be conceptualized as tertiary prevention in that it often is a "last resort" intervention for the family and often takes place when family stress is high.

All of the authors in this section emphasize the importance of caregivers' personal resources. These resources have the potential to be drained as a result of the caregiving role, thus affecting the amount of stress experienced. The balance between the resources the caregiver has and the resources depleted by caregiving appears to be a crucial factor in the amount of stress these caregivers experience. The interventions discussed in this section can be viewed as having the underlying goal of increasing the resources of caregivers either by enabling caregivers to enhance their own resources through more effective coping, or by providing resources to caregivers through respite programs or institutionalization.

A common theme sounded by these authors is that caregiving and distress need not be synonymous. With an increased understanding of the many factors contributing to caregiving stress and coping, and the unique perspectives these authors offer to the caregiving literature, we may be able to move toward more effectively reducing the stress associated with the often inevitable situations that many later-life families face.

13

AN INTERPERSONAL FRAMEWORK FOR STRESS AND COPING: AN APPLICATION TO THE FAMILIES OF ALZHEIMER'S PATIENTS

Anita DeLongis
Tess O'Brien

University of British Columbia

With the aging of the population comes an urgent need to increase our understanding of the stress faced by later-life families and of how older adults and their families cope. Interest in this subject has focused primarily on the cognitive aspects of stress and coping. This focus has proved to be quite fruitful, generating a great deal of research and theory on stress and coping. However, with the notable exception of the literature on social support, little attention has been paid to the extent to which the occurrence of stressful events and their effects are determined by the social context.

In this chapter we consider the social context and describe interpersonal and cognitive processes that generate coping with and adaptation to stressful life circumstances. We draw heavily on cognitive models of stress and coping (Lazarus & DeLongis, 1983; Lazarus & Folkman, 1984, 1987), with the goal of extending the model's predictive ability by elucidating interpersonal dimensions of the stress process. We review literature pointing to a role of interpersonal factors in determining a number of aspects of the stress process: the onset of stress, which coping strategies are employed, the resources that are brought to bear in coping, the efficacy of those coping strategies, and the impact of stress on health and mood. Particularly in stressful situations in which others are involved, interpersonal factors may be important predictors of the individual's ability to manage the situation.

We would like to thank Rick Fabes, Darrin Lehman, Ron Pound, Sandra Parker, and Marianne Schroeder for their helpful comments.

Many of the sources of stress central to the lives of older adults are social in nature (see Chapter 3, this volume). Among the most frequently occurring major life events in old age are the serious illness or death of a loved one (Reich, Zautra, & Guarnaccia, 1989). Our understanding of the impact of network events such as these will be limited if we view the older adult in isolation, outside the context of family and the wider social sphere. In this chapter we highlight the critical role that interpersonal factors play in stress and coping in aging families, drawing on the context of caregiving for a family member with Alzheimer's disease to illustrate.

In describing a model of stress and coping that integrates interpersonal and cognitive dimensions, we discuss a function of coping that deserves attention in light of the interpersonal nature of many of the stressors faced by later-life families. In this chapter we posit the notion of relationship-focused coping, a form of coping directed at maintaining and regulating social relationships. We focus on empathic coping as one mode of relationship-focused coping that could enhance the well-being of later-life families, especially those that are faced with the task of caring for a chronically ill family member.

THE IMPACT OF ALZHEIMER'S DISEASE ON THE FAMILY

In coping with stressful events, we tend to draw not only on our own resources but also on the resources of those close to us. The financial, emotional, and physical well-being of those around us can be utilized in much the same way as our own personal resources to facilitate adaptive coping and ease us through difficult times. Of course, when the resources of others become depleted, as they often do during chronic illness, one effect is that multiple network members experience a loss of available resources. Clearly, the burden of chronic illness is experienced not only by the patient but also has widespread effects on the lives of family members.

As we have noted, many of the major life events most common to aging families tend to be ones that are associated with a decline in health and related resources of a family member. These health problems often generate a great deal of life change, bringing about frequent hassles in daily life and chronic stress across many months or years. One of the most stressful diseases a family can be faced with is Alzheimer's disease.

When a family member develops Alzheimer's disease, other family members face chronic, severe stress in multiple areas of their lives. The progressive degenerative nature of the disease produces cognitive, physical, and emotional deficits that markedly increase the patient's dependency on others. Caregivers often must dress, feed, bathe, and toilet their afflicted relatives (Deimling & Bass, 1986). Around-the-clock supervision is frequently required because of the patient's symptomatic wandering and nocturnal wakefulness (Chenoweth &

Spencer, 1986). Caregivers must also contend with other characteristic symptoms such as forgetfulness, confusion, disorientation, incontinence, and abrupt mood swings (Brody, 1988). Perhaps most devastating for caregivers is that they are providing care for family members who are increasingly unrecognizable as their former selves (Pearlin, Turner, & Semple, in press); in the advanced stages of the disease, victims often fail to recognize their caregivers (Cohen & Eisdorfer, 1986).

Furthermore, the patient's compromised functioning often creates a restriction of social activity for both patients and their caregivers (Haley, Levine, Lane Brown, Berry, & Hughes, 1987; Rabins, Mace, & Lucas, 1982). Several factors contribute to increased social isolation, including the patient's inability to communicate or otherwise take part in social situations, the patient's need for supervision, and the patient's disruptive behaviors (e.g., swearing and inappropriate sexual behaviors), which may cause embarrassment for the caregiver in social settings. Social isolation is an important factor in the development of depression (Coyne, 1976) and may in itself make coping more difficult for caregivers. Along with social isolation, "virtually every psychosocial factor reputed to be conducive to depressive reactions occurs within the context of caring for Alzheimer's patients" (Becker & Morrissey, 1988, p. 303).

Especially when the patient is the caregiver's spouse, the caregiver experiences a gradual and chronic loss of many of the previously supportive aspects of the relationship at a time when the caregiver may be particularly needy. As the disease progresses, the loss intensifies and the demands of caregiving markedly increase (Mace & Rabins, 1981). The spouse caregiver faces the loss of a lifelong partner, companion, and confidant. Many mutual leisure activities and social events can no longer be shared, and sexual relations become disrupted or diminished (Pearlin et al., in press).

For the adult children of Alzheimer's patients, a number of factors can intensify the stress surrounding the illness, which may in turn limit their abilities to provide care for their parents. Adult children, aware of the possibility of genetic transmission, may fear that they are witnessing their own and their children's future demise. Under such circumstances, an ill parent can become a painful reminder of their own frailty, increasing the difficulty and reluctance involved in caring for their parents (see Chapter 2, this volume). Another strain, especially acute among adult children, is that of balancing multiple role demands (such as those involved in marriage, parenthood, and employment) with those demands inherent in caregiving (Brody & Schoonover, 1986).

Clearly, families caring for Alzheimer's patients encounter myriad network stressors. These types of stressors may be unusually difficult, in part, because by their very nature they involve a disruption to the support system. Stressful situations that affect multiple members of a network simultaneously may diminish the amount of support available to deal with the situation and thereby amplify the stressful nature of the situation. Given a chronic degenerative disease such as Alzheimer's, all family members have to cope in some way with the disease. At the same time that each family member is attempting to come to terms with the disease and its implications, he or she typically is expected to provide support to others in the family.

The juxtaposition of the increase in stress and simultaneous decrease in support available from others may account, in part, for the increased family conflict often reported by those with a chronic illness (Niederehe & Fruge, 1984). Among families coping with Alzheimer's disease, disagreements arise over a variety of issues. A frequent source of conflict lies in decisions that must be made on behalf of the afflicted family member. For example, decisions must be made regarding the kind of care to be provided (Sheehan & Nuttall, 1988). Other sources of conflict may include longstanding antagonistic relationships, conflicting loyalties, money, and resolution of who will assume primary care for the patient (Springer & Brubaker, 1984). This increased conflict is likely to be one result of the increased level of day-to-day stress associated with the illness, and it undoubtedly contributes to a further reduction in family members' capacity to support one another. It is a sad irony that stressors affecting the entire family are, by their very nature, those in which its members feel a greater need to rely on one another while simultaneously feeling less able to help one another.

Much research has documented that under periods of stress or life change later-life families experience greater well-being and manage better when they can derive support from social relationships (see George, in press, for a review). In the case of Alzheimer's disease, caregivers who reported satisfaction with their social support system report higher levels of well-being than do those whose support needs are unmet (George & Gwyther, 1986). Findings in the literature on caregiving (Fiore, Becker, & Coppel, 1983; Fiore, Coppel, Becker, & Cox, 1986) are consistent with the host of findings on social support in the general population, which indicate that perception of support adequacy is more predictive of well-being than is actual amount of support received (e.g., Wethington & Kessler, 1986).

However, as the findings of recent studies suggest, the role of close others in the process of adapting to stress is broad and far-reaching, and not limited to what is generally considered to fall under the rubric of social support (Coyne & DeLongis, 1986). Although social relationships can serve many protective functions, they can become sources of stress as well (see Chapter 8, this volume). The literature on coping and support suggests that interpersonal factors can intensify levels of stress, influence coping responses, and have detrimental effects on well-being. These factors include upsetting interactions with others and negative responses from social network members.

The presence of upsetting interactions in the caregiver's support network has been found to be a significant predictor of both depression and general pathology among caregivers (Fiore et al., 1986; Sheehan & Nuttall, 1988). One study (Pagel, Erdly, & Becker, 1987) found perceived help from the support system to be unrelated to caregivers' depression. Rather, the presence of upsetting interactions within the support network predicted levels of depression, and changes in upset over time predicted changes in levels of depression. Thus, upsetting interpersonal events in one's social network may play a critical role in the etiology and maintenance of emotional problems among caregivers. Furthermore, the negative effects of a problematic relationship may be exacerbated among caregivers in that negative interactions with network members may potentiate the effect of other stressors (Kiecolt-Glaser, Dyer, & Shuttleworth, 1988). The chronic stress involved in caregiving may leave them more vulnerable to negative aspects of interactions than are noncaregivers because of their increased need for support. We have found similarly (Bolger, DeLongis, Kessler, & Schilling, 1989) that stress that is interpersonal in nature, such as that caused by a problem in a relationship, has a particularly strong effect on mood. Mood may be more strongly affected by interpersonal than other types of stressors because the very people who could have positively influenced our appraisals and coping may, under such circumstances, be a source of stress in themselves.

THE ROLE OF SOCIAL RELATIONSHIPS IN COGNITIVE APPRAISAL AND COPING

The importance and complexity of the role of social relationships in stress and coping suggests the need to more fully integrate interpersonal factors into theoretical models. Here we describe an evolving framework for the study of stress and coping that incorporates key cognitive and interpersonal factors. This framework complements and builds directly on a stress and coping framework in which the notion of cognitive appraisal plays a central role (Folkman, Lazarus, Dunkel-Schetter, DeLongis, & Gruen, 1986; Lazarus & Folkman, 1984). Within this model, two types of cognitive appraisals of potentially stressful encounters are of particular concern. When assessing a situation, a primary appraisal is initially made of its personal significance for well-being. This involves an examination of what is at stake in the situation. Next, a secondary appraisal is made as the person evaluates the options and resources available to deal with the situation. The process of appraisal is thought to be ongoing throughout the stressful encounter, with the stressor repeatedly reappraised as more information is obtained. These cognitive appraisals are a key determinant of which particular coping strategies will be attempted (Folkman, Lazarus, Dunkel-Schetter, DeLongis, & Gruen, 1986).

Coping refers to a person's cognitive and behavioral efforts to manage demands (Folkman & Lazarus, 1988; Folkman, Lazarus, Dunkel-Schetter et al., 1986). Two primary coping functions have been identified in previous research: active management of the situation (problem-focused coping) and emotion regulation (emotion-focused coping). Seeking information, taking direct action, and planned problem-solving are among ways of coping identified as directed at altering the stressful situation itself, referred to as problem-focused coping. Avoidance, denial, wishful thinking, and positive reappraisal have all been identified as modes of coping that are directed at regulating negative emotions engendered by the stressful situation, referred to as emotion-focused coping.

Cognitive Appraisals of Stressful Encounters

One issue that has not been addressed adequately in the literature is the extent to which there are social factors that influence the appraisal and coping process. Particularly when ambiguity is high in a stressful situation, as it is with Alzheimer's disease, we may be likely to rely on others' views to guide us in our appraisals of stressful situations. Family members of Alzheimer's patients must, as the patient deteriorates, engage in a process of reappraisal, lowering their expectations for the patient and changing their appraisals of what is socially unacceptable and what therefore threatens the fabric of their lives. By hearing about the behaviors and activities of afflicted members of others' families, and getting feedback from others on their own family members' behaviors and activities, they can become better able to put their ill family member's difficult behaviors in a more appropriate social context, with new norms and expectations (Zarit, Todd, & Zarit, 1986).

Of course, cognitive appraisals of the extent to which a situation is threatening depend not only on others' views, but also on our sense of the extent to which we have resources for coping (Folkman, Lazarus, Gruen, & DeLongis, 1986). Yet, cognitive appraisals of the adequacy of resources for coping may depend heavily on the availability of others to provide support (Lazarus & Folkman, 1984), which in turn may be determined largely by the quality of our social relationships.

Appraisals of the Self

Another way in which our social relationships may alter our cognitive appraisals of stressful situations is by influencing our sense of self-efficacy and control. Personal beliefs of efficacy play an important role in mediating the impact of stress on mood and health. People with a greater sense of personal control are more likely to use problem-focused forms of coping, whereas those who perceive control to be outside of their hands are more likely to engage in emotion-focused forms, particularly those involving denial-like and escape-avoidance processes (Lazarus & Folkman, 1984).

We have found (DeLongis, Bolger, & Kessler, 1988) that perceptions of control are predictive of the ways in which people cope with everyday stress. Those with a greater sense of personal control over stressful situations are more likely to engage in active problem-focused coping strategies, more likely to directly confront the situation, and less likely to simply give in. Perceptions of control (DeLongis, Bolger, & Kessler, 1988) and self-esteem (DeLongis, Folkman, & Lazarus, 1988) are also predictive of the effect of a stressor on well-being; those individuals who are high in perceived control and self-esteem exhibit better mood and health in the face of stress.

As we have suggested, however, perceptions of self-efficacy and control may depend, at least in part, on the feedback that others provide. Social relationships serve a protective function by giving us a sense of being loved and valued, which increases our self-efficacy or -esteem (Krause, Liang, & Yatomi, 1989). In turn, high levels of self-esteem are associated with greater subsequent receipt of emotional support (Dunkel-Schetter, Folkman, & Lazarus, 1987). In general, a supportive network that strengthens and reinforces our self-worth has beneficial effects on our perceptions of self-efficacy and control (see Chapter 4, this volume).

Although we are unaware of studies pertaining to the social context of self-efficacy and perceptions of control within the context of Alzheimer's disease, a number of researchers have examined these factors for other disease states. Bandura and his colleagues (Bandura, 1986; Taylor, Bandura, Ewart, Miller, & Debusk, 1985) found that wives' perceptions of their husbands' efficacy following myocardial infarction was highly correlated with the patients' own appraisal of self-efficacy. More important, the wife's appraisal of her husband's efficacy was predictive of the husband's behavior, even after controlling for his own self-efficacy. In another study, Vaughn and Leff (1976) found that although self-blame is considered to be one of the key features of depression, those depressed people who had a positive relationship with their spouse were relatively free of self-blame. These findings suggest that what are typically considered to be relatively stable characteristics of the person are, at least in part, social constructions (cf. Sullivan, 1953).

Coping with Stress

Social relationships influence coping in a number of ways. One way is through the use of social referencing (Bandura, 1986) whereby people turn to others for a sense of what is considered to be appropriate coping in a given situation. Coping behaviors are often modeled by those around us, and we can learn a great deal about their likely effects simply by observing them. This modeling of effective coping may be one reason why support groups tend to be so helpful to their members. As is true for families facing many of the stressors most common in aging, caregivers of patients with Alzheimer's disease will not find readily available coping models in most of their friends, neighbors, and co-workers. They will have to seek these models elsewhere. The support group provides the opportunity to improve coping by teaching more effective ways of managing the special problems of the Alzheimer's patient (see Chapter 11, this volume).

Social relationships also influence coping through the direct provision of information about the likely efficacy of particular coping strategies. Support groups can serve this function as well. Especially in the early stages of caregiving, group members can provide useful information about what to expect of the patient over the course of the disease, enabling caregivers to anticipate challenges and plan successful ways of coping.

One cost of an exclusively cognitive focus is the failure to consider the special requirements of successful coping when others are involved in the stressful situation. When the source of stress is tension or conflict in a social relationship, it may be particularly important to consider the coping of both the individual and involved others. In a study of dyadic coping (DeLongis, Bolger, & Kessler, 1987), the coping of others involved in the problem not only constrained the way in which the person could cope but also was an independent contributor to the person's mood. Furthermore, some coping strategies tended to be effective only when paired with a similarly constructive strategy on the part of the other person involved in the problem. For example, the effects of coping with tension in a social relationship via compromise tended to depend on the coping of involved others. If both people compromised, the effect of the compromise on the person's mood tended to be positive. If one person compromised, but the other person did not (perhaps engaging in either confrontation or withdrawal), the effects of the compromise strategy on the person's mood tended to be negative.

Even in coping with stressful situations that do not represent a relationship problem per se, we have found that the efficacy of a given coping strategy depends heavily on the response of involved others to the strategy. In a longitudinal study (DeLongis, O'Brien, Silver, & Wortman, 1990), the coping behaviors of recently bereaved respondents were studied. The receipt of a negative response from members of the social network was predictive of three aspects of the respondents' coping: (a) reduced *desire* to cope over time, (b) reduced *effort* put into coping over time, and (c) reduced *effectiveness* of the coping strategy when it was used. Bereaved parents' coping efforts tended to be rendered ineffective if others responded negatively to them when they tried to cope. On the other hand, coping efforts that were met with support tended to be highly effective in helping the bereaved parents to recover from their grief. This held even after controlling for their desire to cope, their coping efforts, and their prior level of depression. In a similar vein, among those caring for a family member with Alzheimer's disease, emotional support from family was associated with more effective coping styles among caregivers (Scott, Roberto, & Hutton, 1986). Taken together, these findings point to the importance of social relationships in determining both the manner in which people cope and the effects that those coping strategies have on well-being.

RELATIONSHIP-FOCUSED COPING

Given the importance of social relationships in stress and coping, our ability to regulate and maintain those relationships may be a critical determinant of coping efficacy and outcomes. Successful coping may depend not only on our ability to keep our emotions under control and on our ability to resolve problems, but also on our ability to regulate our relationships with involved others. Given that our well-being is strongly affected by our social relationships, it may be critical for us to cope in ways that solve our problems without alienating or upsetting involved others, or without creating problems for them.

Whereas emotion-focused modes of coping involve intrapsychic regulation processes, relationship-focused modes of coping involve interpersonal regulation processes. We see both intrapsychic and interpersonal regulation as being significant contributors to the successful resolution of stressful encounters. Identifying this relationship-focused function of coping allows us to look more fully at the transactional nature of stress and coping.

Interpersonal regulation involves processes aimed at establishing, maintaining, or disrupting our social relationships (Campos, Campos, & Barnett, 1989). Relationships that further our sense of emotional relatedness, self-esteem, and self-efficacy offer us a great deal. Our ability to establish and then to maintain these sorts of relationships in the face of stress may critically influence our ability to manage stressful situations (see Chapter 6, this volume). For example, maintaining a sense of emotional relatedness with others may be one of the key factors that influences both the ability to sustain caregiving efforts and the caregiver's well-being. Failure to do so often results in depression and withdrawal of efforts and, in turn causes guilt over being unable to cope with the ill family member (Cantor, 1983).

Although it is often beneficial to maintain and enhance our social relationships, there are times when disrupting our relationships may be adaptive. Relationships that are abusive or extremely problematic may have serious detrimental consequences if continued (see Chapter 8, this volume). Modes of relationship-focused coping that may disrupt or damage social relationships include criticizing, ignoring, confronting, or minimizing contact with other people. Jacobson, McDonald, Follette, and Berley (1985) examined the effect of these coping strategies on the health and well-being of either the person engaging in them or the recipient (see, e.g., Manne & Zautra, 1989, for an exception).

However, several studies have shown that when people reported engaging in more confrontive coping they tended to have poorer mood (e.g., Folkman, Lazarus, Dunkel-Schetter et al., 1986). The negative association between mood and engaging in confrontation may be due, at least in part, to the potentially damaging repercussions for social relationships. We can coerce an involved other into yielding to our position or expectations, perhaps getting that person to do what we need to solve the problem. However, if we antagonize the person or damage their sense of adequacy, this can lead to a loss of available support in both ongoing and future stressful circumstances. This reduced support, in turn, can result in an increased risk for mood and health problems (House, Landis, & Umberson, 1988).

Just as we can identify modes of coping that may damage relationships, modes that may enhance or preserve relationships can be identified as well. These include negotiating or compromising with involved others, considering the person's limitations, and being empathic. This latter mode of coping, empathic coping, is one that has been given short shrift in the coping literature, yet may be of importance in managing many of the stressors relevant to aging families, particularly those stressors related to the serious illness of a family member. We focus on it as one form of relationship-focused coping that may be useful in the context of coping with Alzheimer's disease.

Empathic Coping

Although rarely brought into the stress literature, empathy has long been considered a mediator or contributor to positive social interaction and is thought to play a role in the development of affective bonds, understanding, and caring actions between people (Eisenberg & Strayer, 1987). We use empathic coping to refer to attempts to both perceive accurately the affective world of others involved in the stressful situation and to communicate accurately and sensitively one's affective understanding to those persons (see Goldstein & Michaels, 1985). It involves the following dimensions (Macarov, 1978): (a) taking the role of the other through viewing the world as the other sees it, (b) experiencing the other's feelings, (c) adeptly interpreting the feelings underlying the other's nonverbal communication, and (d) expressing caring or understanding in a nonjudgmental or helping way.

The internal processes involved in empathic perception (Marcia, 1987; Reik, 1949; Strayer, 1987) offer clues to coping tasks that need to be accomplished to generate empathic coping:

1. Identification—becoming absorbed in contemplation of the other person while paying attention to the other.
2. Incorporation—internalizing the other and making the other's experience one's own.
3. Reverberation—simultaneously experiencing the other's feelings and evoking one's own affective and cognitive associations to that experience.
4. Detachment—moving away from the merged experience and recognizing the other as separate from oneself.

Empathic coping paradoxically involves both a merging with the other's affective experience as well as a recognition of one's own individuality and separateness from the other (Strayer, 1987).

Maintaining a balance of affective sharing and self–other differentiation may be crucial to the well-being of both caregiver and patient. As the patient's dementia progresses, caregivers may have difficulty understanding their ill family members, and they may consequently disengage and reduce attempts to emotionally connect and relate to the family member. This lack of emotional relatedness can lead to more depersonalized caregiving and to fewer rewards for sustaining care. Conversely, those caregivers who become overinvolved with their afflicted relative, losing their sense of self–other differentiation, may neglect themselves and become burned out by focusing their energies exclusively on caregiving. Burnout may be more likely in caregiving with Alzheimer's patients because caregivers often feel reluctant or guilty about asking for or accepting help or about seeking respite care (Quayhagen & Quayhagen, 1988). In our focus groups, caregivers often report that they started to cope better and feel better when they realized that they had to take care of themselves, too, which led them to seek ways to free their time by utilizing informal and formal support to help with caregiving tasks. Caregivers who are unable to meet their own needs face the danger of losing a fuller involvement in life, wrenching their only sense of meaning and purpose out of a life restricted primarily to caregiving (cf. Coyne, Wortman, & Lehman, 1988).

Despite cognitive impairments, patients still have strong needs for comfort, intimacy, and continued involvement (Cohen & Eisdorfer, 1986). Empathic coping involves an attempt to search for ways to keep the patient included in ongoing interactions. It also involves attempts to communicate affection and understanding to the patient. This might be accomplished through physical touch, facial expressions, or vocal tones.

A particularly important function of empathic coping among caregivers is that it can facilitate positive interactions between the caregiver and the patient. This may occur primarily through a shift in the caregiver's responses away from an excessive reality-imposing orientation to a more accepting orientation that enables the caregiver and the afflicted family member to enjoy a better sense of emotional relatedness. If caregivers persist in pointing out to their forgetful and disoriented family members that they are not in touch with reality, shame, hurt, and increased confusion may result in the Alzheimer's patient. If, on the other hand, caregivers attempt to deal with these symptoms by trying to sense the emotion underlying the patient's statements, they may be able to offer validating understanding that could quell the emotional turmoil of the afflicted family member. Caregivers who can enter the patient's world may be more inclined to accept and validate the family member's emotions than to impose a forgotten reality on the patient. Rather than trying to bring the patient to his or her senses, caregivers may find it more effective to reassure the patient (Safford, 1986).

An elderly retired physician from one of our focus groups provides an example of this type of coping. After a period of regularly bathing his afflicted wife, he found that she started to adamantly object to being bathed by him. She no longer knew him, sometimes thinking he was her uncle, her neighbor, or her son. No longer recognizing him as her husband, she could not permit him to bathe her. Understanding why she now saw him as an inappropriate helper, he engaged the help of a female homemaking service provider. The wife happily agreed to her help.

The Role of Empathic Coping in the Stress Process

Although there are undoubtedly individual differences in tendencies and abilities to engage in empathic processes (Strayer, 1987), situational and interpersonal cues may play an important role in eliciting empathic coping. The distress of another is one obvious cue (Buck, 1989). There are some factors, however, that may inhibit the use of empathic coping strategies. For example, when people are highly distressed or anxious they are unlikely to engage in empathic coping (Batson, Fultz, & Schoenrade, 1987). Caregivers who experience high levels of personal distress when interacting with their demented family members may be more inclined to the exclusive use of emotion-focused forms of coping in order to regulate their anxiety (Katz, 1963).

If an emotion-focused form of coping, such as denial or avoidance, is engaged in and inhibits the experiencing of emotions, the ability to comprehend and empathically respond to another person's emotions might be thwarted. This impediment of denial-like strategies to engaging in empathic coping may be one reason why avoidance strategies are more effective with short-term stressors and relate to poor psychosocial adjustment when used on a long-term basis (Roth & Cohen, 1986). The use of avoidance strategies, such as fantasy, by caregivers of Alzheimer's patients have been found to be associated with greater psychological distress (Dundon, Cramer, & Nowak, 1987; Quayhagen & Quayhagen, 1988) and higher levels of conflict in the caregiver–patient relationship (Stephens, Norris, Kinney, Ritchie, & Grotz, 1988). We are not suggesting, however, that emotion-focused forms of coping are necessarily ineffective. On the contrary, there are numerous contexts in which they are most adaptive (see Lazarus, 1983). Nonetheless, the long-term efficacy of either emotion- or problem-focused forms of coping is not likely to be high if they are engaged in without regard to their impact on key social relationships. Caregivers who rely exclusively on either emotion- or problem-focused coping strategies, ignoring relationship-focused modes of coping, are likely to generate a multitude of problems in their efforts directed at solving that problem.

For instance, in the example of the caregiver who was faced with the problem of his wife's resistance to his bathing her, a wide variety of strategies could be applied to cope with the situation. An exclusively emotion-focused orientation that ignored both the problem (the wife's need for a bath) and his relationship with his wife might result in the husband relying on palliative coping efforts such as drinking or turning to other activities to escape the situation. Alternatively, a purely problem-focused orientation might result in the husband's repeated, albeit frustrated, attempts to bathe his wife. With the addition of a relationship-focused orientation, he would expend effort on strategies geared toward increasing understanding of the source of his wife's distress as a way of regulating and maintaining his relationship with her. Once an understanding of the source of her distress is developed, appropriate and effective emotion- and problem-focused strategies can be implemented that minimize damage to the social relationship.

The Role of Sympathy in Empathic Coping

Sympathy, although related to empathy, can either inhibit or be generated from empathic coping. It is important to distinguish these two related concepts to understand the role that can be played by both empathy and sympathy in caregiving and support processes. Sympathy has been described as a heightened awareness of another's distress that elicits the desire to see that person's distress alleviated. In contrast, empathic coping efforts are geared toward understanding another (Wispe, 1986). When sympathy is paired with empathic coping, it is more likely that there will be a fit between what the other person is seeking and what is being offered. When sympathy is not accompanied by empathic coping, however, support might be offered without adequate understanding of the recipient's feelings or concerns. It is this combination of high sympathy and low empathy that may help to account for the prevalence of support attempts that fail, as has been reported in the literature (e.g., Coyne et al., 1988; Lehman, Ellard, & Wortman, 1986; Wortman & Lehman, 1985).

Caregivers who are primarily moved by sympathy to alleviate their loved one's distress may do more for the patient than is necessary, prematurely taking over any activities that the patient shows any difficulty performing. They may fail to allow the patient to contribute to family or household activities or fail to find ways to sustain the patient's emotional involvement in family life. Empathic coping may facilitate in caregivers the ability to recognize when their help is needed, and when it is not, thus fostering appropriate problem-focused coping in the caregiver.

CONCLUSIONS AND SUGGESTIONS FOR FUTURE RESEARCH

The quality of the relationship that the caregiver is able to sustain with the family member who has Alzheimer's disease may be largely determined by the extent to which the caregiver engages in relationship-focused modes of coping (cf. Tune, Lucas-Blaustein, & Rovner, 1988). The ways in which we regulate our social relationships could critically influence the occurrence of stressful events as well as how we are able to manage stressful circumstances. Research aimed at elucidating the processes of relationship regulation and other interpersonal dimensions of stress and coping could greatly expand the explanatory power of our models.

Too little attention has been paid to the extent to which life's stresses are basically interpersonal in nature. The interpersonal aspects of stress and coping may be all the more important when considering the stressful situations often faced by later-life families. Given that interpersonal sources of stress have, by far, the more serious consequences for health and well-being (Bolger et al., 1989), we advocate a stress and coping framework that integrates key cognitive and interpersonal factors. Such an integrative framework poses a number of issues that future research should address. We must attend to the coping of involved others and ask what the "goodness of fit" is between the coping strategies employed by those involved. Is one person using exclusively denial-like strategies, whereas another is attempting to engage primarily in planful problem-solving? What are the implications of such a mismatch in coping? To what extent does the coping of involved others determine the individual's health and well-being as well as the efficacy of his or her own coping strategies?

In addition, we must ask whether our measures adequately assess the range of strategies used to cope with what are often primarily interpersonal events. To the extent that the social context has been excluded from our models, we cannot expect our current measures to include key variables. We have had success in adding a number of relationship-focused dimensions, including empathic coping, to our measures of coping.

Methodologies that strive to capture the dynamic processes of stress and coping also need to be utilized. We have found that methodologies involving closely spaced repeated measures, often in the form of daily diaries, increase our predictive power by allowing the assessment of changes in stress and coping and well-being over time. Our abilities to advance the well-being of later-life families may be strongly determined by our abilities to capture the reciprocal intrapsychic and interpersonal dimensions of stress and coping.

REFERENCES

Bandura, A. (1986). Self-efficacy in physiological activation and health-promoting behavior. In J. Madden IV, S. Matthysse, & J. Barchas (Eds.), *Adaptation, learning, and affect*. New York: Raven Press.

Batson, C. D., Fultz, J., & Schoenrade, J. (1987). Adults' emotional reactions to the distress of others. In N. Eisenberg & J. Strayer (Eds.), *Empathy and its development* (pp. 163–184). New York: Cambridge University Press.

Becker, J., & Morrissey, E. (1988). Difficulties in assessing depressive-like reactions to chronic severe external stress as exemplified by spouse care-giving of Alzheimer patients. *Psychology and Aging, 3,* 300–306.

Bolger, N., DeLongis, A., Kessler, R. C., & Schilling, E. A. (1989). The emotional effects of daily stress. *Journal of Personality and Social Psychology.*

Brody, E. M. (1988). The long haul: A family odyssey. In L. F. Jarvik & C. H. Winograd (Eds.), *Treatments for the Alzheimer's patient: The long haul.* New York: Springer.

Brody, E. M., & Schoonover, C. B. (1986). Patterns of parent-care when adult daughters work and when they do not. *The Gerontologist, 26,* 372–381.

Buck, R. (1989). Emotional communication in personal relationships: A developmental-interactionist view. In *Review of Personality and Social Psychology: 10: Close relationships* (pp. 144–163). Newbury Park, CA: Sage.

Campos, J. J., Campos, R. G., & Barnett, K. C. (1989). Emergent themes in the study of emotional development and emotion regulation. *Developmental Psychology, 25,* 394–402.

Cantor, M. J. (1983). Strain among caregivers: A study of experience in the United States. *The Gerontologist, 23,* 597–604.

Chenoweth, B., & Spencer, B. (1986). Dementia: The experience of family caregivers. *The Gerontologist, 26,* 267–272.

Cohen, D., & Eisdorfer, C. (1986). *The loss of self: A family resource for the care of Alzheimer's disease and related disorders.* New York: Norton.

Coyne, J. C. (1976). Toward an interactional description of depression. *Psychiatry, 39,* 28–40.

Coyne, J. C., & DeLongis, A. (1986). Going beyond social support: The role of social relationships in adaptation. *Journal of Consulting and Clinical Psychology, 54,* 454–460.

Coyne, J. C., Wortman, C. B., & Lehman, D. R. (1988). The other side of support-emotional overinvolvement and miscarried helping. In B. Gottlieb (Ed.), *Marshaling social support* (pp. 305–330). Newbury Park, CA: Sage.

Deimling, G. T., & Bass, D. M. (1986). Symptoms of mental impairment among elderly adults and their effects on family caregivers. *Journal of Gerontology, 41,* 778–784.

DeLongis, A., Bolger, N., & Kessler, R. C. (1987, August). *Coping with marital conflict.* Paper presented at the meeting of the American Psychological Association, New York, NY.

DeLongis, A., Bolger, N., & Kessler, R. C. (1988, August). *Cognitive appraisal and coping with daily interpersonal stress.* Paper presented at the meeting of the American Psychological Association, Atlanta, GA.

DeLongis, A., Folkman, S., & Lazarus, R. S. (1988). The impact of daily stress on health and mood: Psychological and social resources as mediators. *Journal of Personality and Social Psychology, 54,* 486–495.

DeLongis, A., Silver, R. C., O'Brien, T., & Wortman, C. B. (1990). *The interpersonal implications of personal coping strategies among parents who have lost a child.* Manuscript submitted for publication.

Dundon, M. M., Cramer, S. H., & Nowak, C. A. (1987, August). *Distress and coping among caregivers of victims of Alzheimer's disease.* Paper presented at the meeting of the American Psychological Association, New York, NY.

Dunkel-Schetter, C., Folkman, S., & Lazarus, R. S. (1987). Correlates of support receipt. *Journal of Personality and Social Psychology, 53,* 71–80.

Eisenberg, N., & Strayer, J. (1987). *Empathy and its development.* New York: Cambridge University Press.

Fiore, J., Becker, J., Coppel, D. B. (1983). Social network interactions: A buffer or a stress. *American Journal of Community Psychology, 11,* 423–439.

Fiore, J., Coppel, D. B., Becker, J., & Cox, G. B. (1986). Social support as a multifaceted concept: Examination of important dimensions for adjustment. *American Journal of Community Psychology, 14,* 93–111.

Folkman, S., & Lazarus, R. S. (1988). The relationship between coping and emotion: Implications for theory and research. *Social Science Medicine, 26,* 309–317.

Folkman, S., Lazarus, R. S., Dunkel-Schetter, C., DeLongis, A., & Gruen, R. J. (1986). The dynamics of a stressful encounter: Cognitive appraisal, coping, and encounter outcomes. *Journal of Personality and Social Psychology, 50,* 992–1003.

Folkman, S., Lazarus, R. S., Gruen, R. J., & DeLongis, A. (1986). Appraisal, coping, health status, and psychological symptoms. *Journal of Personality and Social Psychology, 50,* 571–579.

George, L. K. (in press). Stress, social support and depression over the life-course. In K. Markides & C. Cooper (Eds.), *Aging, stress, and health.* New York: Wiley.

George, L. K., & Gwyther, L. P. (1986). Caregiver well-being: A multidimensional examination of family caregivers of demented adults. *The Gerontologist, 26*(3), 253–259.

Goldstein, A. P., & Michaels, G. Y. (1985). *Empathy development, training, and consequences.* Hillsdale, NJ: Erlbaum.

Haley, W. E., Levine, E. G., Lane Brown, S., Berry, J. W., & Hughes, G. H. (1987). Psychological, social, and health consequences of caring for a relative with senile dementia. *Journal of the American Geriatrics Society, 35,* 405–411.

House, J. S., Landis, K., & Umberson, D. (1988). Social relationships and health. *Science, 241,* 540–545.

Jacobson, N. S., McDonald, D. W., Follette, W. C., & Berley, R. A. (1985). Attribution processes in distressed and nondistressed married couples. *Cognitive Therapy and Research, 9,* 33–50.

Katz, R. L. (1963). *Empathy: Its nature and uses.* London: Free Press of Glencoe.

Kiecolt-Glaser, J. K., Dyer, C. S., & Shuttleworth, E. C. (1988). Upsetting social interactions and distress among Alzheimer's disease family caregivers: A replication and extension. *American Journal of Community Psychology, 16,* 825–837.

Krause, N., Liang, J., & Yatomi, N. (1989). Satisfaction with social support and depressive symptoms: A panel analysis. *Psychology and Aging, 4,* 88–97.

Lazarus, R. S. (1983). The costs and benefits of denial. In S. Breznitz (Ed.), *The denial of stress* (pp. 1–30). New York: International Universities Press.

Lazarus, R. S., & DeLongis, A. (1983). Psychological stress and coping in aging. *American Psychologist, 38,* 245–254.

Lazarus, R. S., & Folkman, S. (1984). *Stress, appraisal, and coping.* New York: Springer.

Lazarus, R. S., & Folkman, S. (1987). Transactional theory and research on emotions and coping. *European Journal of Personality, 1,* 141–169.

Lehman, D. R., Ellard, J. H., & Wortman, C. B. (1986). Social support for the bereaved: Recipients' and providers' perspectives on what is helpful. *Journal of Consulting and Clinical Psychology, 54,* 438–446.

Macarov, D. (1978). Empathy: The charismatic chimera. *Journal of Education for Social Work, 14,* 86–92.

Mace, N., & Rabins, P. V. (1981). *The 36-hour day.* Baltimore: The Johns Hopkins University Press.

Manne, S. L., & Zautra, A. J. (1989). Spouse criticism and support: Their association with coping and psychological adjustment among women with rheumatoid arthritis. *Journal of Personality and Social Psychology, 56,* 608–617.

Marcia, J. (1987). Empathy and psychotherapy. In N. Eisenberg & J. Strayer (Eds.), *Empathy and its development* (pp. 81–102). New York: Cambridge University Press.

Niederehe, G., & Fruge, E. (1984). Dementia and family dynamics: Clinical research issues. *Journal of Geriatric Psychiatry, 17,* 21–56.

Pagel, M. D., Erdly, W. W., & Becker, J. (1987). Social networks: We get by with (and in spite of) a little help from our friends. *Journal of Personality and Social Psychology, 53*(4), 793–804.

Pearlin, L. I., Turner, H., & Semple, S. (in press). Coping and the mediation of caregiver stress. In E. Light & B. Liebowitz (Eds.), *Alzheimer's disease treatment and family stress: Directions for research* (NIMH Publication). Washington, DC: U.S. Government Printing Office.

Quayhagen, M. P., & Quayhagen, M. (1988). Alzheimer's stress: Coping with the caregiving role. *The Gerontologist, 28,* 391–396.

Rabins, P. V., Mace, N. L., & Lucas, M. J. (1982). The impact of dementia on the family. *Journal of the American Medical Association, 248,* 333–335.

Reich, J. W., Zautra, A. J., Guarnaccia, C. A. (1989). Effects of disability and bereavement on the mental health status of older adults. *Psychology and Aging, 4,* 57–65.

Reik, T. (1949). *Listening with the third ear: The inner experience of the psychoanalyst.* New York: Grove Press.

Roth, S., & Cohen, L. J. (1986). Approach, avoidance, and coping with stress. *American Psychologist, 41,* 813–819.

Safford, F. (1986). *Caring for the mentally impaired elderly: A family guide.* New York: Henry Hall.

Scott, J. P., Roberto, K. A., & Hutton, J. T. (1986). Families of Alzheimer's victims: Family support to the caregivers. *Journal of the American Geriatrics Society, 34,* 348–354.

Sheehan, N. W., & Nuttall, P. (1988). Conflict, emotion, and personal strain among family caregivers. *Family Relations, 37,* 92–98.

Springer, D., & Brubaker, T. (Eds.). (1984). *Family caregivers and dependent elderly: Minimizing stress and maximizing independence.* Beverly Hills, CA: Sage.

Stephens, M. A. P., Norris, V. K., Kinney, J. M., Ritchie, S. W., & Grotz, R. C. (1988). Stressful situations in caregiving: Relations between caregiver coping and well-being. *Psychology and Aging, 3,* 208–209.

Strayer, J. (1987). Affective and cognitive perspective on empathy. In N. Eisenberg & J. Strayer (Eds.), *Empathy and its development* (pp. 218–244). New York: Cambridge University Press.

Sullivan, H. S. (1953). *The interpersonal theory of psychiatry.* New York: Norton.

Taylor, C. B., Bandura, A., Ewart, C. K., Miller, N. H., & Debusk, R. R. (1985). Exercise testing to enhance wives' confidence in their husbands' cardiac capabilities soon after clinically uncomplicated myocardial infarction. *American Journal of Cardiology, 55,* 635–638.

Tune, L. E., Lucas-Blaustein, M., & Rovner, B. W. (1988). Psychosocial interventions. In L. F. Jarvik & C. H. Winograd (Eds.), *Treatments for the Alzheimer patient: The long haul* (pp. 123–136). New York: Springer.

Vaughn, C. E. & Leff, J. P. (1976). The influence of family and social factors in the course of psychiatric illness. *British Journal of Psychiatry, 129,* 125–137.

Wethington, E., & Kessler, R. C. (1986). Perceived support, received support, and adjustment to stressful life events. *Journal of Health and Social Behavior, 27,* 78–89.

Wispe, L. (1986). The distinction between sympathy and empathy: To call forth a concept, a word is needed. *Journal of Personality and Social Psychology, 50,* 314–321.

Wortman, C. B., & Lehman, D. R. (1985). Reactions to victims of life crises: Support attempts that fail. In I. G. Sarason & B. R. Sarason (Eds.), *Social support: Theory, research and applications* (pp. 463–489). Dordrecht, The Netherlands: Martinus Nijhoff.

Zarit, S. H., Todd, P. A., & Zarit, J. M. (1986). Subjective burden of husbands and wives as caretakers: A longitudinal study. *The Gerontologist, 26,* 260–266.

14

INTERVENTIONS WITH FRAIL
ELDERS AND THEIR FAMILIES:
ARE THEY EFFECTIVE AND WHY?

Steven H. Zarit

Pennsylvania State University

Family care is a pivotal issue for aging individuals and for society as a whole. Medical and public health measures have enabled unprecedented numbers of people to survive into old age. In 1900, about 40% of a cohort could expect to live to age 65 or beyond, whereas currently the figure is approximately 70% (U.S. Senate, 1985–1986). Although the majority of elderly people are able to live independently, significant numbers require some assistance ranging from minimal levels of help (e.g., with shopping or heavy housekeeping chores) to around-the-clock supervision or assistance. Families are the major source of assistance to elderly people who have disabilities, with estimates of as many as 2.2 million family caregivers (Stone, Cafferata, & Sangl, 1987). These care arrangements have implications for the quality of life of both caregivers and care-recipients. Quality of care affects the well-being, morbidity, and mortality of the older person, and the stressfulness of the care situation has implications for the caregiver's own emotional and physical health. Family involvement is also related to the need for formal long-term care services. On the one hand, encouragement and support for family care can reduce the cost of nursing homes and other forms of custodial care. On the other hand, however, it is increasingly recognized that family care is associated with a variety of costs ranging from lost work days and decreased efficiency on the job to increased health problems for caregivers.

Over the past 10 years, numerous studies have documented the stressfulness of family caregiving. Evidence suggests that there is considerable variability in adaptation to caregiving, but as a group caregivers report increased rates of physical and mental health problems and decreases in life domains that support well-being, including social and leisure activities and in the quality of family relationships (Anthony-Bergstone, Zarit, & Gatz, 1988; Cantor, 1983; Deimling & Bass, 1986; George & Gwyther, 1986; Poulshock & Deimling, 1984). There is now general agreement about the stressfulness of caregiving, but surprisingly few studies have focused on what type of interventions can most effectively reduce stress. Innovative programs are described in the literature, but evidence of their effectiveness is often anecdotal, or evaluations are flawed by such problems as inadequate sampling, inadequate or inappropriate measurement, or the absence of a control group. In this chapter I discuss findings about the effectiveness of various interventions, and I highlight the methodological limitations of current approaches to evaluating outcomes. New directions for future studies are proposed.

Interventions are categorized into two broad types based on their primary goal or objective. The first type includes programs that are designed to improve or enhance the caregiver's abilities for managing the patient or care situations. Psychoeducational interventions including support groups are the main example of this approach. The second type of intervention provides new resources that relieve the caregiver of some portion of routine care activities. Examples of this approach include day care, in-home respite, and overnight respite.

IMPROVING THE CAREGIVER'S ABILITIES: PSYCHOEDUCATIONAL INTERVENTIONS

Although a variety of interventions for family caregivers are now reported in the literature, emphasis is often placed on providing information and skills training so that caregivers can cope more effectively with daily stressors and on the development of supportive relationships that buffer stress (see Clark & Rakowski, 1983; Smyer, Zarit, & Qualls, 1990; Zarit, Orr, & Zarit, 1985). A psychoeducational format is often used, which combines didactic presentations and the use of group process to achieve objectives. In contrast to more traditional clinical approaches, psychoeducational interventions operate on the assumption that a client's problems are the result of lack of knowledge or learning, not pathology or deficient habits. Support groups have been the most popular of these interventions and are now available in most communities. Numerous articles have reported case studies of support groups or related kinds of interventions.

The effectiveness of support groups and similar psychoeducational interventions has been evaluated in four controlled studies (Gallagher, Lovett, & Zeiss, in press; Haley, Brown, & Levine, 1987a; Toseland, Rossiter, & Labrecque, 1989; Zarit, Anthony, & Boutselis, 1987). Table 1 summarizes the major features of these studies. Gallagher and her associates (Silven et al., 1986) compared a Life Satisfaction group modeled on Lewinsohn's "Control Your De-

TABLE 1 Four controlled studies of group interventions

Investigators	Conditions	Subjects	Observed outcome
Gallagher, Lovett, & Zeiss, in press	1. Life satisfaction 2. Problem solving 3. Delayed treatment	Any caregiver	Decreased depression and burden
Toseland, Rossiter, Labrecque, 1989	1. Support Group: professional leader 2. Support group: peer leader 3. Respite only	Any caregiver	Decreased psychiatric symptoms; no change in burden
Haley, Brown, & Levine, 1987a	1. Support group: professional leader 2. Support/stress management: professional leader 3. Wait list	Caregivers of dementia patients	No significant changes in depression or life satisfaction; participants rated groups as helpful
Zarit, Anthony, & Boutselis, 1987	1. Individual and family counseling 2. Support group 3. Wait list	Caregivers of dementia patients	Decreases in burden and psychiatric symptoms in all groups; Gains maintained at 1 year

pression" class (Lewinsohn, Munoz, Youngren, & Zeiss, 1978) with a Problem-Solving group modeled on the approach of D'Zurilla (D'Zurilla, 1986; D'Zurilla & Goldfried, 1971). Attention was focused on the caregiver's mood in the Life Satisfaction group, whereas learning strategies to modify identified problems was the focus of the Problem-Solving group. Toseland and his associates focused on the role of support group leadership, comparing the results of groups led by professionals with those led by peers.

Both Haley et al. and Zarit et al. used a professionally led support group that focused on educating caregivers about the patient's disease and care alternatives and training them in problem solving. Supportive interactions among group members were facilitated, and participants were encouraged to try new approaches to managing the patient. In the Zarit et al. study, the group condition was contrasted with a program of individual and family counseling and a wait list, whereas Haley et al. had only a wait list comparison. These studies also differed in terms of the subject population. The Gallagher et al. and Toseland et al. studies accepted any caregiver, whereas the Haley et al. and Zarit et al. studies were limited to caregivers of dementia patients.

The results of these four studies can be analyzed in two ways: by assessing

(a) pretest to posttest gains or (b) the relative benefits of an experimental condition compared to other treatment or control conditions. Using either approach, however, the findings are equivocal. Gallagher et al. and Toseland et al. reported statistically significant improvements for treated subjects compared to control subjects on some dependent measures. Gallagher's team found significant reductions for both measures of depression and burden, with effects somewhat greater in the life satisfaction condition (D. Gallagher, personal communication, September, 1988). Toseland et al. reported that subjects in support groups had significantly lower scores compared to control subjects on an omnibus measure of psychiatric symptoms, the Brief Symptom Inventory, but there were no differences in reported burden, nor were there differences between groups led by professionals and those led by a peer.

In contrast, Haley et al. and Zarit et al. reported no significant differences between treatment and control groups for measures of burden and affect. Haley et al. qualified their findings by noting that participants in the group were very satisfied with the group experience and reported that the intervention was very helpful. Zarit et al. found significant change over time in all three conditions (individual and family counseling, support group, wait list), with wait list subjects having made some of the same changes in their lives that had been targeted in the interventions. Results of a one-year follow-up indicate that gains on the Brief Symptom Inventory and a measure of burden were maintained. No long-term comparison group was available, however, because control subjects received treatment after the initial eight-week waiting period.

Irrespective of whether findings are statistically significant, the magnitude of change on outcome measures in all four studies indicates a clinically modest gain. These findings stand in contrast to the generally optimistic expectations about the value of support groups. A review of these findings suggests both that methodological problems may have led to some underestimation of treatment effects and that expectations of more global and sweeping change may have been unwarranted. In the following sections I discuss several methodological issues related to evaluation of psychoeducational interventions.

Specifying Treatment Goals

A close examination of the current literature suggests that most researchers have used global measures to assess treatment outcome. The overall goal is generally to reduce stress or burden. These constructs, however, are multidimensional, and changes that reduce one dimension of burden may not affect other aspects. Furthermore, most treatments have been brief and time-limited. The expectations that a group or class that lasts 8 or 10 weeks can have far-reaching changes that address all of the possible negative consequences of caregiving may be unrealistic. For example, if we consider perceived burden, that is, the extent to which caregivers subjectively evaluate their involvement as burdensome, we could focus variously on physical strain (how much effort is involved or how tired or fatigued caregivers feel), emotional strain (how distressed, angry, or sad caregivers feel), role overload (the sense of having too many competing responsibilities), role conflict (the sense that caregiving interferes with other family or social relationships), role loss (feeling that one has had to give up valued activities in order to provide care), and financial burden (that financial costs are more than one can assume). A brief intervention may be able to address some of these concerns, but is unlikely to produce changes in every area.

A related issue is that interventions do not directly address the broad issues that are encompassed in outcome measures. Psychosocial interventions for caregivers have grown out of a clinical literature that suggests that an eclectic list of approaches may be helpful. In a review of this literature, Clark and Rakowski (1983) identified education about the patient's illness and providing emotional support as common themes in most studies. As was noted earlier, some interventions have also emphasized training caregivers in problem-solving approaches. The implicit assumption, then, is that certain events, such as supportive exchanges, will result in improved mood or lowered feelings of burden. The effects of these interventions on mood or burden are indirect. That is, we would expect mood to change as a result of the occurrence of some other events, such as supportive exchanges in a group.

It is useful to contrast this treatment model with other approaches whereby the interventions directly affect dependent measures. An example of this type of direct treatment model is the behavioral therapy for depression developed by Lewinsohn and his associates (Lewinsohn et al., 1978). (As was noted earlier, this approach has been modified by Silven et al., 1986, for use with caregivers). In this approach, clients monitor their daily levels of depressive affect and also certain occurrences (pleasant and aversive events) that are correlated with depression. Once associations are established between events and mood, interventions are made to increase pleasant events and decrease aversive events, and the outcome is evaluated against changes in mood. In other words, the primary focus of the treatment is on making changes that have an immediate impact on depressive affect.

In contrast, when a support group discusses causes and treatment of Alzheimer's disease, the expectation is that lack of information has an indirect relation to the experience of daily stress. This information allows caregivers to gain a better understanding of the patient's situation and the alternatives available to them. Some may even change their routines or behaviors in ways that relieve stress, but this result is indirect, rather than the specific outcome of the intervention. Similarly, supportive exchanges may be helpful to the caregiver, but they will only indirectly affect the stressfulness of the caregiving situation. In contrast to information and emotional support, problem solving potentially targets those situations that are most troubling to participants. Again, however, the proposed mechanism for reducing distress is indirect—that is, it is hypothesized that caregivers will learn new strategies that control problem situations and that greater control is associated with decreased distress. However, a treatment focused directly on caregivers' distress would identify antecedents and consequences of distress and target those events.

Four approaches are suggested by this discussion. First, it is important to identify all the various goals that an intervention might have. Thus a psychoeducational intervention has as one of its goals imparting certain information. Another goal might be providing an environment in which subjects feel free to talk about what is on their minds.

Second, we should differentiate between primary and secondary treatment goals. It is not clear that imparting information will have a direct effect on distress, although there may be some weak or indirect effects. Before examining these possible secondary effects, however, we need to first identify whether the primary goals have been met. Did subjects learn a certain body of information? Did they feel they were able to share their feelings and receive support? Do they learn new strategies for managing the patient's behavior?

Both Haley et al. and my associates and I (Zarit et al., 1987) have reported that caregivers are very satisfied with these primary aspects of the interventions. In both studies, participants were enthusiastic in endorsing different features of the interventions as being helpful. Results from the Zarit et al. study are shown in Table 2. The subjects' perceptions of treatment benefits were assessed in two ways: (a) subjects rated the overall degree of change they experienced during the intervention on a 7-point Likert scale, with the midpoint indicating no change; and (b) subjects rated the degree of helpfulness of different features of the intervention on 5-point scales. Four dimensions (therapeutic quality, information, problem solving, and support) were created by summing statements in those respective domains. As can be seen in Table 2, their perceptions of the helpfulness of the treatments were very positive.

After determining whether these primary goals have been achieved, we should then examine secondary effects. In other words, we need to confirm that the treatment has been implemented as planned. This approach is akin to determining blood levels in a drug treatment study, that is, whether there has been enough exposure to a treatment to expect intended effects. We can expect positive results only if there is adequate exposure to the therapeutic processes.

Third, the design of interventions should reflect their goals. If we want to focus primarily on some aspect of emotional distress or burden, for instance, the intervention should specifically target that domain. Just as in "Coping with Depression" classes where the focus is on antecedents and consequences of depressed feelings, the intervention should target specific feelings of burden or distress.

Finally, we should realistically estimate the amount of time that an intervention requires. Longer-term interventions such as 16 or 20 weeks may be needed

TABLE 2 Subjects' perceptions of treatment benefits

	Group			
	Support $n = 44$		Family counseling $n = 36$	
Variable	M	SD	M	SD
Global rating of change	4.74	1.75	5.48	1.77
Caregiver Change Interview				
General therapeutic	3.87	0.72	3.98	0.62
Information	3.97	0.90	4.13	0.65
Problem solving	4.02	0.75	4.35	0.59
Support	3.86	0.67	4.24*	0.34

Note. From Zarit, Anthony, and Boutselis (1987). Reprinted by permission of publisher and author.
*$p < .05$.

to implement a complex treatment program. This longer period has been the norm in depression treatment studies. Longer interventions, however, pose other difficulties, specifically, that caregivers may be reluctant or unable to commit that much time. One solution used by Toseland et al. is to make respite workers available to stay with the care-recipient so that caregivers can attend group meetings.

Ascertaining the Goals of Caregivers

A central question in identifying goals of an intervention is, what do participants want to get from the program? We have generally assumed that the goals of the intervention and the goals of the participants are synonymous, although that is not necessarily the case. To use the comparison with depression interventions, subjects volunteer for a treatment study because they perceive a problem with depression, and they are typically screened to determine that they meet some entry criteria. In contrast, caregiver intervention studies recruit caregivers. Subjects may meet some minimal entry criteria (e.g., evidence of a certain level of involvement with the care recipient, caring for a person with a particular type of disability such as dementia), but they are not being treated for caregiving. Rather, the intervention focuses on some problems associated with the caregiving role, problems that subjects may or may not experience. For example, the goal of the intervention may be to decrease feelings of depression. Although feelings of depression are common among caregivers, they are not universal. In fact, many caregivers who volunteer for treatment programs report little or no depressive feelings (see Anthony-Bergstone et al., 1988; Gallagher et al., 1989; Zarit et al., 1987). The same finding holds true for other emotions, such as anxiety or anger, or for burden.

This situation creates problems for measuring treatment outcome. In the four controlled studies reviewed earlier, subjects varied considerably in their initial levels of functioning on outcome measures, with significant minorities in each study reporting low levels of distress and burden. For those subjects, it is not possible to demonstrate a treatment effect. Indeed, one might predict that subjects with initially low scores on these dependent measures should report increases in stress and burden over time, as a function of the tendency for extreme scores to regress to the mean. The limited amount of improvement reported by these studies may be partly the result of including subjects who could not show improvement on the outcome measures.

One interpretation of these observations is that caregivers engage in a process of denial and do not accurately report distress. This proposition has been suggested in the clinical literature, and has been noted by researchers who find discrepancies between how caregivers present themselves and how they score on paper-and-pencil measures (e.g., Toseland et al., 1989; Zarit et al., 1987). Gallagher and her associates (1989) compared results of assessment of depression through self-reports on the Beck Depression Inventory and through interviewer rating, using the Schedule for Affective Disorders and Schizophrenia interview (Endicott & Spitzer, 1978). The personal interview identified higher rates of depressive symptoms than did the self-report measure. These findings indicate the importance of a multimethod approach to measurement. Beyond the question of underreporting, it is also apparent that at least some caregivers are genuinely not distressed or burdened. Unlike the depression example described earlier, these caregivers do not seek help for depression, distress, or burden. The fact that caregiving and distress are not synonymous suggests reconsideration of the basic research design of intervention studies.

One approach is to target a particular problem for intervention (e.g., depression or specific burdens), and then set appropriate entry criteria so that subjects experience the problem for which they are being treated, Greene and Monahan (1989) have criticized this strategy on the basis that highly stressed subjects will show a regression to the mean. This problem, however, can be dealt with by inclusion of an appropriate control group that has similar initial scores on the variables of interest. The treatment effect should be greater than the effects of normal fluctuations in symptoms (such as are manifested by regression toward the mean). The fundamental point is that if the goal of an intervention is to treat a particular type of problem, participants should report experiencing that problem at the outset.

From a different perspective, nondistressed caregivers who volunteer for interventions obviously have different goals, including preventing the situation from becoming more stressful. Rather than treating them for problems they do not currently have, such as depression, we should focus both on their immediate concerns and on prevention approaches. This group may be especially responsive to a variety of interventions, because they are not in crisis.

Goals may also vary within a sample, including one selected for some characteristic such as depressive symptoms. For instance, even if participants are distressed, their primary goals may concern other issues. One problem in implementing interventions is that many caregivers focus more on the care-recipient than on themselves. They often want to learn how to cure, assist, or control the recipient, rather than to alter their own behaviors. In the Zarit et al. (1987) study, participants were asked to identify the goals that they had for the intervention. The diversity of goals is illustrated in Table 3.

In part, the discrepancy between participants' and researchers' goals is due to an overreliance by researchers on mental health measures, including depression and well-being. In all likelihood, interventions are really directed toward altering the caregiver's feelings of distress or unease over caregiving, that is, feeling overloaded, overwhelmed, uncomfortable, or unwilling to carry out various activities. Mental health measures such as depression are proxies for this more specific focus. However, caregivers can feel strain without also having significant levels of depressive or other mental health symptoms. Indeed, they may seek out treatment specifically to prevent the situation from becoming so out of hand that their well-being suffers. We need measures, then, that target specifically the problems caregivers face. I do not mean to imply that depression among caregivers is not important, but, rather that we should make appropriate distinctions between depression as a syndrome and the daily tension or strain of caregiving. If the focus of an intervention is treating the clinical syn-

TABLE 3 First and second goals of caregivers volunteering for an intervention study

	% of Subjects	
Goal of caregiver	First choice ($N = 170$)	Second choice ($N = 158$)
Evaluation of the patient	2	4
Information	25	16
Learning how to manage problems	21	20
Support	12	10
Obtaining respite services	11	10
Finding a cure	11	7
Help with feelings: guilt, anger	4	9
Other	14	27

Note. Twelve participants did not indicate a second goal.

drome of depression among caregivers, then subjects should be selected who meet specific entry criteria for depression. It follows, then, that depression measures are appropriate measures of outcome. On the other hand, if an intervention broadly focuses on stresses of caregiving, then other outcome measures are more appropriate. The discussion that follows on measurement of burden is one such approach. One other strategy is the use of goal attainment measures that may clarify what caregivers want from interventions and how they perceive the intervention as being helpful. Toseland et al. have used this approach with some success.

Measuring Burden

There has probably been no construct that has generated more interest and controversy in caregiving research than burden. Burden has been defined in many, often mutually exclusive, ways. Burden is, variously, the load borne by caregivers, their appraisals of the care-recipient's behavior, their appraisals of the tasks they perform, and their evaluation of the consequences caregiving has had on different aspects of their lives (Haley et al., 1987b; Hoenig & Hamilton, 1966; Montgomery, Stull, & Borgatta, 1985; Poulshock & Deimling, 1984; Zarit, Reever, & Bach-Peterson, 1980; Zarit, Todd, & Zarit, 1986). Adding to the confusion caused by inconsistent definitions is the suggestion that burden is not a useful construct (George & Gwyther, 1986; Moritz, Kasl, & Berkman, 1989). Despite the conceptual confusion and criticisms, perceived or felt burden is a very important part of the overall picture of caregiving stress, and it may be a critical measure for evaluating outcomes of interventions. Some of the issues and criticisms surrounding conceptualization and measurement of burden are discussed here, and a new approach to conceptualizing burden is proposed (see also Stephens & Kinney, in press).

There appear to be more disagreements about the definition of burden than actually exist. An examination of current research suggests that most investigators identify similar constructs as important for understanding caregiving but call them by different names. Most research has been guided by a general stress and coping model, which includes the following components:

- objective stressors experienced by caregivers, such as the care-recipient's disabilities, the resulting care that must be provided, and disruptive or otherwise impaired behavior;
- primary appraisal of these stressors, that is, the extent to which caregivers perceive particular events or behaviors as being stressful, challenging, or hassles;
- mediating variables such as coping or social support;

- caregivers' appraisals of the effects that these demands have had on different areas of their lives; and
- outcomes such as changes in health or well-being.

There is usually considerable similarity among studies in how the process of caregiving is viewed, irrespective of whether a construct is called burden or something else (see also Stephens & Kinney, in press).

Criticisms of the concept of burden have focused primarily on definitions involving caregivers' appraisals. George and Gwyther (1986) identified three limitations of these types of burden measures. First, burden measures cannot be administered to noncaregivers. As a result, it is not possible to determine the relative effects of caregiving compared to other life situations using these measures. Second, burden measures require caregivers to relate caregiving to its effects, thus confounding stressor and outcome. Third, the use of total scores of burden prevents identification of antecedents of different dimensions of burden (e.g., physical or emotional burden). Because of these limitations, George and Gwyther proposed that caregiving studies should focus instead on measures of well-being rather than using specially constructed measures of burden.

Two of these criticisms can be readily addressed. When comparisons with noncaregiving samples are relevant, it is possible to administer appropriate instruments that provide an estimate of the relative effects of caregiving stress compared to other life situations (see Anthony-Bergstone et al., 1988). Similarly, there is no intrinsic reason why burden measures should be represented by summary scores. The use of summary scores represents an oversimplification, because the impact of caregiving is likely to be multifaceted. One could argue that a summary score of all sources of burden will predict the breakdown of a caregiving situation better than will separate indices, but this is an empirical question that can be tested. As an example, Hassinger (1985) used scales derived from a factor analysis of The Burden Interview (Zarit & Zarit, 1982) to predict institutionalization. She found that two scales, which she identified as anger and perception of patient's demands as excessive, predicted institutionalization approximately as well as the summary score.

The other distinction raised by George and Gwyther, that of the potential confound between stressor and outcome, is more basic. Although separation of stressor and outcome can be argued as desirable on an abstract level, caregivers evaluate their situation in terms of how they perceive that the stressor is affecting their lives. This appraisal is an element of the situation that is not captured by measures of well-being but may be critical for understanding the decisions that caregivers make. A caregiver may not be depressed, or may not differ from other caregivers or from normative samples in current feelings of well-being, yet they may feel that the amount of care needed is more than they can provide. As a result, a caregiver may choose to institutionalize the patient or to make other changes in care. To understand how decisions about care are made, we need some sense of the meaning and significance of the situation to the caregiver.

The use of well-being measures is based on the assumption that caregivers will experience some decrease in well-being relative to normal populations. However, the primary reference point that caregivers use in evaluating their situation is not how their status compares to other people but how they functioned before assuming these caregiving responsibilities. Many caregivers undoubtedly experience some decline in well-being relative to their prior functioning, although this relative decline may or may not cause them to differ from normative samples. For example, a caregiver who previously had high levels of well-being may now be at an average level, thus he or she may not differ from norms on this measure or from other caregivers whose feelings of well-being were average before caregiving and have not changed. Similarly, some caregivers may be concerned about potential threats to their well-being, although no changes have taken place as yet. Thus, whereas well-being measures are important for examining the impact of caregiving relative to other populations, caregivers' appraisals of impact provide a different and potentially useful dimension.

This approach is consistent with how my colleagues and I have defined burden (Zarit & Zarit, 1982; Zarit et al., 1980; Zarit et al., 1986). We have viewed burden as being based on caregivers' appraisals that assisting their relative has had a detrimental effect on their personal and social life, health, finances, and emotional well-being. This focus is derived from pioneering studies (e.g., Grad & Sainsbury, 1963, 1968; Lowenthal, Berkman & Associates, 1967) in which researchers observed that breakdown of the family care situation was not due to the severity of illness alone, but to the family's physical, emotional, or financial exhaustion as well. In these early studies, as well as in our own work, it has been observed that some families with severely impaired care-recipients manage adequately, whereas others are overwhelmed. Similarly, families of elderly people with milder degrees of impairment are sometimes exhausted by the care they are providing.

In developing The Burden Interview, we were concerned with identifying families' feelings that the care they were providing was having undesirable or unwanted effects. We are aware that the attributions caregivers make about the causes of these feelings may be inaccurate. As an example, a caregiver who says her health is suffering because of the amount of care she is providing may or may not be identifying accurately the cause of her decline in health. However, her appraisal that the situation is detrimental is important to understanding her reactions and the decisions she will make about care for her relative.

The Burden Interview was developed in an ad hoc way as a tool for studying the caregiving experience. Because of the considerable advances in our understanding of caregiving that have taken place in recent years, however, a new and more comprehensive approach to measurement of caregivers' appraisals is warranted.

A framework for conceptualizing burden

Caregivers' appraisals of the effects that providing care has had on their lives, or what we refer to as burden, is the outcome of the following process. In order to meet the demands for care placed on them, caregivers draw on various resources. One resource is time. In order to provide care, family members use time that would otherwise be spent in other activities such as social or leisure pursuits or work. Another resource is effort. The caregiving tasks involve varying amounts of physical exertion, which the caregiver expends in carrying out these activities. Third, caregivers may use resources to obtain someone else to carry out various tasks. They may hire someone, thus using financial resources, or call upon family or friends or other sources of voluntary support. Finally, caregivers draw on their own emotional resources when they provide direct care or coordinate the contributions of other care providers.

Caregivers often do not think about the choices they make in using these resources and may perceive that they have little or no control over the process. This perception of loss of control may have important consequences, for example, making caregivers more prone to depression (Pagel, Becker, & Coppel, 1985). Irrespective of whether they feel in control, however, caregivers have made decisions that reflect their strategy to use various resources for meeting care demands.

The use of a particular resource is not necessarily burdensome. For example, some researchers have argued that we should consider restrictions in social and family activities as one negative outcome of caregiving (see George & Gwyther, 1986; Poulshock & Deimling, 1984), yet caregivers may willingly give up certain activities in order to carry out their responsibilities. They may utilize a resource (time) by giving up some activities in order to spend more time with the patient. The loss of social or other activities becomes burdensome when caregivers appraise it to be so, that is, when they have given up more than they are willing or able to do.

Some caregivers feel burdened when care activities result in even minimal changes in their usual routines, whereas others willingly give up these activities. Similarly, some family members may be unwilling or unable to make the physical effort involved in providing care including diverse activities such as heavy lifting or getting up with patients at night. Emotional resources are necessarily related to these other resources. Caregivers will differ in the emotional resources needed to tolerate the various demands placed on them. The amount of time and effort they put into caregiving may also deplete their emotional resources. As an example, caregivers who leave themselves with no diverting or relaxing activities or nothing to look forward to may become resentful of even small demands.

A critical part of this approach is the concept of limits. A limit is the point at which caregivers perceive that the resources they are willing or able to commit to providing care are not adequate. For a caregiver who has a minimal commitment, the limit may come when minimal care demands threaten to disrupt usual social activities. For highly involved caregivers, the limit may occur when the physical demands exceed their ability. In either case, caregivers' perceptions that demands have exceeded resources are critical. Burden, then, is the appraisal that care demands exceed the resources that caregivers have or are willing to use.

This conceptualization of burden is similar to "secondary appraisal" in the Lazarus and Folkman (1984) model—that is, caregivers evaluate whether resources are adequate to meet the perceived threat or demands. Because of the specific context of caregiving, in which family members can choose to assume or not assume responsibility, we need to consider both the appraisal of adequacy of resources and willingness to use resources in that way. Caregivers are burdened, then, if they have to do more than they are willing or if they perceive the situation as demanding more than they are able to give.

In this conceptualization, burden becomes an indicator of the stability or lack of stability in current caregiving arrangements. Caregivers who feel burdened will either make changes in the caregiving situation (e.g., purchase more services or decide to institutionalize) or will increasingly feel frustrated or angry by having to do more than they are willing. In a situation where demands are perceived as exceeding resources, harmful consequences are more likely to result to the caregiver, including development or exacerbation of health or mental health problems.

Burden, then, represents an important mediator between stressors and outcome, in which caregivers appraise the adequacy of the resources available for meeting perceived demands. Development of a measure of burden in this framework involves some confounding of stressor and outcome. That is, caregivers would be required to make attributions about current feelings and emotions. This confounding is a central feature of how people evaluate themselves in a stressful situation. Because people use these kinds of appraisals when making decisions in stressful situations, we should consider them when studying the process by which they adapt to these stressors.

The use of this approach to measurement of burden in intervention studies will depend on the goals of the intervention. Some dimensions of burden may be relatively stable and will not change in the short run. Other dimensions, such as how much effort is required to meet care demands, should be modifiable, for instance, if the caregiver obtains relief. As was discussed earlier, the important consideration is to target the specific concerns of the caregiver. If a particular individual is not burdened by a loss of social activities, then using an intervention to increase the amount of social activities does not make sense.

Sampling Issues

When conducting intervention research, there is pressure to obtain a sufficient sample size to ensure that there is adequate statistical power for conducting data analysis. As the design of the study becomes more complex, the numbers of subjects required for adequate power will increase. As a result, researchers are likely to feel pressure to set broad inclusion criteria to recruit a large number of subjects. As was noted earlier, including subjects who do not have the problem for which they are being treated (e.g., burden or depression) can lead one to underestimate treatment results. Other factors that may affect outcome include family variables and type and severity of the patient's disability.

Whereas the literature has emphasized family caregiving, family variables have generally been ignored, and the focus has been only on a single caregiver. The study of families represents a complex area, with many structural and qualitative dimensions potentially affecting caregiving outcome. For intervention studies, the major structural variables are the kin relationship between patient and caregiver, whether or not the patient and caregiver share the same household, and whether the caregiver is the primary person providing assistance or plays a secondary role to another relative. Two important qualitative dimensions have been suggested by Cohler and his associates (Cohler, Groves, Borden, & Lasarus, 1989): obligation and affection. These qualitative dimensions potentially interact with structural dimensions.

Type of kin relationship is a central issue in caregiving. Relationships vary in terms of expectations and history. Cohler et al. (1989) suggested that spouse caregivers differ from children in their commitment and affective ties to the patient. Among spouses, striking differences in the coping styles of husbands and wives have been described. Wives have tended to be more emotionally involved in caregiving, whereas husbands adopted an instrumental approach (Fitting, Rabins, Lucas, & Eastha, 1986; Zarit et al., 1986). Another difference is the level of burden and psychological distress experienced among husbands, wives, and daughters who are primary caregivers (Cantor, 1983; Fitting et al., 1986; Zarit et al., 1986). Because these dimensions are often used to measure outcome, having disproportionate numbers of husbands, wives, and daughters among treatment groups may confound the results if these variables are not controlled in the analyses. At a more general level, there needs to be consideration of whether intervention goals differ by kin relationship.

The second structural dimension, living in a shared or separate household, overlaps with type of kin relationship. In most cases, spouses will share the same household, whereas caregivers who are adult children are more likely to maintain a separate household. From a stress and coping perspective, it is clear that the type of stressors and amount of exposure to them will differ between these types of arrangements. In a shared household, interaction can be constant, and caregivers will have problems arranging time for themselves. In separate households, caregivers tend to have more concerns about arranging delivery of services to the patient's residence and about the overall safety and security of the elder. The issue of place of residence is complicated further if the care-recipient lives in specialized housing. Again, stressors for caregivers are likely to differ, depending on the type of housing and amount of assistance they provide. In some instances, the differences will be so great that inclusion of subjects in the same intervention would generally not be appropriate without blocking on the dimension of residential status.

Inclusion of families with a relative in the community versus in a nursing home is an example of this type of difference. Family caregivers of nursing home patients have not received adequate attention. They may be under considerable stress because of family conflict over placement or because of their efforts to participate in and influence care in the nursing home. Nonetheless, these are strikingly different concerns than for the caregiver of a relative living in the community. The differences among other types of specialized housing and independent living are not as clear. The researcher should consider the goals of the intervention, and, then determine whether these goals are relevant for residents of specialized housing and their caregivers. As an example, teaching family caregivers how to access support services might be unnecessary if the care-recipient lives in specialized housing that provides meals, housekeeping, and some health-related services.

The third major structural dimension is whether the caregiver is the primary or secondary caregiver. This distinction often arises when a daughter identifies herself as caregiver for a parent, although the other parent provides most of the assistance. Although the secondary caregiver will not have as much ongoing responsibility for assisting with activities of daily living or managing behavior problems, he or she will be more likely to arrange and coordinate outside services. In clinical settings, secondary caregivers have been found to be frustrated by how the primary caregiver carries out his or her responsibilities. This tension between caregivers may be a significant treatment issue.

Researchers have paid less attention to the qualitative issues of obligation and affection. Descriptive studies suggest that affective ties between caregivers and recipients may influence burden and psychological distress (Chenoweth & Spencer, 1986; Deimling & Bass, 1986; Fitting et al., 1986; Zarit et al., 1986). The results of these studies, however, have been somewhat contradictory. Both Cantor (1983) and Robinson and Thurnher (1979) found burden to be higher among caregivers who felt closer to the patient, whereas the opposite results were reported by Zarit (1982) and Jenkins, Parham, and Jenkins (1985). Although these differences may be due in part to sampling and measurement, the implication is that quality of affective ties may have important, but as yet undetermined, effects on caregiving. Quality of relationship may also affect commitment to continue providing care (Hassinger, 1985).

The effects of caregiving may also vary depending on the patient's type of disability. In particular, the differential impact of physical and cognitive disorders on the caregiver should be taken into account. In one of the few systematic studies of this dimension, Birkel (1987) compared caregivers of people with cognitive impairments but no significant physical care needs with caregivers whose relatives were physically but not cognitively impaired. He found that cognitive impairment was associated with higher levels of stress among family caregivers and that there were different mediating factors in these two types of care situations. Household size was associated with greater stress for caregivers of physically impaired patients and lower stress for caregivers of demantia patients.

Birkel limited his sample to subjects who clearly had either physical or cognitive symptoms, and excluded individuals who had both. In planning an intervention study, the most important consideration is probably presence of dementia, with its associated behavioral disturbances and degenerative progression. These characteristics may place sufficiently different demands on caregivers so that their response to treatment should be considered separately from other caregivers. In contrast, the distinction between Alzheimer's disease and other dementias is probably not as important, especially because there can be errors in clinical diagnosis and a certain number of cases have mixed pathology.

Two other dimensions to be considered in sampling are severity of the patient's impairment and duration of caregiving. In progressive disorders such as dementia, these dimensions will tend to be related, although with some important differences that are due to the type of kin relationship. Spouses typically will observe changes and provide care earlier in the disease process than will other family caregivers. To the extent that interventions depend on caregivers having a certain amount of experience with the problem or not yet being burned out, the duration of their caregiving experiences should be taken into account. In addition, some interventions may be more effective earlier in the course of caregiving (e.g., educational programs), whereas others may be effective later on (e.g., a therapy-oriented group stressing expression of emotions).

From a practical perspective, controlling all of the variables discussed or other factors that affect the caregiving context is beyond the scope of most intervention studies. The researcher should control for those dimensions that pose the greatest threat to internal validity for the evaluation at hand. Alternatively, multisite trials of interventions could generate adequate sample sizes for testing hypotheses about differences in treatment responses influenced by factors such as the relationship of the caregiver and care-recipient or the type of disability.

The Importance of Control Groups

The importance of control groups for evaluating treatment is obvious, but there are special considerations in caregiving studies. Although "no treatment" or waiting list groups are often used as controls, there are problems with these procedures. For example, caregivers on a waiting list are not inactive and may make significant changes in their situation during the waiting list period, such as arranging for community services (Zarit et al., 1987). Of course, the longer the waiting period, the greater this tendency will be. Yet, as was observed earlier, short-term interventions may be too brief, given the complexity of problems facing caregivers. The preferred type of control condition in psychotherapy research is attention or interaction. Control subjects would spend as much time with a therapist or leader and participate in some activity that in theory would not affect the outcome. That approach may be problematic given the amount of stress many caregivers experience and the difficulty of developing a credible, long-term placebo. Additionally, in group treatment studies, random assignment of subjects will result in variable waiting periods before treatment, unless large numbers of potential subjects are available at one time.

Single subject design may provide one solution to these problems. An A-B-A design can evaluate the impact of a specific intervention, for example, using a behavioral approach to reduce problem behaviors of the care-recipient. The major limitation of this approach is that reversals are difficult to implement for some types of interventions. Another promising strategy is the use of quasi-experimental designs. Instead of randomly assigning subjects, two or more similar communities could be compared. Subjects in one community would receive an experimental program, whereas people in the other community would be assessed but receive only usual community services (see Grad & Sainsbury, 1963, 1968). In addition to overcoming some of the practical limitations of random assignment, this approach enables an evaluation of long-term effects of the intervention. With a typical waiting list, ethical considerations and practical concerns of recruiting a sample dictate that one provide treatment after the experimental period. With control subjects residing in another community, there would be less need to provide the experimental intervention.

RELIEVING THE CAREGIVER: RESPITE AND SIMILAR INTERVENTIONS

Psychosocial interventions enhance caregivers' personal resources by providing information, support, and strategies for responding to common care problems. These interventions may influence caregivers in making major changes in their care arrangements (e.g., utilizing more paid help). In contrast, some interventions directly provide new resources for assisting the care recipient. Interventions such as day care or in-home respite may alter the caregiver's exposure to stressors and therefore can modify the caregiver's well-being and other outcomes in meaningful ways. Various kinds of respite programs, including day care, in-home care, and overnight respite have been developed to provide relief to the caregiver.

Despite growing interest in respite services, few studies have been conducted that provide rigorous empirical evaluation of outcome. To date, most reports have been anecdotal or single case studies without control groups. Clinical evidence has suggested the value of respite programs, but some critics have questioned whether respite is effective in reducing stress on caregivers or delaying institutionalization. In one of the largest studies to date, Lawton, Brody, and Saperstein (1989) used a randomized design to evaluate the effects of subsidized respite services for caregivers of people with dementia. After an initial interview, subjects were randomly assigned into experimental and control groups. Those in the experimental group worked with a case manager who identified needs and arranged for appropriate respite services, including in-home care, day care, and institutional care, whereas the control group received a list of community agencies that provided assistance. The results showed that subjects in the experimental group kept their relative in the community slightly longer than did control subjects (309 compared to 285 days); however, there were no differences in caregiver burden or well-being. As in other intervention studies, caregivers were generally satisfied with the help they received.

Whereas Lawton et al. concluded that their findings provide evidence of the benefits of respite, Callahan (1989) described the results as discouraging, particularly, because they provide little support for the goals of helping caregivers or reducing institutionalization. In light of the findings from the Lawton et al. study and similar community demonstrations, Callahan suggested that expansion of these services is not justified and that calls for a national respite policy are premature.

This study and the commentary by Callahan suggest four major points about the design and evaluation of respite interventions. First, as Callahan argued, the evidence is too limited to propose large-scale public funding of respite. There have been few studies conducted and even fewer that demonstrate clear-cut benefits. As Callahan proposed, we need tests of different models and approaches to determine relative effectiveness and costs.

Second, the methodology for evaluating community-based demonstrations needs to be improved. The Lawton et al. (1989) study had many of the same problems as did psychosocial interventions. Subjects were selected not because they wanted respite but because they were caregivers of dementia patients. Although this approach allowed the researchers to draw a more representative sample of all caregivers and to construct a no-treatment control group in an ethical way (i.e., the researchers did not want to recruit subjects for respite and then not provide it), it also meant that respite may not have been a pressing need for many experimental subjects. Another major problem is that rates of utilization of respite between experimental and control subjects differed only to a small degree. Many of the control subjects arranged for respite services on their own. In contrast, subjects in the experimental group did not use respite as much as was expected.

Thus the study may suggest only that linking people to respite does not greatly increase utilization over normal rates. Because respite was only partly subsidized, financial considerations may have affected utilization rates. Finally, as in the psychosocial interventions reviewed earlier, the lack of differences at outcome in well-being and burden of the experimental and control groups is probably due in part to variability in initial scores. Because some subjects had low burden and high levels of well-being before the intervention, they could not show improvement on these measures. With the number of people for whom change could be demonstrated reduced, differences between treatment and control conditions were less likely to emerge.

A third implication of the design and evaluation of respite services is that we need to consider how these services are supposed to assist caregivers. Noelker and Bass (1989) have identified four types of linkages between informal and formal caregivers. These four models are as follows: (a) complementary, in which the informal and formal system provide different but complementary tasks; (b) supplementary, in which the formal system provides assistance with tasks also being performed by informal caregivers; (c) substitution, in which formal services take the place of informal assistance; and (d) kin independence, in which informal caregivers receive no help from the formal system.

The particular benefits that a caregiver experiences may depend on how services are used, that is, whether they are complementary or supplementary or result in substitution. To the extent that respite services result in supplementary linkage or substitution, they would provide relief for some tasks provided by the family. In a complementary linkage, however, family caregivers would continue providing the same types of assistance as before. In that situation, respite would be filling some unmet needs, but because the caregiver is still involved to the same extent, the effects on feelings of distress or well-being are likely to be less than if the caregiver is doing less. Another consideration is whether respite services place additional demands on caregivers, for example, having to drive the care-recipient to a service site. Just as we should not assume that support groups are supportive, we cannot assume that respite decreases the amount of involvement between caregiver and patient.

Berry and I (Berry & Zarit, 1988) explored the effects of respite on how family caregivers of dementia patients used their time. Caregivers currently enrolled in two types of respite services, day care and in-home care, were compared. Telephone interviews were conducted with each caregiver on three respite days and three nonrespite days. A time-budget approach was used whereby subjects identified their activities and estimated the amount of time they spent in each activity. Activities were then coded as 1) Caregiving with the patient; 2) Caregiving activities performed when the patient was not present (e.g., filling a prescription); and 3) Time spent away from the patient.

The results are surprising in that family members receiving day care spent more time in caregiving activities with the patient on respite days than on nonrespite days. In contrast, caregivers receiving in-home respite experienced some decrease in caregiving time on respite days. Examination of activities of caregivers indicated that day care users had to carry out many of the same care activities on respite days compared to nonrespite days, such as getting the patient bathed and dressed in the morning before going to day care. In contrast, in-home respite workers provided some of these care tasks.

Interviews with subjects indicated that they were very satisfied with both types of respite. The main advantage of both types of respite was that they provided family members with a block of time when they did not have care responsibilities. Results showed that subjects did, in fact, have more time away from the patient on respite days, and noncaregiving time tended to be in larger chunks. About half of the sample using each type of respite used the respite period to work. Of the remaining subjects, most used respite time to catch up on household and other activities. Few used the time for rest or relaxation.

These findings suggest that the mechanisms of respite may be different than expected. Rather than providing significant relief from care demands, respite allows families to shift caregiving into certain parts of the day, giving them blocks of uninterrupted time to carry out other activities. Thus the primary type of interface provided by respite may be complementary, although in-home respite also functions in a supplementary way. These observations suggest that respite may be most effective for caregivers with specific, competing responsibilities, such as employment. On the other hand, to the extent that respite does not decrease the amount of caregiving time and effort, it may not be helpful to caregivers who are themselves frail or who are becoming overwhelmed by the magnitude of daily tasks they must perform.

The fourth consideration in evaluating respite programs is the organizational arrangements for service delivery. In particular, the way in which service is organized and delivered may affect rates of participation. There is an emerging belief that caregivers underuse services, even when they are educated about them. Low usage was one important feature of the Lawton et al. study. Providers often attribute this reluctance to an unwillingness to accept help; however, structural features of the service may also affect participation. One obvious structural feature is cost. Bass and Noelker (1987) found that usage rates were strongly affected by family income. Those families with higher incomes could better afford community services, and they actually used them more often.

Families themselves provide another perspective on aspects of a service that facilitate or impede usage. In a study of the use of case management by families of dementia patients, my colleagues and I focused specifically on families' attitudes about services (Zarit, Malone Beach, & Spore, 1988). Although families generally found case management to be helpful, they were less positive about home services. They noted problems with the reliability of services and their lack of control over the service. Specifically, they reported that home care aides were often poorly trained and ill-equipped to deal with a dementia patient, that aides were unreliable and often did not show up when scheduled, that the agencies would tell families when to expect an aide rather than coordinating with the family's schedule, and that agencies would not allow families to ask for a particular person. As a result of these frustrations, many families discontinued using the service. Even when they continued using services, they often felt that it added to their stress rather than relieving it. Although this study was conducted on a small scale, it is cited here to illustrate ways in which the service delivery system may affect caregiving outcomes.

CONCLUSION

Development and evaluation of interventions for family caregivers is one of the most important challenges in long-term care of the elderly. Although initial efforts have generated creative ideas, we do not as yet have proven models of service delivery. The growing recognition of the effects of caregiving on the family needs to be coupled with efforts to develop approaches that prevent or relieve strain.

Studies of community interventions need to be based on a partnership among the researchers, agency personnel, and funding sources. Close collaboration is required at every step of the evaluation process. From the researcher's perspective, there should be a clear understanding of the clinical setting, including its goals and processes of intervention. Providers, in turn, have to recognize that systematic research can complement clinical efforts by identifying the strengths and weaknesses of a program. Moreover, it is possible to carry out research in nonintrusive ways. In fact, the typical evaluation instrument often complements and can replace parts of a clinical evaluation that the agency would do anyway.

Funding agencies also need to recognize the importance of good evaluation. Many of the long-term care initiatives developed in recent years with both public and private funds appear either to tack on evaluation as an afterthought or to sacrifice the internal validity of the clinical intervention in order to obtain data. The amount of funding must also ensure adequate integration of research and clinical staff. On the one hand, clinical personnel must be supplemented if they are performing additional tasks related to the research. On the other hand, research personnel should be located on site, both to gain a fuller understanding of clinical operations and to provide continuing supervision of data collection and other research activities. These collaborative arrangements will lead to the development of a body of empirical findings that can guide programs and policies in providing optimal kinds of assistance to caregivers and care-recipients.

REFERENCES

Anthony-Bergstone, C., Zarit, S. H., & Gatz, M. (1988). Symptoms of psychological distress among caregivers of dementia patients. *Psychology and Aging, 3,* 245–248.

Bass, D. M., & Noelker, L. S. (1987). The influence of family caregivers on elders' use of in-home services: An expanded conceptual model. *Journal of Health and Social Behavior, 28,* 184–196.

Berry, G. L., & Zarit, S. H. (1988, November). *Caregivers' activities on respite and non-respite days: A comparison of two service approaches.* Paper presented at the meeting of the Gerontological Society of America, San Francisco.

Birkel, R. C. (1987). Toward a social ecology of the home-care household. *Psychology and Aging, 2,* 294–301.

Callahan, J. J., Jr. (1989). Play it again Sam—There is no impact. *The Gerontologist, 29,* 5–6.

Cantor, M. H. (1983). Strain among caregivers. *The Gerontologist, 23,* 597–604.

Chenoweth, B., & Spencer, B. (1986). Dementia: The experience of family caregivers. *The Gerontologist, 26,* 267–272.

Clark, N. M., & Rakowski, W. (1983). Family caregivers of older adults: Improving helping skills. *The Gerontologist, 23,* 637–642.

Cohler, B., Groves, L., Borden, W., & Lasarus, L. (1989). Caring for family members with Alzheimer's disease. In E. Light & B. Lebowitz (Eds.), *Alzheimer's disease, treatment and family stress: Directions for research.* Washington, DC: U.S. Government Printing Office.

Deimling, G., & Bass, D. M. (1986). Symptoms of mental impairments among elderly adults and their effects on family caregivers. *Journal of Gerontology, 41,* 778–784.

D'Zurilla, T. J. (1986). *Problem-solving therapy: A social competence approach to psychotherapy.* New York: Springer.

D'Zurilla, T. J., & Goldfried, M. R. (1971). Problem solving and behavior modification. *Journal of Abnormal Psychology, 78,* 107–126.

Endicott, J., & Spitzer, R. L. (1978). A diagnostic interview: The schedule for affective disorders and schizophrenia. *Archives of General Psychiatry, 35,* 837–844.

Fitting, M., Rabins, P., Lucas, J., & Eastham, J. (1986). Caregivers for dementia patients: A comparison of husbands and wives. *The Gerontologist, 26,* 248–252.

Gallagher, D., Lovett, S., & Zeiss, A. (in press). Interventions with caregivers of frail elderly persons. In M. Ory & K. Bond (Eds.), *Aging and health care: Social science and policy perspectives.* New York: Tavistock.

Gallagher, D., Rose, J., Rivera, P., Lovett, S., & Thompson, L. W. (1989). Prevalence of depression in family caregivers. *The Gerontologist, 29,* 449–455.

George, L., & Gwyther, L. (1986). Caregiver well-being: A multi-dimensional examination of family caregivers of demented adults. *The Gerontologist, 26,* 253–259.

Grad, J., & Sainsbury, P. (1963). Mental illness and the family. *Lancet I*, 544–547.

Grad, J., & Sainsbury, P. (1968). The effects that patients have on their families in a community care and a control psychiatric service: A two-year follow-up. *British Journal of Psychiatry, 114*, 265–278.

Greene, V. L., & Monahan, D. J. (1989). The effect of a support and education program on stress and burden among family caregivers to frail elderly persons. *The Gerontologist, 29*, 472–477.

Haley, W. E., Brown, S. L., & Levine, E. G. (1987a). Experimental evaluation of the effectiveness of group intervention for dementia caregivers. *The Gerontologist, 27*, 376–382.

Haley, W. E., Brown, S. L., & Levine, E. G. (1987b). Family caregiver appraisals of patient behavioral disturbance in senile dementia. *Clinical Gerontologist, 6*, 25–34.

Hassinger, M. J. (1985). *Community-dwelling dementia patients whose relatives sought counseling services regarding patient care: Predictors of institutionalization over a one-year follow-up.* Doctoral dissertation, University of Southern California, Los Angeles.

Hoenig, J., & Hamilton, M. W. (1966). Elderly psychiatric patients and the burden on the household. *Psychiatria et Neurologia, 152*, 281–293.

Jenkins, T. S., Parham, I. A., & Jenkins, L. R. (1985). Alzheimer's disease: Caregivers' perceptions of burden. *Journal of Applied Gerontology, 4*, 40–57.

Lawton, M. P., Brody, E. M., & Saperstein, A. R. (1989). A controlled study of respite service for caregivers of Alzheimer's patients. *The Gerontologist, 29*, 8–16.

Lazarus, R. S., & Folkman, S. (1984). *Stress, appraisal, and coping.* New York: Springer.

Lewinsohn, P. M., Munoz, R., Youngren, M. A., & Zeiss, A. M. (1978). *Control your depression.* Englewood Cliffs, NJ: Prentice-Hall.

Lowenthal, M. F., Berkman, P., & Associates. (1967). *Aging and mental disorders in San Francisco.* San Francisco: Jossey-Bass.

Montgomery, R. J. V., Stull, D. E., & Borgatta, E. F. (1985). Measurement and analysis of burden. *Research on Aging, 7*, 137–152.

Moritz, D. J., Kasl, S. V., & Berkman, L. F. (1989). The health impact of living with a cognitively impaired elderly spouse: Depressive symptoms and social functioning. *Journal of Gerontology, 44*, S17–S27.

Noelker, L. A., & Bass, D. M. (1989). Home care for elder persons: Linkages between formal and informal caregivers. *Journal of Gerontology, 44*, S63–S72.

Pagel, M. D., Becker, J., Coppel, D. B. (1985). Loss of control, self-blame, and depression: An investigation of spouse caregivers of Alzheimer's disease patients. *Journal of Abnormal Psychology, 94*, 169–182.

Poulshock, W., & Deimling, G. (1984). Families caring for elders in residence: Issues in the measurement of burden. *Journal of Gerontology, 39*, 230–239.

Robinson, B. C., & Thurnher, M. (1979). Taking care of aged parents. *The Gerontologist, 19*, 583–593.

Silven, D., DelMaestro, S., Gallagher, D., Lovett, S., Benedict, A., Rose, J., & Kwong, K. (1986, November). *Changes in depressed caregiver's symptomatology through psychoeducational interventions.* Paper presented at the meeting of the Gerontological Society of America, Chicago.

Smyer, M. A., Zarit, S. H., & Qualls, S. H. (1990). Psychological intervention with the aging individual. In J. E. Birren & K. W. Schaie (Eds.), *Handbook of the psychology of aging* (3rd ed.). New York: Academic Press.

Stephens, M. A. P., & Kinney, J. M. (in press). Caregiving stress instruments: Assessment of content and measurement quality. *Gerontology Review.*

Stone, R., Cafferata, G. L., & Sangl, J. (1987). Caregivers of the frail elderly: A national profile. *The Gerontologist, 27*, 616–626.

Toseland, R. W., Rossiter, C., & Labrecque, M. (1989). The effectiveness of peer-led and professionally-led groups to support caregivers. *The Gerontologist, 29*(4), 457–464.

U.S. Senate Special Committee on Aging. (1985–1986). *Aging America: Trends and projections.* Washington, DC: U.S. Department of Health and Human Services.

Zarit, J. (1982). *Predictors of burden and distress for caregivers of senile dementia patients.* Doctoral dissertation, The University of Southern California, Los Angeles.

Zarit, J. M., & Zarit, S. H. (1982, November). *Measurement of burden and social support.* Paper presented at the meeting of the Gerontological Society of America, San Diego.

Zarit, S. H., Anthony, C. R., & Boutselis, M. (1987). Interventions with caregivers of dementia patients: Comparison of two approaches. *Psychology and Aging, 2*, 225–232.

Zarit, S. H., MaloneBeach, E. E., & Spore, D. S. (1988). *Case management as an approach to dementia: An exploratory study.* Unpublished manuscript.

Zarit, S. H., Orr, N. K., & Zarit, J. M. (1985). *The hidden victims of Alzheimer's disease: Families under stress.* New York: New York University Press.

Zarit, S. H., Reever, K. E., & Bach-Peterson, J. M. (1980). Relatives of the impaired elderly: Correlates of feelings of burden. *The Gerontologist, 20*, 649–655.

Zarit, S. H., Todd, P. A., & Zarit, J. (1986). Subjective burden of husbands and wives as caregivers: A longitudinal study. *The Gerontologist, 26*, 260–266.

15

NURSING HOME CARE AND FAMILY CAREGIVERS' STRESS

Aloen L. Townsend

Benjamin Rose Institute

During the past decade, research on later-life family caregiving has burgeoned. Most researchers have examined noninstitutional, home-based care arrangements. In this chapter I discuss nursing home (i.e., institutional) care for older relatives. My goals are to present an overview of current knowledge about family caregivers' stress and nursing home care and suggest future directions for research and theory in this area. To accomplish these goals, I first place nursing home care in a broader long-term care context and document the increasing prevalence of institutional care as a later-life family experience, despite survey research indicating that nursing home care is rarely the preferred arrangement.

I then review research findings about family caregivers' stress as both a cause and a consequence of nursing home care. This review is organized around two questions. First, what role does a family caregiver's stress play in the older relative's entry into a nursing home? Second, once admission occurs, what are the effects of nursing home care on the well-being of family members? Answers to these questions are drawn from literature on later-life family caregiving and data collected by the Margaret Blenkner Research Center of the

Support for the research reported in this chapter was provided by the Benjamin Rose Institute, by National Institute of Mental Health Grant R01 MH35360-01 through 07, and by Retirement Research Foundation Grant 84-3. The contributions of colleagues Linda Noelker and Gary Deimling and the assistance of Kate McCarthy, Nancy Esker, and Dorothy Schur are gratefully acknowledged.

Benjamin Rose Institute. The focus is restricted to stress experienced by family caregivers—rather than by care-recipients—usually a spouse, adult child, or daughter-in-law (Stone, Cafferata, & Sangl, 1987).

The Margaret Blenkner Research Center (MBRC) recently completed two panel surveys on later-life family caregiving. Both studies were based on purposive samples of families containing an older person (at least 60 years old) living in the greater Cleveland metropolitan area, his or her spouse if married, and at least one proximate adult child (residing within one hour of Cleveland). More than 500 individuals (N = 538) were interviewed, up to six times, between 1981 and 1986. Timing and content of the interviews were coordinated across studies. One difference between studies was that in one the older parent at least initially lived separately from any adult child, whereas in the other most of the parents and adult children lived together.

The two MBRC samples deliberately included a broad range of functional impairments among the older parents. About half initially needed no assistance with any of six activities of daily living (Lawton & Brody, 1969). The rest needed help with at least one activity (i.e., eating, dressing, bathing, toileting, grooming, or mobility). No restrictions were placed on the nature of the physical, mental, or cognitive problems underlying these functional limitations.

One purpose of both studies was to explore causes and consequences of changes in care arrangements, including the transition to nursing home care. A total of 81 family members (15% of the combined samples) experienced a parent's or spouse's entry into a nursing home during the two studies. These 65 adult children and 16 spouses, most (89%) of whom are White, form the basis for the data presented in this chapter. A few questions were asked only during three interview waves. For these questions, findings are based on 65 respondents (51 adult children and 14 spouses). No interviews were conducted with the institutionalized relatives. Data were taken from the first interview after nursing home placement. The modal and mean time from admission to interview was 12 months (M = 12.0, SD = 12.2, range = 1–48 months). Although most data came from structured, closed-ended questions, some qualitative data from open-ended questions or comments volunteered by participants are also presented in this chapter.

UNDERSTANDING THE CONTEXT OF NURSING HOME CARE

In order to understand the relation between family caregivers' stress and nursing home care, it is important to place institutional care in a broader long-term care context. Most older people who need care receive assistance in noninstitutional settings. However, because of the growing numbers of older Americans, their greater longevity, and their increasing incidence of chronic health problems, more families are facing the need for nursing home care than ever before. Presently about 5% of Americans 65 and older live in nursing homes (Hing, 1987). By 1995, this nursing home population is expected to grow by almost 50%, to 1.9 million older people (Doty, Liu, & Weiner, 1985).

The likelihood of nursing home care increases with age. Although only 1% of Americans between 65 and 74 resided in nursing homes in 1985, 22% of those 85 and older did (Hing, 1987). The odds also are greater when the older person is White, female, or unmarried and lives alone (Hing, 1987; Kane & Kane, 1987). Of the 1.3 million older residents in nursing homes in 1985, 6% were Black, 25% were male, and 16% were married at admission (Hing, Sekscenski, & Strahan, 1989). The 5% of older people residing in nursing homes at any given time underrepresents those who will receive institutional care sometime in their lives. Thus between 23% and 38% of individuals 65 or older are projected to spend some time in a nursing home before they die (Liu & Palesch, 1981).

Longer life expectancy affects the likelihood of nursing home care both directly and indirectly, because it has a bearing on the ages, relationships, and resources of family caregivers, as well as the number of older relatives for whom families have caregiving responsibilities (Brody, 1966; Riley, 1983). For example, married, middle-aged caregivers increasingly face the prospect of having in-laws as well as parents who need care. Family caregivers also are getting older, so there is greater likelihood that their own health problems will interfere with extended home care. It is often the caregiver's death or poor health that necessitates nursing home placement (Brody, 1966; Deimling & Poulshock, 1985). In addition, geographic mobility, smaller family size, and women's employment further decrease the availability of family caregivers at home (Stone et al., 1987; Treas, 1977).

Nursing home care is preferred by only a minority of older Americans. Generally, it is viewed as a last resort (Brody, 1977; Tobin & Lieberman, 1976). Most older Americans would prefer to receive help in their own home if they are unable to care for themselves for an extended period of time (Harris & Associates, 1982). As one elderly husband in the MBRC studies poignantly put it, "I would hate like the dickens to have [my wife] go into a nursing home." Yet, many older people recognize that home care may not be possible (Harris & Associates, 1982). After placement occurred, most family members in the MBRC studies (79%) agreed that there were not many choices available about ways to meet their relatives' care needs, and nearly all (95%) felt that there was no alternative to nursing home care. To some extent, these beliefs may reflect post-hoc justification for their decision or a realistic assessment of the necessity of institutional care; however, these beliefs also reflect the limitations of noninstitutional long-term care services. These services are often unavailable, unaffordable, unreimbursed, fragmented, insufficient, and poorly regulated as to quality (Kane & Kane, 1987).

THE STRESS OF CAREGIVING AS A FACTOR
IN NURSING HOME PLACEMENT

There is ample evidence that many caregivers do experience stress from providing care to older family members (Brody, 1977; Cantor, 1983; Zarit, Todd & Zarit, 1986). Yet, despite these findings and policy makers' concerns about caregivers' burnout, surprisingly little empirical research has been done on the stress of caregiving as a predictor of nursing home placement. The two research domains have remained discrete. Most research on the stress of caregiving is confined to families providing home care. Because this research treats burden or stress as the outcome of caregiving, there is little evidence about the implications for institutionalization or, in other words, about how much stress is too much. Thus most research provides no sense of when or why caregivers decide that home care is no longer possible or desirable and nursing home care is necessary. To understand this, current models of stress need to be extended, to include both desire for or consideration of placement and actual admission as outcomes.

If most research on the stress of caregiving has stopped short of predicting nursing home placement, most studies of predictors of institutionalization have paid little attention to the stress of caregiving. Instead, the demographic characteristics, health, and functional abilities of care-recipients are the most commonly used predictors of nursing home use. When family support is included, it is usually operationalized as presence or absence of family rather than as stress on the caregiver. Consequently, it is clear that older people without family—those who are widowed, never married, or without living or proximate children—are more likely to enter nursing homes than are those with family (Hing et al., 1989; Kane & Kane, 1987). However, the reasons why some impaired older people with proximate families enter nursing homes and others do not are poorly understood.

The handful of existing studies that have shown the stress of caregiving to be a predictor of nursing home care have taken three different approaches. First, some studies have focused on the desire to institutionalize rather than on actual nursing home admission. In one study greater subjective caregiver burden was related to greater desire for nursing home placement among caregivers (Morycz, 1985), although the relationship held for White and female but not Black male caregivers.

Second, some studies have included retrospective reports of caregivers' reasons for choosing nursing home placement. In the MBRC interviews, for example, nearly all family members (94%) said one reason that they chose to admit their relative was that the relative needed more care than the family could provide. Also, in approximately 6 out of 10 cases (57%), a caregiver was no longer able or willing to provide care. Reasons for the caregiver's withdrawal included (in descending frequency): caregiving tasks became too difficult emotionally or physically; the caregiver's illness, hospitalization, or death; other job or family responsibilities; problems in the relationship between the caregiver and care-recipient; and dangerous or disruptive behaviors of the care recipient. Other researchers have reported similar reasons for placement (Brody, 1977; Cath, 1972; Kasmarik & Lester, 1984; Powell & Courtice, 1983).

Third, a few panel studies have compared preinstitutionalization differences in stress between caregivers whose relatives were subsequently institutionalized and those whose relatives remained at home. Greater prior subjective caregiving burden (Deimling & Poulshock, 1985; Zarit et al., 1986), more restrictions on leisure activities (Colerick & George, 1986; Deimling & Poulshock, 1985), worse physical health of the caregiver (Deimling & Poulshock, 1985), and greater psychological distress (Colerick & George, 1986) distinguished caregivers whose relatives later entered nursing homes.

A few studies have pointed out variables that may intervene between the stress of caregiving and nursing home placement. Such variables may delay or preclude nursing home care if the caregiver is highly stressed. Conversely, some variables may lead to earlier admission. One possible moderator is attitude toward nursing home care. Deimling and Poulshock (1985) found that relatives of caregivers with positive prior attitudes toward institutional care were more likely to enter nursing homes than were those relatives whose caregivers had negative attitudes. Attitude toward institutional care was a stronger predictor of placement than was subjective caregiver burden. Such attitudes have rarely been considered in prior empirical studies, however.

A second possible moderating variable is family norms or obligations. Promises made by family members never to put a loved one in a nursing home can delay placement and be a source of great emotional distress for caregivers (Brody, 1977). For children, commitment to provide home care sometimes represents a means of repaying the parent for earlier care, and for spouses it often symbolizes a way of fulfilling marital vows. As one elderly husband in the MBRC studies observed, "She's my wife. As long as I'm here, I'll take care of her. Putting her in a nursing home would be a very last resort." Spouse caregivers are less likely than adult children to relinquish home care for institutional care (Brody, 1977; Hing et al., 1989), although spouses usually experience greater caregiving burden (Cantor, 1983). Family norms or promises influencing nursing home decisions have not been the subject of empirical research, however.

Availability of both institutional and noninstitutional services can be another intervening variable. Nursing home care is sometimes infeasible for families who want it because of lack of available beds, admission requirements, or finances. One daughter in the MBRC studies who began searching for a nursing home more than a year before placement reported, "The places we have looked into make us see [my mother] could never afford this type of arrangement. So at this point we are really lost as to what we should do." On the other hand, some families who would prefer home care are unable to find or afford alternatives to institutionalization. National data reveal that 40% of older residents reportedly entered nursing homes because they lacked sufficient funds to purchasing nursing care at home (Hing et al., 1989). Such structural and economic factors, assessed either objectively or subjectively, are missing from most existing research.

There is anecdotal evidence that some families choose institutional care in order to avoid the stress of caregiving (Smith & Bengtson, 1979; Tobin & Lieberman, 1976). These family members should report lower levels of stress prior to admission and earlier institutionalization than families where nursing home care is not used preventatively. Proactive placement is not easy to discriminate, because studies rarely ask family members whether preventing or minimizing the burden on caregivers is a family value and a reason for choosing placement.

The stress of caregiving as a predictor of nursing home care for older relatives has received surprisingly little empirical investigation. The small body of research that does exist indicates that burden on the caregiver is a significant factor in the use of institutional care. At the same time, several variables including attitudes toward nursing home care, family norms and obligations, availability of institutional and noninstitutional alternatives, and family values, may moderate this relationship.

THE IMPACT OF INSTITUTIONALIZATION ON FAMILY MEMBERS

In this section, the focus shifts to the impact of placement on family members' well-being. This topic has received more study than has stress as a predictor of nursing home placement. Although popular belief persists that residents of nursing homes are abandoned by their families (Tobin & Lieberman, 1976), recent research refutes this. Nearly two-thirds (64%) of nursing home residents in one study reported at least weekly visits from family, whereas only 13% said that they were never visited by family, and most residents named an adult child as their primary confidant (Kahana, Kahana, & Young, 1985).

In the MBRC studies, more than three-fourths (78%) of family members named themselves or another relative as the single-most important person providing the nursing home resident with emotional support. The type of family member mentioned usually was an adult child (46%) or a spouse (28%), but occasionally another relative (4%) was mentioned. Thus these studies, along with others (Buckwalter & Hall, 1987; Montgomery, 1982), document that families, especially adult children, remain a central and active part of many residents' support networks after placement.

Considerable evidence exists that a relative's entry into a nursing home is one of the most stressful later-life events (Brody, 1977; Cath, 1972; Hatch &

Franken, 1984; Chapter 3, this volume). For many people, institutionalization symbolizes abandonment and death, and negative attitudes about nursing home care are still prevalent (Powell & Courtice, 1983; Tobin & Lieberman, 1976). The impact of nursing home care on family caregivers' well-being is multifaceted, with effects ranging from emotional or psychological to physical, temporal, and interpersonal. Existing literature and relevant MBRC data on these effects are reviewed next.

Psychological Impact

Psychological reactions of family members to the institutionalization of their relatives include feelings of guilt, anger, helplessness, failure, grief, and depression (Brandwein & Postoff, 1980; Greenfield, 1984; Kasmarik & Lester, 1984). Even when the impaired relative participates in the placement decision and family relationships are good, negative feelings among relatives are reportedly widespread (Brody, 1977; Tobin & Lieberman, 1976). Most prior research on the psychological impact of a relative's nursing home placement has been based on case studies or the clinical experiences of formal service providers rather than on empirical research. Thus, just how common psychological distress really is or how generalizable clinical findings may be to other families is unknown.

The MBRC research provides some empirical support for clinical conclusions that a relative's nursing home placement has a negative impact on the mental health of many family members. After placement, psychological distress was widely experienced by family members in the MBRC studies: 56% agreed or strongly agreed that the relative's entry into the nursing home was the most difficult problem they had ever had to face, and 72% agreed or strongly agreed that it was easy to feel overwhelmed by this. Nearly 6 out of 10 respondents (57%, based on $n = 65$) felt guilty about the relative's care arrangement, and 7 out of 10 (74% of $n = 65$) reported feeling upset seeing the relative in the nursing home.

However, negative emotional reactions to placement may coexist with psychological relief (Brody, 1977; Greenfield, 1984, Kasmarik & Lester, 1984). Although one-fourth (26%) of the 81 family members in the MBRC studies reported that their emotional health got worse because of a relative's entry into a nursing home, another fourth (27%) said their emotional health got better. As one son observed, "I don't worry as much. I know [my mother's] cared for." Seven out of 10 respondents (70%) agreed that their lives were less complicated since the relative entered the nursing home, and 86% disagreed that nursing home care had created more problems than it had solved.

Only a handful of prior studies have empirically investigated the question of whether nursing home care brings family caregivers psychological relief. These studies used either cross-sectional, post-placement comparisons between caregivers with institutionalized and noninstitutionalized relatives or panel comparisons of subjective burden and psychological well-being (generally, depression) before and after placement. Few differences between family members of institutionalized and noninstitutionalized elders or before and after placement have been found (Colerick & George, 1986; Pagel, Becker, & Coppel, 1985; Pratt, Schmall, Wright, & Hare, 1987; Zarit et al., 1986).

Nonetheless, behind these overall similarities lie some subtle differences in the well-being of caregivers across care arrangements. First, there is evidence that family members with institutionalized relatives may experience different sources of stress than caregivers to noninstitutionalized relatives, such as greater financial worries and interactions with formal service providers, even when overall burden levels are comparable (Pratt et al., 1987; Zarit et al., 1986). Second, one panel study (Zarit et al., 1986) revealed that although subjective caregiving burden decreased over time regardless of the care arrangement, the magnitude of decline was greater among caregivers whose spouses were institutionalized. Third, the effects of placement may depend on how caregivers' psychological well-being is assessed. For example, caregivers whose relatives were institutionalized reported more post-admission use of psychotropic drugs but no greater psychological stress than caregivers still providing home care (Colerick & George, 1986). Fourth, panel analyses of family caregivers' mental health in the MBRC studies show that aggregate stability in mean mental health scores from before to after placement may in part reflect equal percentages of caregivers whose mental health improved or deteriorated. In summary, although a minority of family caregivers appear to experience psychological relief when a relative enters a nursing home, most find this arrangement emotionally distressing. There is no clear evidence, however, that nursing home care is necessarily more stressful for family caregivers than is home care.

Physical and Temporal Impact

Little prior work has attended to the consequences of an older relative's nursing home placement for family members' physical and temporal well-being (i.e., time available). Although the psychological effects have been described as largely negative, a few studies have described the physical and temporal impact on caregivers as primarily positive. Thus placement may relieve caregivers of responsibility for time-consuming and physically taxing tasks (Brody, 1977; Smith & Bengtson, 1979). As one son commented, "Placement takes a lot of the physical and emotional burden of [my mother's] daily care and responsibilities off of me."

In the MBRC studies, the relative's entry into a nursing home generally had no effect or a beneficial effect on family members' physical and temporal well-being. Only 27% of respondents ($n = 65$) said that institutionalization had affected their own physical health, and nearly all of those affected reported that their health had improved. Nevertheless, one-fourth (26% of n = 65) reported not getting enough rest because of the relative's institutionalization, and more than one-half (54%) reported difficulty having enough time or energy to devote to the institutionalized relative. The relative's entry into a nursing home may be even more likely to provide family caregivers with physical and temporal relief when the need for 24-hour care or supervision was one of the reasons for placement, as in caring for dementia patients. Thus Colerick and George (1986) found that caregivers of Alzheimer's patients reported more satisfaction with leisure time after their relative entered a nursing home.

Interpersonal Impact

Research on the impact of nursing home placement on interpersonal relationships has generally focused on negative changes and on family relationships. Brody (1977), for example, has argued that institutionalization reactivates long-standing, latent family difficulties, intensifies ongoing conflicts, and creates new family tensions. These tensions center around anger over placement, disagreement about the necessity or timing of this, feelings of abandonment, sibling rivalries, resentment over perceived caregiving inequities, and conflicts over family members' obligations toward each other (Brandwein & Postoff, 1980; Greenfield, 1984; Townsend, 1987).

These interpersonal strains can involve relationships with the institutionalized relative or other family, including extended kin (Brody, 1966; Tobin & Lieberman, 1976). There also is selective evidence that relationships with nonfamily supports may erode after a relative's placement. Caregivers in a study by Colerick and George (1986) reported no change in support from family, but a decrease in support from friends after their relatives' entry into nursing homes.

Family conflict was rarely reported in the MBRC studies: After admission, one-third or less of the sample (n = 65) reported family tension or strain (30%), difficulty getting the institutionalized relative to cooperate (32%), or problems getting family members to visit the resident (33%). On a series of questions about negative changes in family relations due to placement, less than one-fifth of the respondents (N = 81) reported more family arguments (9%), the family not getting along as well as before (10%), greater anger among family members (15%), or family members being disappointed with how matters related to placement were handled (18%). Thus the MBRC studies show little support for negative interpersonal effects of placement.

There also are some studies suggesting that nursing home care can have a benign or positive effect on family relationships. In these studies, new, renewed, or continued closeness among family members was more common than deterioration or continued estrangement (Hatch & Franken, 1984; Montgomery, 1982; Moss & Kurland, 1979; Smith & Bengtson, 1979). More than half of the MBRC respondents reported that, because of placement, family members talked things over more (51%), relied more on each other (56%), thought family relationships were more important (58%), felt closer to each other (60%), and took more time to get together (65%). Overall, then, there is evidence for considerable variation in the effects of institutionalization on interpersonal (mainly family) relationships. Most families experience improvement or continued closeness, whereas a minority experience deterioration or continued conflict.

Predictors of Stress Following Placement

Predictors of the stress experienced by caregivers after their relatives are institutionalized include the quality of family relationships, the process by which the placement decision was made, the resident's health and adjustment after placement, the role relationship of the family caregiver, evaluations of the institution, and duration of institutionalization. Some of these categories have received more attention than others. Again, much of the literature is clinical rather than empirical, and the empirical research has typically used cross-sectional designs.

Estranged or conflictual family relationships prior to placement have been said to make both intrapsychic and interpersonal adjustment to institutionalization more difficult (Brody, 1966). However, no empirical tests of this hypothesis are known. The degree of family support after placement also reputedly affects subsequent stress. Thus, Hatch and Franken (1984) found that relationships with other family members changed only when the others' reactions to placement were perceived to be very negative (e.g., unconcerned or condemnatory) or very positive (e.g., helpful and supportive). In the MBRC studies, greater post-placement family tension and conflict over visiting the resident were correlated with more guilt, more negative affect, and poorer mental health among adult children (Townsend, Deimling, & Noelker, 1988).

Lack of participation in the decision by the impaired relative or family caregivers also has been hypothesized to lead the excluded family member to feel angry, depressed, resistant, or resentful after placement (Brody, 1977; Kasmarik & Lester, 1984). Indeed, Tobin and Lieberman (1976) argued that the relationship between parent and child will inevitably be altered by the way in which the nursing home decision was made, regardless of the relationship's earlier history. Another factor affecting family members' stress is the resident's health after admission. Brandwein and Postoff (1980) concluded that deterioration in the resident's health after placement exacerbates family caregivers' guilt. The feeling that "being in the nursing home is killing my mother," as one daughter in the MBRC studies grimly stated, conveys how stressful a relative's decline after placement can be for family members.

The institutionalized relative's mental or emotional condition is particularly important. Visits to a nursing home are more stressful for family members when the resident is mentally impaired (Moss & Kurland, 1979; Pratt et al., 1987). The MBRC studies showed that adult children's reports of difficulty dealing with their institutionalized parent's mental or emotional state after placement correlated with greater feelings of guilt and more negative affect (Townsend et al., 1988). Stephens and her colleagues (Stephens, Bridges, Ogrocki, Kinney, & Norris, 1988) have documented that the resident's cognitive impairment and behavioral problems are the most prevalent daily hassles for family members of institutionalized Alzheimer's patients and have the greatest negative impact on family members' psychological well-being.

The institutionalized relative's adjustment to or acceptance of nursing home care also influences family caregivers' stress. Behaviors that reflect the relative's despair over or resistance to placement (for example, crying or emotional withdrawal, refusals to eat, or verbal abuse) reportedly intensify family members' feelings of powerlessness, guilt, anger, and grief (Buckwalter & Hall, 1987). In the MBRC studies, perceived problems with the relative's adjustment to nursing home life, such as complaints about staff or other residents, were reported by between one-fifth and one-third of the sample. A significant minority of mentally intact relatives were reported to be dissatisfied with their care arrangement: Of the 47 institutionalized relatives whom family members felt were aware of their surroundings, 32% were not at all satisfied or not too satisfied with their nursing home care, according to the family member. The more difficulties that adult children reported with parents' adjustment to being in a nursing home, the more guilt the children expressed and the less satisfied the children also were with the care arrangement (Townsend et al., 1988).

Conversely, improvement in the resident's physical or mental health after placement has been associated with improved family relationships (Smith & Bengtson, 1979). These improvements sometimes surprise family members. One daughter, who described her mother as previously depressed and "smothered" at home caring for an equally frail husband, observed with wonder after her father's death and her mother's entry into a nursing home, "She can talk and see other people here and has improved so much I can't believe it."

Prior research also suggests that the family role relationship of the caregiver influences the caregiver's post-institutionalization stress. Although most studies have either focused solely on adult children's reactions (Brandwein & Postoff, 1980; Hatch & Franken, 1984) or have failed to differentiate among family caregivers, Brody (1977) has written about the special strain that spouses experience with a husband's or wife's entry into a nursing home. In the MBRC studies, spouses were more likely than children to agree that their relative's placement was the most difficult problem they had ever faced ($t = -2.94$, $df = 79$, $p < .01$), and they reported greater emotional upset ($t = -2.51$, $df = 63$, $p < .01$), less positive affect ($t = 3.20$, $df = 79$, $p < .01$), poorer mental health ($t = 2.59$, $df = 79$, $p < .01$), and more depression ($t = -3.24$,

$df = 79, p < .01$). For adult children, perceived conflict between obligations to the institutionalized parent and to themselves, their own family, or work is especially stressful. Hence, in the MBRC studies, the more these obligations seemed to conflict, the greater were adult children's feelings of guilt and emotional distress (Townsend, 1987; Townsend at el., 1988).

Other predictors of post-placement stress relate to the institutional environment. The transition from home care to institutional care involves considerable loss of control by family members over the relative's care. Consistent with general research on stress (Thoits, 1983), this loss of control has a negative impact on family members' well-being (Brody, 1977; Greenfield, 1984; Pratt et al., 1987). The fact that most families have had no or little prior experience with nursing homes makes them an unfamiliar setting in which family members do not know what to expect. Many family members are unsure about what their role ought to be in this new environment (Brody, 1977; Pratt et al., 1987). This leads to one of the most frequently-reported difficulties after placement: Family members do not know what to do during visits (Brody, 1977). The extent to which the nursing home encourages and assists the family's continued involvement with the resident significantly influences both family members' and residents' adjustment (Buckwalter & Hall, 1987; Montgomery, 1982; Pratt et al., 1987; Smith & Bengtson, 1979).

Family members' perceptions of the quality of care provided by the facility also have been linked to their satisfaction with placement or their distress over this arrangement. Knowing that the relative is in a more protected, secure environment or one where necessary care is being provided can bring considerable relief (Hatch & Franken, 1984; Smith & Bengtson, 1979). Conversely, when family members do not trust nursing home staff to provide good care, the need to monitor and supervise care can become a source of stress. In the MBRC studies, the more difficulties that adult children reported having with the institution (including problems with the quality of care, feelings of discomfort with the facility, and complaints about staff), the less satisfied with the care arrangement they were and the more guilty about placement (Townsend et al., 1988).

Family members' stress related to nursing home care also may change over time, although there have been no known empirical tests of this. Greenfield (1984) and Powell and Courtice (1983) asserted that family members usually adjust to placement between six weeks and a year after admission. Others (Hatch & Franken, 1984; Kasmarik & Lester, 1984) have distinguished more global periods of stress, namely, making the decision and the time immediately surrounding admission. Tobin and Lieberman (1976) proposed that family members' feelings and relationships continue to change throughout relatives' nursing home residence. However, in the MBRC data there were no significant correlations between the duration of institutionalization and family members' mental health or psychological distress over placement (Townsend et al., 1988). Unfortunately, most research has either ignored the relationship between stress and duration of nursing home care or has controlled the effects of time through sample selection criteria.

Prior research on predictors of post-institutionalization stress among family members has typically examined a single predictor and outcome at a time, so little is known about how these sources of stress may interrelate or differentially affect well-being. Factor analysis of the MBRC data from adult children differentiated eight oblique dimensions of stressors: the resident's mental state, the resident's adjustment, the adult child's adjustment, the adult child's other responsibilities, family strain, family visiting patterns, the adult child's perceptions of the institution, and the facility's proximity (Townsend et al., 1988). These factors were, at most, moderately intercorrelated (maximum $r = .41$). Although five of these dimensions parallel the sources of stress predicted by prior research, three others do not. These three were the adult child's self-reported difficulties adjusting to or coping with the parent's placement (e.g., problems getting enough rest, coping with multiple demands, and finding good advice), conflict specifically over getting family members to visit the nursing home, and the distance between the child's home and the nursing home.

The impact of these stressors on children's mental health varied across indicators (Townsend et al., 1988). For example, greater difficulty balancing responsibility to the institutionalized parent with the child's other obligations was correlated with greater feelings of guilt ($r = .50$, $p < .01$) but had no bearing on depression ($r = .16$, $p > .05$). These findings suggest that multidimensional models of both predictors of stress and well-being are needed in order to refine current understanding of family caregivers' experiences with nursing home care.

LIMITATIONS OF PRIOR RESEARCH AND DIRECTIONS FOR FUTURE RESEARCH

My review of existing research on family caregivers' stress as both a cause and a consequence of nursing home care for older relatives leads to the following conclusions. First, greater stress caused by caregiving does increase the likelihood of nursing home placement. However, at least two older persons with equal impairments are estimated to receive noninstitutional care for every older resident in a nursing home (Doty et al., 1985). Clearly, many family caregivers do not turn to nursing home care even under stress. I discussed several factors that may moderate the relationship between the burden of caregiving and nursing home placement, but few prior studies have included such intervening variables.

Second, once it occurs, a relative's nursing home care is indeed stressful for many family members. Psychological distress is the most commonly reported and most widely studied effect. Whether compared to caregivers of noninstitutionalized relatives or their own subjective burden prior to placement, most family members with institutionalized relatives show no significant decrease in psychological stress after placement. As one daughter observed nearly a year after her mother's institutionalization, "I do my best to convince myself that this is the best and only answer to caring for my mother. I just wish I could do more for her. I keep thinking should I have done this?"

Across other dimensions of well-being, however, considerable variability in impact is evident. Institutional care generally has positive effects on family caregivers' physical and temporal well-being, but its interpersonal impact is much more mixed. I reviewed a variety of predictors of family caregivers' well-being after their relatives' admission to a nursing home. There are four features of previous research, however, that limit the confidence with which the foregoing conclusions can be asserted: lack of empirical evidence, inadequate sampling, limited study designs, and lack of theoretical models.

Empirical Evidence and Sampling

Foremost among the limitations of prior research is the scarcity of empirical studies. More research is sorely needed on family caregivers' beliefs, attitudes, intentions, behaviors, and experiences related to institutional care. Although nursing home care is not as widely experienced in later life as is home care, the number of families facing this experience is nevertheless sizable and is growing. Furthermore, evidence of the stressfulness of nursing home care for many families argues for better understanding of this arrangement in order to improve long-term care policies and services.

Sampling strategies also limit the applicability of previous research. Among common shortcomings are results based on small, nonprobability samples of caregivers; sampling from a small number of long-term care facilities, sometimes even a single site; and studies that either disregard differences among care-recipients in impairment or restrict themselves to caregivers of Alzheimer's patients. In addition, because characteristics of the family caregiver, such as role relationship or race, have rarely been criteria for sample selection or subsequent analyses, knowledge about spouses or minority caregivers and nursing home care is especially lacking.

One important goal for future research, therefore, includes designs with larger, probability samples of family caregivers. Another goal is using designs that analyze variability among family caregivers by characteristics such as gender, race, or role relationship. Such distinctions are very important predictors of stress among caregivers of those in noninstitutional settings (Brody, 1977; Cantor, 1983; Morycz, 1985), but they have not been incorporated into nursing home research. A third goal is to sample from a broader array of long-term care facilities. Currently, characteristics of nursing homes used by study participants are infrequently described, let alone incorporated into data analyses or interpretation of results. Theoretical guidance in selecting critical features of nursing home environments for study is currently lacking. Some potential institutional factors to incorporate into future work (such as type of ownership, size, or structure) can be gleaned, however, from the 1985 National Nursing Home Survey (Hing et al., 1989) and from work on institutional environments by Moos and his colleagues (Moos, Gauvain, Lemke, Max, & Mehren, 1979).

A fourth goal for future research is to improve samples by attending to the diversity in care-recipients' impairments. Specifically, we need to know whether findings based on family caregivers of Alzheimer's patients are generalizable to other circumstances and vice versa. The relationship of a care-recipient's impairment to a family caregiver's stress is receiving increasing attention in noninstitutional caregiving (Deimling & Bass, 1986), but it usually is neglected in studies of families and institutional care.

Study Designs

Anecdotal case studies and clinical experiences of formal care providers are far more prevalent than are empirical studies of family members. Although this nonempirical knowledge can greatly enhance and guide future research, more quantitative testing of the validity and generalizability of hypotheses is needed. Clinical hypotheses about how family promises prevent or delay use of nursing homes and about the prevalence of guilt among family caregivers after placement are two key directions for empirical research.

There has also been a paucity of multivariate designs. For example, the importance of stress on the caregiver relative to other potential predictors of nursing home placement is poorly understood, given the limited number of multivariate analyses. Furthermore, even existing multivariate studies (e.g., Colerick & George, 1986; Deimling & Poulshock, 1985) have used statistical techniques, such as multiple regression, which do not illuminate the causal patterns underlying predictors of institutionalization. Existing multivariate analyses also have explored only additive, linear relationships among predictors. Retrospective data suggest that institutionalization is the result of a breakdown in the delicate balance between the older person's care needs and self-care abilities; the primary caregiver's resources, motivation, and other commitments; and the larger caregiving support network. Yet present research is hampered by a dearth of multivariate causal models incorporating these domains, and interactive or nonlinear models may be needed to represent these breaking points.

It also is obvious from existing research that future models need to include multiple dimensions of the stress of caregiving as well as multiple predictors in order to understand both the causes and consequences of nursing home care. A multidimensional approach would help clarify which facets of burden are more likely to lead to institutional care and would better illuminate the mixture of positive and negative effects on family caregivers' well-being that occur after placement.

Overreliance on cross-sectional designs is another shortcoming of present research. The limited longitudinal data on family members' stress prior to institutionalization makes the dynamics of the process leading to placement ambiguous. There currently is no research, for example, investigating whether a prolonged high level of stress is more difficult for caregivers to bear and, hence, is more likely than erratic or escalating burdens to result in placement. Given that there is great variability in nursing home residents' health patterns prior to admission (Hing et al., 1989), there also is probably considerable variation in caregivers' stress levels leading to placement. Conversely, the absence of panel data after placement leaves only speculation about the course and pace of family members' adjustment to nursing home care. Existing cross-sectional studies after admission often do not even descriptively report the duration of institutionalization, let alone incorporate this as a predictor of stress.

Longitudinal models of stress and nursing home care also would require researchers to consider the timing of data collection more explicitly. Measures obtained shortly before a relative's admission may confound stress due to the noninstitutional caregiving circumstances with stress related to the institutionalization decision or process. Although very little is known about how placement decisions are made, there is some qualitative evidence that this may be an extended and highly ambivalent process for many caregivers (Cath, 1972; Townsend, 1987). As one son in the MBRC studies said, a year prior to his widowed mother's entry into a nursing home, "I may have to make a decision for which I'm not prepared."

Another design limitation that future research needs to address is selection of appropriate comparison groups. Although a few recent studies have included family caregivers of both institutionalized and noninstitutionalized relatives, most current knowledge is based on retrospective data from families whose relatives already receive nursing home care. Thus, in addition to the panel question of whether family members' stress changes from before to after placement, the question of how stressed family caregivers with institutionalized relatives are when compared to family members providing noninstitutional care also has received little investigation. Cross-sectional comparisons between caregivers of institutionalized and noninstitutionalized relatives do not provide adequate answers because of possible differences between the two groups prior to placement.

Theoretical Models

Although greater stress on the caregiver predicts a greater likelihood of institutionalization for the care-recipient, theoretical models to explain why are lacking. There are no well-developed models telling us why some families use nursing home care whereas others do not, predicting the psychological breaking point at which family caregivers decide home care is no longer desirable or feasible, or delineating how placement decisions are made. In order to understand the reluctance of so many families to use nursing home care, conceptual models of the symbolic meanings of institutionalization for family relationships seem especially important for future development.

Similarly, after admission, theories predicting how family members' well-being will be affected are missing, as are models for how and why the stress of caregiving may change over time. Theoretical analyses of both the similarities and differences between noninstitutional and institutional care are particularly needed in order to understand how nursing home care affects family members and why stress levels often remain high after placement. Currently, research on families and nursing home care glosses over both an extended process or series of stages families go through (e.g., decision making, application, admission, and subsequent residence) and a highly complex environment, subsuming a diverse array of facilities.

Finally, once the relationship between the stress of caregiving and nursing home care is more fully and clearly understood, this knowledge should be used to design interventions to alleviate stress, before as well as after placement. To be successful, these interventions should target not only individual family caregivers, but also whole or partial family systems, as well as formal long-term care providers, policy makers, and funders of long-term care. It may well be that fundamental changes in the availability, accessibility, funding, staffing, design, and quality assurance of long-term care services across the spectrum will be more effective in making institutional care less necessary and less stressful than will efforts directed toward family caregivers.

REFERENCES

Brandwein, C., & Postoff, R. (1980). A model of intervention for working with adult children of aged parents. *Long Term Care and Health Services, 4,* 173–182.

Brody, E. (1966). The aging family. *The Gerontologist, 6,* 201–206.

Brody, E. (1977). *Long-term care of older people: A practical guide.* New York: Human Sciences Press.

Buckwalter, K., & Hall, G. (1987). Families of the institutionalized older adult: A neglected resource. In T. Brubaker (Ed.), *Aging, health, and family: Long-term care* (pp. 176–196). Newbury Park, CA: Sage.

Cantor, M. H. (1983). Strain among caregivers: A study of experience in the United States. *The Gerontologist, 23,* 597–604.

Cath, S. H. (1972). The institutionalization of a parent: A nadir of life. *Journal of Geriatric Psychiatry, 5,* 25–46.

Colerick, E. J., & George, L. K. (1986). Predictors of institutionalization among caregivers of patients with Alzheimer's disease. *Journal of the American Geriatrics Society, 34,* 493–498.

Deimling, G. T., & Bass, D. M. (1986). Symptoms of mental impairment among elderly adults and their effects on family caregivers. *Journal of Gerontology, 41,* 778–784.

Deimling, G. T., & Poulshock, S. W. (1985). The transition from family in-home care to institutional care: Focus on health and attitudinal issues as predisposing factors. *Research on Aging, 7,* 563–576.

Doty, P., Liu, K., & Weiner, Y. (1985). An overview of long term care. *Health Care Financing Review, 6,* 69–78.

Greenfield, W. (1984). Disruption and reintegration: Dealing with familial response to nursing home placement. *Journal of Gerontological Social Work, 8,* 15–21.

Harris, L., & Associates, Inc. (1982). *Priorities and expectations for health and living circumstances: A survey of the elderly in five English speaking countries* (A study for the Commonwealth Fund). New York: Author.

Hatch, R., & Franken, M. (1984). Concerns of children with parents in nursing homes. *Journal of Gerontological Social Work, 7,* 19–30.

Hing, E. (1987). *Use of nursing homes by the elderly: Preliminary data from the 1985 national nursing home survey, No. 135* (DHHS Publication No. PHS 87-1250). Hyattsville, MD: Public Health Service.

Hing, E., Sekscenski, E., & Strahan, G. (1989). *National nursing home survey* (DHHS Publication No. PHS 89-1758). Washington, DC: U.S. Government Printing Office.

Kahana, E., Kahana, B., & Young, R. (1985). Social factors in institutional living. In W. Peterson & J. Quadagno (Eds.), *Social bonds in later life: Aging and interdependence* (pp. 389–418). Beverly Hills, CA: Sage.

Kane, R. A., & Kane, R. L. (1987). *Long-term care: Principles, programs, and policies.* New York: Springer.

Kasmarik, P., & Lester, V. (1984). A hard decision: When institutionalization is the best answer. In B. Hall (Ed.), *Mental health and the elderly* (pp. 165–184). Orlando, FL: Grune & Stratton.

Lawton, M. P., & Brody, E. (1969). Assessment of older people: Self-maintaining and instrumental activities of daily living. *The Gerontologist, 9,* 179–186.

Liu, K., & Palesch, Y. (1981). The nursing home population: Different perspectives and implications for policy. *Health Care Financing Review, 213,* 15–23.

Montgomery, R. (1982). Impact of institutional care policies on family integration. *The Gerontologist, 22,* 54–58.

Moos, R. H., Gauvain, M., Lemke, S., Max, W., & Mehren, B. (1979). Assessing the social environments of sheltered care settings. *The Gerontologist, 19,* 74–82.

Morycz, R. K. (1985). Caregiving strain and the desire to institutionalize family members with Alzheimer's disease. *Research on Aging, 7,* 329–361.

Moss, M., & Kurland, P. (1979). Family visiting with institutionalized mentally impaired aged. *Journal of Gerontological Social Work, 1,* 271–278.

Pagel, M., Becker, J., & Coppel, D. (1985). Loss of control, self-blame, and depression: An investigation of spouse caregivers of Alzheimer's disease patients. *Journal of Abnormal Psychology, 94,* 169–182.

Powell, L., & Courtice, K. (1983). *Alzheimer's disease: A guide for families.* Reading, MA: Addison-Wesley.

Pratt, C., Schmall, V., Wright, S., & Hare, J. (1987). The forgotten client: Family caregivers to institutionalized dementia patients. In T. Brubaker (Ed.), *Aging, health, and family: Long-term care* (pp. 197–215). Newbury Park, CA: Sage.

Riley, M. (1983). The family in an aging society: A matrix of latent relationships. *Journal of Family Issues, 4,* 439–454.

Smith, K., & Bengtson, V. (1979). Positive consequences of institutionalization: Solidarity between elderly parents and their middle-aged children. *The Gerontologist, 19,* 438–447.

Stephens, M. A. P., Bridges, A. M., Ogrocki, P. K., Kinney, J. M., & Norris, V. K. (1988, November). *Daily stressors for family caregivers to institutionalized AD patients.* Paper presented at the meeting of the Gerontological Society of America, San Francisco.

Stone, R., Cafferata, G., & Sangl, J. (1987). Caregivers of the frail elderly: A national profile. *The Gerontologist, 27,* 616–626.

Thoits, P. A. (1983). Dimensions of life events that influence psychological distress: An evaluation and synthesis of the literature. In H. B. Kaplan (Ed.), *Psychosocial stress: Trends in theory and research* (pp. 33–87). New York: Academic Press.

Tobin, S., & Lieberman, M. (1976). *Last home for the aged.* San Francisco: Jossey-Bass.

Townsend, A. L. (1987). *Family caregivers' perspectives on institutionalization decisions.* Cleveland, OH: The Benjamin Rose Institute. (ERIC Document Reproduction Service No. ED 296 233)

Townsend, A. L., Deimling, G. T., & Noelker, L. S. (1988, November). *Transition to nursing home care: Sources of stress and family members' mental health.* Paper presented at the meeting of the Gerontological Society of America, San Francisco.

Treas, J. (1977). Family support systems for the aged: Some social and demographic considerations. *The Gerontologist, 17,* 361–367.

Zarit, S. H., Todd, P. A., & Zarit, J. M. (1986). Subjective burden of husbands and wives as caregivers: A longitudinal study. *The Gerontologist, 26,* 260–266.

16

ECOLOGICAL PERSPECTIVES ON STRESS AND COPING IN LATER-LIFE FAMILIES

Mary Ann Parris Stephens
Stevan E. Hobfoll

Kent State University

The study of stress in later-life families has focused on a wide array of issues that have challenged researchers and theorists who are concerned with the stressors facing older adults and their family members and with how these individuals cope with such difficulties. Early chapters in this volume have emphasized the kinds of stressors that older adults frequently encounter and how such experiences affect them and the family system in which they are embedded. Later chapters have emphasized helping interactions as a means for coping, both for the older adult whose personal resources may be inadequate to meet the demands of a stressful situation, and for the family as its primary response for coping in such situations. Some chapters have focused on the ways in which help is given and how it is received within such families, and others have emphasized the ways in which giving help on a continuing basis can alter family functioning. What is clear from these chapters is that stressful events and attempts to cope with them do not occur in a vacuum. Rather, they occur within a family network in which members are inextricably linked to one another in such a way that what happens to one family member will in some way affect all others in the family unit. Thus coping efforts, as well as stressors themselves, are often highly interpersonal and complex phenomena and, as such, their impact is necessarily multifaceted.

Although the study of stress in later-life families addresses different aspects of family functioning within these families, there exists a set of basic theoretical assumptions about the nature of stress and social relations within these families. We have three major purposes in writing this chapter. First, we want to make some suggestions for the development of theory concerning stress and coping in later-life families. Many of the suggestions we make are based on the underlying assumptions and values of this volume's contributors. Second, although methodology was not a key issue for most chapters in the volume, we want to address what we see as some of the major problems of research design and measurement that are encountered by researchers interested in assessing family stress and coping. Finally, we deal with several issues pertaining to the application of research knowledge about older families—specifically, how we can apply this knowledge to the development of effective social policy and intervention programs.

In assembling our thoughts, we have drawn heavily from the general stress and coping literature, from chapters appearing in this volume, and from the lively discussions among the chapters' primary authors and other invited guests at the 1989 Kent Psychology Forum. Although we have done the formal writing of this chapter, the ideas that we discuss are in large part the product of a fruitful collaborative effort by Forum participants.

THE NEED FOR AN OVERARCHING THEORY

In social gerontology in general, as well as in the more specific topic area of stress and coping in later-life families, the absence of theoretical integration or even productive communication among related areas of research is striking. Several factors have contributed to the creation of this situation, which renders the development of a comprehensive theory problematic. One major problem inhibiting communication among stress and coping researchers in social gerontology is the lack of a shared language for describing various stress and coping phenomena. Researchers often use different labels to refer to similar phenomena. For example, some researchers use the term *trauma* to refer to stressors that engender extreme psychological and physical reactions in people who experience them. To refer to similar stressful conditions, other researchers use the term *disaster* or *crisis*. Despite the obvious similarities in the nature of these constructs, different literatures and methodologies have emerged around each. Thus, disparate labels that are used to refer to closely related constructs may obscure the shared characteristics of like events or experiences. Furthermore, researchers may be misled into believing that different processes underlie each.

Another factor inhibiting communication among stress and coping researchers stems from their tendency to focus on only a few aspects of complex psychosocial processes and to ignore other, sometimes importantly related, aspects of these same processes. Such decisions are typically made on the basis of pragmatic necessity, or along disciplinary lines. Regardless of the source of this problem, it has the effect of splintering research knowledge. When the focus on these subprocesses is narrow and does not consider the larger psychosocial process of which it is a part, researchers may come to underestimate or overestimate the importance of the phenomena with which they are primarily concerned. Additionally, they may fail to appreciate fully the conditions under which these phenomena occur. As an example from the social support literature, an exclusive focus on either the recipient or the provider of assistance in a helping interaction can obscure the importance or meaning of either partner's behavior or of the interaction within the dyad.

Clearly, what social gerontologists need is an overarching theory of stress and coping that can help delineate critical constructs within the field and describe how they relate to one another. Such a theory could provide a common language for communicating about phenomena and could offer a broader context in which subprocesses could be evaluated. Even though theories currently abound in social gerontology, they typically represent little more than a few loosely connected hypotheses about a rather limited set of constructs. It is obvious that the task of developing an overarching theory will be shared by many individuals over time and is one that is beyond the scope of this chapter. However, as a contribution to this evolutionary process, we would like to make several suggestions about the characteristics that these theoretical developments should include.

CHARACTERISTICS OF A STRESS AND COPING THEORY IN SOCIAL GERONTOLOGY

The topic of stress and coping in later-life families will naturally engender a wide array of models and theories because the phenomena of stress and coping are multifaceted. Depending on the perspective from which the problem is viewed, there will be a need to employ differing explanatory mechanisms. Despite this overall complexity, an ecological paradigm seems to fulfill the need for an heuristic conceptual framework.

What we mean by an ecological paradigm can be illustrated by the biological concepts from which social scientists have borrowed the ecological analogy. An ecosystem is a web of related organisms, plants, and animals that exist together in a particular climate and geography. When one facet of the ecosystem is changed, the change ripples through the various subsystems of the ecological web. Even a slight difference in one part of the system, for example, the climate, will affect the plant life, animal hierarchy, and terrain and ultimately will come full circle to affect the climate itself.

The same principles hold for human ecosystems. The family, for instance, is itself an integrated system that exists within a given economic and social setting that is affected by the laws, institutions, and provisions of the larger society, all of which are nested within a given culture. Any change in any facet of this system will, in turn, reverberate throughout the ecosystem. As an illustration, societal policy concerning home-based care for chronically ill older adults will affect family roles and obligations, work, intrafamilial relations, nursing homes, and how the society views these older people. Eventually, these changes will cycle back to affect policy vis-à-vis home-based care.

Taken as a whole, the chapters in this volume offer considerable support for this ecological perspective. In our discussions with the chapters' authors, the schema in Figure 1 has been developed to illustrate different levels of the ecology of later-life families. We contend that an overarching theory should accommodate each of these levels of analysis. The major point that we want to make here is that the resulting ecological theory will include multiple levels or domains, and it will consider multiple systems within domains in order to provide a more true-to-life understanding of stress and coping in later-life families.

The Macrosocial Domain

The first level of the ecology of later-life families includes the macrosocial context. This domain can be divided into three related areas, the social, cultural, and historical contexts. The social context includes formal societal institutions and organizations. These entities often bear directly on later-life families in ways such as the amount of financial support and service support they provide, how they legislate and make policies, and how they act on the concerns expressed by older adults and their families. Also represented in this level of the ecology are the sociological characteristics of family systems that exist within the society. For example, the nature of family systems within the larger society may be characterized by a concentration of nuclear families that tend to be mobile and spread out. However, a subgroup within that society might be typified by a system of extended families that live in a geographically restricted area and that are only loosely connected.

A second facet of the macrosocial level is the cultural context. Every society reflects a given culture that shapes the values and traditions of its people. Later-life families are affected by the specific aspects of the culture that touch on the lives of the elderly. Currently, our culture is attempting to balance the principles of capitalism and the recognized need to provide some assistance to those who cannot fend for themselves. Many older adults and their families would be unable to survive, in the most literal sense, were it not for the cultural imperatives that press society to support those older people who have already made their life contribution to that society. This emphasis often competes against other cultural imperatives that imply the importance for self-sufficiency, individualism, and the ideal that support for the elderly should rest on the shoulders of their families alone.

The concept of retirement itself is founded on cultural traditions. Until recently in developed nations (and even today in developing nations), the majority of individuals worked from the cradle to the grave. One stopped working only when one became incapable of working or when economic advantage

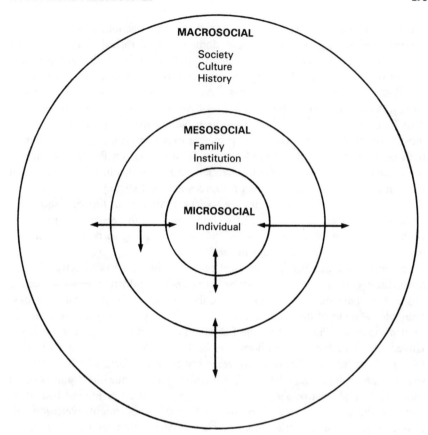

FIGURE 1   Levels of the Ecology of Later-Life Families.

made further work unnecessary (the latter being a much rarer event). Today, retirement is both a reward and a socioeconomic necessity for our society. After long years of service, retirement allows the opportunity to make one's hobbies one's vocation. The ideal picture of fishing trips, visiting with grandchildren, and enjoying the harvest of one's years is evoked. Retirement is also a virtual necessity for our society. Because of increasing life spans for individuals, retirement is needed to clear space in the work force for the entry of young people. The reality of retirement is that it is often forced on those who would choose to work longer, and it is often economically infeasible for those who would like to retire but cannot. Yet, despite all these pros and cons, retirement is a concept deeply rooted in our society and economy, and its specter is raised from the first work day for which individuals pay Social Security tax or invest in a company retirement plan.

The social and cultural fabric of society evolves through a history of interactions of people with their social systems. These interactions provide the basis for the third facet of the macrosocial domain, the historical context. Today's families are steeped in experiences that are products of events that are as distant as World War I and the Great Depression and as recent as the policies of the just-past President. Even more long-term historical trends have a continued legacy. A case in point is the evolution of "rugged individualism" in America. This founding principle has been used to argue against the need for all but the most basic public institutions. This principle experienced a brief hiatus during the Roosevelt New Deal and the Kennedy–Johnson War on Poverty, but it was revitalized in the 1980s. Rugged individualism is a principle that suggests that individuals must rely on their own resources and that society will be strong to the extent that this ethic permeates the society. It affects our thinking about and operation of Social Security, social welfare, and health services programs. It even influences how much we as individuals are willing to depend on family members when we ourselves are in need.

Rugged individualism is a cultural phenomenon that has directly affected historical events. These events may be better understood when we view them in this cultural perspective. History is not only what is recorded in history books. Examples abound of historical events that our history books gloss over, or fail to mention at all. For instance, the Socialist Party had a strong showing in the United States in the early part of this century. Union rights and retirement benefits were fought over for many years just prior to World War II. Additionally, the unemployed marched on Washington, DC, during the Depression in such great numbers that they swelled to the ranks of an army and had to be violently dispersed by federal troops for fear that they might overthrow the government. These histories are reflected in the memories of older adults and in the evolution of our institutions. The realities of these events are present whether or not we recognize them. However, we cannot use them to gain insight about ourselves and our society unless we are aware of their influence.

Even when we are aware of historical events we are not always cognizant of their impact. For example, it is easy to forget how recently Medicare was introduced. Any time such a sweeping change as this occurs, we tend to forget what life was like before it took place.

An understanding of history not only sheds light on our past but also provides valuable information regarding our future. An interesting example of this is the emergence of posttraumatic stress disorders among veterans of World War II, problems that are surfacing more than 40 years after the war's armistice. These men tend to be in their mid-60s, and their stress reactions are emerging as they enter retirement and perhaps have more time to look back on their earlier adult experiences at war. Thus, today's events not only represent tomorrow's history, but also they have the potential for having long-term effects on the people who experience them and on future generations.

The Mesosocial Domain

The next level of the ecosystem is nested between the macrolevel and the individual. It includes the family life cycle and the particular institutions that house, treat, and fund services for the elderly and that assist their families. The family life cycle encompasses the relations between family members and the history and social characteristics of the family. Family size, age of members, social class, education, intimate relations, and past family events are some of the factors that form this level of analysis. One family may be composed of an isolated elderly pair, another may include older people living independently and visiting family, and yet another might consist of an older person living with children and grandchildren. These family constellations are affected by factors such as the age and health of the elderly members, their economic status, and their geographic location (e.g., rural, suburban, or inner-city). It also depends on a variety of historical relations (e.g., norms of reciprocity or feelings of affection) within the family. There has been a tendency in this regard to imagine relations within the family as though they began when the older person entered old age. Strong family ties are developed over a life span of interaction typified by sharing and support.

The second facet of this middle domain includes the institutions with which older individuals and their families interact. Older people often are confronted with dependency on and frequent contact with institutions and their representatives. Retirement villages, Social Security offices, hospitals, and nursing homes are examples of such institutions. These institutions often have a pervasive effect on older people and their family members. Although these institutions play less of a role in the lives of those people who are more independent in terms of health and economics, for the old-old it is rare to avoid their influence.

These institutions often affect families in profound ways, but is should not be inferred that individuals are passively involved with them. Despite the power of these bureaucracies, the ecological back-drop reminds us that people respond resourcefully through self-help groups, political action groups, and personal contacts in order to have an effect on institutions and on how they treat individuals. Some of the mutual influence is informal, as when nursing homes provide better care to residents whose family members visit often. More formal influence can be seen through groups pressing for better care at a particular nursing home, calling state authorities to report alleged infractions of the law, or moving a family member from one nursing home to another with better care services (i.e., pressure from the competition).

Interaction between the family and institutional systems may be frequent. For example, when home-based care services are inadequate, family caregivers may falter under the burden of their older relative's increasing ill health and the concomitant need for care. This situation might lead them to turn to more restrictive institutions for aid or cause adult children to partially or fully give up employment to provide more intensive care. Clearly, efforts to understand the complexities that later-life families experience will necessarily entail focusing on many factors that may interact within a level (e.g., families and institutions), as well as attending to different levels of analysis.

The Microsocial Domain

Finally, Figure 1 illustrates the micro-level of the ecosystem, the individual. The individual is perhaps the most important concern in the study of stress and coping in families with older members. After all, it is the individual person who experiences emotions and physical suffering and who ultimately puts forth coping efforts to adapt to life's difficulties. However, researchers have tended to investigate individuals almost to the exclusion of the other levels that we are suggesting. Attention has been directed primarily at how the individual perceives, processes, and responds. Far less attention has been directed at understanding the context in which these psychosocial phenomena occur. The individual is only a small part, albeit a very important part, of highly complex and interrelated psychosocial processes. Therefore, a comprehensive understanding of the individual cannot be achieved without inclusion of the macrosocial and mesosocial domains.

The individual may well be the best source of information about matters such as subjective feelings, personal satisfaction, and subjective health. However, individuals are all too often the sole source of information about their families, the institutions with which they interact, and the nature of their physical environment. If one is looking for a subjective accounting of these other levels of the ecosystem, then individuals are an excellent source of information. It should be kept in mind, however, that this information does not necessarily represent the actual state of the institutions, neighborhood, or social relations about which knowledge is sought. The ecological paradigm demands that more objective indicators be used to represent the differing levels of the ecosystem. Indeed, the contrast between objective measures and subjective perceptions is in itself a very important nexus of study. Feeling unsafe in a safe versus an unsafe neighborhood indicates very different processes, and entirely different interventions would be called for in each case.

Personal skills may represent one fruitful arena for study in gerontology. The ecological paradigm encourages the investigation of skills because of the underlying assumption that people are not passive objects in their ecosystem. In addition to interpersonal skills, researchers might wish to examine differences between those individuals whose professional or work skills fit later-life demands and interests, versus those whose work skills have little use in later life. A teacher and a carpenter, for example, may both use their skills until they experience a severe decline in health. The teacher's familiarity with and interest in books and the carpenter's manual agility may lead to certain hobbies that are rewarding. Steelworkers and typists may, in contrast, experience poor fit of their skills in their later-life activities and challenges.

Other important areas for future exploration on the individual level include studies of perceived and actual control, self-esteem, mastery, and optimism, among others. Comparative studies of such personal characteristics between middle-aged, young-old, and old-old adults will help to elucidate the psychosocial development of the human organism. Such knowledge has important theoretical and practical implications as it can both facilitate our understanding of ourselves and guide treatment and intervention programs. The study of these personal variables should focus on how they affect stress and coping and on how they are affected by stress and coping efforts.

Although there has been a great deal of gerontological research focusing on the individual level, there are many unexplored areas remaining. We especially advocate study on the individual level in concert with investigation of phenomena at the other levels we have discussed. Such research will have a much greater chance of creating a meaningful tapestry of empirical knowledge that can be applied to the advancement of understanding about later-life families and how best to assist them.

ECOLOGICAL PERSPECTIVES ON HELPING
AND BEING HELPED

To illustrate how the ecological perspective we have been advocating might be used guide research and theory on later-life families, we will concentrate on a key component of functioning within these families: helping interactions. Our aim here is to point out some of the ecological features implied in both giving and receiving support within a family system and how these might be conceptualized by social gerontologists. Social support within later-life families is an important issue in its own right, and a great deal of attention has been devoted to its effects, both for the recipient and for the provider.

Most research in the area of social support has been (and continues to be) nonecological. This line of research has tended to assume that receiving social support is de facto supportive for the recipient, has tended to emphasize cognitions or perceptions of support, and has viewed support as a static variable. Similarly, research on providing long-term support has focused on negative effects for the support provider, has excluded the family history of helping that prevails, and has shown support provision to be a unidimensional construct. These views of support tend to ignore the possibility that social support may have negative consequences for the recipient and benefits for the provider; that supportive exchanges may be mixed with nonsupportive overt and covert messages; that relationships have histories that serve as the back-drop to the interpretation of supportive interactions; and that the self and the environment interact to make a combined contribution to psychological, physical, and behavioral outcomes.

In order to avoid some of the pitfalls of past research on receiving and giving social support, we would like to make a number of suggestions based on the ecological paradigm. We discuss four emphases that we believe could improve the study of socially supportive relationships and could be applied to the study of later-life families more generally.

Emphasis on Social Relationships

Our first suggestion is that researchers emphasize the concepts of social relationships and interpersonal interactions rather than social support. Our suggestion is based on the fact that not all interpersonal exchanges, even those that are intended to be helpful, have the effect of being supportive. The concepts of social relationships and interpersonal interactions not only make fewer assumptions about the nature of interpersonal exchanges, but they also have other advantages. First, these concepts broaden the range of focus in that in the context of any interpersonal relationships there exists the possibility of sharing resources, accepting resources from or giving resources to another, and assisting with problem solving and instrumental tasks or being helped in these ways. Second, by focusing on personal relationships, we can also turn to a rich emerging literature on close personal ties.

When we consider the broader literature on personal relationships, we are immediately reminded that these social acts not only hold the potential for rewards, but they also can exact a price. As has been mentioned throughout this volume, receiving help may evoke feelings of weakness and dependency and the belief that the help was given in the spirit of one-upmanship. In addition, accepting help may incur a sense of indebtedness or obligation to reciprocate. For the older person who is experiencing stress and whose resources may be especially low, there may be feelings that what can be offered in return for help is woefully inadequate. Such feelings would tinge the receipt of aid and make it like a bitter pill—something to avoid if one can cope alone.

One of the most obvious facts of interpersonal relationships has simply eluded researchers of social support until very recently. Specifically, the fact that relationships may be vehicles for negative interaction was ignored because it conflicted with the very name of the construct of social support. Although interactions within social relationships tend to be more positive than negative, most of these interactions are mixed. For example, an elderly parent is likely to perceive some acts of help by an adult child as being beneficial, even while being in conflict with the helper over another issue.

A less obvious fact of interpersonal relationships is that receiving support itself may at times be stressful. Receiving help from others during a crisis may produce a pressure cooker effect, in that support under such conditions may prevent the recipient from diverting attention away from the source of stress, a coping strategy that sometimes has a palliative effect (at least temporarily). Furthermore, being a part of a supportive network may mean that one shares in others' pain and misfortunes. When one then feels the need to help alleviate others' discomfort, the cost of caring is increased, and feelings of stress ensue. In later life, the cost of caring may be exacerbated by the older person's perceived or genuine inability to act against the source of stress or its ramifications. For example, the older adult may feel incapable of helping with needed child care for their grandchildren or may be financially incapable of helping out in a financial crisis. Those older adults with more distant relationships will be less troubled by their inability to remediate the stressors that beset kith or kin.

On the other side of the helping relationship, the literature on close personal ties reminds us that not only is giving help costly, but also it can be of substantial benefit to the support provider. Providing a means by which a loved one is enabled to do things that he or she could not do alone can heighten the provider's sense of self-esteem, can fulfill a variety of social expectations, and can actually strengthen feelings of intimacy in the dyad. In very close relationships, what is given and received may carry a different meaning from what is given and received in the context of more distant relationships. Thus, responses to helping within families, although governed by the involuntary and obligatory nature of these relationships, are affected by feelings of closeness and caring.

Emphasis on Long-Term Involvement

Focusing on personal relationships also forces us to realize that relationships do not begin at the moment social support is given and received. Rather, these relationships have complex and often lengthy histories. Thus, for the recipient, the same act of support may be interpreted in different ways, colored by the meaning of the act in past interactions. A large sum of money may mean an act of generosity or a means of gaining social control. Likewise, emotional support may be interpreted as empathic caring, or an expression of power on the part of the support provider.

For the support provider, giving aid to someone with whom resources have been shared in the past and for whom feelings of deep affection have developed will have quite different effects than in those situations where aid is given out of sheer obligation or duty. For example, although giving care to a husband with severe dementia may be physically exhausting and psychologically distressing for his wife, a lifetime of personal commitment and caring and the feelings that "he would have done the same for me," may help to offset the stress of caregiving. More distant relationships are less likely to be affected by these historical factors and, thus, the commerce of support within them may be conducted on a more face-valid basis.

Emphasis on Action and Choice

An ecological approach also demands attention to the fact that both recipients and providers play an active role in helping relationships. This perspective emphasizes the resourcefulness of individuals and their attempts to act in ways that are beneficial to their own adaptation. Older adults who receive social support from others are not simply passive recipients who take whatever help is offered. Rather, they are also active agents in that they play a part in eliciting this support, either through explicit means (e.g., directly asking for help) or implicit ones (e.g., the extent to which others are attracted to and like them). In a similar fashion, support providers are not simply thrust into their roles but often seek out and choose these roles.

Research on older adults as both receivers and providers of social support may have been influenced by stereotypes of older people as being in continuous need of help or as being overly stressed when they have to provide help. Both of these views depict older people as weak. By recognizing that older adults are influential in the course of their lives, either through active decision making or through their interpersonal skills, the view that they are victims of the social support process will diminish. This perspective will free researchers to focus on other important factors in social relationships, such as those that lead older people to be successful at support mobilization and those that encourage them to become involved with others through the help they can supply.

Emphasis on Casting a Broad Net

Another hidden assumption in research on social support is that support is provided only by other people. This assumption is reflected in the proliferation of social support inventories and questionnaires that have emerged over the past several years. By and large, these instruments do not assess support that might be received from important social institutions, such as churches and synagogues, or from a spiritual source, such as God.

As research has progressed in social gerontology, we have become keenly aware of the important role that religion plays in the lives of the current cohort of elderly people. In fact, many older people spontaneously indicate that their religious beliefs provide valuable support in times of stress. Perhaps as access to and communication with others become problematic due to a decline in health or increases in sensory losses, spiritual support increases in its potency and effectiveness, especially in times of stress. It is wholly reasonable that both organized religion and spirituality contain potentially effective coping resources for individuals. Churches and synagogues embody many people who share a set of values and beliefs, many of which emphasize the virtues of helping others. Furthermore, beliefs in a higher power can offer a sense of life's coherence or purpose, and such beliefs can assist in coping with the vicissitudes of living.

Because researchers have not focused on religion as a source of support, either because they were uncomfortable in doing so or because their initial assumptions about social support were too narrowly focused, we know very little about the extent to which spiritual support bolsters psychological well-being, physical health, or other coping efforts. We encourage researchers to begin "casting a broader net" in their study of older adults and their families by increasing the range of phenomena to be considered. Such efforts will require a reexamination of our working assumptions and a less value-laden approach to the development of new ones. If we are to understand the factors that influence people's health and well-being, we will need to open ourselves to their worlds as they actually are, and not merely as we a priori define them to be.

METHODOLOGICAL CONSIDERATIONS

The second focus of this chapter is on problems of research design and measurement encountered by researchers investigating stress and coping in later-life families. To be sure, the points we raise here are not unique to stress and coping processes occurring in late life, nor do they represent an exhaustive list of problems in this area of study. Rather, we highlight the problems that seemed to be most salient to this volume's contributors at the 1989 Kent Psychology Forum. The most pressing methodological issues for Forum participants centered on the design of research that is sufficiently sensitive to register potential relationships among stressors, well-being, and the processes that intervene between them.

Perhaps one of the most interesting and perplexing features of research on stress is the high degree of variability found in people's responses to potentially stressful events. Not only do different individuals respond to the same event in different ways, but also the same individual is likely to respond to different events in different ways. To add one more layer of complexity to this state of affairs, the same individual may even respond to the same stressor in different ways on different occasions.

After four decades of research on stress, it is abundantly clear that "a stressor is not a stressor, is not a stressor." Rather than being a homogeneous class of events, potential stressors possess a variety of characteristics that distinguish them from one another, including their threat to survival, the degree to which they can be predicted and controlled, and whether their impact is primarily physical or psychological. Despite these distinguishing characteristics, all stressors, by definition, share some important properties, specifically, their ability to threaten or disrupt the health and well-being of people who experience them. Thus, one major problem for stress researchers is to identify the "dose response" of stressful events. That is, how much threat or disruption must an event elicit in order to be classified as a stressor for most people and to be considered along with other known stressors? It is conceivable that some of the inconsistencies in the stress literature have come about through an improper classification of events.

Answers to this question require research efforts that are highly sensitive to the correspondence between potentially stressful events and people's reactions to these events. If a lack of correspondence is found, at least two interpretations can be made. First, it might be concluded that the event was not sufficiently stressful to evoke stress reactions and, thus, the event should not be classified as a stressor. Second, it might be concluded that the research as it was designed was not able to detect the correspondence that existed. Interpreting the null hypothesis is always a risky business and is subject to the values, expectations, and predilections of the individual interpreter. To avoid such dilemmas, we want to suggest several strategies for increasing the sensitivity of research designs for assessing possible relationships between stressful events and well-being.

In our discussion, we do not emphasize statistical power whereby issues of sample size and measurement reliability are paramount. Although we are acutely aware of the importance of this type of research sensitivity, we leave those discussions to others. Our emphasis here is more on the construct validity of research designs. We emphasize the importance of designing research procedures that maximize opportunities for capturing the full impact of potential stressors. Specifically, we focus on the issues related to the timing of measurement and the use of multiple operations and methods.

Just *when* to assess the impact of potential stressors is a serious concern if we are to adequately understand the stress processes occurring in later-life families. If we take our measurements too soon or too late, we are likely to underestimate their impact or even incorrectly judge that their impact was totally benign. Because stressors differ along many dimensions (e.g., magnitude and duration) that could affect the onset and extent of stress reactions, the timing of maximum impact surely differs across stressors. To be certain, the answer to the question of "when to look for" stress reactions is ultimately an empirical one. In some rare but fortunate situations, empirical data are available from previous studies that suggest optimal assessment intervals. In more common and less fortunate situations where such information is not available, we encourage researchers to design their research in such a way that empirical answers can be derived. For example, samples might be split randomly such that half of the respondents are assessed at one interval and half at the next. One group could be assessed at 3 and 9 months post-event (e.g., the experience of a heart attack), and the other could be assessed at 6 and 12 months. This strategy would permit dense sampling of stress effects without unduly burdening respondents.

Because the impact of stressors is not uniform throughout the course of the event, we encourage researchers to sample stress reactions densely as events unfold. For example, assessments of caregivers' responses might be made the day before, the day of, and the day immediately following the placement of a relative in a long-term care facility. Although planning such research implies a certain capacity to anticipate events, such a saturation of assessments would offer new insights into the process of immediate reactions. This procedure would not, however, eliminate the need for assessments of longer-term reactions.

To understand the full impact of stressor events, we also may need to expand the range of outcomes that we are seeking. The classic stress reaction included in most studies of human stress is that of depression. Although depression is known to be a common stress reaction, other emotional states and behavioral responses should be evaluated as well. For example, serious psychosocial disturbances in one's life are likely to produce feelings of anger and anxiety and could lead to maladaptive activities such as excessive alcohol consumption and overeating.

Our last suggestion for improving the sensitivity of research designs to the potential correspondence between stressor events and well-being is to broaden the types of methods used to obtain data on each side of this relationship, as well as on processes that intervene. The modal method used in stress research is the self-report. This method for obtaining research data is fraught with many biases, including problems of recall and the tendency to respond in socially desirable ways. We encourage researchers to use a variety of other methods that do not rely on self-reporting, including assessments of physiological responses, reports from significant others, and direct observation. We also suggest that even within the self-report framework, different instruments be used to assess closely related constructs (e.g., anger and anxiety) as well as the same construct within a single investigation. The logic in each case is the same—to reduce the extent to which observed relationships can be attributed to shared method variance and to increase the confidence with which these relationships can be attributed to the naturally occurring events they are intended to represent.

PRACTICE APPLICATIONS AND IMPLICATIONS

A high priority for theory and research in the area of stress and coping in later-life families is the ability to apply research knowledge to efforts that will improve the quality of life for older adults and their families. This priority demands an emphasis on generating knowledge that can be understood and used by those people who serve older adults and their families. The ecological perspective we have been advocating is useful toward this end because of its emphasis on what people do in their daily lives as they interact with other people and with social institutions. This ecological model also can be helpful in deciding how best to use research information to make life better for older adults and their families. Our aim in this section is to offer some suggestions about how research knowledge on later-life families may be used by those professionals who seek to assist them in a wide variety of arenas.

Just as the ecological perspective encourages us to examine processes occurring within different domains of social organization (the macrosocial, mesosocial, and microsocial levels), it also encourages us to use these domains as points at which social and behavioral changes might be introduced. We strongly encourage psychologists, social workers, and nurses to begin focusing on social policy as a means of affecting changes for many individuals and families. It is clear that although some variability exists in the reactions of older adults and their families to many of the stressors of later life, a great deal of consistency also exists across individuals. Such findings suggest that what might be conceived of as problems of individuals can also be seen as social problems that require social solutions. For example, changes in policies that govern reimbursement for services to individuals with Alzheimer's disease can affect millions of families over time. Increasing service options for these families through increased levels of reimbursement could go a long way toward reducing the financial, psychological, and social burdens frequently experienced by caregiving families. Likewise, increasing funding for already existing programs could assist many more people. Extending "Meals on Wheels" programs to a greater number of older people could enable these individuals to continue living in the community or might prevent the need for an adult child to interrupt employment or a career to care for them.

When we consider the possibility of intervening at the macrosocial level, we are forced to think in terms of prevention. Although some social policies or programs are designed for remediation of existing problems, macrolevel changes strongly imply preventative strategies. Because such changes, usually in the form of social policy modification or changes in the financial support for programs, affect many people over relatively long periods of time, there exists the potential to eliminate the source of some problems before they ever materialize. For example, if respite care services for family caregivers proves beneficial to individuals who have already become excessively burdened by their caregiving responsibilities, then it seems reasonable that providing such services to individuals who have recently assumed their caregiving roles could help prevent similar burdens. Although changes in systems at the societal level often come about slowly and typically require substantial political and public pressure, we think the benefits outweigh the costs in many instances. We encourage greater efforts by psychologists and other mental health professionals (especially those who have as their primary concern older adults and their families) to become more actively involved in this domain.

The meso-level, consisting of smaller-scale institutions, organizations, and groups, including families, offers another fruitful point at which to intervene. Changes at this level frequently are more easily attained than those at the macrolevel, simply because these mid-level systems are less complex and usually are more accessible to mental health professionals who act as change agents. In addition to interventions designed to remediate existing problems, this level also is a productive arena for preventive actions. For example, educational programs might be designed to help the families of older people who have recently experienced a stroke. By enabling these families to anticipate the assistance that their relative will need and how best to provide it, some of the patient's feelings of excessive dependence may be avoided, and more productive interactions in the family as a whole may be facilitated. Similarly, nursing homes might help families who have made the difficult decision of nursing home placement to make this transition more easily. Such transitional programs might provide families with information about the emotional turmoil they will probably encounter at the time of placement and teach them strategies for coping effectively with this major life change.

Finally, changes may be introduced at the level of the individual who is experiencing stress. We believe that such interventions are most effective when one of the major assumptions of the ecological paradigm is used as a guiding principle—namely, that people are not passive reactors to their environments but are active agents in shaping their own worlds. As such, efforts at changing individuals should focus on ways to help these people take charge of their own lives in ways that are maximally beneficial to their adaptation.

It is interesting to note that traditionally the individual has been not only the focus of research on stress and coping, but also the primary focus for change efforts designed to alleviate stress and promote effective coping. The fundamental reasons governing these two situations are probably the same—namely, that the emotional distress and physical suffering of the individual are highly salient to observers. Thus efforts are most often directed at alleviating this distress and suffering by working with the person in a one-to-one fashion. Although we recognize the value of this approach to change, we wish to point out two limitations that this approach often places on our thinking.

First, an exclusive focus on the individual can restrict us from considering the various forces in the social environment that both serve as causes of the individual's distress and could be mobilized to alleviate it. Second, this narrow focus can keep us thinking about how to solve problems rather than how to prevent them. In working with individual clients, we encourage mental health professionals to refrain from this type of myopia and to begin thinking more in ecological terms. The ecology of later-life families reminds us that the individual is embedded in complex social systems, many of which can be used to remediate intrapersonal and interpersonal problems as well as to help prevent their future occurrence.

We also want to emphasize the need to consider the "ambience" of programs and services, as well as the resources they offer. These interventions cannot have their maximum beneficial impact if people do not use them, or if people use them resentfully only when all other resources have been exhausted.

Our point here is that programs and services should be user friendly. More specifically, these services should be accessible and flexible enough to meet the differing needs of older adults and their families. In this regard, we cannot overstate the importance of dependability and quality of service delivery. If families are to benefit optimally from services, they must be able to count on the services being rendered in an appropriate way. For example, in-home respite services that do not take caregivers' needs into account in scheduling visits, that are not punctual in arriving, and that provide inadequately trained aides are not likely to be frequently used by caregiving families, or cannot be expected to generate much relief for those who do. Even more serious is the possibility that families may become so embittered about their experiences with these poor services that they will not seek out higher-quality services even when they are available.

It may very well be that the present cohort of older adults and their families may feel reluctant to seek help in times of stress, for fear that such acts would indicate their own weaknesses or failures. Some socialization of these individuals by mental health professionals may be needed to assure them that what they are experiencing is natural and that, because others in similar situations have responded similarly, their own distress does not reflect negatively on them as individuals. Such assurances also should emphasize that seeking help from programs or professionals is a healthy first step toward alleviating their distress. In reality, the dynamics of helping relationships involving clients and service providers are similar to those involving family members and friends. Therefore, it cannot be expected that every attempt to help by a professional or program will have its intended positive effect or that it always will be appreciated by the recipient. However, every effort should be made to find the most effective ways to help older adults and their families cope with the unique stressors they face at this point in their family life cycle.

Clearly, human civilization is embarking on a new era that will be dominated by many issues related to the rapid aging of the population, including chronic illness and disability, health care, and retirement practices. It is almost a truism by now to state that such issues have implications not only for the older generation, but for their family members as well. We believe that the chapters in this volume have made a substantial contribution to the long-term evolution of knowledge about older adults and their families. This new era will no doubt present many challenges for society as a whole, and it will continue to challenge researchers and practitioners in the social sciences.

Index